1988

Families in Transition

Primary Prevention of Psychopathology

George W. Albee and Justin M. Joffe
General Editors

VOLUMES IN THIS SERIES:

The above volumes are available from
University Press of New England
3 Lebanon Street, Hanover, New Hampshire 03755

Families in Transition

Primary Prevention Programs That Work

Editors

Lynne A. Bond
Barry M. Wagner

Primary Prevention of Psychopathology
Vol. XI

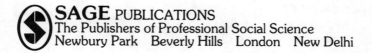
SAGE PUBLICATIONS
The Publishers of Professional Social Science
Newbury Park   Beverly Hills   London   New Delhi

For information address:

SAGE Publications, Inc.
2111 West Hillcrest Drive
Newbury Park, California 91320

SAGE Publications Inc.
275 South Beverly Drive
Beverly Hills
California 90212

SAGE Publications Ltd.
28 Banner Street
London EC1Y 8QE
England

SAGE PUBLICATIONS India Pvt. Ltd.
M-32 Market
Greater Kailash I
New Delhi 110 048 India

Printed in the United States of America

Library of Congress Cataloging-in-Publication Data

Main entry under title:

Families in transition.

    (Vermont conference on the primary prevention
of psychopathology ; v. 11)
    Includes papers presented at a conference held
at the University of Vermont in June 1985.
    Includes index.
    1. Mental illness—Prevention—Congresses.
2. Family—Mental health services—Congresses.
3. Family—Services for—Congresses. I. Bond,
Lynne A., 1949-   . II. Wagner, Barry M.
III. Series.
RA790.A2F36   1987   362.2'0425   86-29795
ISBN 0-8039-2998-6

Contents

Preface

This is the eleventh volume emanating from the Vermont conferences on the primary prevention of psychopathology. The first in this series of conferences was held in 1975 as a result of discussions between George Albee, of the University of Vermont, and Faith and James Waters of the Waters Foundation. Their interests converged on a common desire—to stimulate efforts to foster human development through the prevention of factors known to stress and debilitate human functioning. The Vermont conferences have been a forum for professionals from many disciplines—psychology, medicine, social work, biology, sociology, and education, among others—to discuss models, research, and programs of practice for the prevention of psychological dysfunction.

Through the years, the Vermont conferences and their associated volumes have provided a broad overview of issues relevant to prevention. They have considered environmental influences and psychopathology; building competence and coping skills in infants, children, adolescents and adults; prevention through political action and social change; promoting sexual responsibility and preventing sexual problems; prevention in health psychology; and an overview of the last decade of work in primary prevention. The conferences have also enlarged upon earlier notions of prevention, looking beyond the prevention of dysfunction to emphasize the promotion of well-being.

While prevention has received a dramatic increase in attention over the past decade, considerable skepticism and apprehension persist among some mental health decision makers about prevention program implementation. Some of the prevailing doubts stem from the misconception that prevention advocates and prevention program developers rarely proceed from theory to practice, and that there is too little methodologically sound evidence that prevention programs are effective. With the fiscal restraints being experienced in the field of mental health, time and money are scarce. Mental health workers and administrators feel less able to experiment with *potentially* effective programming, and more pressure to allocate their resources to proven commodities.

In fact, there *is* good evidence that primary prevention programs work. We now have a substantial body of prevention programs that are based on sound scientific theory, are methodologically strong, rigorously evaluated, and demonstrated to be effective. This volume brings together a group of exemplary primary prevention programs to document these accomplishments and provide models for the further development of such efforts.

The contributors to this volume participated in the tenth Vermont conference titled "Families in Transition: Primary Prevention Programs that Work," held on the campus of the University of Vermont in June 1985. Each of the contributors has gone beyond the stages of theorizing and model building to translate ideas into fully operating programs, programs that have been evaluated and demonstrated to be effective. Therefore, this volume brings together a rich store of insights regarding modes for conceptualizing prevention activities, translating these ideas into action, evaluating prevention efforts, and disseminating program information.

The theme of families in transition was selected with the recognition that all individuals are part of some family system, and, more often, a complex and/or overlapping family network that emerges with the development of new partnerships, the arrival of children, divorce, and so on. Families are, undoubtedly, a major source of influence, which mental health prevention and promotion efforts must consider from a variety of perspectives: a source of conflict, resistance, support, strength, and a system that has a development and life of its own—a system that simultaneously shapes and is shaped by its members, and influences and is influenced by the community and its many interrelated systems (political, economic, social, legal, and so on).

The prevention/promotion efforts presented in this volume consider the well-being of individuals, the family unit as a whole, and, directly or indirectly, the broader societal structures in which families are embedded. But in each instance, the family's transition is the point of focus. These transitions represent issues that arise at varied points across the life span of the family (although designating a life span is somewhat arbitrary given the continually evolving structure of the family). The transitions include both normative and nonnormative occurrences, another distinction with blurred boundaries: While an event may be common and anticipated (e.g., the aging of one's parents), it may have unexpected and/or atypical concomitants; and what is predicted based upon statistical data is not necessarily expected or planned for by most individuals (e.g., divorce). By examining the diversity of programs in this volume, and their similarities and dissimilarities, we hope that the

9

reader will develop a greater perspective on primary prevention, family functioning, and what makes prevention programs work.

As has been the case for each of the Vermont conferences and publications, the present work resulted from the efforts of a small group of individuals in the department of psychology of the University of Vermont. They include George Albee and Justin Joffe, members of the conference planning committee and general editors of the series on Primary Prevention of Psychopathology. We are particularly grateful to Barbara York, the conference coordinator, for her tremendous organizational efforts and to Stephen Goldston, who, at the time of the conference, was director of the Office of Prevention at the National Institute of Mental Health and facilitated a contract with NIMH to fund the meeting of contributors to this volume.

—Lynne A. Bond
—Barry M. Wagner

PART I

Today's Family in Perspective

The American family is continuously confronted with change. There are those changes that occur within individual families—each family has a life of its own that involves transitions in its structure and daily workings. There are other changes that have occurred more gradually through the history of our society, changes regarding the meaning of family, and its role in our private and public lives. Before examining efforts for supporting families through their individual transitions, we may find it useful to step back for a moment and consider the family in its broader historical context—where has it come from and where is it going? A reappraisal of the family's viability in our society can serve as a basis from which to consider the characteristics of programs that can best serve them.

In the first section of this book, Howard Bahr examines family change and the mystique of the traditional family. Bahr, a professor of sociology at Brigham Young University, has been a participant in the Middletown III Project, which has compared life in a midwest town (Muncie, Indiana) over a 50-year period, from the 1920s to the late 1970s and early 1980s. Although the demise of the American Family is a well-publicized notion, and a part of daily conversation at every street corner and shopping mall, Bahr challenges the idea that the family has, in fact, decayed from some idyllic form that existed in years past. Drawing from historical accounts of family life over the past three centuries, he argues that the American family is as strong as ever, and perhaps more adaptable than before.

What implications does Bahr's argument have for the importance of programs aimed at supporting families through transitions and difficulties? Need we think of the family as being in a state of decay in order to argue that additional effort and money be directed toward relevant prevention programs? Clearly not. Whether the family is, in fact, in a state of demise, or whether we are simply becoming more cognizant of its needs and difficulties, the fact remains that there is much we can do as individuals, neighbors, professionals, and community leaders to turn potentially stressful and even debilitating transitions into opportunities for promoting the growth of individuals, family units, and communities.

1

Family Change and the Mystique of the Traditional Family

Howard M. Bahr

Since 1976 I have been a participant in the Middletown III Project, an interdisciplinary research program whose primary objective has been to compare Middletown (Muncie, Indiana) in the late 1970s and early 1980s with the Middletown of the 1920s, as carefully documented by Robert and Helen Lynd in this century's first sociological best-seller (Lynd & Lynd, 1929).

Among the major findings from our 50-year comparisons is that although Middletown families have changed in some ways, they remain central to the life of Middletown people, and are at least as strong—and perhaps more flexible—than the city's families of 50 years ago.

This finding does not reflect the opinions of Middletown people about what is happening to today's families. On the contrary,

> Nearly everyone in Middletown knows about the crisis of the modern family and deplores it. Over and over again, they hear from politicians, educators, and neighbors down the street how serious the situation is. The message is gravely proclaimed in television documentaries and in White House conferences, intoned from the pulpit, enshrined in legislative preambles. Any intelligent housewife in Middletown can tick off the degenerative symptoms that make the survival of the family so doubtful: the isolation of the nuclear family, the skyrocketing divorce rate, the widening generation gap, the loss of parental authority, the general dissatisfaction with marriage, and the weakening influence of religion. (Caplow, Bahr, Chadwick, Hill, & Williamson, 1982, p. 320)

The popular wisdom—buttressed by media commentators, politicians, clergy, and other well-informed people—is that we live in an era of family decline, when the forces of godlessness or of technology gone berserk, or both, have weakened that fundamental building block of our

13

civilization—the family—weakened it to the point that its very survival is in question.

For us to suggest that American families are at least as strong as they were 60 years ago flies in the face of a conventional wisdom supported by reports of high divorce rates, family violence, single parenthood, and voluntary childlessness.

Consider divorce, a leading candidate for best indicator of family collapse and decay. The national trends are readily stated. Between the early 1960s and the late 1970s, the divorce rate, however measured, increased substantially, more than doubling between 1963 and 1978. After 1978, the divorce rates plateaued at an annual rate of between 5.2 and 5.4 divorces per 1000 population (the 1981 national divorce rate was 5.3 per 1000 population, compared with 5.2 in 1980).

In 1982, for the first time in 20 years, both the number and the rate of divorces declined rather sharply, to 5.0 per 1000 population; there were 43,000 fewer divorces in the United States in 1982 than in 1981. The divorce rate per 1000 married women aged 15 and over was 22.6 in 1980 and 1981, but 21.7 in 1982. In 1983, the absolute number of divorces declined for the second consecutive year, and in 1984 it declined again. In absolute numbers, 24,000 fewer couples divorced in 1984 than in 1983, and the 1983 figure, just slightly lower than the 1982 total of divorces, was 59,000 or 5% lower than the final total of divorces in the United States in 1981 (National Center for Health Statistics, 1984, 1985).

The more than doubling of the divorce rate during the 15-year period ending in 1978 has been interpreted by many as reflecting drastic and possibly fatal changes in the American family. The relative stability and then modest decline between 1978 and 1984 does not change the fact that the national divorce rate for the past decade has been high by historical standards. But what do these "high" rates tell us about the relative strength and vitality of American families in our time? Practically nothing.

The divorce statistics mean, in fact, that there are more people involved in divorce than there used to be. They say nothing about the quality of American marriage or the relative happiness or commitment to family values of persons who divorce compared with those who do not. When people try to generalize from divorce statistics to statements about the quality or vitality of the family, they are vulnerable to several kinds of error. For divorce rates do not necessarily reflect failures in marriage; nor do rising divorce rates mean that "the family" is necessarily weakened. Sermonizers and propagandists often apply divorce statistics illegitimately, to support a view of social decline or to buttress arguments for intervention programs. In fact, until the historical and social contexts in which the allegedly "high" rates occur have been carefully assessed, *no* interpretation of the meaning of the trend is likely to be valid (see, e.g., Crosby, 1980; Day, 1979).

Is the American family in trouble? From the divorce rates alone, we cannot say. We do assert the relevance of the collective experience of the Middletown III researchers in Muncie, Indiana, and of their 50-year comparisons of numerous indicators of family life and family stability in that specimen community.

We lived in Middletown, collectively, for almost three years. We came to know its families systematically in the statistical profiles we analyzed, and impressionistically, personally, in our neighbors and friends. We read in the local newspapers of their failures and successes, their crimes of boredom and passion; through in-depth interviews with law enforcement officials, ministers, physicians, and social workers, we saw the stresses and crises of Middletown families through the eyes of the professionals who serve them. We experienced life in Middletown during a time of economic recession and high unemployment, and saw families surviving on food stamps and unemployment insurance; we watched 1000 applicants scrabble in a parking lot over 100 application forms for a job at an auto plant. We saw defeat in the eyes of people miserable with their marriages, their jobs, or their lot in life generally. More important, we were able to compare systematically some aspects of family life in contemporary Middletown with similar aspects of Middletown life 50 years ago.

Compared to what it might be—measured against some ideal or against the romantic dreams of its young people—Middletown is a miserable place. But compared to the real past that the Lynds recorded—compared to what it has been—we found Middletown and its families to be in remarkably good condition.

Some critics of this assertion argue that we somehow overlooked the stress and understated the pain that they know afflicts Middletown, and American, families. But stress and pain are relative; the results of literally thousands of individual comparisons between the Middletown families of 1925 and those of 1977-1981, along with an exhaustive assessment of the national family trends for the same period, lead quite convincingly to the conclusion that there is less pain now than there was then.

Underlying both the dire predictions of the deterioration of our families and the less heralded optimism about the future of the family is some notion of what the family has been, and what it ought to be. Usually these notions are vague and implicit. For many years we have lived with an ambiguous image of the "traditional family" of yesteryear, a shadowy image of a warm hearth and a fireplace where the family gathered in quiet contentment, a stable group of mother, father, children, and perhaps grandma.

As we remember our own upbringings, the good times tend to grow brighter and larger in memory. And if our own childhood was not in a traditional family that approximates the nostalgic ideal, we *know* that some of our friends' families, or perhaps those of our grandparents or great-grandparents, had that safe solidarity of kinship and caring, responsibility and love, that the turbulent present seems to offer in such small and untrustworthy dosages.

Only when we get down to particulars and ask precisely what life was like in that traditional family of nostalgic memory do its glistening freshness and warmth begin to recede, and fade, and cool. Forced to look at specific people and places, the rounded corners sharpen a little, and some patches of dry rot may be seen.

Bettmann (1974, p. xiii), creator of an immense graphics archive, writes that his lengthy experience as a pictorial archivist, viewing the world from the "picture window of history," has given him the optimistic and unfashionable idea that the past was, in fact, quite grim. The average citizen of the "Gay Nineties," he says, was a person to be pitied rather than envied:

> Compared with him we are lucky—even if dire premonitions darken our days and we find much to bemoan in our society. . . . Even if we cast but a cursory glance at the not so good old days and bring them into alignment with our own, we will find much to be grateful for. We are going forward, if but slowly.

The Traditional Family, European Style

The traditional family that we look back on, that we view in the distorted and rose-tinged spectacles of collective memory, was not just an American family, but a product of Western European civilization. In looking for benchmarks against which we may measure the widely heralded decline of the modern family—for ways to correct our faulty lenses, as it were—some comparisons with European families are instructive. We have been conditioned by the media to interpret many of the characteristics of modern families as hallmarks of decay and collapse. Let us try to examine the noble edifice of the traditional family before the collapse began.

Whole volumes are devoted to describing the diversity and character of the traditional European family. I recommend in particular Shorter's *The Making of the Modern Family* (1977). Remember that the period of the "traditional" practices we shall consider extends roughly from 1700 to the mid-1800s and, in some cases, until the beginning of the twentieth century. For the moment, we focus on two topics, affection and gender roles in marriage, and then we will look at the care of infants and children.

Gender Roles and Affection in Marriage

The typical division of family labor in the traditional family was unbalanced to the degree that affectionate sharing of burdens and joys was the exception rather than the rule. Indeed, the traditional power relationships in European families impeded rather than encouraged affection between husband and wife. In French peasant society in the early nineteenth century, husbands "ruled the roost." Wives had to treat husbands as superior beings, had to account to them in the slightest matters, and were treated as "chief servants" by their grown sons and male farmhands as well as their husbands (Shorter, 1977, p. 54-55).

Judging from the available evidence, and there is a surprising amount of it—contemporary observation by physicians, amateur historians, the clergy, and government officials—marriage among the common people was usually a relationship of little affection. The essential glue that held families together was not romantic love, but rather considerations of property, lineage, and strictly defined, community-enforced, gender roles.

The relative priority of economics as opposed to affection is shown in numerous accounts of peasant illnesses and medical practices. There are official reports that husbands often refrained from seeking a doctor when their wives were ill, but called the veterinarian at the first sign of sickness in a prized cow or bull (Shorter, 1977, p. 57). A churchman of the 1850s lamented that the French peasant was more grieved over the loss of stable animals than of his wife, because the wife was more easily replaced with another woman, for free, while the animal could be replaced only at considerable expense (Shorter, 1977, p. 58).

These are not isolated examples. The same values are expressed in numerous proverbs of the time (Shorter, 1977, p. 58):

Rich is the man whose wife is dead and horse alive.

Your late wife you so deplore until you enter your front door.

The two sweetest days of a fellow in life are the marriage and burial of his wife.

The ritualized subordination of the wife was a dominant feature of marriage, and had negative consequences for quality of the marriage relationship. Companionship and mutual affection were impeded by rules that the wife did not take meals with her husband, but rather stood and served him until he had finished. Men were taught to regard women as a defective, inferior, beings apart, and their interests and concerns were not to be taken seriously.

The traditional wife did have authority over her own sphere of things, which included her "inside" duties of child rearing, cooking, cleaning, keeping the household accounts, and any cottage industrial work, along with a lengthy list of "outside" responsibilities such as wood gathering, water-carrying, poultry and dairy care, marketing, larding, and all tasks associated with the family garden. The essential point is not that the wife was overworked or that the husband had more disposable time than she did, both of which were usually true, but rather that despite the variety and heavy responsibility of some of her roles, they all were defined as subservient roles (Shorter, 1977, pp. 65-72).

Women were expected to be passive and accepting, acted upon, not acting, as de Beauvoir (1953) eloquently shows in her account of women's role as the "other" throughout history. The traditional woman in the traditional European family did what her men told her to do, and her status depended on how well she served their needs.

She was expected to sacrifice for the family; she was supposed to do more, and give up more, than was her husband. And beyond the passivity and self-sacrifice was the sexual and reproductive role, which meant "sleeping with their husbands on demand and producing babies up to the limits set by community norms" (Shorter, 1977, p. 75).

Infant and Child Care, Traditional Style

Modernization, that process so often linked to the decline of the family, has been accompanied by vast changes in the attitudes of adults toward their children, and, in particular, in the way mothers treat their babies. It is over two decades since Aries (1962) startled family historians by arguing that in traditional European society, parents tended to be indifferent to their young children. Aries argued that the evidence of the neglect and emotional coldness that so often appeared in historical documents was largely a function of the high infant and child death rates: why get attached to someone you are likely to lose? But the indifference went deeper than that. He cited a seventeenth-century neighbor comforting a mother of five "little brats" with these words: "Before they are old enough to bother you, you will have lost half of them, or perhaps all of them" (Aries, 1962, p. 38).

Child neglect in traditional Europe was not merely psychological protection against probable loss. On the contrary, as numerous historians have discovered as they have tried to reconstruct the family life of the common people, indifference, neglect, and sometimes manifestly harmful practices were a consequence of family priorities; the children's welfare simply was not very important in the overall scheme of things.

The traditional mother left her small children alone for long periods while she worked about the farm, and a fair number of infants accordingly were burned to death when their clothing caught fire, died from infections exacerbated by long periods of neglect, or were killed by farm animals. Farm work, or other paid work when available, plainly took precedence over child care, and child mortality rates showed it. There were incredibly high death rates among infants who were sent away to be wetnursed in the countryside; and for a long time sending babies away was very common among families who could afford it. There was a common practice of "exposing" babies, that is, leaving them on the steps of a church, orphanage, or elsewhere, where, presumably, they might be found and cared for. Also worth noting is the marked difference in attitude between the modern couple, for whom the death of a child is a devastating, never-forgotten experience, and the traditional European couple for whom "with the third or fourth child, death would be perceived as a blessing for both children and parents" (Shorter, 1977, p. 173).

According to Laslett (1971), John Locke (1697) argued that the children of the poor English families had to work for some part of the day when they reached the age of three years. Such children amounted to a considerable labor force, for in many villages children under ten made up between one-fourth and one-third of the total population. Yet their numbers gave them little power, and in many ways they were nonpersons. According to Laslett's (1971, pp. 109-111) reconstruction of traditional English village society, although there were children everywhere, "these crowds and crowds of little children are strangely absent from the written record." Why are they absent? Because, while they amounted to almost half of the population of some communities, they were not defined as "counting" the way children count in modern families. The family was not organized around them. Rather, most of them

were living in a condition of semi-obliteration, many of them never destined to become persons at all. Indeed a number of them can never have handled a penny which they could pocket and call their own, even if they actually survived to the age of twenty-one. (Laslett, 1971, p. 111)

We should emphasize that the indifferent traditional mothers were not out of step with their times; they were not monsters or deviants. Their attitudes and priorities reflected their times and circumstances, and one aspect of these circumstances was that one in four infants did not live through the first year of life, and another one in four was not likely to live to become an adult. Nevertheless, it is a mistake to attribute their poor mothering to the high mortality rates. Indeed, Shorter (1977, pp. 203-204) argues that the process runs the other way—the high mortality rates were frequently a consequence of poor mothering:

> The point is that these mothers did not *care*, and that is why their children vanished in the ghastly slaughter of the innocents that was traditional child-rearing. (p. 204)

The Traditional Family in America

So much for the traditional family in Europe. Perhaps we can find the good traditional family of harmonious and equitable division of labor, of enlightenment and empathetic child care in the United States. Perhaps that model, the ideal home that is said to have collapsed or to have been gutted with modernization, existed in America rather than Europe.

We turn to the American Midwest in the mid-nineteenth century, to the American farm family of yore. In the first annual report of the U.S. Department of Agriculture, Hall (1863, pp. 462-470) decried the condition of farm women. He said that "a farmer's wife, as a general rule, is a laboring drudge" who typically worked harder and endured more than anyone else in the household. He urged farmers to treat their wives as people who occasionally need rest and recreation, rather than as machines.

Faragher's *Women and Men on the Overland Trail* (1979) draws upon the written records of overland migration left by midwesterners who traveled to Oregon Territory or California between 1840 and 1870. His object was to try to understand family life in the nineteenth century, using the personal records left by the emigrants. His analysis shows, above all else, that the families of that time were structured in ways that oppressed and subordinated women. In the farming communities from which the overland emigrants came, the labor of both men and women was necessary if the enterprise were to survive, but women were not given status in accord with their contribution.

On the overland trail, as on the farm, men were supreme, patriarchy was the rule: "Society, composed of men and women, was run by the men; women were allowed no formal roles" (Faragher, 1979, p. 111).

The law sustained patriarchy. In the traditional American family of the nineteenth century, husbands had to provide for their wives and children, but wives were legally dependent upon their "husband-guardians." Husbands were responsible to "control and discipline their wives," and "within limits" to punish them physically if necessary. By common law, "reasonable limits" meant that the wife could be beaten by her husband as long as the instrument used was not thicker than a man's thumb. Husbands had the right to control whom their wives saw, and when, to keep them at home or separate them from kin. Divorce favored the husband, who usually retained control of dependent children (Faragher, 1979, pp. 161-162).

In practice, the consequence of the legally sanctioned patriarchy was that men, if they wished, could impose their wills on their wives and children. The decision to migrate westward provides an example of patriarchal decision making in action, for many of the pioneer women who left diaries or reminiscences wrote about how the decision to go west was made. Of the 82 women emigrants' diaries studied by Faragher, there is not one where the wife initiated the idea to emigrate to Oregon or California; it was always the husband. In one-third of the cases, the wife objected, often strenuously, but to no avail (Faragher, 1979, p. 163).

What of romance, the opportunity to pick and choose among potential partners, to find, if not a soul-mate, at least a compatible companion? The evidence suggests that there was little chance for romance in either pioneer or rural life. Usually the crucial issue for a woman was not whom she would marry, but whether she would be married at all. After examining the diaries of the overland emigrants and other sources, Faragher concludes that "the notion of companionate marriage was foreign to the thoughts and feelings of ordinary farm folks."

In the America of the nineteenth century, children learned the "natural" division of family labor, and adopted the values that supported the inequitable division of family power and opportunity. Men and women were seen as different kinds of beings, and their differences were defined as God-given and unchangeable. Men and women occupied separate worlds and grew up within differing subcultures. The family might be the fundamental unit, but the essential connections linking family members with other groupings were same-sex connections. There was men's work and women's work, there were women's concerns and men's concerns, and rarely did the two intersect.

The family might be the essential social unit, but that did not mean that the marriage that created the family was supposed to be a "happy" marriage in today's sense of the word. A good family was a productive unit, a harmony of duty and reciprocity. Romance and passion, rather than being integral to it, were impractical, unrealistic, even dangerous bases upon which to build a "solid" marriage. For women, at least, marriage was the passageway into adulthood, and "those who failed in marriage failed in life" (Faragher, 1979, p. 180).

The definitions of womanhood that permeated traditional American society included belief in female inferiority and some degree of misogyny. The women responded with attitudes of meek acceptance and efforts at mutual support. Their own estimation of the quality of their lives is illustrated in the comment of a pioneer mother who, learning that her ninth baby was a girl, whispered to an older daughter, "Poor baby! She'll be a woman someday! Poor baby! A woman's lot is so hard!" (Faragher, 1979, p. 182).

And what of the much-praised opportunity for children in traditional families to learn useful skills from their parents, the mother-daughter or father-son companionship often assumed to be a positive by-product of the traditional family? We are familiar with the farm-to-city migration, historically massive and still continuing, wherein the daughters and sons supposedly benefited by such treatment opt instead for the less brutal and demanding life-style. Faragher (1979, p. 186) quotes a successful pioneer mother whose chief regret, as she looks back at her traditional family, is that the heavy demands of being a farm wife and mother left her little time for her children:

> The most lingering of my many regrets is the fact that I was often compelled to neglect my little children, while spending my time in the kitchen, or at the churn or wash tub, doing heavy work for the hale and hearty men.

The heavy load borne by the farm wife is characteristic of agricultural societies generally, and was not limited to midwestern or pioneer women. Even in the old South, where womanhood in general and wife and mother in particular were highly pedestaled, the women's lot was difficult. Some southern women, both before and after the Civil War, saw the parallel between women's status and that of Blacks. Said Chesnut (1951), a well-educated woman from one of the first families of Charleston, South Carolina, "There is no slave, after all, like a wife" (p. 49) and "all married women, all children and girls who live in their father's houses are slaves" (p. 486).

One reviewer of women's work in the traditional farm household called farm wives "draft horses of endurance," and shattered the nostalgic image of the charming, sunny kitchen, full of good humor and tempting fragrances (Bettmann, 1974, p. 48). The kitchen stove, Bettmann wrote, was "a penal rockpile on which many a good country wife prematurely spent her beauty and strength," and a variety of physically punishing tasks turned fresh-faced young brides old before their time (p. 48).

That marvelous, healthful, tranquil rural life, where the traditional American family flourished, was abandoned as quickly as possible by most of the young people who were born there. The young voted with their feet and headed, not west, but to the cities. Generally their years growing up on the farm had not prepared them to compete with the city-bred children, and there was some "catching up" to do. Farm labor had matured their bodies. Their minds were notoriously immature.

The liabilities of life on the family farm seem to have been especially repugnant to young women. As girls, they "had toiled along with their mothers—whose hardships were compared with those of oxen" (Bettmann, 1974, p. 56). Having watched premature disfigurement of their mothers, having seen the benefits of the traditional farm firsthand, many young women were convinced that no matter how bad things might be in the factories and sweatshops, they were better than back on the farm.

If the American farm family of the late 1800s does not represent the strong traditional family beside which we can discern the decline almost everyone sees in today's family, perhaps we should look to the city families. Space does not permit a detailed examination of living conditions and family arrangements in the cities of the late 1800s and early 1900s. Suffice it to say that this was the period of child labor, of little government regulation of the quality of the foods and medicines available, of little or no protection against industrial accidents, no health insurance, no unemployment insurance, and abominable conditions of sanitation in most hospitals and health clinics. Living was expensive and among the low-income urbanites, not only was it common for the mothers of small children to be employed, but often the children had to contribute to the family income if the family were to get by. In Syracuse, New York, an observer noted the complaints of local children that "the factories will not take you unless you are eight years old" (Bettmann, 1974, p. 78). In 1900, there were almost two million child workers, not counting street vendors, shoe shine and paper boys, and the like. One-third of all mill employees in the United States were children. The plight of city children—that is, children of low-income city families, and they were a majority of the city's children—was captured in the verse:

> The golf links lie so near the mill
> That nearly every day
> The laboring children can look out
> And see the men at play. (Bettmann, 1974, p.79)

Traditional Small-Town Family:
Middletown, 1924-1925

Robert and Helen Lynd (1929, 1937) described the family life of Middletown in great detail. In fact, their picture of the family life in the two great social classes—the working class and the business class—is one of the best-documented accounts of American family life for any era before the 1950s. Let us examine Middletown families in the 1920s, and then consider whether *these* families might qualify as the traditional models to be emulated by the families of the 1980s.

Surely there is no more depressing portrait of normal, everyday family life in twentieth-century America than the Lynds' description of the lives of working-class Middletowners. Most of the city's citizens are pictured in stark poverty, trapped in perpetual insecurity, and living in hopeless intimacy with companions they do not understand or to which they do not relate. There was a fairly strict separation of the sexes even in the business class, and, in both classes, the subordination of women was practiced and sanctioned.

A few insights from the Lynds' (1929) chapter on marriage (one of four chapters devoted to "making a home") will orient us to the direction of trends in family solidarity and viability since the 1920s. Middletown husbands, the Lynds observe, viewed their wives as morally superior but intellectually inferior. The wives concurred, affirming that women were impractical and intuitive. "Men are God's trees; women are his flowers," read one women's club's motto. As for men's alleged practicality and strength, the women completed the mutual condescension in statements like, "Men are nothing but big little boys who have never grown up and must be treated as such" (Lynd & Lynd, 1929, p. 118).

Companionship in marriage was the exception rather than the rule. Typically at mixed gatherings, the men went off by themselves and so did the women. Working-class couples were even less companionate than the business class, and bickering and apathy were more common than marital congeniality.

Marital intimacy was complicated by natural taboos against open discussion of contraception and a general lack of communication between husbands and wives. Working-class wives typically lived in fear of pregnancy; for many working-class husbands, "their wives have become associated with weariness, too many children, and other people's washings" (Lynd & Lynd, 1929, p. 129).

The Middletown family of the 1920s had other problems. There was a sense that children were beyond their parents' control, that the parents were facing problems their own parents had never confronted, that the "traditional" answers and family practices were no longer relevant.

A decade later, Lynd and Lynd (1937) published a report on how Middletown had adjusted to the Great Depression. The sense that the youth were somehow out of control was even stronger in 1935. And in the rest of the nation, tens of thousands of teenagers were leaving their families because of parental unemployment, frustrated hopes, or parental marriages that had deteriorated because fathers were no longer able to fulfill the male role of provider and therefore had lost the basis of their authority to head the family (see, for example, Komarovsky's [1982] depiction of the effect of the Depression on family structure and power relations).

Looking back, where is there to decline *from*? Surely not from a model family arrangement that fit many American families in the 1920s or 1930s. Was there *ever* a time, for even a brief span—as with Camelot, we'd settle for "one brief, shining moment"—when traditional marriage flourished and really produced all those magnificent qualities and opportunities everyone seems to think it should facilitate?

What about the era of the 1950s? Those were the years when suburban mothers, armed with proper priorities and Dr. Spock, women who had "everything"—a home in the suburbs, lovely children, a new car, a successful husband—took to drink because life had no meaning for them. Or, as Friedan (1963) described, they lay awake at night, while their successful husbands slept beside them, and asked themselves in despair, "Is this all there is?" "Why am I not satisfied?" "Shouldn't there be more to my life?"

No, the companionate family of nostalgia, the traditional family where men and women knew their roles and understood each other and what life was all about, when hearth and home were strong and meaningful, was not the American family of the 1950s or the 1960s.

The Myth of Family Decline

I spent my first postcollege years studying skid-row men and the institutions that try to rehabilitate them. As we studied the life histories of homeless men, we learned that to talk of *rehabilitating* them was foolish. Most of them had never been *habilitated* in the first place. *Re*habilitation programs that were aimed at returning them to life-styles, family statuses, or occupational positions they had *never* occupied usually failed. What was needed was not a return to some situation or status that, for them, had never existed, but a positive plan for *habilitation*—a plan to chart new territory in their life courses.

I encounter the same kind of semantic confusion in talk of the *decline* or *decay* of the family institution. Decline from what? From a lifetime of bondage and drudgery for women, who had to turn to other women or to no one for the companionship and understanding men were unprepared to offer them? Decline from conditions of unequal yoking between men and women, with men supposed to be dominant and women supposed to be subordinate and neither gender able under existing community norms to maximize the companionship that a more egalitarian union might provide? From conditions of ignorance about human sexuality such that people were afraid to talk about their personal medical problems even with their physicians? Decline from situations where people who had married young, in haste and without adequate preparation, found themselves bound for life to incompatible strangers with no recourse possible, given the rules of the communities where they lived?

Contemporary Iran and Saudi Arabia have low divorce rates; yet few of us define their marital situations as superior to our own. Nor would we claim that the options available to American couples as they deal with problems of marital adjustment—including the chance to get out of a marriage one or both partners define as a failure—reflect more "decay" or "moral decline" than do the options available to citizens of Iran.

The entire notion of family decline presupposes a traditional family that was, in most respects, better for all of its members than are today's families. I believe that historically one is hard-pressed to find such families, except in isolated and atypical instances. The fully functioning, warmly supportive traditional family is more of an ideal than a historical reality. It makes no sense to judge the quality of contemporary families by contrast to a model family that never existed, and then lament our fallen states. Comparison with the *real* past, based on the available historical and sociological evidence, shows that our families have been and are likely to continue to be the contexts for much pain, inequity, sorrow, stress, and disillusionment. But there is little evidence that in the American family the levels of pain and disillusionment are higher now than they used to be. There are even some signs that for women and children, at least, there is less pain now than there once was.

All is not well in American families, or in Middletown families. It never was. But much is better than it used to be, and what is truly exciting is that the modern family is entering new territory. The family is changing in ways better symbolized by horizontal movement rather than incline or decline. I like Shorter's (1977, pp. 3-4) metaphor of the family as a ship. Once, he suggests, it was safely moored in port, tightly tied to the docks and safe from harm. Winds might blow and waves crash upon it, but the hawsers were strong and the ship remained safely moored. Then suddenly, surprisingly, the craft was adrift, subject to dangerous tides and storms. What had happened? How had it come loose? The answer, Shorter proposed, is that the crew—parents and children—cut the ties that bound the good ship family safely to community and tradition. They saw the dangers and the opportunities of setting sail, and opted for the freedom to venture into the open sea as an individual family, rather than molder in port.

Why would Dad, Mom, and the Kids do such a thing? Not because they sought decline or decay, but because they found the "traditional family" too constraining, too costly in pain, in unnecessary sacrifice, in dreams unrealized, blessings deferred, joys denied. It was not the idyllic, warm, and effective launching pad for successful living we have imagined. Usually it was not a very nice family for many, or even most, of its members. The traditional family, in reality, stifled creativity and personal choice as often as it fostered them.

The idea that the American family of today represents decline and decay is a myth. The available evidence, including very detailed benchmarks from the 1920s and less extensive but still compelling evidence from earlier times, does not support the metaphor of decay or collapse. Without overlooking the "worlds of pain" that still mar much of our family relationships—relations between spouses, between parents and children, between grown children and their aged parents, between divorced parents who struggle for custody and control over their children's lives, among remarried couples who must deal with foster children and complicated sets of ex-in-laws and ex-mates—I believe the evidence strongly supports the position that a decline in family vitality, strength, solidarity, or positive influence in people's lives has *not* occurred. At worst, today's families are as viable as those of half a century ago, or a century, or however far back you want to reach to find the "traditional" model. More probably, today's families are in many ways stronger, more resilient, and more rewarding units in which to live.

The traditional family of nostalgic memory, that model against which we compare our present families and weep, never existed for most of the people in any place in any time we know about. The traditional family that the hard facts of family history and historical demography reveal usually turns out to have been an intolerant, intractable structure, a network of limits and bounds that in its inflexibility produced a tragic loss of human potential. Sometimes it was tyrannical, with the patriarchal domination or the traditional obligations stifling creativity, opportunity, and growth. Usually it was inequitable, where, at considerable cost to men, women, and children, it was the macho and not the meek who inherited the earth, or at least benefited most from the system.

A traditional family—or rather, traditional families—existed in most parts of the world, and in some societies were remarkably stable for millennia. But they were no pinnacles of progress or enlightened living from which we, in error or ignorance, have declined. The traditional families we know about were as confining as they were liberating.

In a review of *Middletown Families* (Caplow et al., 1982), and of Peter Davis's television series on Middletown, which was first broadcast when the book appeared, Goodman (1982) wondered about the contrast between the findings of numerous recent studies showing the vitality and continuing influence of contemporary American families and the widely held popular view that American families were falling apart. She noted Caplow et al.'s (1982) notion that the myth of the declining family persisted because it made people feel good: when they compared their own situation to the alleged pervasive family collapse and decay, they came off fairly well. In Caplow et al.'s (1982, p. 328) words, "When Middletown people compare their own families . . . with the 'average' or the 'typical' family . . . nearly all of them discover with pleasure that their own families are better than other people's."

Goodman (1982, p. 15) rejected the idea that the myth of the declining family developed "as a subtle way to applaud our own superiority." In her view, the myth of the declining family has deeper, more complex roots:

> I think we all carry around inside us some primal scene of a family Eden, an ideal of family life. . . . In real life, our families fail our fantasies. We know that. But they aren't failures. At best . . . they are complex, powerful, imperfect. And their strength is too easy to forget. (Goodman, 1982)

I have tried to show that the very notion of "family decline" rests upon a mythical, nostalgic idea that at some time in our historical past there was a stable, well-ordered family structure, agreeably run and psychologically supportive of the "natural" needs of its members, and generally superior to today's problem-ridden families. This traditional family of collective nostalgia probably never existed for any sizable portion of any western society, although at all times there have undoubtedly been individual families—oases in the general deserts of pain, depression, and despair—that provided warmth and stability and a supportive context for personal as well as collective actualization and achievement. As Lynd and Lynd (1929, p. 130) reported:

> There are some homes in Middletown among both working and business class families which one cannot enter without being aware of a constant undercurrent of sheer delight, of fresh, spontaneous interest between husband and wife. But such homes stand out by reason of their relative rarity.

And such families seem to have been atypical in all the times and places for which we have even fragmentary data about the family life of the general populace.

In fact, the only way one can come close to an ideal "traditional" family is to talk about the family life of a tiny segment of the population—the moneyed, leisure class—and even then the bulk of the evidence usually does not reveal the values, behaviors, and personal qualities supposedly associated with the traditional family of the Good Old Days. Whenever we get down to specific places—a city, a region, a county, a nation—and to real time, and unearth sufficient evidence to permit reconstruction of the family lives of the common people as well as those of the wealthy, the pictures of family life that emerge almost always reveal units far less democratic, healthful, loving, and supportive of individual growth than those of our own time.

References

Aries, P. (1962). *Centuries of childhood: A social history of family life*. New York: Vintage.

Bettmann, O. (1974). *The good old days: They were terrible*. New York: Random House.

Caplow, T., Bahr, H. M., Chadwick, B. A., Hill, R., & Williamson, M. H. (1982). *Middletown families: Fifty years of change and continuity*. Minneapolis: University of Minnesota Press.

Chesnut, M. B. (1951). *A diary from Dixie*. Boston: Houghton Mifflin.

Crosby, J. F. (1980). A critique of divorce statistics and their interpretation. *Family Relations, 29*, 51-58.

Day, L. (1979). Those unsatisfactory statistics on divorce. *Australian Quarterly, 51*, 26-31.

de Beauvoir, S. (1953). *The second sex*. New York: Knopf.

Elder, G. H., Jr. (1983). A third look at Middletown. *Science, 216*, 854-857.

Faragher, J. M. (1979). *Women and men on the overland trail*. New Haven, CT: Yale University Press.

Friedan, B. (1963). *The feminine mystique*. New York: Norton.

Goodman, E. (1982, April 29). There are strains, but family life today is alive and well. *Boston Globe*, p. 15.

Hall, W. W. (1863). Health of farmers' families. In *Report of the Commissioner of Agriculture for the year 1862* (pp. 453-470). Washington, DC: Government Printing Office.

Komarovsky, M. (1982). *The unemployed man and his family*. New York: Dryden.

Laslett, P. (1971). *The world we have lost*. London: Methuen.

Lynd, R. S., & Lynd, H. M. (1929). *Middletown: A study in American culture*. New York: Harcourt, Brace & World.

Lynd, R. S., & Lynd, H. M. (1937). *Middletown in transition: A study in cultural conflicts*. New York: Harcourt & Brace.

National Center for Health Statistics. (1984, September). Annual summary of births, deaths, marriages, and divorces: United States, 1983. *Monthly Vital Statistics Report, 32*(13).

National Center for Health Statistics. (1985, February 28). Advance report of final divorce statistics, 1982. *Monthly Vital Statistics Report, 33*(11). (Supp.)

Shorter, E. (1977). *The making of the modern family*. New York: Basic Books/Harper Colophon.

PART II

Using Broad Systems to Implement Change

A message that is reiterated many times throughout this volume is the importance of taking a broad, systems perspective to thinking about primary prevention programs. In contrast to more common, individually focused tactics, a systems approach can enhance the ability of a program to reach and affect large numbers of people. Embedded in the very spirit of primary prevention is the insight that there are countless numbers of individuals with the potential for developing problems who are never reached by the traditional mental health system, or are reached only after many of their coping resources have been already depleted. Moreover, integrating prevention activities into existing social systems allows us to sustain broad-scale contact: prevention/promotion efforts become more thoroughly incorporated into the daily lives of individuals, gaining the potential to exert a greater influence. The two chapters in this section of the book offer examples of how preventionists can make use of broad social structures in both of these ways.

Charles Roppel is founder and Chief of the Promotion Branch of the California Department of Mental Health. He and Marion Jacobs, Co-Director of the California Self-Help Center (a center developed by the Promotion Branch to further the use of self-help groups) describe the development of the Promotion Branch and a number of the programs that the Branch has developed. Perhaps the most extraordinary aspect of the efforts of this office is its effectiveness in marketing the concept of prevention as well as prevention materials, and particularly the attention that it has devoted to ensuring the utilization of its prevention programs.

The story of the development of the Promotion Branch in California includes important examples of how preventionists can promote their work. At each step in the development process, Roppel and his staff took every opportunity to increase public exposure to their efforts and to garner the support of influential people. Roppel has emphasized the importance of creating media products that are well produced and highly entertaining, and thus better able to catch the attention of the

31

public. One particularly successful and innovative effort was the creation of a contest in which schools across the state competed to win prizes for the development of the best wellness-promotion activities or programs. Two elements were key to the success of this project: First, Roppel secured the endorsement of the State Department of Education, which legitimized schools' participation; and second, he persuaded a large bank to sponsor the contest and provide the prize money.

Roppel and Jacobs believe that their most important achievement thus far has been the creation of the California Self-Help Center, a referral, public education, and research and development center for self-help programs. The Self-Help Center has produced a program of audiotape and print materials designed to provide individuals with all of the resources they will need to build a self-help group without the presence of a mental health professional.

Sylvia Schmidt, a private consultant in Davis, California, and Deanna Tate, Associate Professor in the Department of Child Development and Family Living at Texas Woman's University, present a model of the dynamics of employer-supported child care. The model incorporates variables at several hierarchically arranged systems levels, including the family, the workplace (e.g., employer and attitudes, benefits), the community (e.g., child care facilities, support networks), and the state and federal governments (e.g., laws, programs, and services). The authors review the history of employer-supported child care, with a particular emphasis on the 1981 Economic Recovery Tax Act (ERTA), which arranged federal tax laws so as to offer incentives to businesses for providing child care services. Consistent with their dynamic model, they argue that the ERTA has affected variables at all levels of the child care system, including business practices and attitudes, community attitudes, employer attitudes, community child care practices, and so on. Currently, there are a number of alternative ways that such services can be offered, from on-site child care centers to a voucher system that allows parents to choose from a variety of child care options.

Schmidt and Tate review the research on knowledge and attitudes toward employer-supported child care, and present three brief case studies consisting of cost-benefit analyses for instituting employer-supported child services at different business settings. The authors make the case that employer-supported child care services will continue to expand in the future, and urge us to support this expansion by disseminating information in our own contacts with business persons.

2

Multimedia Strategies for Mental Health Promotion

Charles E. Roppel
Marion K. Jacobs

Background

Eight years ago, staggering under the awesome mandate of preventing all mental illness in California, the Mental Health Promotion Branch of the Department of Mental Health set out to create a presence of primary prevention throughout the state. The process and products of that effort are the story of this chapter—a story I hope is of interest to others in the mental health industry. I use the word *industry* in its Hollywood sense, because the Promotion Branch is fashioned to function as a producer, generating appealingly packaged mental health programs that are conceptualized by us and brought into creation by a host of talented specialists with whom we contract.[1]

Everything that comes out under the Promotion Branch label—be it a film, tape, radio or TV spot, brochure, board game, or teachers' curriculum guide—contains sophisticated mental health information sleekly and attractively packaged for popular and easy usage. Technical information drawn from top specialists in health, mental health, and education receives first-rate artistic treatment and professional marketing, the final product being owned and distributed by the State.

Recognizing that many readers are not in a position to think in terms of such a statewide enterprise, I first want to share with you a process that I and my staff have undergone over the last eight and a half years, not only because I think the process may be as important as our products in promoting mental health, but because components of the process may have applicability to your personal work endeavors.

California is a large state, with a population of almost 25 million people spread over 58 counties, and a 1985-1986 state budget approaching the $32 billion mark. I work in a department that is also very large, with an annual budget of approximately $700 million, most of which is earmarked to meet the agency's responsibility to provide *treatment* services for the emotionally disturbed residents of the state. So when I was asked to put together a statewide program that would focus on *prevention* strategies in the mental health system, I felt like a gnat under the upraised toe of an enormous treatment monster. Prevention is considered a luxury—last to arrive and first to go when things get tough. With that in mind, our first year was spent putting together mechanisms that we felt might make prevention a chic kind of enterprise in which people would want to become engaged.

First, I gather together a small staff (the original group are all still there) consisting of myself as a kind of manager, a psychiatrist, a psychologist, an office manager, and an administrative assistant. Next, we did a statewide inventory of the amount of money and the kinds of prevention programs that were currently available. It was not an evaluation, simply an inventory, because, on the books, California counties and local mental health programs were spending something like 30 million dollars in the area of prevention. We wanted to see what kinds of programs were being offered and whether anything close to 30 million dollars was actually being spent on prevention. The inventory confirmed our suspicions and documented that only about 2 to 3 million of the 30 million dollars was being spent on primary prevention programs per se. The rest was actually funding early intervention, crisis intervention, emergency services, some administrative costs, and a contingency fund for future crisis needs. But the important thing about that inventory process is that we began to establish a relationship with local programs and to find those individuals in the community who wanted to get involved in prevention programming. Without threatening anyone, we were creating the beginnings of a network.

Next, we arranged for a public opinion survey of 1000 California adults. Basically, they were asked what they did when things weren't going well for them—what kinds of strategies they used to stay well, if you will. One of the beneficial outcomes of that particular enterprise was that it allowed us to have a press conference and announce the findings, as a result of which we began to get some exposure. We also discovered something interesting from the poll. As of 1979, about 75% of Californians thought that, when they were experiencing a stressful life problem, it was a very good idea to find someone else who had had that same experience and get together with them to talk. Only 9% of the respondents, however, had actually ever *done* that. This suggested that people had an unfulfilled need to find other people with whom they could share a common concern, and that they needed help in actually connecting with others. We decided that facilitating that process would be one of our major priorities.

At this early point in our development, we knew that we had to secure the future of our prevention work because the monies that were set aside by the Director of Mental Health were intended only to help us get started. I began a process of talking with some legislators who were known to be friendly to our perspective and, after considerable and complicated negotiations, legislation passed in 1979 and funding was established. The legislation mandated that the California Department of Mental Health "develop a statewide mental health prevention program directed toward a reduction in the need for utilization of the treatment system and the development and strengthening of community support and self-help networks." It was as critical to have that mandate as it was to have the $750,000 that was awarded to the California Department of Mental Health to carry the mandate out. As a result, despite Proposition 13, a departmentwide loss of 100 positions, budget reductions of about 30% over the last five years, a variety of internal crises, and six different mental health directors, we have never lost one cent of funding. The reason that this program has never been touched is that *prevention was mandated*. The department was required to do it, and our money could not under any circumstances be diverted to feed the treatment monster. The legislative intent was very clear.

The legislature did not demand specific actions of us; they concurred with our broad goals and expected that we would act responsibly and effectively. We rejected the traditional approach of dividing the money up and allocating it to local programs to use as they saw fit, because $750,000 divided 58 ways would not give enough to anyone. In our inventory process of local programs, we had asked local programs what, aside from money, was the most needed. Almost unanimously, they asked us to teach them how to create prevention strategies and give them the tools and resources to do it. That critical piece of information helped us avoid the temptation to create three or four extensively evaluated pilot demonstration projects. We reasoned that so few projects, however ingenious, were not enough, and we had no assurances we could provide long-term funding to evaluate them properly. Also, taking such an approach would not provide us with the level of visibility we felt was needed in this touch-and-go formative period.

Our need for visibility, coupled with the community's desire to use our assistance to create prevention strategies at a local level, led to the decision to keep all the money and become a resource center for the state of California and its local mental health programs. Our job would be to develop resources, including print and electronic media tools and programs, to influence people positively to behave in ways that would reduce the incidence of illness. Our hope was that by providing these resources to local county groups, we would stimulate ongoing interest and programming at the local level. Essential to the plan was that the products be of the highest quality, which also meant that some of them were going to be expensive. These products had to contain positive, sound information, and—what is more difficult—they had to be generic in nature to allow the user to adapt them personally to the local situation. We have maintained those standards over the years, which I think is one of the reasons the materials developed by the Promotion Branch are so well received and used by so many people, throughout California and around the country.

Our original name was the Office of Prevention. After two years of living with that title, we decided there were good political and attitudinal reasons to change it to the Mental Health Promotion Branch. When I told the legislature or civic groups that I was from the Office of Prevention, they invariably asked what I was preventing, and how I was preventing it. This is a question to which it is virtually impossible to offer an adequate response. Also, the term *prevention* connotes negativity, in that it implies an effort to stop something bad. It is much more effective and much better received by mental health directors, the state legislature, mental health advisory boards, and an array of other constituencies to be in the positive business of promoting mental health and enhancing the quality of life.

The remainder of the chapter will highlight four of our projects, to provide the reader with some sense of how our ideas have been applied.

Friends Can Be Good Medicine

Much of our work is based on the impressive research literature that has been evolving over the last decade regarding social support systems. Study after study indicates that when individuals have an interpersonal support system, however one defines that, the incidence of all kinds of mental and physical illness is significantly reduced, irrespective of age, ethnicity, or socioeconomic status. In 1979, the idea that interpersonal relationships play a role in staying well or becoming ill was brand new, and we wanted to bring this significant health fact, framed as a piece of new health information, to the California public. Our message was really very simple: Support systems are important to staying well, particularly in times of crisis, so pay attention to and nurture your relationships. We carefully avoided "how-to's" or specific prescriptions, instead limiting ourselves to a very simple public education program.

To help spread the message, we devised a series of multimedia print and electronic materials. Among the print materials was a little magazine known around our office as the "Green Book," but officially titled *Friends Can Be Good Medicine*, a phrase that became the theme of this statewide campaign. The Green Book is the most popular print piece we have ever done, with a half-million copies in circulation all over the country. It offers health information and contains exercises that provide readers with an opportunity to explore their personal relationships within the context of health promotion. We also developed a brochure called *Can Friends Help You Stay Well*. This is a "stress-test" exercise that talks about social support networks and contains clues and tools to get people to pay greater attention to relationships and help them understand the links between relationships and health status.

We also developed a little green brochure called, *Can Friends Be Good Medicine*, with versions in Spanish and English, which includes a form that people can sign to declare that they are going to pay more attention to certain relationships. In addition, a series of electronic materials have been developed, including a very popular 9-minute film called *Friends*. This warm and friendly film graphically portrays people of all ages engaged in supportive relationships. Our 20-minute film, *Relations*, narrated by Ed Asner, talks about barriers to relationships. It contains brief vignettes, and is designed to be stopped at various points to allow for discussion of the barriers that keep the people in the stories from relating well. The film can be shown to groups of any size to get them involved in discussing the notion of relationships, particularly supportive relationships, and how such relationships might be used to help individuals stay well and avoid illness. In addition to these generic products, we created a series of materials about social support for specific populations. These include an array of materials to serve the native American, Asian/Pacific, elderly, Hispanic/Latino, and the Black communities. All are self-contained, packaged materials designed by task forces drawn from these various populations.

In 1981, we combined all this material and set up training programs at 12 different sites around California to train trainers who could then spread the word about social support in a pyramid effect around the state. The "training trainers" models worked extraordinarily well, and in less than a year we had 1200 people who were trained, including members of the clergy, members of civic clubs, teachers, law enforcement personnel, and community volunteers. Armed with information and free material that we supplied, they carried the "Friends" campaign forward in their own settings and social networks around the state.

To determine the effects of this program, we did a systematic pre-post evaluation study in a six-county region, looking for specific indicators of change. One indicator was whether there was increased community agreement with the basic message. After the campaign, 73% of the sample, as compared to 64% before, agreed that friends can indeed be good medicine (note that we do not say *are* good medicine).[2] A sample item from this domain of the study is, "People with no close friends are likely to have more health problems." In the attitude domain, 65% attached a high degree of importance to friendship after the program (e.g., believed it was important to "talk with one or two friends every week") compared with 51% before. As for behavioral intentions, the percentage of people expressing a great likelihood of engaging in friendship-related activity (e.g., visiting someone, spending more time with friends or family) in the coming two weeks increased from 50% to 65%. All of these pre-post differences were statistically significant. We conducted a follow-up assessment a year later and were encouraged to find that, for the most part, gains were maintained, though to a lesser extent. These findings do not, of course, prove that there was actual behavior change or less illness in California. They do indicate, however, that the public had new information. Over a six-month period, almost six million people in California were exposed to well over 150 different media events run by the trainers of trainers, including many radio and TV talk shows. From the standpoint of dissemination of information, we know that "Friends" was a very successful project.

The Promotion Branch then developed a document called *Tools for Staying Well*, which is a catalog describing all the materials we have produced to date. It includes a film rental library, with 12 of the films available in video as well as film format; all films are available free to California residents. In addition, there is a wide assortment of printed materials that we now sell all over the United States. The politics of that are very good, because we both make these resources available to other states and generate some revenue. The California legislature likes to see a financial return on the dollars it invests, predisposing it kindly, we hope, toward future requests for funding.

Another related project that will be briefly highlighted here was the brainchild of Dr. Robert Taylor of the Promotion Branch, who saw the potential for harnessing the currently very popular medium of radio to bring health promotion information to the general public. Over a one-year period, we developed a series of 200 90-second radio vignettes that focused on staying well; taken together, these comprised the *Staying Well Radio Series*. Each vignette is about social, physical, or emotional health. We peddled our 200 vignettes to radio stations all over California, asking them to run one per day as a public service, until all 200 had been aired. About 80 radio stations agreed, which meant that during the time these "spots" were running, we had an exposure audience of one million people *a day* for a period of six months. To give the reader the flavor of these spot announcements, the texts of two of them, one on physical health and one on emotional health, are included.

"Genes"

> Announcer: This is Dr. Robert Taylor. She's Cindy Spring. They're talking about staying well. Let's listen in.
> T: What about genes . . . how much do you think genes affect your health?
> S: I like the design on the back pockets . . . but I hadn't considered them a health risk.
> T: Very funny. I don't mean designer jeans. You know—genes. G-E-N-E-S.
> S: What difference does it make? You can't do anything about your genetics!
> T: Now see, that's probably what a lot of people think . . . it's not true.
> S: Taylor, come on, you're telling me I can change the shape of my nose . . . or the color of my skin?
> T: No, look. I don't mean *that* kind of change! But you *can* alter the effect of your genes. By finding out what diseases run in your family, you can fashion a life-style that resists those diseases.
> S: All right. Say I've inherited a risk from my grandmother . . . a risk for high blood pressure. What can I do about it?
> T: You're probably at risk too. But by limiting your salt, watching your weight, getting regular exercise . . . you definitely improve your chances of not getting high blood pressure.
> S: Makes sense . . .
> T: And it can probably work for other things . . . obesity . . . or, say, alcoholism that runs in families. . . . When you're at risk genetically for a disease, it's worthwhile to try to head it off.

OUTRO

> S: So I guess the key is to know . . . uh . . . the design of my genes, so to speak . . .
> T: And if you don't know what runs in your family, make it a point to go find out.

"Friends Can Be Good Medicine"

> Announcer: This is Dr. Robert Taylor. She's Cindy Spring. They're talking about staying well. Let's listen in.
> S: Look at these grocery bags . . . the slogan on the bags, "Friends Can Be Good Medicine" . . . nice idea, huh?

T: Actually, more than just a nice idea.

S: Seems like common sense to me . . . but I'm sure you know some research studies on it, right?

T: [taking the tease] In fact, I do. . . . Studies from all over the world show that people closely connected with other people are less likely to get sick, physically as well as mentally . . . they even tend to live longer than people who go it alone.

S: Now wait. You're not telling me that all people who are alone are doomed to be sick, are you? That's not reasonable.

T: No, I'm not saying that. It's just a matter of odds. If you've got satisfying personal relationships, friends, or family, your chances of staying well are improved.

S: So, friends—like diet and exercise—affect our health . . . wonder how it works?

T: It's a mystery . . . no one really knows for certain. Could be friends encourage us to live healthier lives . . . maybe it's the help they give us when we're stressed.

S: What about just having someone to listen . . . keep us from giving up when things get tough.

OUTRO

S: Friends can be good medicine . . . I like the sound of it.

T: From a health perspective—Friends are definitely worth the effort.

Wellness Programs for Children and Adolescents

Realizing that the "Friends" program really contained nothing usable for children and adolescents, we contracted to develop some products to serve that population. "Friends Can Be Good Medicine," a curriculum guide for teachers of grades K through 12, focuses on social support systems. It contains a "Friends Can Be Good Medicine" book, lessons, and activities, catalog of materials, and exercises. The teacher response to this product has been extraordinarily positive.

We also commissioned the Wellness Race, a board game for K through Adult, which is much like Trivial Pursuit, but deals with emotional, physical, and social health, and aims at knowledge transfer through social interaction. It was pilot-tested, as were all the other materials, and the results very clearly showed that children knew more health information after they played the game than before.

The third project for younger age groups evolved from the radio series. We asked a group of teachers of grades 5 through 12 to survey the 200 vignette messages and identify those subjects that had the most relevance for adolescents. In this manner, 30 topics were selected and were developed into the "Staying Well Resource Package: Topics on Behavior and Health," a discussion guide and audiotapes for teachers of grades 5 through 12. There are three broad topic areas—Physical Health, Emotional Health, and Social/Behavioral Health—with 10 vignettes related to each. Subjects include acknowledging feelings, blaming the victim, breaking unwanted habits, disclosure, and male friendships.

The next task was to figure a way to get teachers to use these three programs. We did not want to simply "dump" them on teachers, knowing from experience that doing so might lead to the programs being shelved and forgotten. Our solution was to develop a contest among all California schools that evolved into a program called "Staying Well: The Chance of a Lifetime." After some effort, the Department of Education agreed to cosponsor the enterprise with the Department of Mental Health, which basically meant endorsing it and giving us their mailing list. We then approached Citicorp, the nation's largest bank, which was aggressively moving into California and seeking a good public image. They agreed to donate $27,000 for wellness awards for the schools, because our public funds could not be used for prizes. In each of three categories—elementary, middle, and senior high—schools received a $5000 first-prize Wellness Award; $2000-second prize; $1000-third prize. There were also 10 honorable mention prizes of $100 each in each of the three categories. We sent to every public and private school principal, PTA president, school board president, and school superintendent in California an invitation to participate in the "Staying Well: Chance of a Lifetime" statewide contest among schools. All the school had to do over the next five months was develop and document a program, an event, or an activity that focused on wellness and involved the entire student body. Any school that entered the contest was given, free of charge, a "Friends Can Be Good Medicine" curriculum guide, the Wellness Race Game, and the Staying Well Resource Package. We also distributed a competition handbook that explained all the required documentation, a roster of 205 trained individuals to serve as resource people for the schools, and a monthly wellness newsletter. In all, 1807 schools, representing a total student population of almost one million, signed up to participate. The competition lasted through the end of March 1985, and the winning schools received their awards in the Governor's conference room from representatives of the Department of Education, the Department of Mental Health, and Citicorp. The work of the three first-prize winners gives a sample of how creatively young people throughout the state were involved in a wellness process.

First prize in the senior high category went to San Pedro High School, a comprehensive public high school serving over 2300 students. The school began with a wellness committee, which included teachers, administrators, school psychologists, a school nurse, and the student body president. Each of the 12 members of the committee took complete responsibility for developing an activity he or she felt they could best lead. For example, the principal wrote a regular wellness column for the *Pipegram*, a newsletter to parents. The school dean organized a turkey trot before Thanksgiving, with students, parents, and staff jogging or walking a preset course around the school, and those completing the course winning a chance for a Thanksgiving turkey. Humor was an important part of San Pedro's Staying Well program, as evidenced by announcement boards urging all to "Be true to your teeth, or they will be false to you," and "Smile, it increases your face value." Student involvement was particularly evident at San Pedro. The school news-paper contained an article on wellness each month, and students organized a local chapter of Students Against Driving Drunk (SADD). Other schoolwide activities included a schoolwide health survey, a group assembly on drug abuse, an assembly on setting goals, which featured Olympic Gold Medal Winner Paul Gonzales, and dramatic skits emphasizing wellness. San Pedro staff participated in staying well by developing a weight loss program organized by the school nurse. One of the highlights of San Pedro's program was the development by the school psychologist of a suicide prevention program, which reportedly was responsible for saving the life of one of the school's students during the Stay Well program. San Pedro High School plans to use its wellness award to establish a permanent health resource center on campus, which will house books, pamphlets, and other materials to be utilized by staff, parents, and students.

Faye Ross Junior High was the first prize winner for the middle schools. This seventh- and eighth-grade school, with a highly diverse socioeconomic and ethnic population, emphasized self-responsibility in its Staying Well program, especially in programs concerning attendance, weight control, nutrition, and suicide prevention. A variety of programs were offered in this Los Angeles area school, with the expectation that all students would be reached by at least one approach. Creative classroom activities included health classes utilizing UCLA's tobacco and alcohol prevention program, drama classes presenting health-related skits, writing classes penning wellness essays, science classes teaching wellness software, and art classes developing Staying Well theme posters.

Atherwood, the winning elementary school, located in the Simi Valley of Ventura County, chose as its wellness goal improving the school climate. Atherwood had recently become a magnet school for the district's gifted and talented education program (GATE). By the end of the 1983-1984 school year, there was a serious problem with teasing and fighting between the regular students and the GATE students. The Staying Well program at Atherwood had the specific goal of integrating regular and GATE students and improving their interactions. A wellness committee, led by the PTA, included the school psychologist, school staff, and students. "A healthy life is a happy life" was chosen as the theme, and the following areas of wellness were targeted for two months each during the school year: healthy relationships, nutrition, mental health, and physical well-being. A monthly newsletter was sent to all parents, with school board members and district personnel regularly writing about the staying well activities in the school. (What wonderful outreach!) Atherwood is particularly proud of the "natural snow cones" they pioneered by locating a company that agreed to create natural fruit flavors; other schools in the district now plan to use the fruit flavoring to make these healthy snacks. An all-school Olympics focused on physical fitness and generated excitement and warmth among the students, their parents, and other community members. Other highlights of the program included a lunchtime visit to students by the Banana Lady—parents dressed as a banana and a paper bag—to promote the idea of healthy lunches, a seat belt campaign, wellness posters and essays, a child abuse program for the third and fourth grades, and an assembly on "Laughter—the Best Medicine." Students also chose pen pals in other classes in order to find a new friend with whom to participate during good deed week. Atherwood plans to spend its $5000 wellness award to erect an outdoor multipurpose friendship pavilion that will be used for lunchtime recess and after school activities for students, teachers, and community members.

California Self-Help Center

During the last three years, we have established what I believe will be our most important program: the California Self-Help Center. After several years of promotion work, we decided that although teaching people about the role of social support systems in staying well and avoiding illness was important, it was not enough. We also wanted to provide a mechanism to enable people who were coping with serious, life-disrupting personal problems to have easy access to a support system—if they needed one. Self-help groups were the specific type of support we had in mind, partially because they are plentiful, inexpensive, and do not carry the stigma sometimes associated with seeking professional psychological help. But our main reason for promoting self-help groups was the accumulating evidence that people who share a common concern can be powerfully helpful to each other.

Thus the Promotion Branch made the decision to fund and establish, within the Psychology Department at UCLA, the California Self-Help Center, under the codirectorship of Professors Marion Jacobs and Gerald Goodman. Its mandate is clear and direct: "To foster the mental and physical health of Californians coping with life-disrupting personal problems by promoting the appropriate use of self-help, mutual support groups." To achieve this goal, the Center supports and promotes the use of self-help groups through services it provides in four areas. The first is the Referral Service, which began functioning on a statewide basis in January 1985. A toll-free number, (800) 222-LINK, offers California residents potential referral to any of over 2000 identified, verified, and surveyed groups that are listed and described in the Center's computerized data base. The groups, from all 58 counties, cover over 150 different specific issues within the broad categories of physical illness, mental problems, addictions and compulsions, violence, bereavement, parenting, life-style, and periods of transition. The Referral Service links individuals to currently existing groups, helps groups contact other groups, and helps individuals form groups where none exist in their area. After six months of operation, the Center was receiving 1000 calls per month, and that number is continuing to rise.

The second service is the statewide Public Education Service, designed to educate the public, professionals, and the self-help community about self-help and the self-help group process. This unit works with the media, conducts conferences and workshops, collects and distributes information on self-help, publishes a quarterly statewide newsletter, and conducts the Center's promotional campaign. As an organization, the Center is particularly interested in promoting liaisons between the professional community and the self-help community, believing they both have important expertise to share.

The third service is called Resource Development. It surveys groups to assess their needs and, based on these findings, develops multimedia training materials and training workshops to fill those needs. Phone and in-person consultation for newly forming and existent groups is also available. A particularly important training resource developed by Center staff is the Common Concern Program, which will be described separately in the next section.

The fourth service component is the Research Service, which seeks to study and disseminate information about self-help groups and their processes. Recognizing that there is much we do not know about self-help groups—for example, why they in some cases work well and in other cases result in casualties, or who can best use them, or under what conditions they should be used—I intentionally located the California Self-Help Center at a major university to bring strong educational and research capabilities to bear on such questions. Our research efforts are driven by a sense of ethical responsibility, community concern, and scholarly interest in learning how to make the best possible matches between help-seekers and support groups and providing the groups with tools to enhance their help-giving efforts. Toward that end, some of the Center's research focuses on the internal communication process of groups. This little-studied area holds great promise for providing self-help group participants with technical information on how best to engage in the helping process. The Common Concern Program described in the next section is evidence of the major investment the Promotion Branch has in developing such tools.

We predict that there is about to be an explosion of scholarly interest in, and rigorous research on, self-help groups. We welcome and look forward to being a part of it, but not without some trepidation, hoping mightily that professionals will be sensitive to the special issues connected to working with these groups, and will feed their findings to the self-help community in a readily usable form.

Common Concern Program

I have referred a couple of times to the Common Concern Program, a production that is so important it could even be revolutionary. We do not know that yet, but field tests are extremely encouraging.

Four years ago, in my usual role as producer, and committed to the idea that we needed to help people find and form support groups, I funded Professors Gerald Goodman and Marion Jacobs of UCLA to create a package of audiotape and printed materials that could teach a group of 8-10 people who share a common concern how to organize successfully, run, and maintain a self-help group, relying solely on their own resources and the information on the tapes and in the manuals. In other words, no professional leadership was to be required (though it was not to be precluded either); this fits nicely with the spirit of self-governance, one of the defining characteristics of self-help groups.

Basically, this inexpensive, portable package consists of six master audiocassette tapes. Each of the 12 sides of the master tapes guides the groups through one session. The package also includes a Coordinator's Manual to assist the person who first organizes the group, and a Leader's Guide. Each member receives a copy of the Leader's Guide, which provides preview and review material as well as detailed instruction about what to do when it is the member's turn to be the group's rotating leader or assistant leader. For some populations, there is also an item we call a specializing tape, which introduces into each session a 5-7 minute segment containing material of a psychological nature about the group's particular common concern, thus "customizing" the otherwise generic program.

Through brief lectures and structured exercises, the tapes weave training in communication skills and group management procedures into the ongoing process of discussing the group's common concern and providing support. A typical session lasts one-two hours, and the maximum tape time is 30 minutes (usually less), providing guidance and structure but leaving plenty of room for the group to meet its personal needs. The tapes are designed to sell even skeptical members on the idea of training and to present the training material artfully enough to be palatable to a group of people who have many other things on their minds and are intensely struggling with some major life-disrupting problem.

Here is how the package works. Somebody interested in starting a group—it could be someone suffering with a problem, a professional, or just someone with an interest in helping—is mailed the package of six cassettes, the Coordinator's Manual, ten Leader's Guides (one for each member) and a specializing tape if one is available for the specific population. The organizer or coordinator, following the Coordinator's Manual as much as is necessary, recruits, screens, organizes, and eventually forms a group. The coordinator may be a group member, but that is not necessary.

From the very first meeting, the members are in charge and conduct the session by following the instructions on the tape and in the Leader's Guide. The tape for each session is devoted to a separate communication or group management topic. Short lectures and instructions take a maximum of 30 minutes and are interspersed with exercises and discussions to keep the process interesting and the members actively involved. To provide plenty of time for them to discuss common concern issues or any other topics of immediate interest, the last hour of each meeting is reserved for an unstructured open discussion. Just prior to the open discussion, the group may listen to five minutes of specializing tape material (if available) containing specific psychological information pertinent to its concern.

The master tape instructs the group to shut the tape off whenever members are to engage in active participation and then to turn the tape back on as soon as the activity is over. When it is time to listen to the specializing tape, instructions are given to replace the master tape with the specializing tape, listen, and then have an open discussion. Where no specializing tape exists, the leader for the session brings in material of interest.

The materials have been tested with groups for divorced women, incest survivors, couples coping with infertility, recent widows, breast cancer patients, hospice workers, parents coping with the death of a child, and parents of learning disabled children; we are encouraged to see that each of these populations is capable of creating self-contained, cohesive, ongoing, effective support groups. Groups generally have no difficulty following the procedure under the direction of a rotating leader team that has prepared ahead of time by reviewing the Leader's Guide and the upcoming tape. After 12 sessions, Common Concern groups typically have impressively sophisticated helping skills, are firmly committed to the tape format, like being self-governing, are proud of their leadership abilities, and highly recommend the program. If effective ways to promote the Common Concern Program can be devised, people who might never be touched by the mental health system could be helped to form effective support networks. In both rural and urban areas, meeting in church basements, hospitals, and living rooms, the public will have access to quality professional guidance for only the cost of the tapes. In addition, Common Concern has important research implications, as it represents the first standard stimulus for running and studying support groups.

Three Other Projects for
Mental Health Promotion

In quick succession, I will note three other Promotion Branch productions to round out the picture of our multimedia approach.

One is a brochure to deal with unemployment issues, which was developed several years ago during a period when that problem was very severe. Called "Unemployment Success," it is a self-help tool for the unemployed. The most important thing about this tool is what we did with it. Believing that departments within government should work together, we persuaded the State Department of Employment Development to make these brochures available in unemployment offices throughout the State. Although most people who are unemployed are unwilling to go to mental health centers for help, they do go to unemployment offices, where we were able to distribute a quarter of a million brochures.

Currently, we are sponsoring a contest among county mental health directors to select the best local primary prevention and mental health promotion programs, as judged by a panel of peers. This contest gives people the opportunity openly to take pride in their prevention work, and also generates interest and increased involvement in the process.

Finally, there is the 12-minute film, "Danny's Song." It was lifted from a longer 30-minute film that we made to promote the mental health of the physically disabled. "Danny's Song" does that, but has also turned out to be a film about wellness. So when anybody asks what we mean by wellness, this film is what we show them. It is very personal and beautifully portrays what support means in promoting health.

I wish I could prove that all of this works. I think that it works, but I can't prove it. I can tell you that the response is very positive, funding is secure, and people like it. I personally believe from what I have seen that a lot of people have been assisted through this kind of effort. What we told the legislature initially is true—the money they give us to promote physical and mental health is a wise investment.

Notes

1. Use of the first person in this chapter refers to Mr. Roppel.

2. Note that we do not say friends *are* good medicine, because that isn't true. Friends *can* be good medicine. They can also be a great source of stress, and not necessarily good medicine at all. But the potential is there, so we always stress that they *can* be.

3

Employer-Supported Child Care: An Ecological Model for Supporting Families

Sylvia E. Schmidt
Deanna R. Tate

Imagine yourself sitting over a microscope peering intently at a slide. The slide is filled with churning organisms. You are watching the movement very closely. Now, mentally move yourself out of your body to watch yourself peering into the lens. While you are in a state of concentration on the slide, you are not simultaneously aware of yourself as sitting in a room, in a building, in a city, in a state, in a nation.

The view seen through the microscope is a "micro" view of phenomena. The examination of an individual in the context of family, neighborhood, workplace, community, state, and nation constitutes a "macro" view. This chapter focuses upon the "macro" view.

Employer-supported child care is affecting many levels of the ecosystem in which families live. Employer-supported child care, a powerful tool, has the potential to support the strengths and wellness of families.

The term *family wellness*, as used in this chapter, describes the concept of "flourishing" as families (as opposed to "coping" as families). Wellness is a growing movement that is a step beyond prevention (Ardell, 1984). Wellness is characterized by positive direction, systematic action, balance of forces, and optimization in use of resources.

Using the ecological model to examine the impact of family-workplace interaction, this chapter focuses on:

— History of employer support for child care
— Tax legislation regarding employer-supported child care

49

— Employer-supported child care options
— Summary of current research
— Current trends and what they mean
— Future trends and what we can do

Suggestions for cooperation between business, family, and mental health professionals will be presented.

**Ecological Model for
Family-Workplace Interaction**

Those who use the ecological model do so in order to view phenomena in context. The model has been used widely by physical, biological, and social scientists; however, only recently has it been applied to studies of families.

While classic studies have viewed variables in isolation, and then postulated various relationships, ecological studies view interaction in context from the onset.

Figure 3.1 illustrates the components of the ecological model applied to family-workplace interactions. The interactions between all levels of the ecosystem are not linear, but are circular, involving a continuous feedback loop. Each level affects every other level. The interfaces are dynamic rather than static. Once equilibrium is established, an event affecting any level results in changes at every other level.

The following example illustrates how the model applies to family-workplace interactions. Consider an individual family, composed of two earners, and the event of childbirth. This event will require communication between each parent-earner and each employer, with feedback about how the child will affect employment. At the community level, interaction will occur between parents, caregivers, and community agencies. Even federal laws and policies will shape the family's decisions about the baby. Each decision made during these exchanges will set in motion the dynamics that will eventually reestablish equilibrium to the ecosystem.

It may be that one or the other parent will use maternity or paternity leave. Or, if work policies do not facilitate child care, that parent may choose a new employer whose policies and benefits support child care. Agencies that provide information about child care or financial support will interact with the family if community services are requested. Increases in the numbers of families using these services affect state and federal policies about work and family interactions.

Other applications of the model have been made to general studies of

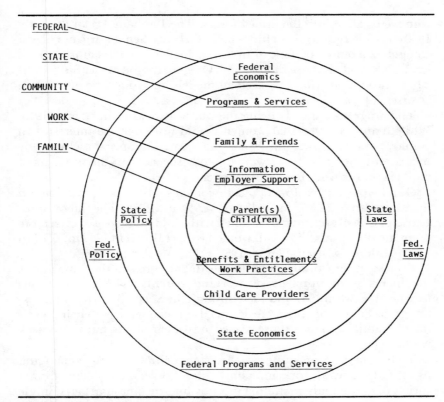

Figure 3.1   Ecological Model for Family-Workplace Interaction

the human ecosystem (Bubolz, 1979) and to studies of families of the handicapped (Bubolz & Whiren, 1984). Those interested in further discussion of the ecological model are referred to Auerswald (1975) and Wood and Jennings (1985).

History of
Employer-Supported Child Care

The changes that have occurred in child care, family composition, work-family interactions, and local, state, and federal laws and policies can be traced in the history of employer-supported child care. When women were seldom employed outside the home, the need for child care was limited and casual. Child care needs became critical during World War II when women were needed in the work force to replace the men who were called into the armed forces. The Lanham Act in the early 1940s provided government funds for child care when the urgency of war compelled women to work in industry. Centers were established near work sites, such as those in Portland, Oregon, for the Kaiser Shipyards. These are still described as excellent models for group care of children (Zinsser, 1984).

The programs funded during the war were discontinued after 1945. While many expected that women would no longer be interested in employment following the war's end, yearly figures show a steady increase in the numbers of women, and especially in the numbers of mothers, in the work force since that era.

Of all women aged 16 and older, women's labor force participation increased from 31.8% in 1947 to 51.7% in 1980. The labor force participation of ever-married women with children increased even more dramatically, from 18.6% of all women with children in 1947 to 56.7% in 1980 (Children's Defense Fund, 1982).

Even so, public funds for child care did not grow at the same rate as the increases in numbers of working parents. The public funds legislated between 1947 and 1980 through the Social Security Administration or Education Acts were designed as social services to help lower-income families, mainly those headed by women, obtain training or seek work.

Today's families are quite varied in composition. Society is changing its attitudes toward work and family life. Workers today come from a variety of households, including those of dual-income marriages, single wage-earners, and mixed groups who share living arrangements. Each of these family compositions may include children.

This heterogeneous work force has very different benefit needs from the traditional household composed of working husband and home-making wife. In fact, no more than 11% of American families currently have this "traditional" composition (Washington & Oyemade, 1984). The dissatisfaction of employees with traditional benefit programs designed for homogeneous, traditional families was reported in a recent *Wall Street Journal* article (Apcar, 1985). According to Opinion Research Corporation, which was cited in the article, the lowest satisfaction was expressed for long-term disability, life and health insurance, sick leave, and pension plans.

The need for child care, new family compositions, and dissatisfaction with traditional benefits has affected the ecosystem at the level of family-work interactions. The response by employers who take a holistic view of work and family is to offer new kinds of benefits. Group plans have been joined or replaced by individualized benefits, such as health and fitness memberships, grants for education, child care, and others. Some employers offer a cafeteria plan, so-called because it allows a personalized package of benefits taken from a "menu" of choices (Lampert, 1984; Wojahn, 1984).

The benefit occurring more and more frequently is that of child care. In fact, child care benefits have been described by the National Chamber of Commerce as the fastest growing benefit of the 1980s.

The growing need for child care for all working parents stimulated a change in federal policies and tax laws. The passage of the 1981 Economic Recovery Tax Act (ERTA) structurally changed the financing of child care benefits. The tax act and emerging policies resulted in recognition of the cost of child care as a legitimate expense of doing business. Businesses in the private sector could support child care as an employment benefit. This change at the highest level of the ecosystem joined tax law with social service law to affect national child care policies.

The Impact of
Tax Law on Child Care

The 1981 Economic Recovery Tax Act added a new avenue for funding ongoing child care costs for working parents. Using tax acts as a means of generating financial support for child care changed the emphasis from child care as a social service to child care as a business service (Schmidt, 1984). The designation of child care expenses as tax-free benefits served two purposes: it recognized child care costs as an expense of earning a living, and it also provided a means of subsidizing the costs of such services for lower-income taxpayers (Hargrave, 1982). From an ecological view, the nation responded to the growing numbers of workers who require child care in order to work by expanding tax laws, thus involving the private sector as well as the public sector in funding child care. A complete review of tax treatments of child care costs and public policy has been reported elsewhere (Hargrave, 1982).

Though the legislation was not intended to exclude or reduce social service funding for child care of the unemployed, some have been critical of the purpose of the act. Such critics view cuts in social service funds that occurred at the same time as an indication of congressional intent that corporations should take some responsibility for subsidizing child care of all kinds (Samoff, 1985).

A closer look at the potential funds available to all working parents through tax legislation shows this criticism to be shortsighted. The funds available through tax legislation are new funds, for a new purpose (Tate & Schmidt, 1984). They provide a means of support for the child care costs of parents who were not previously eligible for social service child care. The group most economically vulnerable, lower-wage workers, who may enter the work force with the assistance of social service child care, can now more easily afford to remain employed.

Child care benefits, called dependent care assistance plans, are written using Internal Revenue Service terms (IRS, 1981). Such plans must be written and made available to all employees. Plans cannot pay more than 25% of the total cost of the benefit to owners or highly compensated workers. The amount provided by the employer for each employee must be determined and reported annually, as other tax-free benefits always have been. Commerce Clearing House, a tax information service, has detailed the tax incentives for employer-sponsored day care programs (Commerce Clearing House, 1982).

The ERTA and other tax acts have been successful in stimulating the economy, and in establishing new benefit programs and work-family interactions. On the other hand, elimination of tax-free benefits in the name of "tax reform" has been considered. Employers have seen demonstrations of the value of child care to such an extent, however, that even if it lost its tax-free status, it would likely still be seen as a useful management tool. The cost savings to agencies such as nonprofit hospitals demonstrate that child care plans are a good investment even without the tax advantages (Schadt, Walling, & Schrag, 1984).

Employer-Supported Child Care Options

Direct Child Care Programs

The most commonly known child care programs are those that are on-site child care centers, directly operated by a company for the benefit of its employees. Child care centers at work sites are especially suited to the company whose workers need child care seven days a week, evenings, or at other unusual hours. They are also expedient in cases where few child care facilities are located near the company. The ERTA provides an accelerated plan for recovering the cost of building a child care center when it is part of a new corporate building project. Beginning in 1980, this provision stimulated the creation of many on-site centers.

Business park developers are a recently growing segment of the business world to include on-site child care facilities in new constructions. In fact, legislation has been proposed in some states to fund model projects in rapidly growing commercial areas. The states see such efforts as a means of attracting new and desirable industries.

To date, on-site child care centers have been built and used by manufacturers with swing shifts, hospitals with 24-hour operating schedules, unions, employee benefit associations, and the military. Work site child care centers, however, though useful, have not always been successful. In her 1978 research describing on-site programs, Perry found that some centers had closed, due to underutilization, costs, or operating hours that did not meet the needs of the work force.

Indirect Child Care Programs

Employers can financially support child care by contracting services for their employees' children in community centers or home-based programs. Where a variety of child care services are needed by employees, or where workers live in several residential areas, vendored child care makes sense. It is also suited to situations in which an infant may be cared for by a day-home provider for a year or two, after which he or she is transferred to a group care facility with a nursery school component. The advantages of the vendored child care approach also apply when children reach school age and can be enrolled in an after-school child care program. The employer contracts for several child care spaces in different programs, paid in advance. This option provides flexibility not only to the working parent, but also to the employer.

Vendored care avoids high start-up or building costs, and allows more choices in the type of care, thus providing for the various needs of different families. It is an option that also allows smaller businesses to offer child care benefits without the direct operating costs of on-site care.

The most flexible child care option of all is the use of a voucher system, whereby all or part of the cost of the employee's child care expenses are reimbursed by the employer through a coupon, or voucher, of designated value. This option functions somewhat like the method used for reimbursing travel, hotel, or food bills that are costs of business trips.

The dependent care assistance plan using a voucher is not limited to any one type of child care. The care can be provided by an individual in the child's home, or any other setting chosen by the parent. Some restrictions apply. For example, care provided by a nonworking spouse or dependent family member is not reimbursable.

Other Service Options

Other child care services exist that aid in implementing a dependent care assistance program. One option is parent seminars for groups of employees. Such seminars may address a variety of parents' needs; for example, they may offer information regarding how to choose good child care services, they may teach parenting skills, or they may provide for developing skills designed to improve how parents manage work and family interactions.

A second service is an information and referral service, or I&R. Networks for coordinating information about local child care programs and services have developed at the local, state, and national levels. An employer-supported I&R system was developed by IBM after a survey of employees reported that this service would be the most useful in finding and using good care. It consists of an in-house software package for computerized use in IBM's multisite corporate locations.

The oldest state level I&R system is in California. Initially, the service advised parents about public child care services; currently, it provides information to the general public about all licensed child care programs and other related matters.

A bill recently considered by Congress would aid in funding child care I&R on a federal level. In addition, the National Association for the Education of Young Children recently implemented a national referral service to identify the expertise of its membership, and to provide referrals to programs, speakers, consultants, and other children's services in response to public inquiries.

Child Care-Sensitive Business Practices

An examination of personnel policies can help redesign business practices involving work schedules and vacation and sick leave, so that more flexibility is available to parents with child care responsibilities. Flex-time, regular part-time work, job-sharing, and use of sick leave for children's illnesses are all examples of child care-sensitive business practices.

The child care options for employer-supported child care described here may be used separately or in combination. The ecological model would suggest that the context in which the child lives, including the child's family, the parent's place of employment, the services in the community, and the relevant state and local laws and practices, should all be considered by businesses in choosing from among the options.

Summary of Current Research

Employer-supported child care, primarily in the form of on-site child care centers, has been in existence for many years. Only a few studies, however, have reported actual numbers of existing programs. Perry (1978) reported that 105 company child care centers responded to her national survey in 1978. In 1982, 415 programs were described (Burud, Aschbacher, & McCroskey, 1984). In 1984, about 1850 child care assistance programs were known to exist, with another 500 to 1000 companies providing financial contributions to local centers, and an additional 500 to 1000 companies providing parent seminars (Friedman, 1984). This great increase in numbers over the last few years reflects the influence that ERTA has had since its inception.

A line of research initiated and directed by Deanna Tate at Texas Woman's University (TWU) has tracked the impact of tax legislation on employer-supported child care. TWU researchers (LaRue, 1984; Oakley, 1983; Schiller, 1982; Schmidt, 1984; Wyatt, 1985) examined the state of knowledge of and attitudes toward ERTA and employer-supported child care held by randomly selected employers, whereas previous studies surveyed only employers with existing programs (Burud et al., 1984; Perry, 1978).

Currently, five studies on employer-supported child care have been completed, and two more are underway. The dimensions included in the studies are knowledge of ERTA and employer-supported child care, attitudes toward ERTA and employer-supported child care, models for needs assessment in communities of varying sizes, ERTA effects on child care professionals, knowledge and attitudes of child care providers and parents toward ERTA and employer-supported child care (see LaRue, 1984; Oakley, 1983; Schiller, 1982; Schmidt, 1984; Wyatt, 1985), and cost-benefit analysis of employer-supported child care under ERTA (Tate, 1985).

Knowledge and Attitudes

The research results are summarized here in categories relating to the levels of interaction described in the ecological model. While the majority of TWU studies report findings related to business attitudes, some report findings related to families, family-work interaction, community child care providers, and the economy.

Regarding the knowledge and attitudes of parent-workers, Wyatt (1985) found that less than half of such parents had knowledge of the ERTA, but that 80% of those that did had a positive attitude toward it. The relationship between percentages of parent-workers in a given firm and attitudes toward employer-supported child care was mixed, depending on the size of the firm. In smaller firms, the relationship was a positive one. The higher the percentage of parent-workers, the more positive the attitude. In larger firms (100-plus employees), results were more variable. That is, families that work in smaller firms are more routinely positive about employer-supported child care than those that work in larger firms. In addition, positive attitudes toward employer-supported child care and ERTA were highest in firms already utilizing a variety of family-supportive benefits and practices. Use of other family-supportive benefits may be an indicator of receptiveness to providing child care benefits.

A survey of community child care providers (Wyatt, 1985) found that less than one-fourth of the providers had functional knowledge of ERTA. As with the parents surveyed in the same study, however, over half of the providers had a positive attitude toward the general concept of employer-supported child care in the ERTA. The study thus suggested that although parents and providers had a positive attitude toward the ERTA, they lacked the knowledge to avail themselves of its benefits. In other words, they liked the idea, but did not know much about it.

Of particular interest in the series of studies at TWU was the knowledge held by randomly selected business persons (Oakley, 1983; Schmidt, 1984). Managers of both large and small businesses had very little knowledge of employer-supported child care, and even less knowledge about ERTA. The child care model with which they were most familiar was the on-site model. The source of knowledge about employer-supported child care was primarily news media reports. No one reported having received knowledge of the ERTA from tax advisers. Those who reported knowledge of ERTA were sometimes erroneous in their perceptions. Follow-up questions indicated that tax provisions for individual child care tax credits were often confused with ERTA provisions for dependent care assistance.

Knowledge was easily increased. In one study (Schmidt, 1984), a 20-minute educational presentation providing an overall understanding of ERTA provisions was given to each business person interviewed; the presentation was associated with an increase in degree of positive attitude regarding ERTA and employer-supported child care.

Overall, employers of both large and small businesses were generally positive in their attitudes toward ERTA and employer-supported child care. When asked to choose a preferred option, the order of options from most to least preferred were voucher, vendor, information and referral, charitable contributions to community child care facilities, and on-site care.

Cost-Benefit Analyses

A long-term study currently in progress at TWU is a negative case analysis of the costs and benefits of providing employer-supported child care utilizing the tax provision of the ERTA. A negative case analysis uses a research technique that compiles a list of the potential explanations (hypotheses) about the costs and benefits in question. When case data are obtained, those explanations that do not fit the cases examined are eliminated. This results in a compilation of explanations of costs and benefits common to all cases reviewed. A protocol has been developed for calculating the costs of stabilizing turnover before and after implementing a child care benefit program. Preliminary data is reported here in the form of three case studies of different businesses (Tate, 1985).

Case study one. The system for the calculation of the costs of implementing a child care benefit program was developed using as a prototype a printing business with approximately 50 employees. The business had a ratio of nonexempt, or blue-collar workers, to exempt, or professional or administrative workers, of 2: 1.[1] The business was quite young, and although profitable, was not paying a large amount of taxes because of initial purchases of capital equipment. Such equipment is costed for tax purposes over several years, and qualifies the business for depreciation allowances (Morgan, 1982). The primary reason for interest in employer-supported child care, however, was to maintain the stability of a skilled work force; it was costly to recruit and train workers.

The calculations, when completed, yielded a ratio of 1:4. In other words, for every dollar committed to employer-supported child care, the business would yield four dollars in cost-containment and tax savings. The business was too small to expect to operate an on-site child care program; therefore, it would benefit most by implementing a voucher or vendor system.

Case study two. Another case that was used to generate cost data was that of a small manufacturing concern with approximately 85 employees (Burud et al., 1984). This business had on-site child care that had been available to employees for approximately three years. Fortunately, this company had been collecting for many years the type of information that made possible a calculation of the benefits over time.

The geographical area, which included many comparable businesses, had an unemployment rate of 1.5%-3.0%. Turnover per year ranged from 50%-100%. The manufacturing enterprises utilized a high percentage of unskilled female workers. Much movement of workers from plant to plant was occurring.

The primary motivation of this company to commence an employer-supported child care program was to help stabilize this highly mobile work force. The company purchased a house that adjoined the parking lot and converted it into a child care facility, spending $42,500 on renovation and start-up. They budgeted $30,000 annually for ongoing center-related expenses. Parents paid for part of the costs in fees. Not all parents needed the center: 26% of workers had 39 children in the center. The parents were split between exempt and nonexempt workers.

In the first year of operation, turnover, which had been much like the prevailing patterns in the area, dropped to between 7%-8%. By the third year, it was 5%-6%. Whereas before the program the firm had four applicants for each position, the pattern changed to 20 applicants for each position, 95% of whom reported applying because of the presence of the employer-supported child care program. Absenteeism went from 5%-10% to 1%.

The firm discovered several other areas of savings. They were able to maintain the same level of production with ten fewer production workers and five fewer clerical workers. They generated savings in reduced expenditures for salaries, fringe benefits, equipment, workstations, and training costs for these workers. The value of media coverage due to the child care program was estimated at $12,000 per year.

The cost-benefit analysis for this business, utilizing the research protocol, yielded a ratio of 1:6, or six dollars in savings for each dollar spent. This estimate is conservative. It is clearly a case of spending money to make money, however.

Case study three. The case study of a nonprofit community hospital was undertaken in order to determine whether a nonprofit organization would benefit from employer-supported child care when tax advantages are not an issue. The hospital is in a major metropolitan area, and has approximately 4000 employees. The primary motivation for considering an employer-supported child care program was to assist in the recruitment and retention of highly skilled allied health professionals such as nurses and various types of therapists. Any such program would be available to all employees, however.

Although the analysis of the case is not complete, preliminary calculations indicate that the ratio of cost to benefit is likely to be 1:3. For each dollar spent, three dollars in savings would occur. The ratio is expected to be stable regardless of the model of employer-supported child care selected.

The cost-benefit studies, when completed, will provide factual information about the effectiveness of employer-supported child care in solving problems of absenteeism, turnover, productivity, recruitment, job satisfaction, and cost containment of personnel. At present, the only available analysis of the relationship of child care benefits to these problems (Miller, 1984) does not express the outcome in terms of dollar savings.

Current Trends and What They Mean

The trends below illustrate the responses of individuals, families, businesses, and communities to the advent of employer-supported child care. They include increasing knowledge through advocacy, the need for child care business consultants, discussion of family needs at work, new profit-related questions about child care, and new linkages for sharing expertise between the fiscal and human service communities.

Increasing Awareness

The ERTA provisions for dependent care assistance positively affect businesses and families in those situations where the provisions are implemented. Not enough businesses or employees, however, are knowledgeable concerning the ERTA and employer-supported child care. Because attitudes are basically positive once the benefits to businesses have been described, a logical first step in advancing employer-supported child care is providing information to both management and employees. While all professionals in various human service fields can be advocates for employer-supported child care, a trend is developing for more formal communication with businesses.

Child care consultants help businesses to identify fiscal resources currently used and lost to turnover, training, and absenteeism. Developing, planning, designing, implementing, and evaluating employer-sponsored programs have become a long-term process requiring child development, research, and business expertise. Many independent child care consultants have begun informal networks for sharing information useful in working with employers considering child care benefits. For example, consultants who are members of the National Association for the Education of Young Children (NAEYC) gave papers on the context of consulting at a preconference session of that organization in New Orleans in November 1985 (Tate & Nelson, 1985).

Surveys for Planning Services

Child care planners and consultants survey corporations and communities to determine the cost, availability, and use patterns of community child care, and its quality. Consultants use their expertise in creating surveys, projecting costs and savings, and evaluating usage of existing services before new facilities or programs are implemented. An experienced consultant acts as a broker for the child care system, consulting with providers, and representing the child care services they provide to the business community.

Corporate surveys used for planning employment-related child care focus on the feasibility of the service, and the business problems and concerns that the benefit will address. Because work-related surveys are conducted in relation to the goals and purposes of individual businesses, they resemble market research reports rather than traditional social service needs surveys. In fact, the success of encouraging employers to continue child care benefits may rest on how well such reports support the goals and purposes of the business (Schadt et al., 1984).

Increased Parent-Employer Communication

There is also a trend toward increased discussion of family needs in the workplace. A new openness is developing on the part of both parents and employers that allows discussions of the need for child care. Interactions between parents and employers are an important part of the planning process. The expression by workers and managers of attitudes and concerns about child care arrangements is both necessary and desirable.

Cost-Benefit Analyses

The interface of child care with employment will mean more than sharing concerns; it will also mean asking new profit-related questions. Employers today have an increased awareness of the human resource value of their employees (Burud et al., 1984). Business managers desire workers who stay on the job, work at maximum productivity, and are interested in knowing and supporting corporate goals.

These profit-related questions will require analyzing employment costs. How much money is lost when workers with training and experience leave employment because child care is not available or is inadequate? Formulas exist for calculating the costs (Burud et al., 1984). Consultants working with small businesses will need to introduce the subject of costs to managers who may lack personnel departments or related business data.

Communication Between Professional Groups

A fifth trend is developing that requires interaction between previously unconnected groups of professionals. That is, feedback loops are needed between tax planners, fiscal advisers, lawyers, business managers, and professionals in the human services. This is vital, because professionals giving advice about business and tax legislation are not experts in the delivery of child care and human services, and seldom act as advocates for the human services possible within the tax laws. Human service and mental health professionals, on the other hand, have long taken an advocacy position for children and families, but they do not all have business expertise. Feedback loops will allow interactions that combine the fiscal expertise of the financial community with the psychological expertise of the human service and mental health communities.

Future Trends: What Can We Do?

As individuals, we are all part of a family, part of a business community, and part of a state and a nation that has been deeply affected by the advent of child care as a necessary service for working parents. Trends for the future include advocacy activities for each of us at all levels of interaction with our own ecosystems.

One future trend will be the use of economic language to describe the costs of child care and its impact on the ecosystem. Every business is part of a community's social system. Employers are interested in worker availability, business expansion, and worker productivity. Child care affects each of these areas of interest.

As members of a community social system, employers are affected by high costs for public services that could be reduced by the availability of child care. For example, communities that support a strong child care system are less likely to pay for crimes such as vandalism committed by unsupervised children. As well, when good child care is readily available and affordable, the need is reduced for public funds for the care of child crime victims, including victims of child abuse and neglect, and for children who suffer serious accidental injuries (Phillips, 1984).

What can be done by mental health professionals to further the process? Each person interested in advocating for employer-supported child care can use business and professional networks to raise the consciousness of the community. Persons using the services of mental health professionals may themselves be a business employer. Further, a family problem that presents itself may be alleviated through child care at the client's place of employment. Parents can also benefit from professional help in learning how to talk with their employers about their work-related child care needs. Parents can persuade employers about the necessity for child care and the dollar benefit of the service to the parent and the employer.

It is also useful for mental health professionals to be aware of ways in which employer-supported child care can assist families with retarded or disabled children. In neighborhoods where mental health/mental retardation facilities provide day services for the children of working parents, the parent's employer may be willing to provide vendored or vouchered financial support for the cost of care. One of the few available studies reporting on the benefits of child care in terms of the savings for families describes the economic impact of child development day programs for families of retarded children (Liberman, Barnes, Ho, Cuellar, & Little, 1979). The cost of institutional care of older children was reported to be four to eight times as much per year as the initial cost of early intervention.

A collection of readings examining work and family life in the future (Children's Defense Fund, 1983) can assist in designing family impact research. These readings report declining fertility rates, growing numbers of women entering the work force, and the impact of these trends on family size. Such trends will change interactions between work and family life. These changes will include alterations in family stability, the division of domestic labor, and child-rearing patterns.

In coming years, there will be a growing need for child development professionals to become specialized in the area of employer-supported child care. Some preventionist psychologists may wish to pursue the specialized training required to work in this field. Others may serve as mentors for individuals who exhibit the skills needed to work long hours with groups of young children. With increasing numbers of children in group care, child care professionals will play a central role in the lives of a wide range of young children; their training and career development will need to include experiences with both typical and exceptional children. Child development specialists will be identified through professional referral services, such as that being implemented by the National Association for the Education of Young Children.

Conferences and special educational sessions for child care professionals have already been held. The need for specialized skills for working with businesses and their employees will increase in the future. The next steps in the development of this profession will be the institution of a recognition process, new career preparation at the graduate level, and an increasing output of research in the field (Tate, Schmidt, & LaRue, 1984).

One last potential trend of importance to the mental health profession is the notion of dependent care assistance to support the cost of day care services for older dependent family members, or an incapacitated spouse. The expertise of the preventionist and the human development specialist will be required in order to sustain such a trend for including other dependent family members in employee benefit programs.

A strong network of quality child care for all children and dependent family members has great potential for preventing family disorders and promoting family wellness. Future questions are not limited to who will finance child care, but must also address how children will be guided and educated in order to thrive in the uncertain, dynamic ecosystem of the future.

In closing, the statistics regarding families in the work force are telling. The trends are unmistakable. More and more women—and, specifically, more and more mothers—are in the work force, more than at any time since employment records have been maintained. The data speak with such clarity that authorities can confidently predict that such trends will only intensify.

The nation's work force needs the talents and energy of these working women, and yet because women have responded to this need, society is presented with the demand for an increasing quantity of quality child care. No longer can society count on available home workers such as grandmothers, aunts, or neighbors to provide child care. They are in the work force, too. The ERTA has a great deal of potential for helping to provide a solution to the great need for affordable quality child care. The outcomes can be good for the economy, for business, and ultimately for the nation's families.

The trend toward increasing numbers of employer-supported child care programs is likely to continue. As the numbers of programs increase, the impact on family wellness, business profits, and the nation's economy will reflect the new balance obtained by the ecosystem.

NOTE

1. The Fair Labor Standards Act (U.S. Department of Labor, 1975) defined standards for classifying employees other than professional (exempt), who were required to be paid minimum wage and overtime (nonexempt). This act extended the categories to include child care and other previously unincluded workers.

References

Apcar, L. M. (1985, April 30). Labor letter. *Wall Street Journal*, p. 1.
Ardell, D. (1984). The history and future of wellness. *Wellness Perspectives Journal of Individual, Family and Community Wellness, 1,* 3-23.

66   Schmidt, Tate

Auerswald, E. (1975). Thinking about thinking about mental health. In G. Kaplan (Ed.), *American handbook of psychiatry: Vol. 2. Child and adolescent psychiatry, sociocultural and community psychiatry* (pp. 316-338). New York: Basic Books.

Bubolz, M. (1979). The human ecosystem: A model. *Journal of Home Economics, 71,* 28-31.

Bubolz, M., & Whiren, A. (1984). The family of the handicapped: An ecological model for policy and practice. *Family Relations, 33,* 5-12.

Burud, S., Aschbacher, P., & McCroskey, J. (1984). *Employer-supported child care: Investing in human resources.* Boston, MA: Auburn.

Children's Defense Fund. (1982). *Employed parents and their children: A data book.* Washington, DC: Author.

Children's Defense Fund. (1983). *A corporate reader: Work and family life in the 1980's.* Washington, DC: Author.

Commerce Clearing House, Inc. (1982). *Tax incentives for employer-sponsored day care programs.* Chicago, IL: Author.

Friedman, D. (1984). *Update on employer-supported child care initiatives.* New York: Conference Board Work and Family Information Center.

Hargrave, E. (1982). Income tax treatment of child and dependent care costs: The 1981 amendments. *Texas Law Review, 60,* 321-354.

Internal Revenue Service (IRS). (1981). *Highlights of 1981 tax changes* (Dept. of the Treasury, Internal Revenue Service Publication 553). Washington, DC: Government Printing Office.

Lampert, H. (1984, November). Just tell us what you want. *Savvy,* pp. 69-71.

LaRue, K. (1984). *The economic recovery tax act of 1981 effects on child care professionals.* Unpublished master's thesis, Texas Woman's University, Denton.

Liberman, A., Barnes, E., Ho, E. S., Cuellar, I., & Little, T. (1979). The economic impact of child development services on families of retarded children. *Mental Retardation, 17,* 158-159.

Miller, T. (1984). The effects of employer-sponsored child care on employee absenteeism, turnover, productivity, recruitment or job satisfaction: What is claimed and what is known. *Personnel Psychology, 37,* 277.

Morgan, G. (1982). *Managing the day care dollars: A financial handbook.* Cambridge, MA: Steam Press.

Oakley, M. (1983). *Employers' interest in child care services study.* Unpublished master's thesis, Texas Woman's University, Denton.

Perry, S. K. (1978). *Survey and analysis of employer sponsored day care in the U.S.* Dissertation Abstracts International, 39, 5305-A. (University Microfilms No. 79-05048)

Phillips, A. (1984). *How can we work and take care of our children?* Report to the Orange County Board of Supervisors from the Orange County Commission on the Status of Women. Orange County, CA: Orange County Commission on the Status of Women.

Samoff, R. (1985, Spring). Child care: A call for corporate response to the Reagan policies. *News from the Coalition for Employer-Supported Child Care,* p. 1.

Schadt, K., Walling, L., & Schrag, L. (1984, November). *Justification of corporate expenditures for employer-supported child care programs.* Paper presented at the annual conference of the National Association for the Education of Young Children, Los Angeles.

Schiller, P. (1982). *Employer-employee perceptions of organizational responsibility for employee child care programs and benefits.* Unpublished doctoral dissertation, Texas Woman's University, Denton.

Schmidt, S. (1984). *The 1981 economic recovery tax act and child care: Attitudes and practices of small business in Texas.* Unpublished doctoral dissertation, Texas Woman's University, Denton.

Tate, D. (1985). Turning a new leaf: The economic recovery tax act and employer-supported child care. In *Improving child care services: What can be done?* (pp. 65-75). Washington, DC: Government Printing Office.

Tate, D., & Nelson, E. (1985, November). *We've only just begun: Issues in employer-supported child care.* Preconference workshop at the annual meeting of the National Association for the Education of Young Children, New Orleans.

Tate, D., & Schmidt, S. (1984). New resources for children and families: The 1981 economic recovery tax act. In R. Williams et al. (Eds.), *Family strengths 6: Enhancement of interaction* (pp. 319-329). Lincoln: University of Nebraska-Lincoln, College of Home Economics, Department of Human Development and the Family.

Tate, D., Schmidt, S., & LaRue, K. (1984, November). *Employer-supported child care: Marketing strategies derived from research.* Paper presented at the annual conference of the National Association for the Education of Young Children, Los Angeles.

U.S. Department of Labor. (1975). *Handy reference guide to the Fair Labor Standards Act.* Employment Standards Administration, Wage and Hour Division Publication 1982. Washington, DC: Author.

Washington, V., & Oyemade, U. (1984, Winter). Employer-sponsored childcare: A movement or a mirage? *Journal of Home Economics,* 11-15, 27.

Wojahn, E. (1984, March). Beyond the fringes: How smaller companies are profiting from flexible-benefit plans. *Inc.,* pp. 61-66.

Wood, B., & Jennings, G. (1985, May). *An ecological model for strengthening families: Individual, family, community, state, and world.* Paper presented at the National Symposium on Building Family Strengths 8, Lincoln, NE.

Wyatt, S. (1985). *Knowledge and attitudes of child care providers and parents toward the economic recovery tax act and employer-supported child care.* Unpublished doctoral dissertation, Texas Woman's University, Denton.

Zinsser, C. (1984, October). The best daycare there ever was. *Working Mother,* pp. 76-78, 80.

PART III

Supporting Families Through Normative Transitions

During the development of any family unit, certain transitions are common, if not inevitable: the entry of new family members, the deaths of others, and certainly changing roles and relationships as each family member encounters new experiences and develops physically and psychologically. But while we anticipate many of these transitions in a general sense, it is difficult to foresee the specific demands and opportunities each will involve. The fact that these transitions are normative does not necessarily suggest that we truly have planned for them. For example, the death of a spouse may be recognized as an inevitable event, but it is one for which few individuals prepare themselves. The young child's struggle to establish autonomy from the parents, and the adolescent's attempt to define an individual identity are both predictable and well-publicized events, but leave many families feeling overwhelmed. Each of the chapters in this section of the book addresses a specific primary prevention project that has been effective in supporting families through normative transitions.

The first chapter describes the Infant and Family Focus Project, a service and research project that examines two models for providing home-based prevention programs for families of newborns. The authors, Sandra Mitchell, Diane Magyary, Kathryn Barnard, Georgina Sumner, and Cathryn Booth, are part of an interdisciplinary team of professionals in nursing and psychology at the University of Washington. Their project systematically compares a Mental Health service delivery model, which emphasizes a process approach to maternal-child competence with an Information and Resource Utilization model, which is characteristic of traditional public health efforts. Their findings suggest the importance of focusing upon interactive processes in the family rather than individuals and information, per se.

In their chapter, Mitchell and her colleagues address issues that must be considered in all prevention efforts. In describing their work, the authors provide insights into the ways in which sound programming and experimentation can be constructed from a theoretical model (in this case, a model of maternal competence). Moreover, they illustrate the care with which the individual components of a program must be considered in developing a coherent intervention. They conclude by considering four unanswered questions: Who should be the target of prevention programs? How should you define program outcomes? When should you attempt to measure the desired program outcomes? How can you best evaluate prevention efforts, given that their goal is often the nonoccurrence of certain events? These are issues with which all preventionists struggle.

The second chapter in this section of the book is authored by Bernard Guerney, Professor of Human Development and Founder and Head of the Individual and Family Consultation Center at the Pennsylvania State University. Noting the awesome power of the family to shape the destinies of its individual members, Guerney emphasizes the importance of using this power to facilitate the functioning of individuals as well as the entire family unit. His Family Relationship Enhancement (RE) Program is designed to train specific relationship skills that may build upon already existing strengths in the family. It is designed to empower family members, individually and as a unit, by fostering the development of alternative modes for thinking, feeling, and acting that, in turn, facilitate effective coping with stress and conflict and promote mutual support among family members.

Guerney begins his chapter with an overview of the Family RE Program, and discusses the similarities and dissimilarities between this and other programs. After elaborating upon the specific Family RE skills that are trained, and commenting upon the formats in which the training has been accomplished, Guerney reviews, at length, the varied and numerous research projects that have documented the effectiveness of his program. The flexibility of Family RE training is noteworthy—it has been used as primary, secondary, tertiary, and therapeutic intervention; it has been conducted by mental health professionals, paraprofessionals, and lay volunteers; it has been used at mental health facilities, churches, drug and alcohol treatment agencies, and women's resource centers, among other settings. The ability of this program to retain its integrity throughout these adaptations suggests the particular strength of this approach.

In the next chapter, Kerby Alvy, the Executive Director of the Center for the Improvement of Child Caring (Studio City, CA), addresses the training of parenting skills. As he points out, the notion of parent education programs dates back more than a century, with recent interest centering particularly upon those programs that emphasize skill-building. Like Guerney in the previous chapter, Alvy highlights the importance of providing individuals with specific skills that will enable them better to foster the development of their own family members.

Alvy has been concerned with developing parenting programs that are sensitive to the values of minority populations, particularly urban Blacks. In addition to discussing the issues that must be addressed for successful cultural adaptations of services, Alvy shares a personal account of some of the growing pains that are involved in such a process—the racial strains, issues surrounding cultural bias, and the struggle to develop mutual trust among program staff as well as recipients.

The following chapter is authored by Myrna Shure, Professor in the Department of Mental Health Sciences at Hahnemann Medical College, and Coprincipal Investigator of the Hahnemann University Prevention Intervention Research Center. She and her colleague, George Spivack, have spent the past 15 years developing and refining a program for training Interpersonal Cognitive Problem Solving (ICPS) skills. In comparison to the programs of Guerney and Alvy, Shure sees her work as a more generic approach in that it focuses on thought rather than action. Like Mitchell et al., Shure emphasizes a process approach; she focuses on the process of thought—how to think rather than what to think.

In her chapter, Shure describes various ICPS skills and their relationships to behavior. She also considers the more controversial question of the relationship between the process and content of thinking. Presenting evidence for the interrelationships between mothers' ICPS skills, their child-rearing styles, and their children's skills, Shure describes the success that she and her colleagues have had in training mothers to support the development of problem-solving skills in their children. Hers is clearly an empowerment model—teaching thinking skills that allow the parent and child to solve their problems in their own ways.

In concluding, Shure considers the conditions under which the ICPS approach has and has not been effective, emphasizing the necessity for taking multiple perspectives in order to ensure success: (1) a scientific perspective, (2) a practical, or logistical, perspective, and (3) a personal, or consumer, perspective.

In the final chapter of this section, Phyllis Silverman, an Associate Professor at the Massachusetts General Hospital Institute of Health Professions, discusses issues involved in facilitating the accommodation to widowhood. Silverman stresses the need, in designing preventive interventions, to consider carefully the experiences of the targeted population from its present and past perspectives. For example, she notes that, contrary to popular belief, grief is not a condition from which people "recover" with appropriate treatment; rather, it is an experience to which people accommodate, and an experience that can lead to potential growth and redefinition of the self, given appropriate supports. Moreover, the supports that are needed for this development and reconceptualization of the self will vary as a function of the roles that the individual has occupied in the past. Thus the needs of men and women will differ given their contrasting marital roles and experiences.

In her chapter, Silverman explains why mutual support, self-help groups can be so successful for both widows and widowers. She draws from rich descriptive data collected from over 100 members of two such groups in order to let these members, themselves, explain the ways in which their participation in mutual support efforts has facilitated their growth. Again, the theme of empowerment is strong; in working through their own and others' experiences, the widowed discover their own powers to shape the course of their future accommodation and growth.

4

A Comparison of Home-Based Prevention Programs for Families of Newborns[1]

Sandra K. Mitchell
Diane L. Magyary
Kathryn E. Barnard
Georgina A. Sumner
Cathryn L. Booth

No prevention program can be more *primary* than one that begins before birth. In fact, some of the most successful efforts at health promotion among high-risk families have been those that emphasized good prenatal care and nutrition (for example, Kessner, 1973; Pakter, Rosner, Jacogziner, & Greenstein, 1961). Good parenting and healthy child development require more than just a good start based on physical health, though: they require interpersonal and social skills; the help of concerned relatives, friends, and professionals; specific and general knowledge about child development; a healthy emotional climate; and a family environment in which stability and continuity outweigh change and disorder.

In this chapter, we shall describe the Infant and Family Focus Project (Barnard, Bee, Booth, Mitchell, & Sumner, 1981), a service and research project that has attempted to address the issues raised by primary prevention for newborns and their families. The overall project is a field experiment comparing two different models for providing home nursing services to these families, and it developed out of careful consideration of three separate, but overlapping, questions. First, we developed a model of maternal competence based both on published research and on the clinical experience of our staff. (We focused solely on mothers because many of the women eligible for our project did not have husbands or partners.) Second, we tailored a nursing intervention program focused on the competencies identified in the model. That is, we assume that the best way to ensure a healthy environment for child development was to foster and nurture competence in the mothers (see Bromwich, 1976, for a similar conclusion). Finally, we embedded the new program in a research context that serves both to evaluate the program and to expand our understanding of maternal competence, parent-child interaction, and healthy child development.

Maternal Competence

Our own research (Barnard, Booth, Mitchell, & Telzrow, 1983), and our reading of the scholarly literature, convinced us that successful parenting of infants is a complex matter, requiring a variety of integrated skills on the part of the mother. These skills can be conceptualized as falling into five general categories.

Successful Interaction with Individuals

By *interacting successfully*, we mean nothing more complicated than participating in social conversations, sending and receiving interpersonal messages in ways prescribed by culture and custom. In White middle-class American culture, for example, successful interaction requires orienting bodies toward one another, maintaining eye contact, responding appropriately to questions, and using various facial expressions and voice inflections to convey meaning.

Such basic communication skills are vital if mothers are to interact in growth-fostering ways with their children. A number of researchers have found that maternal responsiveness (especially her contingent responsiveness to the infant's cues) is related to later positive social and intellectual development of the child (Blehar, Lieberman, & Ainswoth, 1977; Clarke-Stewart, VanderStoep, & Killian, 1979; Lewis & Coates, 1980; Thoman, Becker, & Freese, 1978). In particular, maternal interactive responsiveness appears to be instrumental in fostering a secure emotional attachment of the child to the mother (Ainsworth & Bell, 1969; Blehar et al., 1977; Egeland & Farber, 1984), a finding that appears especially significant in light of the reported links between the security of a child's attachment at 12-18 months and later skill in peer interaction and in problem-solving behavior (Arend, Gove, & Sroufe, 1979; Easterbrooks & Lamb, 1979; Lieberman, 1977; Waters, Wippman, & Sroufe, 1979).

Being a good mother requires a woman to communicate not only with her baby, but also with other people on the infant's behalf—health care providers, friends, and relatives and other professional helpers.

Poor social interaction skills can interfere with a woman's ability to use these sources of information and support effectively.

Social skills can be assessed both directly and indirectly. In our own work, we make observations of mothers and infants during feeding and teaching interactions, using specially designed scales (Barnard, 1978) that focus on the mother's sensitivity to infant cues, response to infant distress, cognitive growth fostering, and social-emotional growth fostering behaviors and on the infant's clarity of cues and responsiveness. Similarly, we make direct observations of the mother's social behavior with another adult during interviews.

Successful Interaction with the Community

To be a good parent, a woman must be able to manage her own life in her community—obtaining shelter, food, and other necessities, and dealing with various businesses, agencies, and institutions. She needs also to be able to provide for the special physical, social, and developmental needs of her child. The more adept a parent is at meeting these needs through what Bronfenbrenner (1979) has called the macro-environment, the better the outcome for the children.

The assessment of community life skills is very straightforward, normally being done by direct questioning of a client about her daily activities. Questionnaires that assess satisfaction with social networks and social support (such as the Personal Resources Questionnaire, Brandt & Weinert, 1981) are another way of assessing this domain. Archival records (such as health department records, medical charts, or even credit bureau ratings) may also have information about the skill with which a woman is managing the community life of her family.

Gathering and Using Child Care and Development Information

At the very least, a woman must have the cognitive capacity (what we usually refer to as "intelligence") to learn relevant facts about child care and development. For example, routine care procedures such as mixing formula or doing laundry may be a real problem for mothers whose reading level is limited. And more complicated procedures, such as taking the infant's temperature or administering medications, may be almost impossible.

Factual knowledge about infants and children is also an important consideration. Although books and classes about child development are widely available, poorly educated women in disorganized families are much less likely to take advantage of these resources. Good parenting often requires good basic information.

Finally, the parents' broader understanding of what parenting is all about and their general beliefs about children's abilities play an important part in determining parenting behavior. For example, mothers who believed that prenatally their children could see, hear, and understand things early in infancy had children who subsequently scored higher on developmental tests at ages one and two years (Snyder, Eyres, & Barnard, 1979). In a similar vein, Newberger (1977, 1980) has demonstrated that parents who have been referred for abuse of their children show cognitively less mature understandings of parenting and child behavior than a matched group of controls. Sameroff and Feil (1985) have reported similar findings.

Managing Emotional Life

It is well established that severe disorders of maternal emotional expression present a hazard for healthy infant development (Rutter & Garmezy, 1983; Zahn-Waxler, Cummings, McKnew, & Radke-Yarrow, 1984). Less clear, however, are the effects of temporary and less serious emotional problems. Depression is a particular concern, but the contribution of emotional upset to levels of conflict and disorder in households is also probably important.

Emotional health is usually assessed by questionnaires or symptom checklists. We have found it very useful to include physical symptoms as well as emotional ones in these assessments.

Managing Stress and Life Change

The lives of many high-risk families are characterized by a large number of life changes and high levels of stress. It seems obvious that the demands associated with such emergencies (changing residence, people moving in and out of the household, conflict with intimate and extended family members) interfere with good parenting.

Most studies of health and stress (for example, Sarason, Johnson, & Seigel, 1978), have focused on life change—new events that require coping or adaptation. In our work, we have also begun to assess two other sources of stress: ongoing events (Difficult Life Circumstances) that make chronic (rather than acute) demands upon family members, and everyday events (Hassles) that cause stress by their frequency rather than their severity. We expect that good parenting takes place more frequently in households where life change is no more than moderate, in which Difficult Life circumstances are minimal and well handled, and hassles are not excessive.

Maternal Competence as the
Basis for Intervention

There is reason to believe that many women in high-risk families show deficits in one or more of these aspects of maternal competence. Our goal as prevention specialists is, then, to provide interventions that will support, enhance, and, where necessary, develop these competencies.

It may seem that focusing on maternal competencies—some of which are rather remote from the infant's actual experience—is an awfully indirect way of making an impact on the family of a newborn. Nevertheless, there are several compelling reasons for doing so. First, it is actually more efficient. Working with an infant for a hour a week provides only one hour's worth of intervention, but working with a parent for the same amount of time can provide many hours worth of intervention from the parent to the infant. In a more practical vein, many of the child outcomes of interest (such as school learning or behavior problems) cannot be assessed for many years. Moreover, some of these outcomes are *non*events, such as not getting sick, not requiring special services, or not having behavior problems. Concentrating upon the mothers' skills and behaviors—which are positive attitudes and behaviors that can be assessed here and now—makes it possible to evaluate the effects of the intervention much sooner and more easily. Finally, our research (Barnard et al., 1983) has shown that there is probably a substantial lag between the time a parent's behavior changes and the time that the results of those changes can be seen in children's behavior. For example, when a mother becomes more socially responsive to her infant it may still be several months until the child, in turn, responds to that parental change.

In some cases, where a parent shows serious and/or multiple deficits, working only with the mother may *be* too indirect. In these instances, supportive or alternative care for the infant may be necessary while the parent participates in skill-building treatment. In general, though, prevention programs for families of new babies need to be based on the same principles as those for other groups of clients—providing skills that will allow them to function over the long term as well as in the short run.

A Mental Health Model for
Services to Families of Newborns

The *Mental Health Model* to be described here is the product of combining careful concern for the health and physical development of infants in high-risk families with equally careful concern for their mental health and social-emotional development. Although the program was designed and carried out by community-health nurses, it differs in some important ways from traditional *Information and Resource Utilization Models* delivered in a similar format.

Strength, Integrity, and Effectiveness

Before turning to a more specific description of the Mental Health Model (and of the Information and Resource Model with which it can be contrasted), it will be helpful to consider some characteristics of intervention programs in general. Sechrest and Yeaton (1981; also Yeaton & Sechrest, 1981) have suggested three such dimensions: strength, integrity, and effectiveness.

A program has *strength* to the extent that it includes "large amounts in pure form of these ingredients leading to change" (Yeaton & Sechrest, 1981, p. 156). Although it is not obvious how strength should be precisely measured, it does seem reasonable that interventions that are longer, more intensive, more closely linked to theory, delivered by better trained personnel, and more carefully planned and delivered ought to be stronger than those that are shorter, less intensive, less closely linked to theory, delivered by less-well-qualified staff, and less well designed and executed.

A program of intervention has *integrity* if it is delivered as intended. It has been suggested (Boruch & Gomez, 1977) that when laboratory-proven treatments are moved to field settings, a lack of program integrity may account for failures to demonstrate positive outcomes. For well-planned and documented programs, it is easy (albeit not yet common) to collect data on how accurately study procedures and protocols are carried out—and such data are needed to demonstrate program integrity.

Finally, a program's *effectiveness* is the extent to which it actually produces differences of the desired kind and of sufficient magnitude. The sufficiency of program effects can be assessed in a number of ways (Sechrest & Yeaton, 1981, suggest judgmental, normative, and statistical methods as among the possible alternatives), but the basic logic is that the more and larger the changes produced, the greater the effectiveness.

Every practitioner would like to have a program that is high on all three of these dimensions—but this is not very realistic. The program we have designed for families of newborns is an attempt to use the most effective strategies available, with maximum integrity, but with probably only moderate strength. We accepted moderate strength, because most of the factors that make a treatment very strong also significantly increase its costs—duration, frequency of contact, training of staff. Because this program is designed for use by public health agencies—whose resources are increasingly limited—it is especially important that it not be prohibitively expensive.

Two Models for Home-Based Care

The two treatment programs to be described here—the traditional Information and Resource model and the innovative Mental Health Model—were both designed to meet the special needs of high-risk families and their infants from midpregnancy through the first year of life. We define families as high risk if the mothers show a pattern of youth, poverty, low education, and social isolation, or if the family has a history of alcohol or drug abuse, or abuse or neglect of another child.

Program similarities. The two programs share several important features. First, both are based on high quality basic health care during pregnancy and the first year of infant life. Aside from prenatal medical care, all women in our study received specialized nursing care and nutritional guidance during pregnancy, and postpartum and well-baby care during the year following the baby's birth.

Second, both programs used some home visits for the delivery of services. A survey of resources in our community had shown us that women in high-risk families were rather unlikely to make use of classes and groups designed to help pregnant women and new mothers. Home visits, on the other hand, have traditionally been used in community health nursing, because of their effectiveness in providing services for "hard to reach" clients. In both the programs, these visits began during the second trimester of pregnancy and continued to the end of the first year of the baby's life.

Next, services in both programs were provided by a single consistent caregiver for the duration of the project. Each client had her "own" nurse whom she saw regularly, and the development of the relationship between the client and the nurse became part of the treatment in its own right.

Another important common element in the two programs was their organization into written protocols with specific goals and objectives. These goals, which were separately specified for pregnancy and the infant's first year, gave structure to the work done with the clients at each home visit. Careful records were kept by all of the visiting nurses about when each goal was introduced and when (or whether) it was attained.

Both programs provided families with a great deal of information about child care and about managing family life in general. As will be seen, the ways in which this material was presented differed, but the quantity was substantial for both models. Similarly, both programs made a good deal of use of record keeping beyond that which is normally part of health record charting. Some of this record keeping was related to assessing the integrity of the programs, and some was related to keeping track of the goals and objectives for each client.

Program differences. The chief differences between these two programs can be seen against the background of these similarities of format and content. This contrast is primarily in the philosophy and methods of providing services.

The Information and Resource model can be characterized as a didactic approach centered upon the physical health of the mother and child. It is a didactic approach, because it focuses on providing information—facts, procedures, practices—to the mother in a direct and straightforward way. Along with direct teaching, the nurse also provides referrals to other community agencies and sources of service, so that she serves as a resource coordinator as well as a caregiver. Both the information and the referrals made in this program tend to be about the physical health of the mother and child, including a strong element of health promotion and disease prevention as well as the diagnosis and alleviation of physical problems.

The Mental Health Model, on the other hand, can be characterized as process-oriented, centered upon the interpersonal therapeutic approach, and providing comprehensive health care. The nurse fosters an explicitly therapeutic relationship, and in that relationship the nurse can demonstrate ways of handling family relationships and problems. The client is seen as an active participant, rather than as a comparatively passive learner or resource user. The emphasis throughout is upon the process of dealing with family problems and developmental issues. And although physical health is one important content area, social-emotional health and maternal social competence are also emphasized.

Protocol Development

The written protocols for the two models of care reflect somewhat different processes of program development.

The Information and Resource model protocol is a systematic and explicit version of traditional public health and community health practice. The written protocols for the present study were prepared by staff nurses from the Seattle King County Public Health Department, working together with faculty from our project. The staff nurses reviewed their own work and drafted a series of nursing activities and desired outcomes, and these were discussed, revised, and edited until consensual agreement about their content was reached.

The written protocol for the Information and Resource model was organized in four time periods: antepartum, postpartum (covering the immediate postpartum period), newborn (birth to six weeks), and infancy (six weeks to twelve months). For each of these time periods, there was a set of 10 to 15 broad categories, each with one or more specific items. The nurse home visitor kept a record of when work on each specific item was begun and when it was accomplished.

The Mental Health Model evolved from a series of nursing research projects (Barnard et al., 1983; Barnard & Douglas, 1974; Barnard & Eyres, 1979; Barnard, Wenner, Weber, Gray, Peterson, 1977; Eyres, Barnard, & Gray, 1979). In particular, the model is an attempt to integrate the best of research and theory on maternal and child health with the strongest and most effective ways of delivering the relevant services. Both the specific content of the program (which is organized around the model of maternal competence presented earlier) and the process of delivering services borrow heavily from developmental, social, and clinical psychology and related human services professions.

The overall goals of the Mental Health model are shown in Table 4.1. It is noteworthy that the first two goals of the program are process-oriented—they describe the ways in which the nurse will develop and make use of a therapeutic relationship with the mother. The remaining goals are more content-oriented, and they describe the domains of concerns that the nurse and mother will address over the course of the intervention.

The use of the therapeutic relationship as the organizing theme of the intervention is partially based on the work of Brammer (1973), who describes the development of such relationships over the course of therapy. During the stage of "Relationship Building," the caregiver and client enter into a partnership; clarify the goals, expectations, and responsibilities of each partner; formulate a structure (often a specific contract); and develop mutual trust and respect, open exchange of information, sharing of thoughts and feelings, and mutual active participation.

Following successful building of such a relationship, the nurse and mother are able to proceed to "Facilitating Positive Action." In this stage of their work together, the mother is helped to apply her new skills in problem solving, including testing out new behaviors and reexamining thoughts and feelings associated with these skills and behaviors. Gradually, the client becomes able to manage these sequences by herself, which signals the appropriateness of terminating the particular helping relationship.

TABLE 4.1
Mental Health Model Superordinate Goals

---

1. To develop a trusting, supportive, nurturing, interpersonal relationship between mother and nurse.
2. To provide maternal physical and emotional support.
3. To increase maternal social competence with adults.
4. To generalize maternal social competence to parenting situations.
5. To foster maternal attachment to her infant.
6. To optimize the infant's physical, cognitive, and socio-emotional development.

Naturally, the stages of Relationship Building and Facilitating Positive Action do not always occur neatly in chronological sequence, nor are they easily achieved. Our own experience is that building such a relationship is often particularly difficult for high-social-risk women. Consequently, much of the content of the Mental Health model is aimed at those skills (such as social interaction behaviors) that will, in turn, help the building of the relationship.

The written protocol for the Mental Health model was developed by project staff to reflect all of these concerns. It was organized in four time periods: antepartum, intrapartum (concerned with labor and delivery), early infancy (birth to three months), and later infancy (four to twelve months). Each time period was characterized by three to nine broad categories, with specific items in each. As with the Information and Resource model, the nurse home visitors kept records as to the beginning and ending dates for dealing with each of the specific goals and objectives.

Goals and Objectives

Prenatal goals. The contrast between the Information and Resource Model and the Mental Health Model can be seen in their respective goals for the prenatal period of care. (These are listed in Table 4.2.) It should be noted that patients receiving care under both of these models were also receiving prenatal care from a physician.

One contrast that can be made is that the Information and Resource model focuses on the *what*—knowledge about health practices, about labor and delivery, and about personal and community resources. The Mental Health model, on the other hand, focuses much more on the *how*—fostering decision making, reducing anxiety, increasing self-image, and enhancing attachment. Although the realm of issues considered is very similar between the two, the way in which the issue is addressed is quite markedly different. The more didactically based

TABLE 4.2
Goals for the Prenatal Period

Information & Resource Model

1. Kept scheduled appointments regarding pregnancy care.
2. Demonstrated knowledge and use of health practices that lead to optimal wellness.
3. Demonstrated knowledge of the normal anticipated course and potential complications of pregnancy, labor, and delivery.
4. Demonstrated knowledge and use of personal and community resources according to need.
5. Demonstrated positive feelings toward pregnancy.

Mental Health Model

1. Increased support of mother's affiliative system.
2. Fostered decision making of mother in relation to delivery options.
3. Reduced anxiety about situation events related to pregnancy.
4. Increased self-image and confidence for coping with pregnancy, labor, and delivery.
5. Enhanced mother-infant attachment.

program has goals—and services—based upon *information* while the more interpersonally based program is based primarily upon *process*.

A second contrast can be made in terms of the specificity of the program goals. In the Information and Resource model, the goals are explicitly linked to the particular situation of being pregnant. There would be no reason at all for a patient in some other circumstances— such as having a chronically ill child or recovering from surgery—to deal with these goals. In the Mental Health model, however, the goals are somewhat less specific to pregnancy. A woman dealing with another problem might indeed also have to work on increasing her support, fostering decision making, reducing anxiety, and increasing self-confidence. While these are worded in terms of the situational demands of pregnancy, they clearly are oriented to processes that are more general.

Finally, it must be said that it is considerably easier to evaluate the attainment of the goals in the Information and Resource model than those in the Mental Health Model. Appointment keeping and knowledge are a good deal easier to measure than decision making, anxiety, and self-image. These easier-to-measure goals are also probably easier to justify to policymakers—partly because they are so concrete, and partly because they seem so clearly desirable. Nonetheless, the fact that the Mental Health model goals are process-oriented and more generally applicable means that we might expect the positive effects of the program to be generalized more broadly than would be true for more specific and information-oriented objectives.

First-year goals. The goals for each program during the first year of the infant's life are shown in Tables 4.3 and 4.4. The distinctions noted between the two in prenatal goals are still apparent: content versus process, specific versus general, more easily versus less easily assessable. What is also apparent is that the Mental Health model places more emphasis on *dyadic* issues than the Information and Resource model. The goals in the Mental Health program center on relationship and interactive processes between mother and adults as well as between mother and infant. By setting goals about the mother-infant dyad (rather than for each of them separately), the Mental Health model follows the lead of family therapy in seeing the unit of intervention as the interactive system, rather than the individuals in that system (Minuchin, 1985).

Evaluating the Intervention

The research component of the Infant and Family Focus project was designed both to provide a sound and realistic evaluation of the program models' effectiveness and to explore further the relationships among maternal competencies and child and family outcomes. The general design is that of a field experiment, in which clients were randomly assigned to one or the other of the home nursing care models (Mental Health or Information and Resource). Data were collected from the mothers, and after their births, the babies, from the time of intake into the study until the children were three years of age (though the interventions themselves lasted only through the babies' first birthday). The overall research strategy reflects the recommendations made by Gray and Wandersman (1980) in their review of home intervention programs for young children. These recommendations included

(1) systematic data collection concerning the family's ecological sur-roundings, including measurement of preintervention functioning;
(2) detailed study of control or comparison groups;
(3) investigation of the processes of interaction among home visitors, mother, child, family, and social network; and
(4) use of an array of measures: child, family, and social network.

Because the research is still in progress, what follows is a preliminary report of the findings. First we shall describe the research design and data collection, and then look at data currently available reflecting the strength, integrity, and effectiveness of the intervention models.

TABLE 4.3
Information and Resource Model Goals
for the First Year of Life

Maternal Postpartum

1. Completed postpartum checkup by eight weeks.
2. Demonstrated knowledge of physical care of self and the emotional changes and stresses of postpartum period.
3. Demonstrated knowledge of physical complications of postpartum period and when to seek medical care.
4. Demonstrated knowledge of birth control methods and has interim method available if needed and desired.
5. Demonstrated knowledge and use of personal and community resources according to need.
6. Demonstrated recognition and support of role adjustments of family members.

Parenting

1. Demonstrated knowledge of infant illness, basic home health care techniques, and when to seek medical care.
2. Demonstrated knowledge and use of appropriate basic care-giving techniques.
3. Demonstrated knowledge and use of safety measures related to developmental abilities.
4. Demonstrated knowledge and use of appropriate type and amount of infant stimulation through toys, activities, and socializing.
5. Demonstrated attachment behaviors to infant and found pleasure in infant-related care activities and play.

Infant

1. Received at least three physical examinations, of which one occurred by six weeks of age and one occurred after nine months of age.
2. Gained height and weight according to standard growth grid for first year of life.
3. Received initial series of immunizations.
4. Taken a full range of food (type, texture, variety) during the first year.
5. Performed all "midpoint" Denver items for age at one year.

Research Design

Subjects in the study were recruited during the middle trimester of pregnancy from public health clinics in King County, Washington. Women were invited to participate if they met any of the following criteria:

(1) history of alcohol or drug abuse;
(2) diagnosed psychiatric illness;
(3) mental retardation;
(4) history of abuse or neglect of previous child;

TABLE 4.4
Mental Health Model Goals
for the First Year of Life

Maternal

1. Enhanced maternal understanding of the social and reciprocal nature of interactions.
2. Increased maternal social competence and affiliative relationships with others.
3. Facilitated maternal participation in community resources offering child care support.
4. Facilitated maternal use of personal and community resources according to need.
5. Facilitated maternal adaptive and coping behaviors that minimize disruption of parenting.

Parenting

1. Increased parental support of infant self-regulating behaviors in sleeping and eating.
2. Maximized parent-infant interactions and reciprocal affective involvement with each other.
3. Enhanced parental knowledge of realistic expectations for development and provision of environmental input that ensures variety of sensory experiences and temporal organization.
4. Increased parental ability to provide a safe environment for the child.
5. Encouraged avoidance of restrictive care-giving patterns.

(5) low education (high school or less) and low support (no partner, or an abusive partner);
(6) young (19 or less) and low support;
(7) low income and low support; and
(8) young, low income, and low education.

Not surprisingly, these women also tended to reside in crowded living conditions and to move frequently; to have chaotic and disorganized family lives with little schedule or regularity; to experience many crises, accidents, and illnesses; to have high levels of marital (or partner) discord, conflict, and arguments; and to have difficulty in obtaining medical care.

After subjects were recruited, they were randomly assigned to either the Mental Health model (conducted by project staff nurses) or the Information and Resource Utilization model (conducted by the staff nurses from the Seattle-King County Public Health Department). Each woman was visited in her own home (or occasionally, at another place of her choosing) throughout her pregnancy and the first year of the infant's life. The number of visits varied quite widely from one client to another, but all mothers were visited within two weeks of recruitment into the study, within six weeks of the birth of the baby, and within four weeks of the baby's one-year-old birthday.

Evaluation data were collected at regular intervals, beginning at the time of intake into the project. A partial schedule for data collection through the child's three-month birthday is shown in Table 4.5 (data were also gathered about the physical health of the mother and infant, demographic characteristics of the family, father involvement, early contact between mother and infant, and the like). It is noteworthy that several different methods were used to get information: interview, observation, and questionnaire. This variety means that correlations among variables cannot be explained as simply due to shared "method variance" among them. The information gathered at six weeks post-partum was collected by the nurse who was working with the family, but all other data were obtained by staff members not involved with the delivery of services. Insofar as possible, these evaluators were unaware of which care model each family received. Although these families are being followed until the children are three years of age, only the results through the baby's three-month birthday are complete and will be reported here.

In addition to this ambitious plan for assessment of the families in the project, extensive data were collected about the content and process of the interventions themselves. Each home visit (and each phone contact and clinic visit) was recorded in some detail, including the subjects discussed, the nursing process used to deal with each subject (information, support, monitoring, therapy), and the focus of the visit (mother, child, mother and child, other family members). These data were gathered in order to document the strength and integrity of the program as it was actually delivered.

Program Strength

The data pertaining to program strength are currently available only for the prenatal period—from midpregnancy to the time of birth. During that time, each participating family received about five home visits (mean 5.04, SD 3.37, range 0-16), each one about an hour long (mean 63.53 minutes, SD 16.15, range 0-101 minutes), and between three and four phone contacts (mean 3.48, SD 4.98, range 0-29). Not surprisingly, the two intervention models differed significantly in strength on all three of these measures. Families in the Mental Health model received more home visits (6.86 versus 3.32 for the Information Resource model; $t = 7.09$, $p < .001$), and the visits were longer (69.74 versus 57.32 minutes for the Information Resource group; $t = 4.66$, $p < .001$). Nurses in the Mental Health Model also made more phone contacts with their patients (5.23 versus 1.84 for the Information

Resource nurses; t = 4.08, $p < .001$). The total amount of contact (in minutes) during the prenatal period was 630 minutes for the Mental Health group and 240 minutes for the Information and Resource group.

In spite of the differing *amounts* of treatment that the two groups of clients received, the *kinds* of topics dealt with during the visits were quite similar for the two groups (see Figure 4.1). Nurses in both groups spent a considerable proportion of their efforts on physical health, resources, and psychosocial concerns of the mothers, with consequently less emphasis on development, nutrition, parenting, and miscellaneous concerns. In other words, although the process of care delivery differed between the two groups, both received comparable levels of information in these key areas.

Another way of assessing the strengths of a treatment is in terms of the supervision necessary to carry it out successfully. Nurses using the Mental Health model had supervision of two kinds—ongoing involvement with the development and implementation of their program from experienced nurses on the project staff, and biweekly consultation with a clinical psychologist. This latter arrangement served several purposes: it provided a forum for the nurses to receive regular support from their coworkers and the psychologist as they dealt with difficult cases; it provided information and expertise about the mental status of some of the more worrisome clients; and it helped to clarify the nursing goals of the care model, as contrasted to a psychiatric or psychological focus. The nurses in the Information Resource model received their regular staff supervision from the Health Department, and had no regular access to additional consultation.

These data indicate that the Mental Health program shows moderate to high levels of strength. The number of visits and phone calls made by nurses in the Mental Health Model was greater than standard practice in the Health Department (the Information Resource model), but not so much greater as to represent an impossible goal for a public agency. Moreover, the topics covered (though not necessarily the manner in which they are covered) seem quite similar and compatible with those in the traditional program. Finally, it seems probable that the use of effective supervision and consultation has increased the strength of the intervention offered in the innovative program.

Program Integrity

One unique aspect of this program is the effort made to ensure program integrity through record keeping of each home visit and phone contact. One of the most pertinent of these records is a set of program

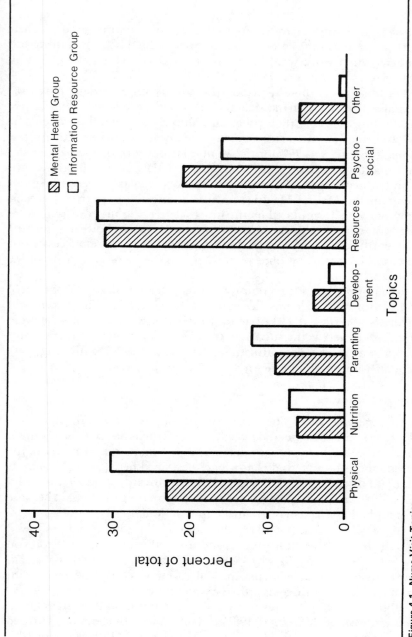

Figure 4.1 Nurse Visit Topics

89

objectives, defined separately for each of the intervention models. Each nurse kept track of each client's progress on these goals by noting the date at which work was begun and the date at which the goal was achieved.

During the prenatal period (the only complete data currently available), the clients in the Mental Health model achieved a significantly greater proportion of their program's objectives than did the clients in the Information Resource model. The completion rate during the prenatal period was 79% for the Mental Health group, and 60% for the Information Resource group ($t = 4.78$, $p < .001$). Some of this difference is undoubtedly due to the greater number of contacts between nurse and client in the Mental Health model. Because the objectives for each program were formulated by the nurses delivering the care, who were aware of their own limitations of time and expertise, however, it is still noteworthy that the Mental Health model was more successful at reaching its goals and objectives than was the Information Resource model.

It is impossible, at this point, to judge whether 60% or 79% protocol completion reflect adequate levels of program integrity. The percentages themselves reflect the skill with which the written protocols were designed as well as the success with which they have been carried out. Either way, these data illustrate the usefulness of gathering data explicitly on program integrity.

Program Effectiveness

Changes over time. There was evidence of positive overall change for all of the families in the study, regardless of which intervention program they received. These positive changes were demonstrated in three of the five domains of maternal competence described here (see Table 4.5). A small (and only marginally statistically significant) decrease was found in one area, and change could not be assessed in the fifth domain because no repeated assessments were made in that domain.

Mothers' social skill with another adult was the one area that showed a slight decline over the beginning months of the intervention. Scores on the Social Skill Scale (Mitchell & Bee, 1983), a 73-item checklist of verbal and nonverbal social behavior, showed a decline of only about one point from intake to the three-month assessment visit.

Both Social Support (as measured by the Personal Resources Questionnaire, Brandt & Weinert, 1981) and the number of Resources Utilized increased over the period being discussed here. Mothers reported a general increase in their satisfaction with their social networks over the

TABLE 4.5
Partial Data Collection Schedule and Preliminary Results

Measures	Occasions	Significant Differences		
Interpersonal interaction:				
social skills	Intake, 3 months	Time	$F(1, 102) = 3.1*$	
feeding interaction scale	6 weeks			
teaching interaction scale	3 months			
Community life:				
community life skills scale	Intake			
personal resources	Intake, 3 months	Time	$F(1, 99) = 11.2***$	
questionnaire		G X T	$F(1, 99) = 3.0*$	
resources utilized	Intake, 3 months	Time	$F(1, 102) = 5.1**$	
Child care knowledge:				
developmental expectations	Intake			
child development	Intake			
questionnaire				
Emotional stability:				
Beck depression inventory	Intake, 6 weeks	Time	$F(1, 96) = 5.0**$	
locus of control scale	Intake			
symptom list	Intake			
Stress and life change:				
life experiences scale	Intake, 3 months			
positive events		Time	$F(1, 98) = 9.6***$	
		G x T	$F(1, 98) = 5.3**$	
negative events		Group	$F(1, 98) = 3.0*$	
difficult life circumstances	Intake			

$*p < .10$; $**p < .05$; $***p < .01$.

course of the intervention. Mothers in both groups also tended to use a slightly greater number of community resources at three months than they had during their pregnancies.

Only the Beck Depression Inventory (Beck, 1972) among the measures of emotional stability showed a change over time, with the average score for all mothers showing a decline over the time of treatment.

Finally, there was an increase over time in the number of life events that the women rated as being positive changes in their lives. Because the number of events rated as negative changes simultaneously decreased (albeit this difference was not statistically significant), it appears that the critical change is not in the *number* of life events, but in the way the events are *perceived* by the client.

Group differences. While it is encouraging that there were so many positive overall changes among the women in the project, it is also important to look at comparisons between the women in the two alternative intervention programs. It can be seen (also in Table 4.5) that group differences (either main effects or Group X Time interactions) occur in two of the five maternal competence domains.

Scores on the Personal Resources Questionnaire, reflecting satisfaction with social support, show evidence of a Group X Time interaction. Scores for mothers in the Mental Health group show about a nine-point improvement on this scale, while those in the Information Resource group improve only about two points.

Both positive and negative life events show evidence of group differences. The number of positively evaluated changes increases more for the Mental Health group than for the Information Resource group (a Group X Time interaction). Negative life events, on the other hand, show a marginally significant group main effect, with mothers in the Information Resource group reporting more such events than those in the Mental Health group.

While these group differences are not of great magnitude, they are important for two reasons. First, all are in the direction of showing an advantage to the Mental Health Model. Second, they are spread across several of the domains of maternal competence, suggesting that improvements in the participants are general as well as specific.

It should also be noted that the data reported here do not directly reflect any of the infant's competencies. If our premise is correct, then these improvements in maternal competence will be associated with good performance in a variety of developmental assessments to be conducted later in the course of the research.

Effectiveness as a function of strength and integrity. It would seem reasonable that the effectiveness of a program would be related to its strength and integrity. Although data are currently available about strength and integrity only through the prenatal period, and about effectiveness only through the third month of the infants' lives, it seems valuable to take at least a first look at the correlations among these variables.

The index of program strength is the total number of contact minutes during the prenatal period. This variable includes clinic visits and telephone conversations as well as home visits. The correlations between program strength and various maternal variables is shown in Table 4.6.

The amount of contact in the Mental Health program is not correlated with any of the mother's incoming characteristics. In dramatic contrast, the amount of contact in the Information and Resource program is related to the mother's social support, resource utilization, depression, and negative life events. Correlations between

TABLE 4.6
Correlations between Program Strength and Maternal Variables

Maternal Variable	Intake Assessment		Later Assessment	
	MH	IR	MH	IR
Social skills				
Social support		−.35**	−.24*	−.39**
Resources utilized		.28**	.22*	.26*
Depression		.39***		.35**
Positive life events				
Negative life events		.26*		.21*
Feeding interaction	NA	NA		
Teaching interaction	NA	NA		.27*

NOTE: MH = Mental Health Group; IR = Information Resource Group. Later assessment was three months for all variables except Feeding and Depression, which were measured at six weeks.
*p < .10; **p < .05; ***p < .01.

these same maternal variables assessed after the birth of the infant are also shown in Table 4.6. It would be misleading to think of these correlations as describing only the effects of the intervention programs, because the maternal characteristics show considerable stability over the time from intake to later assessment (stability coefficients ranged from 0.42 to 0.81 for these variables). Among the mothers in both groups, higher nurse contact is associated with lower levels of social support and greater use of other resources during early infancy. For the mothers in the Information and Resource group, higher nurse contact is also related to more severe depression, more negative life events, and (encouragingly) greater skill during the teaching interaction.

These findings reflect the restriction of resources available in the Information and Resource program, which forced the nurses using that model to focus their attention on those women whose needs seemed the greatest. Because of their separate funding and somewhat lighter caseloads, nurses in the Mental Health model did not have to focus their efforts in this same way.

The index of program integrity was the proportion of the prenatal protocol that was completed by the nurse and client. Correlations between this measure of integrity and various maternal variables are shown in Table 4.7.

Among those in the Mental Health group, the women with better intake social skills were likely to complete more of the program objectives than those with poorer skills. Among those in the Information and Resource group, it was the women with comparatively more social

TABLE 4.7
Correlations between Program Integrity and Maternal Variables

Maternal Variable	Intake Assessment		Later Assessment	
	MH	IR	MH	IR
Social skills	.32***			.24**
Social support		.19*	−.21*	
Resources utilized				.20*
Depression				
Positive life events		.29**	.21*	.28**
Negative life events				
Feeding interaction	NA	NA	.27**	
Teaching interaction	NA	NA	.18*	

NOTE: MH = Mental Health Group; IR = Information Resource Group. Later assessment was three months for all variables except Feeding and Depression, which were measured at six weeks.
*p < .10; **p < .05; ***p < .01.

support and more positive life events who were likely to complete more of the protocol.

The relationships between protocol completion and functioning at six weeks and three months are somewhat curious. Higher rates of completion are associated with positive life events for women in both groups. For the Mental Health group, high rates of completion were also associated with good skills during feeding and teaching interactions. Completion, however, is also related to comparatively low levels of satisfaction with social support from others. One possible interpretation is that women without large social networks of their own may have relied upon the nurse for their social needs. This would have facilitated completion of the protocols, but not increased their satisfaction with their own support networks. Finally, high completers in the Information and Resource group utilized more resources and reported more positive life events.

These relationships among strength, integrity, and effectiveness are not as "tidy" or robust as we might wish, but they do provide some encouraging evidence that program characteristics interact in systematic ways with participants' initial characteristics.

The Unanswered Questions

The data presented here confirm that it is possible to design and deliver a strong and effective program of intervention based on a model of maternal competence. In doing so, however, our project staff have repeatedly confronted some of the more basic issues about preventive interventions for families of infants and young children. To those issues we now briefly turn.

First, we ask, at *whom* our interventions should be aimed. There is certainly a moral and ethical imperative to provide services to the most disorganized and chaotic families in which we believe the children are at highest risk for developmental problems. At the same time, these are the families who need the *strongest*—and therefore the most costly and time-consuming—kinds of treatments we can devise. Should we (as practitioners and citizens) choose to spend our resources on these families, or should we turn our attention to less distressed families who may be helped by less strong (and presumably less costly) programs? Should we (as researchers) choose to test our theories on individuals and families who represent extremes in many ways, or should our research focus on the larger number of less dysfunctional relationships?

Our own choice for *whom* to serve was guided by our sense of which families in our community were both needy and currently underserved. We attempted to multiply the "strength" of the treatment by involving family members, other care providers, and community agencies. We have tried to develop a theory of maternal competence that addresses the special problems of dysfunctional families, but that is also applicable more widely.

A second set of issues focuses on *how* to define and *when* to measure the desired outcomes of a prevention program. Are the most important outcomes the ones predicted by our theory, or the ones that save taxpayers the most money, or the ones that reflect the happiness or commitment of our clients? Is it better to use assessment tools that imperfectly match our aims but are well-known and psychometrically sound, or to use those that are less robust but closer to our goals? Should we look for results as soon as possible, or in the near future, or perhaps wait until the far future?

In our own research, we have had the privilege of doing many of these things at one time: the mothers and children are assessed over a wide number of domains of competence, using many different methods, and for a comparatively long time. But most prevention workers and researchers do not have this luxury, and the choices to be made are not easy ones.

A final set of issues concerns how we can reconcile our habitual ways of doing research with the special problems of assessing the effectiveness of prevention. To evaluate prevention, we need to measure accurately how functions and characteristics are maintained, not just how they are improved or removed or "fixed." But most social scientists have been trained to think of stability as either an impediment to change, or a source of error in scores that reflect change. To evaluate prevention, we need to count up events that don't happen. But most researchers have expertise only in counting things that do occur. To evaluate prevention, we need to combine rich and varied data sources to reflect idiosyncratic aspects of adaptation. But most of our most powerful analytic tools for doing that require sample sizes and mathematical sophistication quite beyond the scope of even ambitious projects.

Our own response to these issues is to be as inclusive of analytic methods as we can—to invite the use of case studies, of small group analysis. We are trying to see stability as a useful characteristic of families and individuals, and to use group-defining variables (those clients who vary less than one standard deviation from one data point to another, for example) to better understand our data. And we try to borrow all of the good ideas we can find!

One metaphor for a good prevention program is a patchwork quilt. A quilt is made up of many pieces that differ in size and shape and color—but it isn't a useful bed covering unless all the pieces are there and skillfully stitched together. The Infant and Family Focus Project is a quilt constructed from one theory-shaped piece (the construct of Maternal Competence), one practice-shaped piece (the Mental Health Model of home based nursing intervention), and one empirically shaped piece (the research design and data analysis). If it turns out to be a prize-winning quilt (and we hope it will!), it will be because all three pieces fit together harmoniously.

Note

1. The research reported here was supported by National Institutes of Mental Health grant MH 36894, "Clinical Nursing Model for Infants and Their Families," Kathryn E. Barnard, Principal Investigator. The Mental Health model was developed and used by Charlene Snyder, Anita Spietz, Nia Johnson-Crowley, and Rebecca Kang, all of the University of Washington School of Nursing. The Information and Resource model was developed by Margaret Eagan, Ruth Hockenbery, Beverly Huchala, Suzanne Limerick, and Anita Pitts.

References

Ainsworth, M.D.S., & Bell, S. M. (1969). Some contemporary patterns of mother-infant interaction in the feeding situation. In A. Ambrose (Ed.), *Stimulation in early infancy*. London: Academic Press.

Arend, R., Gove, F. L., & Sroufe, L. A. (1979). Continuity of individual adaptation from infancy to kindergarten: A predictive study of ego-resilience and curiosity in preschoolers. *Child Development, 50,* 950-959.

Barnard, K. E. (1978). *Nursing child assessment satellite training project learning resource manual.* Unpublished program materials, University of Washington.

Barnard, K. E., Bee, H. L., Booth, C. L., Mitchell, S. K., & Sumner, G. A. (1981). *Clinical nursing model for infants and their families.* Proposal to National Institutes of Mental Health, Research on Mental Health Clinical Services for Infants and their Families.

Barnard, K. E., Booth, C. L., Mitchell, S. K., & Telzrow, R. W. (1983). *Newborn nursing models.* Final report of Project RO1-NU-00719, Division of Nursing, Bureau of Health Manpower, Health Resources Administration, Department of Health and Human Services. Washington, DC: Government Printing Office.

Barnard, K. E., & Douglas, H. B. (1974). *Child health assessment, part 1: A literature review* (DHEW Publication No. HRA 75-30). Washington, DC: Government Printing Office.

Barnard, K. E., & Eyres, S. J. (1979). *Child health assessment, part 2: The first year of life* (DHEW Publication No. HRA 79-25). Washington, DC: Government Printing Office.

Barnard, K. E., Wenner, W., Weber, B., Gray, C., & Peterson, A. (1977). Premature infant refocus. In P. Mittler (Ed.), *Research to practice in mental retardation: Vol. 3. Biomedical aspects.* Baltimore: University Park Press.

Beck, A. T. (1972). *Depression: Causes and treatments.* Philadelphia: University of Pennsylvania Press.

Blehar, M. C., Lieberman, A. F., & Ainsworth, M.D.S. (1977). Early face to face interaction and its relation to later infant-mother attachment. *Child Development, 48,* 182-194.

Boruch, R. F., & Gomez, H. (1977). Sensitivity, bias, and theory in impact evaluations. *Professional Psychology, 8,* 411-434.

Brammer, L. M. (1973). *The helping relationship: Process and skills.* Englewood Cliffs, NJ: Prentice-Hall.

Brandt, P., & Weinert, C. A. (1981). The PRQ—A social support measure. *Nursing Research, 30,* 277-280.

Bromwich, R. M. (1976). Focus on maternal behavior in infant intervention. *American Journal of Orthopsychiatry, 46,* 439-446.

Bronfenbrenner, U. (1979). *The ecology of human development.* Cambridge, MA: Harvard University Press.

Clarke-Stewart, K. A., VanderStoep, L. P., & Killian, G. A. (1979). Analysis and replication of mother-child relations at two years of age. *Child Development, 50,* 777-793.

Easterbrooks, M. A., & Lamb, M. E. (1979). The relationship between quality of infant-mother attachment and infant competence in initial encounters with peers. *Child Development, 50,* 380-387.

Egeland, B., & Farber, E. A. (1984). Infant-mother attachment: Factors related to its development and changes over time. *Child Development, 55,* 753-771.

Eyres, S. J., Barnard, K. E., & Gray, C. A. (1979). *Child health assessment, part 3: 2-4 years.* Final report of Project RO2—NU-00559, Division of Nursing, Bureau of Health Manpower, Health Resources Administration, Department of Health, Education, and Welfare. Washington, DC: Government Printing Office.

Gray, S. W., & Wandersman, L. P. (1980). The methodology of home-based intervention studies: Problems and promising strategies. *Child Development, 51,* 993-1011.

Kessner, D. M. (1973). *Infant death: An analysis by maternal risk and health care.* Washington, DC: Institute of Medicine, National Academy of Sciences.

Lewis, M., & Coates, D. L. (1980). Mother-infant interaction and cognitive development in twelve-week-old infants. *Infant Behavior and Development, 3,* 95-105.

Lieberman, A. F. (1977). Preschoolers' competence with a peer: Relations with attachment and peer experience. *Child Development, 48,* 1277-1287.

Minuchin, P. (1985). Families and individual development: Provocations from the field of family therapy. *Child Development, 56,* 289-302.

Mitchell, S. K., & Bee, H. L. (1983). *Making and using social networks: The assessment of social skills.* Unpublished manuscript, University of Washington School of Nursing.

Newberger, C. M. (1977). *Parental conceptions of children and child-rearing: A structural-developmental analysis.* Unpublished doctoral dissertation, Harvard University.

Newberger, C. M. (1980). The cognitive structure of parenthood: Designing a descriptive measure. *New Directions for Child Development, 7,* 45-67.

Pakter, J., Rosner, H., Jacogziner, H., & Greenstein, F. (1961). Out of wedlock births in New York city, II. Medical aspects. *American Journal of Public Health, 51,* 846-865.

Rutter, M., & Garmezy, N. (1983). Developmental psychopathology. In P. H. Mussen & E. M. Hetherington (Eds.), *Handbook of child psychology: Vol. 4. Socialization, personality, and social development.* New York: John Wiley.

Sameroff, A. J., & Feil, L. A. (1985). Parental concepts of development. In I. E. Siegel (Ed.), *Parental belief systems: The psychological consequences for children.* Hillsdale, NJ: Erlbaum.

Sarason, I., Johnson, H., & Seigel, M. (1978). Assessing the impact of life changes: Development of the Life Experiences Survey. *Journal of Consulting and Clinical Psychology, 46,* 932-946.

Sechrest, K., & Yeaton, W. H. (1981). Assessing the effectiveness of social programs: Methodological and conceptual issues. In S. Ball (Ed.), *New directions in evaluation research, No. 9.* San Francisco: Jossey-Bass.

Snyder, C., Eyres, S. J., & Barnard, K. (1979). New findings about mothers' antenatal expectations and their relationship to infant development. *American Journal of Maternal Child Nursing, 4,* 354-357.

Thoman, E. B., Becker, P. T., & Freese, M. P. (1978). Individual patterns of mother-infant interaction. In G. P. Sackett (Ed.), *Observing behavior: Vol. 1. Theory and application in mental retardation.* Baltimore, MD: University Park Press.

Waters, E., Wippman, J., & Sroufe, L. A. (1979). Attachment, positive affect, and competence in the peer group: Two studies in construct validation. *Child Development, 50,* 821-829.

Yeaton, W. H., & Sechrest, L. (1981). Critical dimensions in the choice and maintenance of successful treatments: Strength, integrity, and effectiveness. *Journal of Consulting and Clinical Psychology, 49,* 156-167.

Zahn-Waxler, C., Cummings, E. M., McKnew, D. H., & Radke-Yarrow, M. (1984). Altruism, aggression, and social interactions in young children with a manic-depressive parent. *Child Development, 55,* 112-122.

5

Family Relationship Enhancement: A Skill Training Approach

Bernard G. Guerney, Jr.

There is no institution more universal than the family that rears us; no more powerful forger of our destinies. There are no authors, dramatists, composers, artists, or movie directors who can create more than a faint shadow of the emotions this family can generate—indeed, this family provides the set of inner tuning forks against which all future experiences must resonate in order to create powerful feelings. There is no clergyman, no politician, no teacher who can plant a deep conviction in us unless this family has wittingly or unwittingly provided in us the type of soil in which it can take root. The only force that rivals it in determining our life directions, our attitudes, our feelings, and our behavior—and even the nature of this rival force is partly preordained by our original family experiences—is our next, our adult, our chosen family.

I am not preaching an attitude of predeterminism. All our good friends and mentors, among whom I emphatically include mental health professionals, may offer us genuine opportunities to improve the quality of our lives dramatically and help us to develop morally, spiritually, emotionally, and socially. What I *am* saying is that those of us who wish to help others improve the quality of their lives, help others to resolve problems, to become stronger, to be able to avoid psychosocial problems—or, if you prefer, to avoid psychopathology—can do so best if we recognize the awesome power for good or bad of family members: parents, mates, siblings, and, not to be forgotten, children.

No outside person is likely to hold more or longer or better fulcrumed levers of power for creating problems or for promoting strengths than the members of an individual's family. If we wish to help others, to strengthen them, whether as a psychotherapist, a consultation and education specialist, a caseworker, a counselor, or a designer of preventive, enrichment, or therapeutic programs, it pays to consider the question: "Is there a way I can use the power of family members to aid me in my efforts to be of help?" Such aid from the family may be sought at any stage of intervention; it can be for recruitment, or for secondary support, or for very active collaboration and assistance in producing change, or to reinforce or maintain changes provided by the intervention.

Or, it could be that changing the way in which the family functions is *itself* the goal of the intervention. The goal can be to change the family to help its members to reach higher levels of psychosocial functioning; to strengthen their mental health. The idea could be to use the strengths the family already has, and to build in new strengths. That is the goal of family prevention and enrichment programs. The Family Relationship Enhancement (RE) program is one such program. Given the power of the family, it is surprising that changing the family system is as recent and rare a type of structured programmatic intervention as it is.

Perhaps the special problems of working with families have something to do with the time it has taken for us to develop family problem-prevention/enrichment programs. In working with a family as contrasted with unrelated individuals, or even with couples, the task is more difficult and complex. That is so because you are dealing with a group in which the general culture and each family's particular history has established customs, roles, and rules of operation that are very powerful, yet at the same time so much taken for granted by the participants, that the family members are hardly aware that these may be open to choice and to change. In a group of unrelated individuals, the program leader generally *creates* the group's style, that is, the leader sets important rules of interaction, more or less from scratch. In working with families, the groups already exist. A family has its own well-established rules of operation, and the unwary or unprepared leader may find him- or herself overwhelmed or engulfed by a family's system of operating rather than being the one able to shape the course of events as planned. The deeper the level of change the leader seeks and the more the leader's goal is to change the system permanently, the more difficult it becomes to sidestep or to overcome this danger.

There are not many generic problem-prevention/enrichment programs that work with parents and their children together on their relationship skills that have been systematically prepared and field-tested and fewer still that have been evaluated or researched. For a bibliography containing all family prevention/enrichment programs we were able to find in dissertations as well as publications, see B. G. Guerney, Guerney, and Cooney (1985). Some of the better known ones will be described briefly in this chapter before I describe the Family Relationship Enhancement method.

L'Abate has developed a broad spectrum of programs called Structured Enrichment programs. These programs, described in three manuals (L'Abate, 1975a, 1975b; L'Abate & Rupp, 1981), address either general enrichment needs, such as feeling awareness or problem solving, or more specific problems such as alcoholism and depression, or specific stages in the family life cycles such as premarital problem solving, and widowhood. Blechman and Olson (1976) have developed a unique Family Conflict Game approach to problem prevention/enrichment. Robin (1979, 1980) has conducted well-designed research on his behavioral approach to training families in problem-solving communication. Hoopes, Fisher, and Burlow (1984) have written a book that outlines a wide variety of programs targeted for specific groups such as victims of incest or stepfamilies. Carnes (1981) has developed a program called "Understanding Us," which is targeted toward families in general. Coufal and Brock (1983), also aiming at the general population, have adapted Louise Guerney's (1977) Parenting Relationship Enhancement to involve younger children (i.e., children under 12) intensively, along with the parents. Margaret Sawin's Family Cluster program (1979) also involves young children. It is used almost exclusively with religiously oriented families.

Similarities and Differences with Other Programs

The Family Relationship Enhancement program is one of a number of RE programs. While similar to the Marital RE program (B. G. Guerney, 1977a, 1984) in many respects, it differs mainly in that the family program is built around a set of guidelines governing communication for any number of family members, whereas the marital program is built around a dyadic communication pattern.

Family RE differs more dramatically from the Child-Parent RE and the Filial RE programs. The Child-Parent RE problem-prevention program (Coufal & Brock, 1983) and the Parenting Skills RE program (L. F. Guerney, 1980) upon which it was based, draw a great deal from Filial RE therapy (B. G. Guerney, 1964; L. F. Guerney, 1976a, 1983). While these programs deal with children under 12 years of age, Family RE, generally speaking, does not because the children are asked to learn the same skills and to use them in the same way as their parents. A certain level of understanding and verbal fluency is required to do this successfully. The child's communication in Filial RE therapy and the Child-Parent RE program is largely through the medium of play, whereas in Family RE, ordinary conversation is the communication medium. In Filial RE therapy and Child-Parent RE problem-pre-vention/enrichment, all the responsibility for skill-learning and performance is placed on the parents; it is the parent who is responsible for bringing about all the desired changes in the relationship and in the child's behavior. In Family RE, this responsibility is shared equitably.

How does the Family Relationship Enhancement program differ other non-RE-based programs and, indeed, from other parenting programs? Each of the nine behavioral modes taught are unique to RE programs. There are some similarities between the sets of guidelines for some of the skills and those taught in some other programs. For example, Empathic skill and Expressive skill in the RE programs are derived from Rogerian psychotherapy. So are the core skills of Gordon's Parent Effectiveness Training program (1970). Hence, there are significant similarities. But even in instances where there is overlap, there are differences that we regard as highly significant in the skill-guidelines and hence the nature of the skills themselves. Except for the fact that enhanced communication, as each program defines it, usually is a major goal of such programs, there is little similarity between the RE program as a total package, and any other family problem prevention/enrichment programs (and, indeed, little similarity with one another among those other programs). Few of the nine RE skills are used in other programs. The integrated, interlocking fashion in which the skills are used also is unique.

RE also differs from most other family programs in the extent to which it relies on skill-training as the medium for producing change. We place all our eggs in that one incubator because we believe it hatches the most real-life change. Whereas lecture and discussion are a major part of some other programs, RE makes use of lecture and discussion, audiotapes or readings, only to the extent necessary to allow participants to understand what the skills are, and why it is to their advantage to learn them, and to demonstrate the skills. Beyond that, RE programs rely entirely on skill-training. By *skill-training*, we mean demonstrating the skills, and then having the family members put them into practice with each other, first in the sessions under direct supervision and then at home under indirect supervision. Direct word-by-word corrective feedback and reinforcement of participants' good effort and good performance are the major teaching tools. Unlike most family programs, no exercises at all are used. Also, in RE, group members don't comment on issues discussed by other families. Instead, the participants use the skills to work only on their own family's real-life relationship problems and conflicts and enhancement goals. If the skills are actually to become an integral part of the social being of the participants, it is our view that it will only be because the family members come to see how useful the skills are to them in dealing with real-life issues.

Values and Goals of Family RE

While every effort is made to influence the behavior of the participants in an RE program, it is very important to note that participants are not instructed in how they should run their lives. The behaviors the participants are urged to adopt are *process* behaviors to help them make their *own* choices about how they should live. They are taught not the life-style choices themselves, but efficient and effective means to arrive at their own decisions. As mentioned elsewhere in this volume by Myrna Shure in describing the Interpersonal Cognitive Problem-Solving program, we are not teaching participants what to decide, but how to decide; not what the solutions to certain conflicts or problems should be, but how to arrive at solutions that will work and that will last; not what behaviors vis-à-vis other family members they should change, but how to implement successfully and help others implement the changes that *they* decide they want to make. The idea is to empower the participants to use some of the same skills that professionals use to offer support, help, or guidance.

Nevertheless, the process variables promoted by RE are based on certain values. Although program designers seldom consider the question or define the values on which their programs are based, it is impossible to design a value-free intervention program. The values on which RE programs are based, and the values that they promote, are compassion and honesty. When put into play, these values tend to promote a third value: equity. The first two of these values are concordant with those held (though not always applied) by nearly everyone. Within American society, however, and indeed most cultures worldwide, there are some subcultures, in which equity is not valued or even deemed appropriate in marital or parent-child relationships, or is viewed in a way very different than the way in which it should be promoted by an RE program. Examples of these different values are expressed in the view that "a child should be seen, but not heard," or the view that the husband is the head of the household and that it is the wife's duty to obey him regardless of her personal wishes.

When it is clear that such value differences are present, we believe it only fair that they should be pointed out and discussed with family members, as early as possible, preferably before the individual embarks on the program. Even where such contrasting values do exist, and are discussed, it has been our experience that there are goals held by the participants (e.g., a less conflicted, disruptive, emotionally painful home environment) that motivate them to undertake the program, despite the value conflict. The application by the family members of the values of compassion, honesty, and equity, as exemplified by the core skills of the RE program, helps participants to fulfill the goals of the RE program. What are these goals?

The goals of the RE program are very ambitious; hence, even if we achieve them only fractionally, we still may accomplish a good deal. We try to change the way in which family members will henceforth interact with one another week in and week out, for the rest of their lives. We are trying to help them *decrease* drastically those types of interpersonal interactions among family members that mental health professionals see as creating anxiety and emotional insecurity. We are trying to help them to *increase* those kinds of attitudes and behaviors significantly, especially relationship behaviors, which seem to build self-esteem, enhance their capacity to show love and to win love, deepen their understanding of themselves, promote understanding and appreciation of those who are important to them in love and in work, allow them to acquire better control over their life-styles, permit them to help others achieve mutually desired goals, and, in general, allow them to deal more realistically with each other—and by extension also to deal more realistically with others outside the family.

General Methods

To achieve these goals, RE leaders deal with three areas: thoughts, feelings, and behavior. Cognition is most important in the very beginning of the program in helping to motivate the participants. It is essential to help couples to see the value that learning to employ a new system of social interaction has for them, that is, how and why changing their ways of interacting will help them to achieve their own individual and familial goals. The objective is one of changing attitudes enough to bring participants to the point where they will willingly struggle through the hard work of attempting to acquire new skills. Also, their ideas and attitudes must be changed sufficiently for them to take the risk of embarrassment; that is, the risk of not performing the skills adequately in the eyes of their mentor and, more important, in the eyes of other family members. Cognition continues to be of great importance each time the guidelines of a new skill need to be mastered. Finally, cognition is involved each time the participants must learn the cues and the new things they must begin to say to themselves that will help them to put their new skills to work in the real world.

Feelings are also important from the beginning. Empathic perception and overt recognition and acceptance of the clients' wishes and fears is a major ingredient of effective leadership of an RE program. In the beginning it is especially important for the leader to recognize family members' wishes, doubts, and fears about the program and what it will mean for them. Later, the clients are called upon to develop among themselves the same capacity for acceptance of feelings as the leader displays. Such sensitivity and acceptance, they will learn, fosters understanding, compassion, respect, honesty, and love.

Changes in an individual's cognition and attitude are invisible to those around him or her until they are reflected in the person's behavior. Only then can they have impact. Only then can they lead to what the changed individual will see as reciprocal changes in the behavior (and hence attitudes) in those others. It is this perceived improvement in the reactions of others to one's new behaviors that, above all else, strengthens the individual's determination to stick with the hard labor of self-change. The cognitive, attitudinal change that prompted the effort toward self-change is tentative and fragile until it is validated by such visible behavioral effects. Lasting change must come from within, be self-discovered. It is mainly by means of behavioral observation and validation that such self-discovery takes place.

For similar reasons, the behavioral realm is central to the training process. Attitudinal change and intellectual understanding, though absolutely essential, cannot be validated until the learner tries to put the new understanding into interpersonal play. The leader, as coach, has to see the attitude and the understanding translated into action before he or she can provide the necessary feedback to perfect the skills being learned. The skill of talking *about* what to do is not the type of skill sought by the RE leader; it is the participants' good, reliable real-life *performance* for which the RE leader strives. Behavioral demonstration and behavioral coaching are seen as the most reliable and efficient route toward that end.

Another important aspect of the general methodology used in Family RE programs is that the emphasis is always on the *system*, that is, the interpersonal context. Moreover, even if some members of the family never physically come to the session, they nevertheless can be included in the program. An absent member is not talked *about*, but, by proxy, actively included. This can be done by means of their parts being role-played by the other participants or by the leader. Also, bit by bit, absent members can even be taught the skills, because one of the skills

(Facilitation) learned by the attending family members is how to teach the skills to others formally or informally.

The specific methods used to train participants in RE cannot be described here because of space limitation. They are spelled out elsewhere (B. G. Guerney, 1977a, 1982, 1984, 1985; Preston & Guerney, 1982). There also are films/videotapes that illustrate the methods used (Figley & Guerney, 1976; Vogelsong & Guerney, 1978, 1979) and audiotapes that demonstrate how the basic skills may be applied by adolescent-parent, premarital, cohabiting, and married couples to parent-child, feminist, sexual, work-related, and dozens of other areas of interpersonal conflict or enhancement (B. G. Guerney & Vogelsong, 1981).

The RE Skills

Within the context of interpersonal interaction, RE participants are taught nine sets of skills; really nine *modes* of thinking and behaving. By using their skills when engaged in significant interpersonal interaction with intimates, they can generate ideas and feelings and outcomes very different than would be generated without the use of the skills. Using the skills changes interactions in the direction of greater mutual respect, support, cooperation, appreciation, and love.

The first skill is *Expressive* skill. Expressive skill carries two benefits to the learner and their family members: (a) it makes the learner more aware of his or her own conflicts, wishes, and feelings as they arise in a relationship or situation, and (b) it allows the learner to express those conflicts, wishes, and feelings to others in such a way as to reduce sharply the chances that the other person will become defensive or angry, and to increase greatly the odds that the other person will understand the speaker's point of view, and be willing to do something to help.

The second skill is *Empathic* skill—a capacity for compassionate understanding. This skill also has two benefits to the learner and his or her intimates: (a) it increases an individual's ability to appreciate the conflicts, wishes, and feelings of significant others, and (b) it encourages those significant others, first, to understand better, and, second, to express more honestly their deepest conflicts, wishes, and feelings. Such understanding is beneficial both to the empathic person and to his or her intimates, because knowing these things permits better mutual support and better solutions to problems and conflicts. In the real world of competing desires and strong emotions flowing between family members, however, it is extremely difficult, almost impossible, to put these two skills into play when they are most needed unless the individual acquires a third skill.

This third skill is *Discussion/Negotiation* skill. This skill (previously called "Mode-Switching" skill) permits the individual to know, in an ongoing dialogue, under what interpersonal and emotional circumstances to use the empathic and the expressive modes, and when and how to change back and forth between the two modes. Without this skill, significant interpersonal exchanges between intimates—especially those associated with underlying anxiety or conflict—are likely to deteriorate, to leave the track, and end in frustration or disappointment. This skill enables one to avoid more frequently unproductive digressions and to focus on progressively more relevant, more important, aspects of the topic under discussion. When one, and especially when all, of the individuals involved in a problem or conflict use the skill, discussion or negotiation is likely to be more meaningful, productive, and satisfying to the participants.

The fourth skill is *Problem/Conflict Resolution* skill. Mastery of this skill helps family members who have a problem or conflict to formulate together a concrete plan as to what should be done about it. Compared to unskilled attempts at achieving resolution, such a plan is likely (a) to meet the needs of each party better in light of the needs of every other party involved, (b) to be practical and workable, and (c) to be long enduring.

The fifth skill is *Facilitation or Teaching* skill. This skill enables the learner to encourage, teach, coach, and assist other family members generally—both those participating in the formal program and those not participating in the program—to learn RE skills and to put them into practice.

The sixth skill is *Self-Changing* skill. Consider a situation in which, after using conflict resolution skill, a solution is worked out wherein somebody makes a commitment to change a behavior that has been causing strife. As everyone knows, even the sincerest desire to change one's behavior does not ensure that one can actually make that change instantly or consistently. Think about how difficult it is to change an ingrained habit such as shouting or interrupting when angry, smoking, eating sweets, or drinking too much alcohol. Self-change skills help the learner to change his or her behavior more quickly and reliably.

But even after learning some self-changing skills, a commitment to behave differently is still not likely to lead to flawless performance. Initially, one is likely to forget to perform as desired; later, relapses may occur. When such failure occurs, the manner in which others in the family react may make the difference between whether the individual abandons the effort, or renews it with greater vigor than before.

That brings us to the seventh skill: *Other-Changing* skill. Consider a situation in which the person who promised to change fails early on, or later lapses into the old pattern. The person to whom the new pattern of behavior has been promised, if he or she did not have other-changing skills, would be likely to feel and to act as if betrayed, to become vituperative, or even to retaliate. These behaviors are generally counterproductive for both parties and for the relationship. Other-changing skill helps one to avoid such counterproductive reactions to another's failure to change instantly and flawlessly. Even more important, other-changing skill allows one, right from the beginning—even before any failure has occurred—to behave in ways that will help the other person change more quickly and reliably.

The eighth skill is *Generalization and Transfer* skill. As stated earlier, our goal is to have RE skills used in daily living whenever they are called for. Generalization/transfer skill is designed to help participants recognize those situations in which the skills are likely to be useful and to put those skills into play at those times. RE skills are usually useful when one experiences significant feelings. This includes both positive feelings—for example, love, pride, and admiration—especially toward an intimate, and negative feelings—for example, loneliness, neglect, frustration, anger, and depression—whether these have anything to do with family members or not. We encourage family members to use their skills to share significant feelings with family members. The reason for that is that our goal is to make the family a *primary support group* for every member of the family.

The ninth and last skill is *Maintenance* skill. Entropy—the breakdown of the more complex to simpler and more primitive forms—is one of the major laws of nature. This applies also to unpracticed interpersonal skills. Therefore, clients are taught the principles and methods for preventing this; that is, how to maintain their skills.

Family RE Formats

With respect to length, a program teaching all the skills fully and ensuring that they have taken firm root in the family's home life should last about 30 hours. But, an abbreviated version omitting the two change skills and spending less time on generalization skill can be conducted in about 15 hours, and in-between lengths can be used to fit particular situations. A variety of time formats can be used. An example of an *intensive* or marathon format would be a single weekend. An example of an *extensive* format would be two-and-a-half-hour sessions once a week for eight to twelve weeks. An example of what is called a *front-loaded* RE format would be a weekend followed by several two-and-a-half-hour evening sessions. For primary prevention programs, a *time-limited* program—one lasting a predetermined length—generally is used. For secondary and tertiary prevention programs (and RE therapy programs), a *time-designated* format (B. G. Guerney, 1977a, p. 71f) generally is used; that is, a tentative time of completion is set, an evaluation is made at that time, and it is then determined whether more sessions may be needed, resulting in another tentative specified time of completion.

The *number* of participants also may vary (and influences how long a group needs to last). In a setting in which payment of leaders is not a prohibitive factor—for example, in a training facility or in a church with volunteer leaders—it would be practical to conduct the program with even one family at a time. In other circumstances, as many as 20 people at a time could be trained, even more if necessary. If desired, subunits from larger families—for example, a mother and one son from a larger family—may be mixed in the same program with families in which all members are participating.

Primary, Secondary, and Tertiary Prevention

Family RE is applicable at all three levels of psychopathology prevention as these have been defined by Caplan (1964, p. 26). It can be used for primary prevention by changing the kinds of parenting practices and family interaction patterns that seem to lead to psychopathology. Using RE-based programs to prevent emotional disturbances or to prevent substance abuse (Rose, Battjes, & Leukefeld, 1984) would be examples. They can be used for secondary prevention when at-risk children have been identified or when very early diagnosis of disturbance or delinquency has been made (e.g., B. G. Guerney, Vogelsong, & Glynn, 1977; Vogelsong & Guerney, 1980). And they can be used for tertiary prevention, for example, to reduce the residual effects of damage that already has taken place and might be partially irreversible. To this end, RE programs have been used with the learning disabled (L. F. Guerney, 1979) and the mentally retarded (Sywulak, 1984). RE has also been used for prevention of relapse, for example, with a family member who has suffered a psychotic breakdown (Vogelsong, Guerney, & Guerney, 1983), and with alcoholism (Matter, McAllister, & Guerney, 1984; Waldo & Guerney, 1983).

When primary prevention is desired for young children (here defined as under 12), the Coufal and Brock (1983) program would be appropriate. When secondary or tertiary prevention is called for with young children, the Filial Relationship Enhancement program is appropriate. When older children or adults are to be the targets of primary, secondary, or tertiary prevention, the Family RE program is the most appropriate RE program. For primary prevention, a time-limited format usually is used. For secondary or tertiary prevention, the time-designated format is usually used.

Settings, Recruitment, and Referrals

RE populations have been successfully recruited through the schools for sibling (Seidenberg, 1978) and student-teacher RE programs as well as for Family RE programs. Many Family RE programs (as well as pre-Marital RE programs) have been run through local churches wherein Family RE has been referred to as a "Learning to Love" program. The public has been recruited to Family RE programs by announcements in newspaper articles and on the local TV cable's "bulletin board." For secondary and tertiary prevention programs or therapy, Family RE also has been used in psychiatric hospitals and drug and alcohol treatment agencies and treatment centers. Many families are referred by child welfare and child and youth service agencies as well as by physicians and privately practicing mental health professionals. A women's resource center serving families with abuse problems is another referral source. Examples of national organizations—old and new—with chapters that could be served by Family RE programs are Parents Without Partners, the National Alliance for the Mentally Ill (see Vogelsong, Guerney, & Guerney, 1983), and the National Federation of Parents for Drug-Free Youth. Family RE programs would also be very appropriate for the employee assistance programs now rapidly developing nationally (see Schmidt, this volume).

Use of Volunteers and Paraprofessionals

Paraprofessionals and volunteers who have been through the program may be trained to conduct Family RE prevention programs. An example of this is volunteers who had been through church-run programs, received training, trained others, and thus maintained a self-perpetuating system of primary prevention over many years. Another example is probation workers who were trained to conduct Family RE with the families of young adjudicated delinquents. Perhaps quasi-families should also be mentioned here: workers in residential settings for the mentally retarded and delinquents also have been trained to use Family RE with their charges.

RE Training and Certification

Professionals and paraprofessionals may receive training to conduct RE programs in a two- or three-day Introductory workshop available through the not-for-profit Institute for the Development of Emotional Life Skills (IDEALS) and related institutes and centers in New Jersey, Pennsylvania, and Virginia.[1] The training programs are skill-centered: trainees see a skill demonstrated, then apply the new skill in a role-play situation. Training groups are kept small to allow for individual feedback on skill performance. For those who wish advanced training, further one- or two-day workshops also are available. Those wishing to be certified by IDEALS as RE problem-prevention/enrichment leaders follow such training with supervision of an RE group they lead. If an individual is near a training center, live supervision may be possible. If not, supervisees may mail audio- or videotapes of RE sessions and receive supervision by phone or by return audiotapes. Certification is the first step toward becoming a trainer as a faculty member of IDEALS, and toward establishing an RE Institute or Center.

Research

The research to be summarized here includes participants who already are experiencing emotional problems as well as those who are not. Because our topic here is prevention, this requires some explanation. In RE research, as in RE practice, there has not been much concern (except for the format used) with whether clients have as yet experienced no problems, are early diagnosed as having emotional problems, are experiencing severe problems, or are in remission from severe problems (see B. G. Guerney, 1977b). The task of RE programs is seen as one of promoting psychosocial strengths and wellness, regardless of where the program participants initially lie on this dimension. In a program such as Family RE, distinction among primary, secondary, and tertiary prevention and, indeed, between prevention and therapy, are difficult to make (Morello & Factor, 1981). For example, when one works with children who have been diagnosed as having emotional, social, or behavioral problems, in order to remove those problems, should that be considered therapy or, given the young age of the children, should that be regarded as secondary prevention of adult psychopathology? Is the use of Family RE with families of recently dried-out alcoholics therapy, or is it tertiary prevention? Second, it must be remembered that the whole family often is involved in RE programs. In Filial or Family RE therapy, for example, the parents of the emotionally disturbed child learns skills (e.g., empathy) that are helpful not only to their children, but to their marriages and other relationships and thus to their own mental health. Also, in Filial RE therapy, every child in the family in the appropriate age range receives the same kind of play sessions or quality-time sessions from their parents as the diagnosed child. In Family RE, other participating children in the family receive the same skill training as the diagnosed child. Hence, what may be considered "therapy" for one child in the family may be considered primary prevention for the parents and for the other children in that family. Because there usually are more people without problems than with problems benefiting from the skills taught in the program, it is even possible to view a diagnosed young child or adolescent not only as a client, but as the means by which other family members are drawn into a primary prevention program.

In considering the conundrum, Caplan's (1964) definitions, and Albee's (1968) views, it seems reasonable to conclude that the type of criteria that should be used to define whether a program is preventive in nature should not be mainly the type of population seen, but whether the method used is one that is capable of efficiently and inexpensively providing a community-based, communitywide programmatic service—as opposed to an individualized clinical approach—and whether or not the program builds strengths as well as resolves problems. The reasoning underlying this conclusion and the criteria that may be used to determine whether an approach warrants the label "preventive" (or "enriching") are described elsewhere (B. G. Guerney, Brock, & Coufal, in press; B. G. Guerney, L. F. Guerney, & Cooney, 1985). It suffices here to say that RE seems to meet those criteria.

In further justifying the fact that some of the studies reported here include disturbed clients either exclusively or among others, it should be stated that results from the area of therapy—provided it is of a type that also meets the criteria of mass application to all families—is not without relevance to assessing that program's usefulness in preventing problems from emerging or becoming worse. If a systematic skill-building program works well for disturbed clients, does not that strongly suggest (albeit certainly not prove) that learning and applying such skills will also work to prevent problems? (We believe the reverse also is true; that is, if skills are useful in preventing psychosocial problems, they also will be useful to people already suffering from such problems.)

Therefore, we have included in the following review studies conducted in which some participants were already considered disturbed. For similar reasons, we have included studies of subunits of the family system, such as premarital and marital couples in addition to cross-generational applications. Finally, the potential of an intervention system—indeed, in part whether it may qualify as such—is related to the possibility that volunteers and paraprofessionals, indigenous and otherwise, may be trained to administer it. Therefore, this research review also considers the area of training such personnel to administer RE programs.

Group Filial RE Therapy

In Filial RE therapy (B. G. Guerney, 1964; L. F. Guerney, 1976a, 1983), parents are trained in relationship skills derived from Rogerian theory (especially Rogerian-based play therapy) and in child social-izing/management skills derived from Rogerian and behavioral prin-ciples. A study of group Filial RE therapy was conducted with 51 emotionally disturbed children between four and ten years of age and their mothers (B. G. Guerney, 1976; B. G. Guerney & Stover, 1971). Coding of maternal responses showed that early in the training process, mothers' behavior in the play sessions manifested significant changes in all the skills they were expected to learn: reflection of feeling, allowing self-direction, and involvement with the child. The children showed highly significant improvement on all the measures of adjustment studied: Problem Check List; the Wichita Guidance Check List (and each of its subscales, which are inner tension, school failure, parent conflict, teacher conflict, and peer conflict); the Des Moines Parent Ratings scales; the Children's Adjustment Inventory; and a Parental Dissatisfaction measure. Clinician's rating on the Rutgers Maladjust-ment Index showed that 100% of the children were at least somewhat improved and 78% were "much" or "very much" improved. In a companion study, Oxman (1971) studied a group of 77 presumably nondisturbed children matched to the Filial RE therapy children for geography, age of parents and children, size of family, and socioeconomic status. The Filial RE children showed significantly more improvement on the variables studied (symptomatology and maternal dissatisfaction). The method of analysis used ruled out the possibility that this difference was due to the poorer initial scores of the therapy group.

In a study by Sywulak (1977) of Filial RE Therapy, 19 mothers or fathers and their emotionally disturbed children served as their own controls. A four-month waiting period was followed by an assessment of gains four months after Group Filial RE therapy began. From prewait testing to the pretreatment testing four months later, there were no significant changes. After an additional four months, which were the first four months of treatment, there was a significant gain in comparison both to the initial testing and to the pretreatment testing. Also, the gain from pre- to posttreatment was significantly greater than the gain (really the lack of gain) from prewait to pretreatment on two measures of children's adjustment: The Filial Problem Check List and the Wichita Parent Check List. A third measure, the Des Moines Parent Rating Scale, narrowly missed significance ($p < .06$). Also, with treatment, parents showed greater change in parental acceptance. An interim testing showed that after only two months of treatment, some gains (the Problem Check List and Porter Parental Acceptance) were already greater than the gains during the waiting period. Thus group Filial RE therapy can produce significant gains in a time frame comparable to the time frame of short-term therapies and probably could be used as such if necessary. Sensué (1981) tested the participants in Sywulak's study after six months of treatment. The clients continued to gain on all measures from the fourth to the sixth month and, at that time, the Des Moines Parenting Rating measure, like all the others, did reach statistically significant gains over the pretreatment and prewait testings.

A follow-up study of the B. G. Guerney and Stover (1971) study was conducted by questionnaire approximately 15 months after completion (L. F. Guerney, 1975a). Three parents could not be located, and only six mothers failed to return their questionnaires. Of the 41 parents who responded to a question concerning the child's adjustment, only one reported the child to have a greater problem than when entering therapy or said that they had since sought additional therapy for the child. Only four were reported to have shown any slippage at all from their level of adjustment at termination. Four were at the same level as at termination and 32 were said to have improved further after termination. Parents attributed such further improvement primarily to their improved ability to deal appropriately with their children (as contrasted, for example, with their children's outgrowing their difficulties).

Sensué (1981) followed up Sywulak's (1977) study approximately three years after termination of treatment. Sensué sought to determine whether the children who had had the Filial treatment remained at a normal level of adjustment. She found that they did. That is, there were no differences between the follow-up sample and a normative sample on measures of child adjustment and parental acceptance. Also, questionnaire data indicated that the parents considered their children's posttherapy adjustment as having continued to be normal and acceptable to them. Other questionnaire data indicated that the parents felt they had learned valuable child-rearing skills, and that they continued to use them in interacting with their children. Parent interviews supported these findings. Interviews with the children revealed that nearly all of them felt the sessions helped them to get closer to their parents, and reduced arguments and fighting. They also believed that having such play sessions would be helpful to other parents and children.

Group Family RE

Ginsberg (1977) studied Group Family RE (then called PARD, for Parent-Adolescent Relationship Development) using ten two-hour meetings of three-pair groups. Randomly assigned, 14 father-son pairs were in the RE group, and 15 pairs in the no-treatment control group. (The no-treatment group later received treatment in a quasi-replication, own-control study.) In discussing emotionally significant topics, the RE group showed significantly more improvement in empathic acceptance, and in the expression of views in ways deemed to show greater self-awareness, sensitivity to feeling, and to be less threatening to others. This was true for unobtrusively observed interactions between fathers as well as in discussions in which they were aware they were being studied. Hypotheses that the RE trained pairs would show greater improvement in various patterns of general communication also were confirmed. The general quality of their relationships also showed greater improvement. The quasi-replication study, using the group that had originally served as a control group to serve as their own controls, generally confirmed the results reported above. This latter study also demonstrated that there was significant improvement in the self-concepts of both fathers and sons trained in RE, a finding that narrowly missed significance in the group-comparison study.

In another Family RE study, B. G. Guerney, Coufal, and Vogelsong (1981) randomly assigned 54 mother-daughter pairs to one of these three conditions: Family RE (i.e., "PARD"), Traditional (group discussion), or Control (No-Treatment). The Traditional and the RE methods were carefully equated and the leaders, who were the same for both groups, were perceived by the clients as being extremely similar in empathy, warmth, genuineness, enthusiasm, and competence. The groups met approximately 13 times for two hours weekly in groups of three pairs. On questionnaire, quasi-behavioral, and behavioral measures, three basic hypotheses were confirmed. The RE participants were superior to both the Traditional and the Control groups in (a) their specific empathic and expressive communication skills, (b) their general patterns of communication, and (c) the quality of their general relationship. In addition to showing that RE is superior to traditional discussion groups, this study showed that treatment factors specific to RE rather than only generic factors (attention, placebo, and so on) account for the improvements that result from RE training.

In a follow-up study (B. G. Guerney, Vogelsong, & Coufal, 1983), six months after termination, mothers and daughters in the Traditional treatment showed no greater gains over pretreatment in specific communication skills, general communication patterns, or the general quality of their relationship, than did mothers and daughters who had received no treatment. Participants in RE showed significantly greater gains in all these areas relative to both the other groups. This indicates that the treatment-specific gains of RE endure over a significant stretch of time. (The study also demonstrated that a booster program is effective in enhancing gains.)

Group Marital RE

The first study of Group Marital RE therapy (then called Conjugal therapy) was conducted by Ely, Guerney, and Stover (1973), who randomly assigned 23 couples to RE or no-treatment. The objective was primarily to determine whether the couples were able to learn the skills taught in the program. It was found that the trained couples made more use of the skills they were taught in responding to hypothetical, critical incidents on a questionnaire and in role-played marital incidents. In a quasi-replication, clients gained more on these variables in treatment than they did in a comparable time period before treatment began. The results also showed significant gains in general communication patterns and in the general quality of their relationship. Collins (1977) also found that in comparison to an untrained control group, couples in Group Marital RE showed greater gains in marital communication and marital adjustment.

Rappaport (1976) studied intensive Group marital RE using an own control design. Twenty married couples were tested, waited two months, were tested again just prior to beginning the two-month, four-session program, and then posttested. The sessions, conducted on weekends, alternated between four- and eight-hour sessions, and totaled twenty-four hours. On all variables studied, the participants showed greater gains during the treatment period than they had during the wait period. In discussions of emotionally significant topics with their partners, couples showed more empathic acceptance of their partners. They expressed themselves in ways deemed more sensitive to their own feelings and less likely to induce argument from their partners. They showed greater improvement in marital adjustment, marital harmony, and marital communication, trust, and intimacy. They showed a greater rate of change in their overall relationship patterns, in their satisfaction with their relationships, and in their ability to resolve relationship problems satisfactorily.

Wieman (1973) compared RE with his Reciprocal Reinforcement program. The Reciprocal Reinforcement program drew upon principles and techniques used by Knox (1971), Rappaport and Harrell (1972), and especially Stuart (1969a, 1969b). The RE program was an abbreviated one of eight weeks duration. Participation in both treatments showed significant improvements over a waiting list control group in measures of marital communication, marital adjustment, and cooperativeness. A follow-up at ten weeks showed that married couples in both programs maintained their gains very well. Ratings on 16 semantic differential scales were, in general, positive for both treatments. Participants in the Reciprocal Reinforcement program, however, saw their experiences in treatment as being more light, safe, easy, cold, and calm than did clients in the RE program. RE program participants perceived their treatment as being significantly more deep, good, worthwhile, exciting, strong, fair, important, comfortable, and professional than did the clients in the Reciprocal Reinforcement program. Because these were both highly credible treatments, such results are not attributable to nonspecific treatment variables.

Another comparative study was conducted by Jessee and Guerney (1981). Thirty-six couples were randomly assigned to Group Marital RE or to a Group Gestalt Relationship Facilitation treatment, each lasting two-and-a-half hours a week for 12 weeks. There were significant gains for the participants in both groups on all variables studied: marital adjustment, communication, trust and harmony, rate of positive change in the relationship, relationship satisfaction, and ability to handle problems. RE participants achieved greater gains than Gestalt Relationship Facilitation participants in communication, relationship satisfaction, and ability to handle problems.

Brock and Joanning (1983), using random assignment, compared Group Marital RE (N = 26) to the Minnesota Couple's Communication program (N = 20). On both self-report and behavioral measures, RE was shown to be more effective in the areas of marital communication and satisfaction. The RE couples maintained their greater gains at follow-up three months later.

Giblin (1982) conducted a meta-analytic study involving 85 studies of marital and family problem-prevention/enrichment programs and nearly 4000 participants. RE was found to be far more powerful in producing positive changes than any other program, including Couple's Communications and Marriage Encounter. Indeed, RE was the only program found capable of producing very large outcome effects.

Dyadic Marital RE

Ross, Baker, and Guerney (1984) conducted a study of Dyadic Marital RE in a mental health center. The five marital therapists working there were all eclectic; their predominant influences within that eclecticism ranged from psychodynamic through client-centered to behavioral approaches. They were given a three-day training program in Marital RE, their first exposure to the method. (Plans to continue the training through supervision had to be abandoned for administrative reasons.) After this training, using strictly random assignment, half of the maritally distressed couples each therapist saw were treated only with RE and half by the therapist's own preferred eclectic approach, adjusted to the needs of that particular couple as the therapist saw fit, but not including RE methods. After the predetermined 10-week experimental period, the 24 participants in each condition were posttested, and the results compared with their pretests. The clients receiving Dyadic Marital RE therapy showed significantly greater gains than the clients receiving the therapist's own preferred treatment approach on all measures used. They gained more in the quality of their communication, the general quality of their relationship, and their marital adjustment.

Schindler, Hahlweg, and Revenstorf (1983) studied the treatment of distressed couples using three conditions: a dyadic communications training program, a group format for the same program, and a waiting list control group. The study is included here because the communications program apparently used the Expressive and Empathic modes of the RE program (as well as a programmed text and a problem-solving approach of their own devising). There were 14 sessions of unspecified duration. The couples in dyadic communication training showed significant gains in tenderness, communication, conflict reduction, general happiness, and positive behavior in problem solving, and also showed a reduction of negative behaviors in problem solving. The couples in the group format showed significant improvement in general happiness and in reduction of negative behaviors in problem solving. The waiting list group showed no significant changes. By one year after termination, five of the sixteen couples (31%) from the dyadic group had separated, while only one couple of the eighteen from the group format

(5.6%) had separated. For a follow-up, the separated couples were not included on either pretest or follow-up samples. With this selected sample, gains were maintained for a full year by both the dyadic and the group format couples in conflict reduction and by the group format couples in general happiness. Schindler et al. (1983) concluded that the dyadic format is superior to the group format, making this the focal point of their discussion. With a five-times-greater rate of marital separation for couples in the dyadic format as opposed to the group format, this seems a strange conclusion, especially because the separated couples are not included in the comparisons! (The differential rate of marital breakup in the two formats was not pointed out by the authors.) Although the superiority of a dyadic format is hardly justified from the results of this study, the dyadic format probably will eventually prove to be superior if effectiveness is measured by hours of time per se put in by client or by therapist. But quite possibly, a group format will prove superior to a dyadic format if one uses as a basis of comparison the time in therapy devoted by clients to their own problems, cost per hour to the client for gains achieved, or the therapist's time per client. The last two are probably the fairest ways to compare dyadic and group formats (see Ross, Baker, & Guerney, 1984, for a further discussion of this issue). The major conclusion that we can draw from Schindler et al.'s study seems to be that both dyadic and group marital communication training can be successful forms of intervention and that, for couples who do not separate, at least some of the impact of these interventions can be maintained for a minimum of a year.

Premarital RE

The first study of Group RE as a problem-prevention/enrichment program for dating and premarital couples was conducted by Schlein (1971) and reported also by Ginsberg and Vogelsong (1977). In this study, couples met weekly for two-and-a-half hours over a period of eight to twelve weeks. The college student couples were randomly assigned to an RE training group and a waiting list control group. As hypothesized, in discussing emotionally significant topics, RE participants showed greater gains than participants in the untrained group in empathic acceptance and in their ability to express themselves in less threatening ways. Participants in RE training showed greater improvement in the general quality of their relationship, in handling problems, in self-perception of warmth, genuineness, and satisfaction with their relationships. The hypothesis that the trained couples would show greater improvement in their general patterns of communication was not confirmed. The mean differences were in the expected direction, and

120   Bernard G. Guerney, Jr.

it is possible that the nonconfirmation was due to a ceiling effect, because the initial scores of the participants were near the top of the scale.

In a companion study, D'Augelli, Deyss, Guerney, Hershenberg, and Sborofsky (1974) coded the emotionally significant dialogues of the premarital couples in the Schlein study by using behavior scales developed by Carkhuff (1969) that have been widely used to assess the performance of counselors, counseling students, and paraprofessionals. The RE group improved significantly more on these scales than the untrained group. After less than 20 hours of training, these college undergraduates moved from a level of skill typical of college students to the level typical of professional counselors.

Ridley, Jorgensen, Morgan, and Avery (1982) compared Premarital couples in RE to couples in a discussion-based treatment designed to improve relationships. They used five measures of relationship quality that assessed one or more of these variables: satisfaction, communication, trust, intimacy, sensitivity, openness, understanding, empathy, warmth, and genuineness. Relative to the couples in the discussion treatment, couples in RE showed more improvements on all measures.

A study by Avery, Ridley, Leslie, and Milholland (1980) compared Group Premarital RE with a lecture/discussion program designed to improve relationships. Both programs were conducted for 24 hours over an eight-week period. Codings of verbal interactions in discussions of emotionally significant topics revealed that the RE couples showed significantly greater improvements on empathy and appropriate self-disclosure. A follow-up six months after termination showed a significant decline in performance from the levels attained at posttesting. Nevertheless, the RE couples maintained their superiority in providing empathy and in making appropriate self-disclosures as compared to couples who had been in the lecture/discussion-based treatment and as compared to their own pretest level.

A study by Ridley, Avery, Dent, and Harrell (1981) compared Group Marital RE, a Premarital Problem Solving Skills Training Program (Ridley, Avery, Harrell, Leslie, & Dent, 1981), and a non-skills-oriented Relationship Development program that the authors developed to promote better understanding among couples. After the eight-session, 24-hour, three- or four-couple group meetings, one significant difference was found: the RE couples showed significantly greater gains than the couples in the Relationship Development group in self-perception of success levels in opposite-sex relationships.

Sams (1983) compared an intensive (one weekend) Premarital RE program with an Engaged Encounter program of the same length, with

18 couples in each program. Engaged Encounter is a nationally used adaptation for engaged couples of Marriage Encounter (Durkin, 1974). It is predominantly sponsored by the Catholic Church. Both programs were administered by the same lay couple volunteers (see Most & Guerney, 1983). Participants in the RE program showed greater gains on all variables studied: empathic and expressive skills and problem solving.

An RE-Related Program for Divorcees

Thiessen, Avery, and Joanning (1980) developed a five-week, 15-hour communication skills training program for recently divorced women. The program was developed from their own experience in divorce adjustment counseling, from divorce adjustment seminars (Weiss, 1976; Welch & Granvold, 1977), from the work of Tubesing and Tubesing (1973), and from RE. Subjects were assigned by convenience of time scheduling to a training or no-treatment group. Training was done in groups of seven or eight. The trained participants showed greater improvement in overall divorce adjustment, in self-esteem, and in empathic responsiveness as measured by subjects' indications of what they would say in situations relevant to divorced women. (No differences were found on self-disclosure or perceived social support.)

Foster Parent, Parent, and Related Skill Training Program

Louise Guerney's (1976d, 1977) Foster Parent Skills Training Program has its own manuals for trainers (L. F. Guerney, 1976b) and for foster parents (L. F. Guerney, 1975b), as well as its own training films (L. F. Guerney, 1973, 1974). Nevertheless, it is part of the RE family of programs: it has much in common with Filial RE therapy, the Parent Skill Training program, and the Child-Parent RE Program. Thus a brief summary of research on this program is appropriate here.

In the first year of a statewide application of this program, B. G. Guerney, Vogelsong, and Wolfgang (1977) studied trainees (mainly caseworkers in child welfare agencies, sometimes foster parents) who were trained to be trainers of foster parents. A control group that did not receive training during a comparable period was matched to the paraprofessionals being trained. These controls came from the same general working settings and were matched on a number of pertinent demographic variables. On a Training Problems Situation measure developed by Louise Guerney (1976c), which assessed the ability of the trainees to deal effectively with a variety of frequently encountered situations and problems in leading skill training groups, the trained group showed greater gains than the control group.

The paraprofessional trainees also were rated on a Trainer's Supervisory form (L. F. Guerney, 1976c) by experienced supervisors watching them conduct training sessions with foster parents. They judged the trainees to be weak in none of the 20 areas covered, and to be very strong in a number of areas. Areas of special strength included sensitivity of the leaders to the feelings of the foster parents in the group, their knowledge of appropriate techniques, and their ability to reinforce the participants. Also, in interviews, trainees indicated that the skills they had learned for conducting these training sessions were very beneficial to them not only in leading the groups, but also in other aspects of their lives and working careers such as intake, home visits, interviewing prospective foster parents, and in daily relations with clients, colleagues, and friends.

A follow-up study of the trainees was conducted by B. G. Guerney, Wolfgang, and Vogelsong (1978). In the original study, the trainees had improved in learning and applying specific training skills including reflective listening skills, reinforcement, using proper leader messages, using various structuring techniques aimed at handling problems, reorienting the group to the scheduled task, clarifying course content, balanced leadership, and avoiding nonaccepting and rejecting statements. One-and-a-half years later, the trained group showed no significant decline in their performance and remained superior to the control group.

The ability of the trainees to effect changes in the foster parents that they trained also was investigated. In comparison with an untrained control group, the foster parents whom the trainees had trained showed significantly greater gains on all three aspects of parental acceptance measured: acceptance of the child's feelings, valuing the child's uniqueness, and acceptance of the child's autonomy. They showed significant improvement in their perceptions of their skills as foster parents. They saw themselves as superior after training in comparison with their pretraining status with respect to such things as coping with children's withdrawal, making and enforcing rules, reinforcing appropriate behavior, structuring appropriately, understanding feelings, and coping with misbehavior.

A follow-up study by B. G. Guerney, Wolfgang, and Vogelsong (1978) found that, seven months to approximately a year and a half afterward, the 32 foster parents who had participated in the earlier study showed no significant fall off in their perceptions of their own competence as described earlier. A Parenting Program Follow-up Questionnaire indicated general acceptance and use of each of the skills as a result of training. Also, 84% of the parents indicated that what they learned in the Foster Parent Skill Training Program "much" or "very much affected" the way they acted with their foster children in a variety of ways. Further, the participants still retained highly significant gains in acceptance of their foster child in comparison with their pretraining attitudes. Additional information about the long-range effects of the Foster Parent Skills Training Program are provided by L. F. Guerney and Wolfgang (1981).

Brown (1980) compared the Foster Parent Skills Training Program with the widely used Issues in Fostering program (Ryan, 1979; Ryan, Warren, & McFadden, 1977). Trainees were randomly assigned to the two programs. The foster parents trained in the Foster Parenting Skills Training Program showed significantly greater gains in their use of effective responses in hypothetical problem situations with children and showed more gains in acceptance of their foster children. Brown also concluded that the Foster Parent Skills Training Program offered more help with a larger percentage of the foster parents' problems with their children.

Coufal (1982) studied 93 biological parents and randomly assigned these parents to three groups: (a) a skills-only program adapted from L. F. Guerney's (1980) Parent Skill Training program, which is in turn similar to the Foster Parent Skill Training program, (b) the Parent-Child RE Training program (Coufal & Brock, 1983), in which play sessions between the parent and child like those used in Filial RE therapy become the primary skill training medium, and (c) a no-treatment group. The groups of six-to-ten parents met for two hours a week for ten weeks. The skills-only group was superior to the no-treatment group parents in verbally expressed acceptance and in reducing nonaccepting responses, indicating the effectiveness of that program. The parents in the Parent-Child RE groups scored significantly higher than both the other groups in behavioral interaction measures of empathy and warmth. They also produced significantly more acceptance responses on the quasi-behavioral measure than parents in both of the other groups. Thus the results indicate that adding the type of play sessions and "special quality times" used in Filial RE therapy to a RE-based parent training improves the effectiveness of such training.

RE in Public School Settings

B. G. Guerney and Flumen (1970) established that elementary school teachers could be trained in the play therapy skills, techniques, and principles used in Filial RE Therapy. After training, 11 volunteer teachers conducted weekly 45-minute sessions for 14 weeks with nine of their most withdrawn pupils. Independent, naive judges coded the children's classroom assertiveness. The hypothesized statistically significant rise in assertiveness was found. A control group of six similarly withdrawn children showed no such change. Generalization of the increased assertiveness was suggested by the fact that the children's assertiveness was more notable with peers than with the teachers themselves. There was a significant correlation between teacher's therapeutic role performance and degree of child's improvement, which offered additional evidence that the specific technique used was the instrumental factor in bringing about the increased assertiveness.

Eric Hatch (1973) also studied teachers and their elementary school students. The teachers were trained in the basic empathic and expressive skills of RE and in democratic classroom management (B. G. Guerney & Merriam, 1972; Merriam & Guerney, 1973). Tape recordings made of classroom meetings held to discuss class problems and coding of teachers' behaviors confirmed hypotheses that, relative to an untrained control group, trained teachers would solicit more feelings and ideas. Also, coding of student statements in these meetings revealed that the students of trained teachers expressed their views more freely.

Carole Hatch (1983) trained six indigenous public school paraprofessionals, using Guerney's *Parenting: A Skills Training Manual* (1980), which is designed, in terms of typography and vocabulary, to be suitable for lower-level readers as well as normal readers. Of the six paraprofessionals, four were deemed successfully trained. They then led parent training groups involving 45 rural impoverished Black mothers of first-through sixth-graders. The mothers were randomly assigned to the training program or a no-treatment control group. Formative evaluations by parents, group leaders, and an observer were highly favorable. Summative evaluations yielded the following results. On a quasi-behavioral measure, trained parents showed greater improvement on measures assessing sensitivity to children. In actual, at-home parent-child interactions, trained parents showed a greater reduction in undesirable statements to children. (There was no significant difference in number of positive statements). On a questionnaire measure, the trained parents indicated greater improvement in parent-child relationships. Teachers, unaware of which children had parents who were trained, rated appropriateness of the children's behavior in the classroom. A significant reduction in problem behaviors occurred among the children of trained parents. A nonsignificant reduction, however, also took place in the no-treatment children, and the difference in change between the two groups was not significant.

Essman (1977) compared female high school students in three programs: a Filial RE-based skill training program, a non-skills-training-oriented practicum program, and a lecture-discussion program. As determined by quasi-behavioral measures of interaction with children, the Filial RE-based program resulted in significantly more improvement than the other two programs in levels of empathic skill and expressive skill, and child management skills (limit setting and imposition of appropriate consequences).

Rocks (1980) used an abbreviated RE program to train teachers along with students nominated by them as noncommunicative underachievers. Trained students were compared to similarly selected students who, by random assignment, had received only brief, non-RE instruction in communication (without their teachers). RE trained students improved more in classroom behavior and school attendance (though not in academic ranking).

Vogelsong (1978) conducted a study in which half of the 16 children in a fifth-grade public school classroom were randomly assigned to the empathy training stage of RE training (with simplified vocabulary and procedures) and half to a control group that spent an equivalent amount of time working together on craft projects. After 10 45-minute weekly meetings, the trained group showed significantly greater posttesting gains in empathy than the control group.

A 16-hour training program, which makes use of some RE skills and training methods, was developed by Haynes and Avery (1979) for high school students. One of two junior English classes was randomly selected for training, with the other serving as a no-treatment control. Coding of 20 minutes of dialogue between a participant and a randomly assigned same-sex partner from the same class provided the data. The trained students showed more improvement on appropriate self-disclosure and empathy. Generalization was assessed by having the students indicate what they would say when confronted with hypothetical situations involving peers, parents, and dating partners. Again, the trained group showed more improvement on self-disclosure and empathy. In a follow-up to this study, Avery, Rider, and Haynes-Clements (1981) showed that the superiority of the trained adolescents in empathy and self-disclosure, and the generalization effect, were maintained five months after the conclusion of training.

In sum, these and other studies lend empirical support to the notion that RE programs can be effective in public school settings (Andronico & Guerney, 1967, 1969; B. G. Guerney, 1979, 1981; B. G. Guerney & Guerney, 1981; B. G. Guerney, Guerney, & Sebes, 1983; B. G. Guerney,

126   Bernard G. Guerney, Jr.

Stover, & Andronico, 1967; Hatch & B. G. Guerney, 1975; Vogelsong, Most, & Yenchko, 1979).

Training of Volunteers and Paraprofessionals

RE is systematic and programmatic. It specifically defines the kinds of responses that are appropriate and those that are inappropriate for leaders to use. Moreover, the types of situations in which one would use various types of leader responses are spelled out (B. G. Guerney, 1977a, pp. 122-167). Therefore, it is not extremely difficult to teach volunteers, including indigenous volunteers or group leaders. In this section, some of the research that has been conducted with such volunteers and paraprofessionals will be briefly summarized.

Residence hall counselors. Avery (1973) trained 20 potential residence hall counselors in core RE skills with an additional 15 serving as a control group. The training was conducted over a nine-week period in two- to two-and-a-half-hour weekly meetings. Training was conducted in groups of approximately six. Both groups were given a 15-minute audiotaped helping interview with a confederate at the outset of the study and again following the training, or following an equivalent time period for the control group. Reliable expert coders who were appropriately naive coded random segments from the audiotapes of these interviews. The trained group showed significantly greater improvement on the Carkhuff (1969) Scale for empathic understanding. The superiority of the trained over the untrained prospective dormitory counselors was maintained six months after the completion of training (Avery, 1978). Waldo has developed a program based largely on RE in which residence hall counselors are trained to train dormitory residents in relationship skills. The program includes manuals for the training of the counselors (Waldo, 1984a), for the counselors to train the students (Waldo, 1984b), and for the students themselves (Waldo & Saidla, 1984).

Drug abusers. Cadigan (1980) adapted RE to train former drug addicts who were staff members in a residential, therapeutic-community drug rehabilitation center. These staff members then trained 16 randomly assigned residents, who were compared with an untrained control group of 24. Some of the hypothesized significant differences favoring the trained residents were found: they used more positive interpersonal responses to hypothetical peer problem situations, and they developed more positive perceptions of the way staff members behaved toward them.

Probation workers. An uncontrolled, empirical evaluation of the effectiveness of probation officers who had had one week's training in RE methods plus weekly supervision sessions was conducted by B. G.

Guerney, Vogelsong, and Glynn (1977). They assessed 17 family members from five families who were treated by these probation workers. Improvement was shown in family harmony, family satisfaction, and ability to handle family problems.

Senior citizens. Levine (1977) trained 12 volunteer senior citizens to conduct growth-enhancing play sessions with children in a day care center. The program was based on Filial RE therapy principles and training methods. Using an own-control design, he found significantly greater increases with training in the senior citizens' positive involvement, empathic behavior, and capacity to allow self-direction with the children. On a quasi-behavioral measure, he also found evidence of generalization of their empathic skills to situations other than play.

Married couples. Most and Guerney (1983) trained five married lay couples who were experienced Engaged Encounter leaders to conduct an RE training program. Their RE training essentially consisted of two weekends spaced one month apart. The second of these training weekends consisted of hands-on training with the trainees acting as junior leaders and the trainers acting as senior leaders. Their training was highly successful as assessed in four general areas: skill acquisition by the trainees, evaluation of the trainees of the program, skill acquisition by 12 couples who participated in a Premarital RE program led by the trainees after their training, and experts' judgments of the trainees' competence in leading that premarital program.

Since the inception of RE prevention-enrichment programs, I have believed that married couples who have already been through an RE problem-prevention/enrichment program could be trained to become leaders not just of premarital but of marital and family RE prevention-enrichment groups. It also has been my belief that such leaders could, mainly by an "apprenticeship" system, train other leaders. Although it has not been researched, such a self-perpetuating system has been going on for some time in some local churches. The potential of RE as a problem-prevention/enrichment program probably would be greatly enhanced if this sort of self-perpetuating training and group leadership were to take place on a much larger scale.

The Future

However the typical family structure may change—for example, the trend toward more single heads of households—the importance of family for the psychosocial well-being of every one of us will not diminish in the foreseeable future. The increased stress that such changes bring only makes it all the more important that family members

128   Bernard G. Guerney, Jr.

learn to reduce the destructive influences they can have upon one another and learn to increase their ability to help one another become stronger emotionally. Such learning can not only enhance the well-being of individual family members, but can also have a favorable impact on social problems such as drug and alcohol addiction and crime. Indeed, it is hard to see how society can overcome such problems unless the vast majority of families learn how to build one another's sense of self-esteem, trust, competence, and psychosocial maturity. The tools are at hand to bring about such learning; the question: How can they be made available to more families?

Note

1. The address of IDEALS is P.O. Box 391, State College, PA 16804.

References

Albee, G. W. (1968). Conceptual models and manpower requirements in psychology. *American Psychologist, 23,* 317-320.

Andronico, M. P., & Guerney, B. G., Jr. (1967). The potential application of filial therapy to the school situation. *Journal of School Psychology, 6,* 2-7.

Andronico, M. P., & Guerney, B. G., Jr. (1969). A psychotherapeutic aid in a Headstart program. *Children, 16,* 14-122.

Avery, A. W. (1973). *An experimental program for training paraprofessional helpers.* Unpublished master's thesis, Pennsylvania State University, University Park, PA.

Avery, A. W. (1978). Communication skills training for paraprofessional helpers. *American Journal of Community Psychology, 6,* 583-592.

Avery, A. W., Rider, K., & Haynes-Clements, L. (1981). Communication skills training for adolescents: A five month follow-up. *Adolescence, 16,* 289-298.

Avery, A. W., Ridley, C. A., Leslie, L. A., & Milholland, T. (1980). Relationship enhancement with premarital dyads: A six-month follow-up. *American Journal of Family Therapy, 8,* 23-30.

Avery, A. W., & Thiessen, J. D. (1982). Communication skills training for divorce. *Journal of Counseling Psychology, 29,* 203-205.

Blechman, E. A., & Olson, D. H. (1976). The Family Conflict Game: Description and effectiveness. In D. H. Olson (Ed.), *Treating relationships.* Lake Mills, IA: Graphic.

Brock, G. W., & Joanning, H. (1983). A comparison of the Relationship Enhancement program and the Minnesota Couple Communication program. *Journal of Marital and Family Therapy, 9,* 413-421.

Brown, D. L. (1980). *A comparative study of the effects of two foster parent training methods on attitudes of parental acceptance, sensitivity to children, and general factor parent attitudes.* Unpublished doctoral dissertation, Michigan State University.

Cadigan, J. D. (1980). *RETEACH program and project: Relationship enhancement in a therapeutic environment as clients head out.* Unpublished doctoral dissertation, Pennsylvania State University.

Caplan, G. (1964). *Principles of preventive psychiatry.* New York: Basic Books.

Carkhuff, R. R. (1969). *Helping and human relations: A primer for lay and professional helpers: Practice and research* (Vol. 2). New York: Holt, Rinehart, & Winston.

Carnes, P. J. (1981). *Family development I: Understanding us.* Minneapolis, MN: Interpersonal Communication Program, Inc.

Collins, J. D. (1977). Experimental evaluation of a six-month conjugal therapy and relationship enhancement program. In B. G. Guerney, Jr. (Ed.), *Relationship enhancement: Skill-training programs for therapy, problem prevention, and enrichment.* San Francisco: Jossey-Bass.

Coufal, J. D. (1982, October). *An experimental evaluation of two approaches to parent skills training: Parent-Child participation versus parents only.* Paper presented at the annual meeting of the National Council on Family Relations, Washington, DC.

Coufal, J. D., & Brock, G. (1983). *Parent-Child Relationship Enhancement: A ten week education program.* Menomonie, WI: Department of Human Development and Family Living.

D'Augelli, A. R., Deyss, C. S., Guerney, B. G., Jr., Hershenberg, B., & Sborofsky, S. (1974). Interpersonal skill training for dating couples: An evaluation of an educational mental health service. *Journal of Counseling Psychology, 21,* 385-389.

Durkin, H. P. (1974). *Forty-four hours to change your life: Marriage encounter.* New York: Paulist Press.

Ely, A., Guerney, B. G., Jr., & Stover, L. (1973). Efficacy of the training phase of conjugal therapy. *Psychotherapy: Theory, Research, and Practice, 10,* 201-207.

Essman, C. S. (1977). *Preparental education: The impact of a short-term, skills-training course on female adolescents.* Unpublished doctoral dissertation, Pennsylvania State University.

Figley, D., & Guerney, B. G., Jr. (1976). *The Conjugal Relationship Enhancement Program* [Film, 15 mm., or ¾ or ½ inch video, 34 min.] (Available from Individual and Family Consultation Center of the Pennsylvania State University, University Park, PA 16802).

Giblin, P. R. (1982). *A meta-analysis of premarital, marital, and family enrichment research.* Unpublished doctoral dissertation, Purdue University, IN.

Ginsberg, B. G. (1977). Parent-adolescent relationship development program. In B. G. Guerney, Jr. (Ed.), *Relationship enhancement: Skill-training programs for therapy, problem prevention, and enrichment.* San Francisco: Jossey-Bass.

Ginsberg, B. G., & Vogelsong, E. (1977). Premarital relationship improvement by maximizing empathy and self-disclosure. The PRIMES program. In B. G. Guerney, Jr. (Ed.), *Relationship enhancement: Skill-training programs for therapy, problem prevention, and enrichment.* San Francisco: Jossey-Bass.

Gordon, T. (1970). *The parent effectiveness training.* New York: P. H. Wyden.

Guerney, B. G., Jr. (1964). Filial therapy: Description and rationale. *Journal of Consulting Psychology, 28,* 303-310.

Guerney, B. G., Jr. (1976). Filial therapy used as a treatment method for disturbed children. *Evaluation, 3,* 34-35.

Guerney, B. G., Jr. (1977a). *Relationship enhancement: Skill-training programs for therapy, problem prevention, and enrichment.* San Francisco: Jossey-Bass.

Guerney, B. G., Jr. (1977b). Should teachers treat illiteracy, hypocalligraphy, and dysmathematica? *Canadian Counsellor, 12,* 9-14.

Guerney, B. G., Jr. (1979). The great potential of an educational skill-training model in problem prevention. *Journal of Clinical Child Psychology, 3,* 84-86.

Guerney, B. G., Jr. (1981). Foreword. In A. W. Borgen & H. L. Rudner (Eds.), *Psychoeducation for children: Theory, programs, and research.* Springfield, IL: Charles C Thomas.

Guerney, B. G., Jr. (1982). Relationship enhancement. In E. K. Marshall & D. Kurtz (Eds.), *Interpersonal helping skills*. San Francisco: Jossey-Bass.

Guerney, B. G., Jr. (1984). Relationship enhancement therapy and training. In D. Larson (Ed.), *Teaching psychological skills: Models for giving psychology away*. Monterey: Brooks/Cole.

Guerney, B. G., Jr. (1985). *Relationship enhancement: Marital/family therapist's manual*. (Available from IDEALS, P.O. Box 391, State College, PA 16804)

Guerney, B. G., Jr., Brock, G., & Coufal, J. (in press). Integrating marital therapy and enrichment. In N. Jacobson & A. Gurman (Eds.), *Clinical handbook of marital therapy*. New York: Guilford.

Guerney, B. G., Jr., Coufal, J., & Vogelsong, E. (1981). Relationship enhancement versus a traditional approach to therapeutic/preventative/ enrichment parent-adolescent programs. *Journal of Consulting and Clinical Psychology, 49*, 927-939.

Guerney, B. G., Jr., & Flumen, A. B. (1970). Teachers as psychotherapeutic agents for withdrawn children. *Journal of School Psychology, 8*, 107-113.

Guerney, B. G., Jr., & Guerney, L. F. (1981). Family life education as intervention. *Family Relations, 30*, 591-598.

Guerney, B. G., Jr., Guerney, L. F., & Cooney, T. M. (1985). Marital and family problem prevention and enrichment programs. In L. L. Abate (Ed.), *Handbook of family psychology*. Homewood, IL: Dow-Jones Irwin.

Guerney, B. G., Jr., Guerney, L. F., & Sebes, J. M. (1983). Towards family wellness through the educational system. In D. R. Mace (Ed.), *Prevention in family services: Approaches to family wellness*. Newbury Park, CA: Sage.

Guerney, B. G., Jr., & Merriam, M. L. (1972). Toward a democratic elementary school classroom. *Elementary School Journal, 72*, 372-383.

Guerney, B. G., Jr., & Stover, L. (1971). *Filial therapy: Final report on MH 1826301*. [Mimeograph, 156 pp.] State College, PA.

Guerney, B. G., Jr., Stover, L., & Andronico, M. P. (1967). On educating the disadvantaged parent to motivate children for learning: A filial approach. *Community Mental Health Journal, 3*, 66-72.

Guerney, B. G., Jr., & Vogelsong, E. (1981). *Relationship enhancement demonstration dialogues* [Audiotapes]. (Available from Individual and Family Consultation Center, University Park, PA 16802)

Guerney, B. G., Jr., Vogelsong, E., & Coufal, J. (1983). Relationship enhancement vs. a traditional treatment: Follow-up and booster effects. In D. H. Olson & B. C. Miller (Eds.), *Family studies review yearbook*. Newbury Park, CA: Sage.

Guerney, B. G., Jr., Vogelsong, E., & Glynn, S. (1977). *Evaluation of the family counseling unit of the Cambria County Probation Bureau*. (Available from IDEALS, P.O. Box 391, State College, PA)

Guerney, B. G., Jr., Vogelsong, E., & Wolfgang, G. (1977). *Foster parent skills training program: First year evaluation*. (Available from IDEALS, P.O. Box 391, State College, PA)

Guerney, B. G., Jr., Wolfgang, G., & Vogelsong, E. (1978). *Foster care systems training project: Second year evaluation*. (Available from IDEALS, P.O. Box 391, State College, PA)

Guerney, L. F. (1973). *What do you say now?* [Film] Pennsylvania State University University Park, PA, in cooperation with the Pennsylvania Department of Public Welfare.

Guerney, L. F. (1974). *The training of foster parent trainers*. [Film] Pennsylvania State University University Park, PA, in cooperation with the Pennsylvania Department of Public Welfare.

Guerney, L. F. (1975a, April). *A follow-up study on filial therapy.* Paper presented at the annual convention of the Eastern Psychological Association, New York.

Guerney, L. F. (1975b). *Foster parent training: A manual for parents.* (Available from IDEALS, P.O. Box 391, State College, PA 16804)

Guerney, L. F. (1976a). The Filial Therapy program. In D. H. Olson (Ed.), *Treating relationships.* Lake Mills, IA: Graphic.

Guerney, L. F. (1976b). *Foster parent training: A manual for trainers.* (Available from IDEALS, P.O. Box 391, State College, PA).

Guerney, L. F. (1976c). *Foster parent training project, Final report, Part II.* State College, PA: Institute for the Study of Human Development.

Guerney, L. F. (1976d). A program for training agency personnel as foster parent trainers. *Child Welfare, 55,* 652-660.

Guerney, L. F. (1977). A description and evaluation of a skills training program for foster parents. *American Journal of Community Psychology, 5,* 361-371.

Guerney, L. F. (1980). *Parenting: A skills training manual.* (Available from IDEALS, P.O. Box 391, State College, PA)

Guerney, L. F. (1979). Play therapy with learning disabled children. *Journal of Clinical Child Psychology, 9,* 242-244.

Guerney, L. F. (1983). Introduction to filial therapy: Training parents as therapists. In P. A. Keller & L. G. Ritt (Eds.), *Innovations in clinical practice: A source book* (Vol. 2). Sarasota, FL: Professional Resource Exchange.

Guerney, L. F., & Wolfgang, G. (1981). Long-range evaluation of effects on foster parents of a foster parent skill training program. *Journal of Clinical Child Psychology, 10,* 33-37.

Hatch, C. (1983). *Training parents of underachieving black elementary students in communication, child management, and tutoring skills utilizing community parapro-fessionals.* Unpublished doctoral dissertation, Pennsylvania State University.

Hatch, E. J. (1973). *An empirical study of a teacher training program in empathic responsiveness and democratic decision making.* Unpublished doctoral dissertation, Pennsylvania State University.

Hatch, E. J., & Guerney, B. G., Jr. (1975). A pupil relationship enhancement program. *Personnel and Guidance Journal, 54,* 102-105.

Haynes, L. A., & Avery, A. W. (1979). Training adolescents in self-disclosure and empathy skills. *Journal of Counseling Psychology, 26,* 526-530.

Hoopes, M. H., Fisher, A., & Burlow, D. (1984). *Structured family facilitation programs: Enrichment education and treatment.* Rockville, MD: Aspen System Publications.

Jessee, R., & Guerney, B. G., Jr. (1981). A comparison of Gestalt and Relationship Enhancement treatments with married couples. *American Journal of Family Therapy, 9,* 31-41.

Knox, D. (1971). *Marriage happiness: A behavioral approach to counseling.* Champaign, IL: Research Press.

L'Abate, L. (1975a). *Manual: Enrichment programs for the family life cycle.* Atlanta, GA: Social Research Laboratories.

L'Abate, L. (1975b). *Manual: Family enrichment programs.* Atlanta, GA: Social Research Laboratories.

L'Abate, L., & Rupp, G. (1981). *Enrichment: Skills training for family life.* Washington, DC: University Press of America.

Levine, E. T. (1977). *Training elderly volunteers in skills to improve the emotional adjustment of children in a day-care center.* Unpublished doctoral dissertation, Pennsylvania State University.

Matter, M., McAllister, W., & (unlisted) Guerney, B. G., Jr. (1984). Relationship enhancement for the recovering couple: Working with the intangible. *Focus on Family and Chemical Dependency, 7,* 21-23.

Merriam, M. L., & Guerney, B. G., Jr. (1973). Creating a democratic elementary school classrooms: A pilot training program involving teachers, administrators, and parents. *Contemporary Education, 45,* 34-42.

Morello, P. A., & Factor, D. C. (1981). Therapy as prevention: An educational model for treating families. *Canada's Mental Health, 29,* 10-11.

Most, R., & Guerney, B. G., Jr. (1983). An empirical evaluation of the training of lay volunteer leaders for Premarital Relationship Enhancement. *Family Relations, 32,* 239-251.

Oxman, L. (1971). *The effectiveness of filial therapy: A controlled study.* Unpublished doctoral dissertation, Rutgers University.

Preston, J., & Guerney, B. G., Jr. (1982). *Relationship enhancement skills training.* Xeroxed manuscript. [Available from junior author.]

Rappaport, A. F. (1976). Conjugal relationship enhancement program. In D.H.L. Olson (Ed.), *Treating relationships.* Lake Mills, IA: Graphic.

Rappaport, A. F., & Harrell, J. (1972). A behavioral exchange model for marital counseling. *Family Coordinator, 21,* 203-212.

Ridley, C. A., Avery, A. W., Dent, J., & Harrell, J. (1981). The effects of relationship enhancement and problem solving programs on perceived heterosexual competence. *Family Therapy, 8,* 60-66.

Ridley, C. A., Avery, A. W., Harrell, J. E., Leslie, L., & Dent, J. A. (1981). Conflict management: A premarital training program in mutual problem solving. *American Journal of Family Therapy, 9,* 23-32.

Ridley, C. A., Jorgensen, S. R., Morgan, A. C., & Avery, A. W. (1982). Relationship enhancement with premarital couples: An assessment of effects on relationship quality. *American Journal of Family Therapy, 10,* 41-48.

Robin, A. L. (1979). Problem solving communication training: A behavioral approach to the treatment of parent adolescent conflict. *American Journal of Family Therapy, 7,* 69-82.

Robin, A. L. (1980). Parent-adolescent conflict: A skill training approach. In D. P. Rathjen & J. P. Foreyt (Eds.), *Social competence: Interventions for children and adults.* Elmsford, NY: Pergamon.

Rocks, T. (1980). *The effectiveness of communication skills training with underachieving low communicating secondary school students and their teachers.* Unpublished doctoral dissertation, Pennsylvania State University.

Rose, M., Battjes, R., & Leukefeld, C. (1984). *Family life skills training for drug abuse prevention.* Rockville, MD: National Institute on Drug Abuse.

Ross, E., Baker, S., & Guerney, B. G., Jr. (1984). Effectiveness of relationship enhancement therapy versus therapist's preferred therapy. *American Journal of Family Therapy, 13,* 11-21.

Ryan, P. R. (1979). *Issues in fostering.* Ypsilanti, MI: Eastern Michigan University.

Ryan, P. R., Warren, B. L., & McFadden, E. J. (1977). *Training foster parents to serve dependent children: Summary progress report.* Ypsilanti, MI: Eastern Michigan University.

Sams, W. (1983). *Marriage preparation: An experimental comparison of the premarital relationship enhancement and the engaged encounter programs.* Unpublished doctoral dissertation, Pennsylvania State University.

Sawin, M. M. (1979). *Family enrichment with family clusters.* Valley Forge, PA: Judson Press.

Schindler, L., Hahlweg, K., & Revenstorf, D. (1983). Short and long-term effectiveness of two communication training modalities with distressed couples. *American Journal of Family Therapy, 11*, 54-64.

Schlein, S. (1971). *Training dating couples in empathic and open communication: An experimental evaluation of a potential preventive mental health program.* Unpublished doctoral dissertation, Pennsylvania State University.

Seidenberg, G. H. (1978). *The sibling interpersonal improvement program and its impact on elementary and junior high school children.* Unpublished doctoral dissertation, Pennsylvania State University.

Sensué, M. E. (1981). *Filial therapy follow-up study: Effects on parental acceptance and child adjustment.* Unpublished doctoral dissertation, Pennsylvania State University.

Stuart, R. B. (1969a). Operant-interpersonal treatment for marital discord. *Journal of Consulting and Clinical Psychology, 33*, 675-682.

Stuart, R. B. (1969b). Token reinforcement in marital therapy. In R. D. Rubin & C. M. Franks (Eds.), *Advances in behavior therapy.* New York: Academic Press.

Sywulak, A. E. (1977). *The effect of filial therapy on parental acceptance and child adjustment.* Unpublished doctoral dissertation, Pennsylvania State University.

Sywulak, A. E. (1984). Creating a whole atmosphere in a group home for retarded adolescents. *Academic Psychology Bulletin, 6*, 325-327.

Thiessen, J. D., Avery, A. W., & Joanning, H. (1980). Facilitating post divorce adjustment among women: A communication skills training approach. *Journal of Divorce, 4*, 35-44.

Tubesing, D. A., & Tubesing, N. L. (1973). *Tune in empathy training workshop.* Milwaukee: Listening Group.

Vogelsong, E. L. (1978). Relationship enhancement training for children. *Elementary School Guidance and Counseling, 12*, 272-279.

Vogelsong, E. L., & Guerney, B. G., Jr. (1978). *The relationship enhancement program for family therapy and enrichment* [Film, 16 mm., ¾ or ½ inch video, 45 min.] (Available from Individual and Family Consultation Center of the Pennsylvania State University, University Park, PA 16802)

Vogelsong, E. L., & Guerney, B. G., Jr. (1979). *Filial therapy.* [Film, 16mm, ¾ or ½ inch video, 40 min.] (Available from Individual and Family Consultation Center of the Pennsylvania State University, University Park, PA 16802)

Vogelsong, E. L., & Guerney, B. G., Jr. (1980). Working with parents of disturbed adolescents. In R. R. Abidin (Ed.), *Parent education and intervention handbook.* Springfield, IL: Charles C Thomas.

Vogelsong, E. L., Guerney, B. G., Jr., & Guerney, L. F. (1983). Relationship enhancement therapy with inpatients and their families. In R. Luber & C. Anderson (Eds.), *Communication training approaches to family intervention with psychiatric patients.* New York: Human Sciences Press.

Vogelsong, E. L., Most, R. K., & Yenchko, A. (1979). Relationship enhancement training for pre-adolescents in public schools. *Journal of Clinical Child Psychology, 3*, 97-100.

Waldo, M. (1984a). *Leadership skills workshop outline.* (Available from IDEALS, P.O. Box 391, State College, PA)

Waldo, M. (1984b). *Relationship skills workshop outline.* (Available from IDEALS, P.O. Box 391, State College, PA)

Waldo, W., & Guerney, B. G., Jr. (1983). Dyadic marital relationship enhancement therapy in the treatment of alcoholism. *Journal of Marital and Family Therapy, 9*, 321-322.

Waldo, W., & Saidla, D. (1984). *Relationship skills manual.* (Available from IDEALS, P.O. Box 391, State College, PA)

Weiss, R. S. (1976). Transition states and other stressful situations: Their nature and programs for their management. In G. Caplan & M. Killilea (Eds.), *Support systems and mutual help: Multidisciplinary exploration.* New York: Grune & Stratton.

Welch, G. J., & Granvold, D. K. (1977). Seminars for separated/divorced: An educational approach to postdivorce adjustment. *Journal of Sex and Marital Therapy, 3,* 31-39.

Wieman, R. J. (1973). *Conjugal relationship modification and reciprocal reinforcement: A comparison of treatments of marital discord.* Unpublished doctoral dissertation, Pennsylvania State University.

6

Parenting Programs for Black Parents

Kerby T. Alvy

Educating parents to promote their children's welfare and development is a venerable idea that has recently taken on new forms, new urgencies, and new critics. The idea dates back to the 1800s and we Americans have evolved a variety of parent education activities and programs that have been offered through a variety of institutions (Brim, 1965).

Over the last 15 years, certain programs have received special attention. These are the parenting skill-building programs that are being taught to small groups of parents in agencies, schools, places of worship, and homes. These programs emphasize positive and accepting attitudes toward children. They use a variety of role playing and multimedia techniques to teach parents how to use basic reinforcement, problem-solving, and communication skills to deal with a wide range of child-rearing problems and challenges.

Several of these programs are being used in different communities throughout the United States and have taken on the status of standard parent training interventions. Some of the more widely used programs include the Rogerian psychology-oriented Parent Effectiveness Training program created by Gordon (1970, 1975, 1976), the Adlerian-oriented Systematic Training for Effective Parenting program created by Dinkmeyer and McKay (1976), and various behaviorally oriented child management programs such as those created by Patterson (1971, 1975, 1976), Becker (1971), and Aitchison (1976; Eimers & Aitchison, 1977).

These programs emerged primarily out of the mental health field and they represent an attempt to share with parents the skills and attitudes that mental health practitioners have found useful in relating to children. The accepting attitudes and positive practices that these programs teach are very similar to those that the research literature on parent-child relations has found to be related to high self-esteem and stable social adjustment in children (Coopersmith, 1967; Maccoby & Martin, 1983; Martin, 1975). Thus these programs appear to teach parents many of the things they need to know and do in order to put their children at a psychosocial advantage in our society.

This new parent training technology came into existence at a time when many voices were calling for more and better parent training. In the early 1970s, the Joint Commission on the Mental Health of Children stressed the need to establish more preventive services like parent training (*Mental Health of Children*, 1973). In the mid-1970s, another federally supported study revealed that parent training was considered by child mental health experts to be the number one community service to promote the mental and emotional development of America's children (Mitre Corporation, 1977).

Also in the 1970s, our country began to acknowledge the widespread abuse and neglect of children by their parents. The growing awareness of this tragedy led authorities in the child welfare fields to advocate for parent training as a primary strategy for preventing child abuse (Alvy, 1975a; Fontana, 1973; Gil, 1973; Helfer & Kempe, 1974, 1976). Federal agencies like the National Center on Child Abuse and Neglect (DHEW, 1976a, 1976b, 1976c) and other national organizations like the Education Commission of the States (1976) echoed this plea.

Juvenile delinquency authorities have also looked to parent training as a promising prevention strategy (Fraser & Hawkins, 1982). Research on delinquency has implicated poor parent-child relations and poor family management as contributing factors, and training parents has much appeal (Patterson & Stouthamer-Loeber, 1984).

Research on the etiology of substance abuse has also revealed a linkage between ineffective parenting and alcohol and drug abuse. The national institutes that focus on these enormous problems have also advocated for parent training as a prevention strategy (NIAAA, 1983; Rose, Battjes, & Leukefeld, 1984).

Thus parent training is now seen as a prevention approach that can affect a wide range of social and health problems. The practitioners and service engineers that must deal with these pressing and costly problems on a day-to-day basis are clear that parent training is a necessary component of any comprehensive prevention plan. In addition, they see parent training as an essential component of treatment plans.

These individuals are also critical of the existing parent training technology. They note that the standard programs are designed primarily for White middle-class parents and they need to be reworked or adapted for ethnic minority and low-income populations (Alvy, 1981b; Mitre Corporation, 1977). Our organization, the Center for the Improvement of Child Caring, has responded to this need and has begun evolving culturally adapted versions for Black and Hispanic parents (Alvy, Fuentes, Harrison, & Rosen, 1980). The majority of this chapter will be devoted to describing the development and current status of adapted programs for Black parents.

Criticism has also been directed at the standard programs for being too complex for use with highly dysfunctional and abusive families, though some practitioners do report successful outcomes in using these programs with abusive parents (Martin & Beesley, 1976). Others have created special program versions just for abusive parents (Bavolek, Comstock, & McLaughlin, 1983; Schuster, Amdurer, Fallon, & Hare, 1981; Wolfe, Kaufman, Aragona, & Sandler, 1981).

In addition to these types of program criticisms, the practitioners and service engineers have also noted that very few persons who work in family-serving public agencies have been trained to deliver and evaluate these programs. This criticism has spoken to the need for developing instructor training programs. Our organization has responded in this area also, and we have developed and field-tested a model training program for preparing mental health, social service, and education personnel for delivering parenting skill-building programs through their agencies and schools (Alvy & Rosen, 1984; Alvy & Rubin, 1981). That model served as the basis for proposed legislation in California (Assembly Bill 251, *The Parent Development Act*, 1985) and is being used by the California Department of Alcohol and Drug Programs.

Advocates and critics of the skill-building programs have also raised questions about their effectiveness, and there have been hundreds of evaluation studies and several literature reviews of these evaluations (Atkeson & Forehand, 1978; Berkowitz & Graziano, 1972; Cobb & Medway, 1978; Croake & Glover 1977; Eyeberg & Johnson, 1974; Moreland, Schwebel, Beck, & Wells, 1982; Reisinger, Ora, & Frangia, 1976; Rinn & Markle, 1977; Tavormina, 1980; Tramontana, Sherrets, & Authier, 1980). Issues regarding the value and effectiveness of these programs have also been raised in the many parent training survey books that have been published recently (Abidin, 1980; Arnold, 1980; Dangel & Polster, 1984; Fine, 1980; Harmon & Brim, 1980; Haskins & Adams, 1983; Kaplan, 1980; Mash, Handy, & Hamerlynck, 1976).

Results of the evaluation studies have been generally positive but they have left many questions unanswered. The behaviorally oriented child management programs seem to be the most consistently effective programs in terms of teaching parents reinforcement ideas and skills that they use to modify their children's behaviors, and these programs have received the most research attention and support. The communication skill training programs have shown positive results in some studies but not in others. It is unclear from these studies which type of parent, parent-child dyad, or families benefit most from the various programs. It is clear, however, that some parents in some programs appear to gain a great deal from participating. We know from our own studies that some parents transform their relationships with their children in very dramatic ways as a result of participating in parenting skill-building programs, while others do not (Alvy, Rosen, Harrison, & Fuentes, 1980; Timnick, 1980).

The lack of clear results from all of these studies is largely a product of the inherent complexity and costliness of conducting quality research on the effectiveness of group parent training programs. There is such a wide array of relevant variables that beg for control and examination that it is almost impossible to make clear statements unless you have measured all of these variables.

There are many, many program variables. The programs differ in terms of theoretical or philosophical underpinnings. Even within the same theoretical approach, such as in the behaviorally oriented child management, there are many program versions of the approach that teach different blends of parenting ideas and skills. Other programs that represent different approaches not only vary in terms of content but also in terms of teaching methodology and instructor role and qualifications. The programs also differ in terms of the amount or length of training that they provide, though most of these programs run for only one three-hour session a week for two or three months.

There are important implementation variables to consider. These programs are offered under an array of institutional auspices, included through court referral. Parents in some programs pay for the services while others do not. Some programs offer incentives for participation and attendance. Getting parents into these programs is often an arduous and time-consuming task. These programs compete for parental attention with the entertainment and sports media, with the need for relaxation, and with many other family and personal matters that often make going to a parent training class a rather low priority.

Then there is the wide range of subject variables that should affect the effectiveness of these programs and that need to be examined. The age and stage of development of the parents' children are important factors, as are the children's personality, intellectual, and behavioral styles. Because these programs are designed to help parents in guiding their children's development, their children's developmental characteristics are obviously of major importance. And so are the individual characteristics of the parents, their personalities and intellectual capacities.

Related subject variables that are also pivotal include the family structure, whether nuclear, single, or blended. The parent's and family's socioeconomic status, religion, and ethnicity are important variables, as is marital harmony or disharmony, and the various environmental stresses that the participating families might be experiencing.

Further complicating factors are group composition and group dynamic factors. No two parent training groups are alike because no two groups have the exact same mix of parent and child characteristics. The dynamics of each group also differ, and instructor and parent characteristics interact to make each group experience unique in its own right.

Given these inherent complexities and given the costs that would be involved in accounting for all the relevant variables, it is no wonder that the results of the available studies are not as clear as would be desirable. More extensive and intensive research is needed, especially now that parent training is being seen as pivotal in ameliorating so many costly and tragic social and health problems.

In turning now to a description of how we went about adapting standard parent training programs for Black parents, I will also report on a recently funded study to research the effectiveness of the adapted programs further. This new study holds the promise of providing clearer results, because it measures a wider range of relevant variables.

Development of
Black Parent Training Programs

The journey that led to the creation of the programs for Black parents was very personal. It was a journey through the racial mine fields in our country that keep people of different color from getting to know each other and from appreciating our common humanity. It was a highly personal and socially revealing journey that could only happen in America.

Program Context and History

It began in 1970 when this White psychologist, the son of Jewish immigrants, received his doctorate and was pursuing employment in Los Angeles. I had several opportunities to work in established and prestigious White institutions but I chose to take a position in the newly formed community mental health center in Watts where I was one of the only two White persons on a staff of 50 professionals and paraprofessionals. By that time in my life, I had developed strong convictions about human rights and fairness, and Dr. Martin Luther King embodied the values and vision that I had come to cherish. Working in Watts was the right thing for this White man to do and it provided a profound postdoctoral education.

As a clinical child psychologist in the children's service, I spent most of my time with Black children and their parents. Upon working with so many parents who were struggling to maintain positive relationships with their children and to raise them in the best way possible, I was struck by the simple fact that they had received no formal education or training to help them. This seemed ironic, given the fact that I had just received an extensive education to learn how to be most productive in relating to children. Yet I was with the children and parents only one hour a week, and they were with each other every day. It seemed to me that the wrong people were being trained.

This realization led me to find ways of sharing with Black parents what I knew about relating to children and I looked into the parent training materials that were available at that time. I found several parent training manuals and programs but none dealt specifically with the issues and challenges that were particular to Black parents. I wasn't even sure at that time how to conceptualize the issues but I knew that the existing programs did not even attempt to address them.

I began using existing materials to run training sessions with the parents, who were very receptive. Many of the parents were relieved that they could be taught skills and procedures that would improve their relationships with their children. Some were desperate and were eager to try whatever might work to turn around a strained and troublesome relationship. Their desperation stemmed not only from the tragedy of not being able to relate to their own children but also from their children's problems at school and in the community. Some were not as receptive, as their relationships with their children had deteriorated so greatly that they were unwilling to do much about it. But none of the Black parents who were involved in these training sessions even mentioned that what they were being instructed to do with their children could be considered as White folks' ways. This didn't come up as an issue. What seemed to matter to these parents was that what they were learning was helpful.

But it did matter to many of the Black staff members of the agency and they let this be known in very critical and racially charged ways. It was not that they were critical about the activity of educating Black parents to be more effective. Their criticism was with the fact that a White man using "White ideas" was training Black parents to raise Black children. In the heat of this type of criticism, there was no time or opportunity to explore the issues or to get beyond the surface of things.

This experience further alerted me to question the cultural fit of the existing programs and parenting ideas, and to realize that something should be done to make them more acceptable and relevant. The first attempt was in developing a job training program for low-income Black parents, Indigenous Mental Health Workers for Children's Services (Alvy, 1975b). This program was funded by grants from the National Institute of Mental Health and the Department of Labor. It consisted of training unemployed Black parents to use the reinforcement skills of the then-existing parent training programs in their counseling of children who were referred to the mental health center and in their relationships with their own children. This program prepared Black parents for human service jobs and the majority of graduates found employment in mental health or educational settings. The program, however, did not deal with adapting the parenting skills to the Black experience. Whatever adaptations took place were the result of the parents themselves making intuitive changes.

It was in 1974 during the conduct of this program that the Center for the Improvement of Child Caring (CICC) was founded. I had been asked to testify at a California senate hearing on child abuse and I had suggested that wide-scale parent training was a good prevention approach. My testimony was picked up by the local and national media, and I was contacted by a private foundation to discuss my ideas. I was asked what type of institution should be created to help with these problems and this question stimulated me to evolve the basic ideas and values of CICC. Then, along with some colleagues and family members, I founded CICC as a private, nonprofit service, research and training corporation.

CICC is a multiethnic organization that is based on values that all children have rights to the opportunity to fulfill their developmental potential. Secondarily, and as one of the many strategies for ensuring that the rights of children are upheld and fostered, we also believe that parents and other caregivers have rights to receive the best education, training, and support. In terms of programmatic objectives, we committed ourselves to developing and refining programs and opportunities for parents and other caregivers to improve and enhance how they care for children. Part of this self-imposed mandate included the idea of adapting current parent training programs to the unique history, needs, and characteristics of ethnic minority parents.

It was four years after the founding of CICC that this idea took programmatic shape. Between 1974 and 1978, CICC was involved in delivering parenting programs to a wide array of parents, including Black parents. It was also during this time that we began to develop the

142   Kerby T. Alvy

national model for training parenting instructors that I mentioned earlier (Alvy & Rosen, 1984; Alvy & Rubin, 1981). We had received a training grant from NIMH and we were in the process of training over 100 instructors to deliver standard parent training programs through their agencies. We also were conducting research on the effectiveness of the standard, nonadapted programs with low-income ethnic minority parents.

Then in 1978 I was asked to speak at an NIMH-supported conference in Louisiana on Improving Mental Health Services for Blacks in the South. There I met Dr. James R. Ralph, who was the head of NIMH's Minority Group Mental Health Center, and we discussed the need to adapt the standard programs for ethnic minorities. Dr. Ralph encouraged me to meet with the leaders of the NIMH-supported minority group research centers in Los Angeles to evolve such a project. The meetings were very exciting and key individuals from the Black and Hispanic centers worked closely with us to develop the project, which we called Culturally Adapted Parent Training (Alvy et al., 1980). The project proposal was reviewed at NIMH by a committee of ethnic minority mental health authorities, and it was approved for three years of funding beginning in September of 1979.

Important Issues

Before describing this project and its results, I would like to share with you some key issues and problems that are involved in such an undertaking.

When you take on the task of designing parenting programs, you are operating in very sensitive areas. Parent training deals directly with how individuals and groups rear their children, and it is through child rearing that many of our most cherished personal, religious, and cultural values are transmitted. Choosing to focus on parent training is a choice to confront our society's most personal and possibly most important activity.

When the focus is on parenting programs for ethnic or racial groups that have been persecuted and oppressed, the task takes on an additional meaning. Blacks and other groups have managed to survive the most opprobrious inhumanities because of the strengths of their families and their will to overcome. When you talk about programs to affect Black families, you are talking about influencing the same social units that have provided the intimate support that nurtures the will to overcome. And you better be damn sure that what you are proposing will enhance that capacity to overcome.

Assuming that what you have to offer will indeed be helpful, you are then faced with the complex task of adapting or designing programs that address parenting themes that are relevant to the Black experience in America. And in so doing you must be knowledgeable about and respectful of the diversity of Black experiences in America and of the diversities within Black communities.

Though the majority of Blacks live in poverty or on the margins of poverty, there is socioeconomic diversity in the Black community. There are Black business leaders, doctors, lawyers, and scholars. The educational and material resources that these individuals can bring to child rearing are markedly different from that which their impoverished brothers and sisters can. This diversity has many implications for designing parenting programs.

Fully one-half of all Black children in America are now growing up in single-parent families headed by women (Children's Defense Fund, 1985) and this fact has many implications for designing and implementing parenting programs. Programs for Black parents must address the special issues of single parenthood in order to be relevant.

There are diversities of outlook and opinion regarding cultural issues that need to be considered. While most Blacks share a special consciousness about what it means to be Black, there are different levels of cultural or ethnic consciousness, different degrees of ethnic identification and even ethnic denial and ethnic self-disparagement. Blacks also differ in their awareness and opinions concerning Ebonics or Black dialect; while some deny its existence, others promote its usage. These matters are obviously relevant to any programs that assist Black parents in rearing Black children. How to address this rich diversity of cultural issues and opinions is a major challenge.

There is also diversity within Black communities regarding intergroup relations. Historically, Blacks in America have struggled with the question of integration versus separatism. Black nationalism is a powerful force in some segments of Black communities but not in others. As Senator Kennedy found out on his recent well-intentioned trip to South Africa, not all Blacks look kindly on White folks who want to be helpful (Kennedy, 1985). Indeed, Blacks who associate with Whites are viewed suspiciously by many of their brothers and sisters.

These intergroup diversities with their undercurrents of reverse racism are important to the content, implementation, and institutional sponsorship of Black parenting programs. I will speak to these issues more fully later in this chapter, but now I just want to indicate that they have created unique problems in developing the adapted programs. Because CICC is not a Black organization and because I am White, the

Black folks who have worked on this project have had to do so at some personal discomfort and risk. I too have experienced these discomforts and risks.

All of our shared uneasiness emanates from our country's history of White racism and discrimination. And this is a critical issue in programs for Black parents. It not only gets expressed in terms of who should develop the programs but also in terms of questioning the nature of the programs themselves and why the programs are needed at all.

An important issue in regard to the nature of the programs is their value orientation. The standard programs are based on values of individual responsibility and individual achievement (Alvy, 1981b). They are not based on other relevant value orientations such as the more communal African values that emphasize shared responsibility and shared achievement (Johnson, Brown, Harris, & Lewis, 1980; Myers, 1982). Therefore, the very task of adapting the standard programs for Black parents, a task that appears to keep the underlying value orientation of the programs intact, is a source of controversy in and of itself.

The need for the programs is also a source of controversy. And what seems to be behind the question of why the programs are needed is a sensitivity to being considered inferior or deficient. Given the history of White racism and its many ugly manifestations, it is certainly understandable why Black Americans would have this type of sensitivity.

Thus any program for Black parents is closely scrutinized to see whether it is based on assumptions of inferiority or deficiency. In terms of adapting parenting skill programs, this issue gets expressed through asking whether the programs imply by their existence that Blacks are deficient in parenting knowledge or skills.

But this question could just as easily be asked of the original programs and of White parents. That is, do the original programs, because they teach particular parenting ideas and skills, imply that White parents are inferior and deficient in parenting know-how and skills?

And the answer to both of these questions is "no." The answer is "no" because the question is inappropriate when applied to educational programs that teach new ideas and skills. It is like asking whether teaching a new subject to college students implies that they are inferior or deficient. Of course, it doesn't. It only implies that there is some new or better organized information that should be helpful, and that is why the course is being taught.

A more productive question in terms of racial discrimination and parenting programs is the question of equity or equal opportunity. If the majority group has available parenting programs that seem to help them raise children who succeed in this society, shouldn't minority groups have equal access to this social opportunity? And here the answer is a resounding "yes!"

And making these programs more relevant to minority groups through program adaptations is one way of promoting this type of equal opportunity.

The Culturally Adapted Parent Training Project

The project to adapt the programs consisted of a series of research and development activities (Alvy et al., 1980). There were parallel activities in developing the adaptations for Black and Hispanic parents but only those that went into developing the Black programs will be described here.

The project began by assembling a multiracial staff, and a distinguished consultant group of Black mental health, child development, and educational experts. The consultants played crucial roles as critics and advisers. Their first task was to supply written critiques of the parenting texts from the standard programs. They scrutinized the texts in terms of whether the parenting ideas in each chapter should be reworked or emphasized for use with Black parents (Alvy, 1981c).

While the consultants were doing this critical review, the project staff was conducting intensive child-rearing interviews with Black and White parents (Alvy, Harrison, Rosen, & Fuentes, 1982a). The data from these in-home interviews were intended to provide an empirical basis for making program adaptations. We had reviewed the handful of prior studies on Black parenting (Baumrind, 1972; Cahill, 1966; Durrett, O'Bryant, & Pennebaker, 1975; Duvall, 1971; Elder, 1962; Geismer & Gerhart, 1968; Levine & Bartz, 1979) and had not found them particularly useful for our purposes. We wanted to obtain more descriptive data on the types of parenting practices and child-rearing situations that were covered in the standard programs, and we wanted some measures of each group's worldview or frame of reference regarding child rearing. We also wanted some data on how Black parents relate to issues of Blackness in their relationships with their children. None of the previous studies had dealt with specific Blackness issues.

After the interview data were collected and summarized, the consultants and staff came together for three days to review and discuss both the data and the consultant's program critiques. These were heated, illuminating, and exciting sessions. They helped focus the project on the need to make the context of Black parenting a major issue, and a project monograph was eventually written on this topic (Harrison & Alvy, 1982). The main point was that what makes Black parenting different and unique is the context of racism and discrimination within which it is forced to take place. This point took on chilling significance during these working sessions because they were occurring at the same time that the bodies of murdered Black children were being discovered in Atlanta.

Many of the observations and issues that were raised by the consultants were similar to those that scholars on Black parenting had addressed in their books and articles (Comer & Poussaint, 1975; Harrison-Ross & Wyden, 1973; Johnson, Brown, Harris, & Lewis, 1980; McLaughlin, 1976; Rosser, 1978). These scholars carefully and poignantly documented how the history of racial discrimination had left its mark on Black parenting, especially in terms of creating a traditional Black approach to disciplining children in which discipline had come to be equated with punishment, spanking, and whipping. They spoke to the problems of developing positive personal and racial identities in the midst of White racism. They showed how much of the themes and practices in Black parenting were developed as survival techniques, and they were ample in their respect for the courage and resourcefulness of Black parents and families. These scholars also commented that many of the survival strategies of the past were inappropriate for the modern era where there are more opportunities and where upward mobility requires more sophisticated educational attainments. They stressed the need for changes in Black parenting, and they advocated the use of many of the parenting ideas and skills that are taught in the standard programs. They strongly emphasized that cultural change was essential for continued cultural viability and survival. The basic ideas of these scholars were eventually distilled into a Profile of Effective Black parenting, which helped inform the program adaptations (Alvy, 1981a).

Many of the observations of the Black parenting scholars found empirical substantiation in the data from the parent interviews (Alvy, Harrison, Rosen, & Fuentes, 1982a). The interviews were with 100 Black lower- and middle-class parents whose preschool children were enrolled in Head Start programs (Black Head Start), 100 predominantly lower-class White parents (White Low Income), and 100 predominantly upper-middle-class White parents (White Higher Income).

The measure of worldview or cultural frame of reference was a projective technique called the Associative Group Analysis technique, where parents give their word associations to various parenting concepts, and their associations are then combined into components of meaning (Szalay, 1978; Szalay & Bryson, 1973; Szalay & Maday, 1973). Figure 6.1

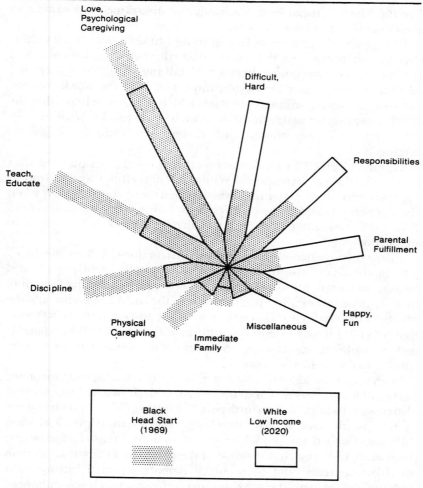

Love,
Psychological
Caregiving

Difficult,
Hard

Responsibilities

Teach,
Educate

Parental
Fulfillment

Discipline

Happy,
Fun

Physical
Caregiving

Miscellaneous

Immediate
Family

Black Head Start (1969)	White Low Income (2020)

NOTE: The size of each meaning component of the semantograph is the percentage of responses (weighted associations) for the components. The total weighted associations or concept score is the key.

Figure 6.1 Semantographic Presentation of Raising Children, Comparing Black Head Start (BHS) and White Low Income (WLI) Parent Groups

contains the components of meaning and their relative salience for the Black Head Start and White Low Income groups in regard to the concept of Raising Children. For Whites, themes of love, difficulty, parental fulfillment, responsibility, and happiness are almost equally as salient.

For the Black parents, love, teaching, and discipline predominate in their outlook on raising children.

In regard to the concept of Disciplining Children, Figure 6.2 reflects that, for the low-income Whites, punishment, spanking, difficulty, and patience are the most salient themes, with talking, consistency, necessity, educating, and loving also being important. For the Black parents, punishment and spanking dominate, which seems to reflect what the Black parenting scholars referred to as traditional Black discipline. The Black image is also infused with themes of educating, obedience, talking, and love.

Figures 6.3 and 6.4 contain data on the reported parenting practices for the Black Head Start and the White Low and High Income Groups. Figure 6.3 details the parenting practices that each group employs when their preschool child does what they say or follows parental instruction. Figure 6.4 shows what the parents do when the same child is disobedient in a major way.

In regard to when children follow instructions, 24% of the Black parents choose to do nothing. The reactions most frequently mentioned by those Black parents who did respond was to show global appreciation, global praise of the child, specific praise of the child's behavior, and the giving of material rewards. The major ethnic and class differences were that fewer Whites choose to do nothing and that more White parents delivered global appreciative comments and praise that were more specific to the child's behavior.

With respect to major disobedience, the main reported reaction on the part of Black parents was to spank or slap with the hand. Black parents also reported a high usage of ordering and hitting children with objects, as well as discussion and preaching. The main ethnic and class differences were that more White parents of both classes reported using discussion, ordering, and removal of the child from the situation than did Black parents, and more Black parents reported hitting their children with objects, though this latter difference was less pronounced when comparing the Black parents and the White low-income group.

Other interview data on hitting children revealed that the vast majority of all parents (99% of the Black, 95% of the White low-income, and 82% of the White higher-income parents) have hit their young children at one time or another. The Black parents explained hitting more in terms of being a useful technique for achieving a wide range of child-rearing objectives, and were more certain of its positive value. The White parents tended to hit more out of anger and frustration, and to be ambivalent about hitting.

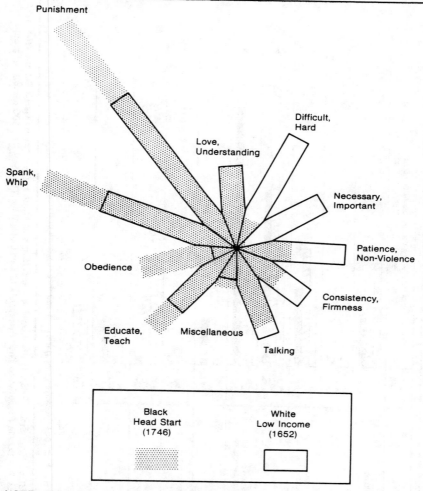

NOTE: The size of each meaning component of the semantograph is the percentage of responses (weighted associations) for the components. The total weighted associations or concept score is the key.

Figure 6.2 Semantographic Presentation of Disciplining, Comparing Black Head Start (BHS) and White Low Income (WLI) Parent Groups

Other interview data dealt with Blackness issues and aspirations for child achievements. When asked if in raising their children they had done or said things to help their children know what it is to be Black, only 51% of the Black parents indicated that they had done so. When

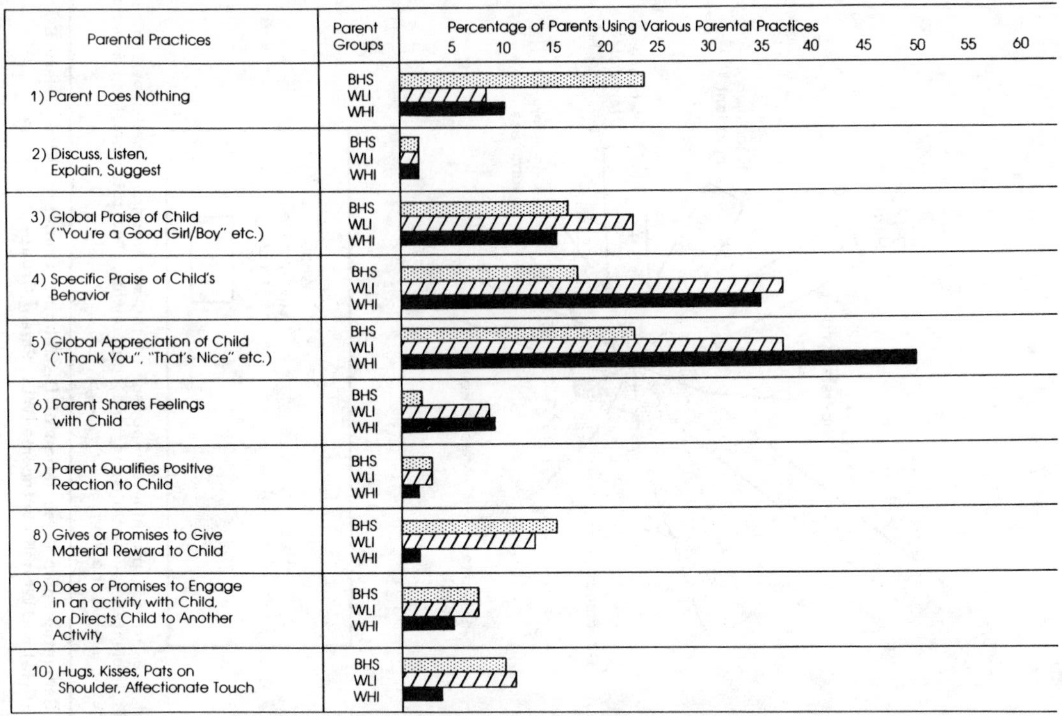

150

Percentage of Parents Using Various Parental Practices

5 10 15 20 25 30 35 40 45 50 55 60

Parental Practices	Parent Groups
1) Parent Does Nothing	BHS / WLI / WHI
2) Discuss, Listen, Explain, Suggest	BHS / WLI / WHI
3) Global Praise of Child ("You're a Good Girl/Boy" etc.)	BHS / WLI / WHI
4) Specific Praise of Child's Behavior	BHS / WLI / WHI
5) Global Appreciation of Child ("Thank You", "That's Nice" etc.)	BHS / WLI / WHI
6) Parent Shares Feelings with Child	BHS / WLI / WHI
7) Parent Qualifies Positive Reaction to Child	BHS / WLI / WHI
8) Gives or Promises to Give Material Reward to Child	BHS / WLI / WHI
9) Does or Promises to Engage in an activity with Child, or Directs Child to Another Activity	BHS / WLI / WHI
10) Hugs, Kisses, Pats on Shoulder, Affectionate Touch	BHS / WLI / WHI

NOTE: Percentages total more than 100% because some parents used more than one practice.

Figure 6.3 Percentage of Black Head Start (BHS), White Low Income (WLI), and White Higher Income (WHI) Parents Who Used Various Types of Parental Practices in Response to Their Preschool Children Doing What They Say (N = 100 parents per group)

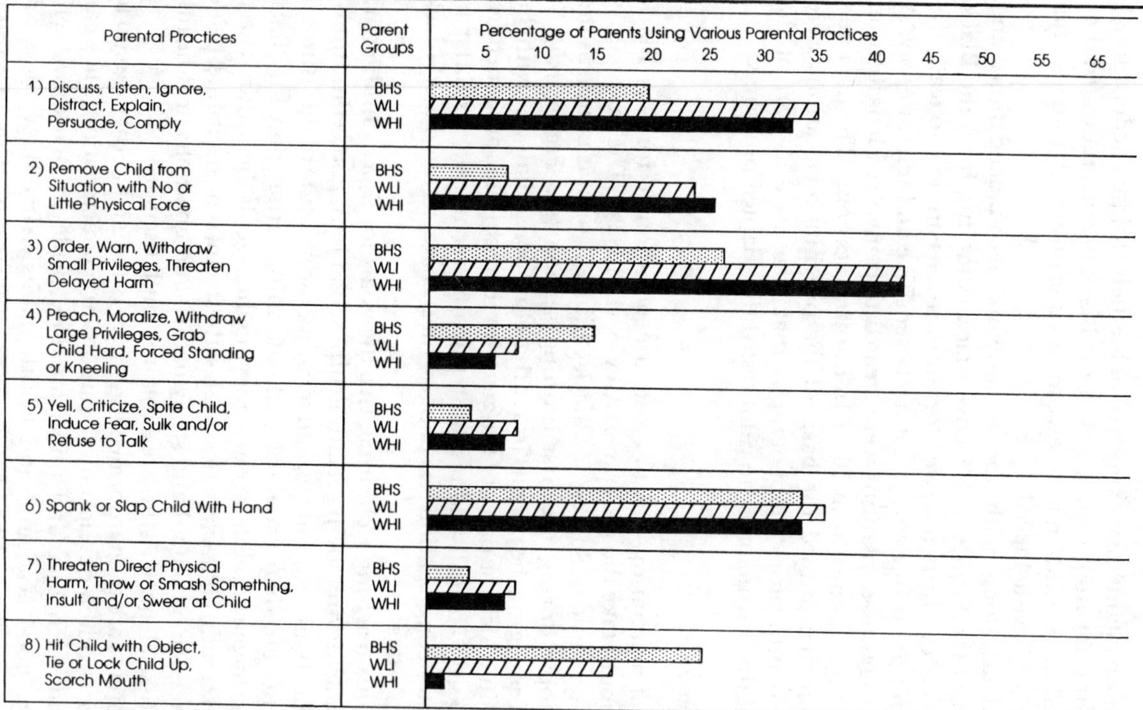

NOTE: Percentages are based on the total out of 100 parents per group who reported that a major disobedience had occurred: BHS = 67 parents, WHI = 100 parents. Percentages total more than 100% because some parent used more than one practice.

Figure 6.4 Percentage of Black Head Start (BHS), White Low Income (WLI), and White Higher Income (WHI) Parents Who Used Various Types of Parental Practices in Response to a Major Disobedience on the Part of Their Preschool Children

asked questions about their expectations for their children's educational and occupational attainments, 94% of the Black parents indicated that they wanted their children to receive more education and higher status jobs than they have achieved.

These data, along with the consultants' recommendations and writings, and the Profile of Effective Black Parenting from the Black scholars, were carefully reviewed for implications on how to teach the standard programs in a more culturally sensitive and relevant way. A series of program adaptations were created that involved lengthening the standard programs from 10 to 15 training sessions. The data and information that formed the basis of the program adaptations were transformed into project monographs that were used as part of the training of the instructors who pilot-tested the adapted programs.

Program Adaptations

The first adaptation was to create a new rationale for why Black parents should take the programs (Alvy et al., 1982b). The rationale is called the Pyramid of Success for Black Children and it is taught as the opening topic during the first training session (see Figure 6.5). It consists of engaging the parents in a call-and-response dialogue with the instructor in which the parents' life goals for their children are generated and discussed. The call-and-response teaching technique is similar to the minister-congregation exchanges that characterize many Black church meetings.

Using this teaching technique, five life goals for Black children are identified: achieving loving relationships, good jobs, good educations, helping the Black community, and resisting the pressure of the "street." The parents are then provided with the information that for Black children to have a good chance at achieving these goals the children need to develop certain characteristics: high self-esteem, self-discipline, pride in Blackness, good school and study habits, and good physical health habits. These characteristics are explained and discussed.

The parents are then informed that there is much that they can do to help their children develop these important characteristics. They can model and teach love and understanding, pride in Blackness, self-discipline, good academic and health habits. After these ideas are explained and discussed, the parents are informed that the programs will provide them with some additional child-rearing skills and ideas to help them model and teach. And in so doing the programs will help them stimulate the development of the child characteristics that are necessary for achieving the life goals for Black children.

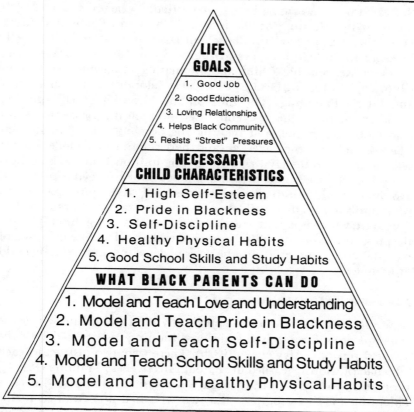

Figure 6.5 Pyramid of Success for Black Children

The second adaptation was to relate regularly the skills that are taught in the standard programs to the Pyramid of Success, so as to reinforce regularly the idea that as the parents are learning and using the skills they are moving their children toward the life goals. This is done by drawing the parents' attention back to the Pyramid every time a new skill or idea is taught, and showing the parents how the use of the idea or skill can promote the development of one or more of the important child characteristics.

The third major modification consisted of a series of new instructional units on topics of particular relevance to Black parents. These units, which consume anywhere from 45 minutes to an hour and a half of instructional time, are intended to be presented at relevant junctures in the teaching of the standard program curricula. The units covered such topics as the Meaning of Disciplining Children (Traditional Black Discipline versus Modern Black Self-Discipline), Developing Self-Esteem and Pride in Blackness, Drugs and Our Children, Developing Sexually Responsible Children, Stimulating Academic Growth in Children, Stimulating Healthy Physical Development, Chit Chat Time, and Single Parenting. The unit on the Meaning of Disciplining Children includes the use and discussion of the projective word association technique, and relating the development of traditional Black discipline to the slavery era and the development of modern Black self-discipline to the civil rights era. The unit on Pride in Blackness raises consciousness and provides strategies for conveying pride and avoiding ethnic self-disparagement, as well as helping parents to communicate with their children over real-life examples of racism. The drug unit, which is taught within the context of helping the child resist the pressures of the "street," is concerned with the modeling influence of parental drug usage and with the ways of detecting and avoiding child drug usage.

Pilot Testing of Adapted Programs

Several instructors who had previously been trained to deliver the standard programs received additional training in how to deliver the adapted versions (Alvy et al., 1982b). There were two instructors each who had previously learned the Parent Effectiveness Training (P.E.T.) program, two who had learned the Systematic Training for Effective Parenting (STEP) program, and two who had been trained in the behaviorally oriented child management program, Confident Parenting (CP). Half of the instructors were Black and half were White. Their retraining included learning the new program content and teaching techniques, as well as some highly personal explorations of their ethnic and racial biases and understandings.

Each instructor was assigned to teach an adapted version of their particular program with a group of Black Head Start parents from the Watts area of Los Angeles. Everyone was alerted to the possibility that there would be inconsistent parental attendance, as this had been CICC's and other agencies' experience in running multisession, voluntary parenting classes in low-income communities. And parental participation and attendance did turn out to be a major problem. One of the participating Head Start agencies was unable to attract enough parents to begin a class, and there was irregular attendance at the five classes that were run.

The evaluation procedures included a relatively brief pretest interview and a more extensive posttest interview. A total of 48 parents were available for both interviews. Of this group, 19 had attended only three to six of the training sessions and they were designated as the Low Attendance Group. The other 29 parents had attended seven or more sessions and they constituted the High Attendance Group. Only two parents had attended all of the 15 training sessions.

The evaluation included a pre- and posttest administration of a measure of parental acceptance, Rohner's Parental Acceptance-Rejection Questionnaire (1980). The main reason for looking at program effects on parental acceptance was that research on parent-child relations has indicated that parental acceptance is a universally significant phenomenon. Parental acceptance and rejection has been shown to influence many facets of child development: acceptance has been consistently associated with high self-esteem, stable social adjustment and academic achievement in children, and rejection in its various forms has been consistently associated with low self-esteem and emotional, behavioral, and academic problems in children (Martin, 1975; Rohner, 1980).

Table 6.1 presents the pre- and posttest acceptance/rejection scores for the Low and High Attendance groups. It shows that there were significant improvements for the High Attendance group but not for the Low Attendance parents. In looking at the subscales that make up the total acceptance-rejection score on this measure (scales having to do with parental warmth, aggression, neglect, and rejection), we found that what was reflected in the significantly improved acceptance scores for the High Attendance group was a greater sensitivity to their negative treatment of their preschool children and a stronger orientation to approach them in more positive ways. The High Attendance parents saw themselves as being less hostile and aggressive, less neglectful and rejecting, and as being more accepting of their preschool children.

During the posttest interview, all of the parents were asked to reflect back on their relationships to their children prior to starting the class, and to rate and describe those relationships now. Table 6.2 contains the parental ratings of relationship changes with their preschool and older children. In every instance, the High Attendance parents rated their relationships as having improved more than the Low Attendance group. Statistical tests showed that the greater overall improvements in the total High Attendance group with both their preschool and older children were significant.

When asked to explain exactly what they meant by saying that their relationships had improved, the High Attendance parents gave a variety of explanations, most of which reflected a change in themselves or in

TABLE 6.1

Total Parental Acceptance-Rejection Scores
on Pre- and Posttests and Tests of Significance
of the Difference Scores between Pre and Post Scores

Parenting Group	N	Pre	Post	T Score	P
Low attendance	13	103.6	95.9	.50	NS
Total high attendance	25	101.4	90.5	4.34	.01
Confident parenting	6	110.5	94.5	2.95	.05
STEP	9	103.1	97.7	1.19	NS
PET	10	94.5	81.6	3.91	.01

NOTE: A lower score means both more parental acceptance and less parental rejection.
N includes only those parents for whom there were both pre and post tests.

their interactions with their children. They offered global explanations ("I learned the correct way to raise my child"), reasons that reflected improved communications with their children ("we talk to each other better now"), reasons that reflected better parental understanding ("I listen more to what he has to say and I understand him better"), reasons that showed better control of parental temper and less use of corporal punishment ("I learned to control my anger," "I whip less"), and reasons that reflected increased affection ("I like her more," "I'm more affectionate"). The vast majority of parents attributed these changes to what they had learned in the programs, with the parenting skills that were taught in the programs the most frequently mentioned feature.

The parents were also questioned on whether they discussed the programs with people outside the class and whether they attempted to teach any of the parenting skills from the programs to these people. Among the High Attendance parents, all but one parent had discussed the program and two-thirds had attempted to teach the skills. These 29 parents had discussed the program with a total of 162 people and had attempted to teach the skills to a total of 85 persons.

In terms of actual child-rearing practices, more of the High than low Attendance parents reported using discussion and other nonforceful methods to deal with child disobedience, and fewer of the High Attendance parents indicated that they used corporal punishment. High Attendance parents in the behaviorally based child management program (CP) were the least likely to use physical force.

The High Attendance parents also reported fewer child behavior problems at the posttest, but the differences between the High and Low groups were not large enough to reach statistical significance.

The parents were also questioned about how they deal with Blackness issues, and were asked their reactions to each of the new instructional

TABLE 6.2
Parental Ratings of Relationship Changes

Parenting Groups	Preschool Child			Oldest Child		
	N	Mean	SD	N	Mean	SD
Low attendance	19	3.89	.80	11	3.54	1.29
Total high attendance	29	4.41	.68	21	4.29	.78
Confident parenting	7	4.43	.78	6	4.33	.52
STEP	11	4.45	.68	5	4.00	1.00
PET	11	4.36	.67	10	4.40	.84

NOTE: Scale: 5 = much better, 4 = better, 3 = same, 2 = worse, and 1 = much worse.

units. In regard to discussing Blackness issues with their children, a very high percentage of High Attendance parents (83%) reported that they had discussed such matters as cultural heritage, racism, discrimination, and racial pride with their children. They indicated that the cultural specifics that were taught in the programs and the generally positive value that the programs placed on discussing racial identity issues were their main reasons for sharing these matters with their children.

The reactions to the other new instructional units were uniformly positive. Of particular interest are the reactions of the parents who attended the sessions that included the unit on Drugs and Our Children. This unit not only presented basic information on drug usage and detection, but it also emphasized that, by using and modeling the positive parenting skills that are taught in the programs, parents would be helping their young children develop the self-discipline that is required to resist overtures to use drugs.

Nearly all of the parents who attended these sessions commented on how useful they were, including those parents who knew most of the information and saw the sessions as "helpful refreshers." The comments of the less knowledgeable parents indicated that they learned about the extent of the drug problem in the Black community and how destructive drugs can be. They learned some of the motives that stimulate children to use drugs, the early warning signs, and how to talk to children about drugs. The sessions appeared to make the parents more vigilant about drug usage, and, as one parent commented, to begin drug discussions very early with their children ("I learned to discuss drugs with the youngest earlier than with the oldest").

Overall, the parents who attended most of the sessions appeared to benefit in a variety of ways. They seemed to use what they learned from the programs both to expand and to improve their relationships with their children. And there was also evidence that the parents became advocates for what the programs taught, because the majority shared and taught what they learned in the programs with other people in their families and community. Given the fact that so few of the High Attendance parents were actually exposed to the entire adapted programs, and the fact that this was the first time that the instructors taught the adapted versions, the results of the pilot test were very encouraging.

The programs, however, need further testing. The small number of parents involved in the pilot test, the attendance problems, the absence of control groups and longer-term follow-up data, the nonstandard measures of program effects, and the paucity of information on parent and child characteristics all speak to the need for a more thorough evaluation of the programs. CICC has been trying since 1982 to evolve a high quality evaluation project and to find an appropriate funding source.

I am happy to report that such a project has been developed and that the National Institute of Drug Abuse (NIDA) is supporting it with a three-year research grant that began June 1, 1985 (Alvy & Myers, 1985). The new research project will enable us to test the effectiveness of the adapted version of the behavioral child management program, Confident Parenting, with 300 Black parents and their first-grade children.

NIDA Research Project

As was indicated earlier, NIDA is interested in parent training as a drug abuse prevention strategy. They are also interested in prevention strategies that are appropriate for ethnic minority populations. These interests took concrete shape in 1983 when NIDA published a research initiative in this area and convened a Technical Review conference to arrive at a state-of-the-art assessment of the potential of parenting and family life skills training programs to prevent drug abuse. I was fortunate to be asked to participate at that Technical Review conference, which was sponsored by NIDA's Prevention Research Branch (Rose et al., 1984).

The challenge in developing a parent training drug abuse prevention research project is to create a project that draws directly on the existing research and theories about drug abuse.

Research on drug-taking behavior has specified different stages (initiation into drug use, continuance, cessation, and relapse) and has shown that a wide range of influencing variables are involved. Various theories have been offered to explain drug-taking behavior and different theories focus on different sets of influencing variables (Lettieri, Sayers, & Pearson, 1980). All theories implicate family and parent variables as either distal or proximal influences in promoting or inhibiting drug-taking behavior.

The complexity of the phenomena is reflected in the Huba-Bentler (Huba & Bentler, 1982) developmental theory of drug abuse. Their research-based theory specifies 13 domains of influencing variables:

(1) Intimate Support System, including family, friends, and peers;
(2) Psychological Status Variables, like introversion-extroversion, rebelliousness, social adjustment, autonomy, depression, achievement striving, and so on;
(3) Environmental Stress;
(4) Socioeconomic Resources;
(5) Sociocultural Influence System;
(6) Social Sanctions;
(7) Social Expectations;
(8) Self-Perceived Behavioral Pressure;
(9) Behavioral Availability;
(10) Product Availability;
(11) Psychophysiology;
(12) Genetics; and
(13) Organismic Status.

These domains of influence are interrelated in complex ways and some domains may be more important for different stages of drug-taking behavior. For example, "it appears that the intimate support system influences may be particularly important in the initiation of drug-taking behavior while organismic status changes due to the drug may more fully account for continued drug ingestion" (Huba, Wingard, & Bentler, 1980, p. 31). The creators of this theoretical model contend that "any effective primary prevention program will have to address themes in many of the domains since the influences combine in many different ways to cause or preclude the initiation of use" (Huba et al., 1980, p. 34). Our NIDA study represents an application of this prevention strategy because it is designed to explore whether parent training can have an impact in several of the critical domains.

Our study also draws on the longitudinal research with Black parents and children that has been conducted over the last decade by Sheppard Kellam and his associates in Chicago. Kellam showed that certain social, psychological, and academic characteristics of Black first-grade children and certain family characteristics were related to substance use 10 years later (Kellam, Brown, Rubin, & Ensminger, 1983). For example, they found that first-graders who were rated by their teachers as being either aggressive or both shy and aggressive, were the highest users of marijuana 10 years later. They also found that isolation and aloneness in mother-headed single-parent families was related to teenage substance use.

These results complement those from other retrospective and prospective studies that have found that a lack of parental acceptance, poor rule enforcement, parental substance use, parental depression, as well as a variety of family and life stresses, are risk factors for children's teenage substance use (Gorsuch & Butler, 1976; Kandel, 1975; Newcomb, Huba, & Bentler, 1983; Wingard, Huba, & Bentler, 1980).

Putting all of this together, we can reasonably assume that a young child's future substance use, and particularly a young poverty-level Black child's future use, involves a complex combination of sociocultural variables (e.g., poverty, racial discrimination), parent variables (parental substance use, personality, and child rearing), child variables (child's personality, social and academic status), and family variables (family structure and stresses).

The adapted program can conceivably affect all of these variables either directly or indirectly. Figure 6.6 illustrates the expected program effects.

The program should directly influence parenting skills because its main purpose is to assist parents in refining and using positive parenting skills. If the skills are used regularly and properly, this should serve to enhance the quality of the parent-child relationship and promote consistent rule enforcement. Because the program places so much emphasis on the Black parents' role as a model for Black children, and because it conveys important information about drug abuse as part of a broader endeavor to enhance parent-child relations, the program should have direct effects on parental substance use. Being confronted with how important their behaviors are in shaping their children's behaviors, the parents may very well reduce, inhibit, or stop their own substance use and/or become more vigilant in monitoring their children in this area.

Through the expected parental changes in drug-taking behavior and through their increased skillfulness in cultivating positive relations with their children, the program should also produce a variety of indirect effects. It is reasonable to assume that the expected parental changes in drug-taking behavior should have an influence on young children's attitudes toward drugs. It is also reasonable to expect positive changes in the children's behavior at home as a result of more skillful parenting.

Other indirect program effects, which could result from both the social support potential of the parenting group and the skills that are

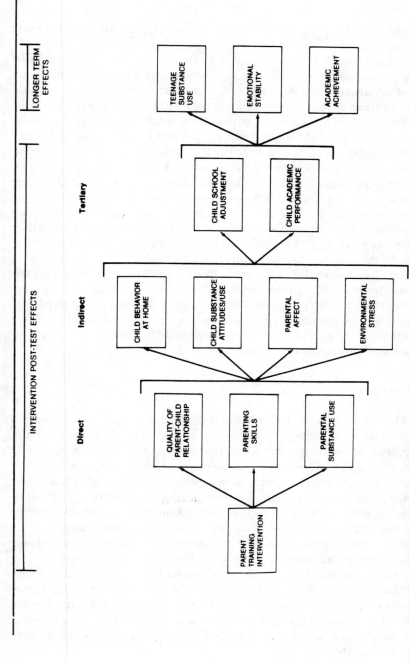

Figure 6.6   A Model of the Project's Expected Intervention Effects

161

taught, may be increases in the parents' ability to cope with environmental stresses and to elevate their affective or emotional states.

A third type of program effect may include improvements in child functioning at school. The anticipated changes at home should have some influence on the children's adjustment and performance at school, though there are obviously many teacher and school issues that would also be operating. If there were program-related school improvements, the program would be an exceedingly powerful intervention.

If the program turns out to have all or some of these effects, it is not unreasonable to expect that the children will be better prepared as they grow up to resist overtures to use drugs, and that their drug-taking behavior during the teenage years would be different than that of children whose parents did not have an opportunity to take the program. It is also not unreasonable to expect that these children will be more emotionally stable and academically effective than peers whose parents didn't have this opportunity.

But these potential long-term effects are beyond the scope of the NIDA project. The project will only allow for follow-up tests immediately after the programs end and one year later. If the results in regard to direct, indirect, and tertiary effects are positive, however, it seems likely that NIDA or another concerned agency would want to support a longer follow-up study.

Conclusions

The NIDA Project and its anticipated continuation will provide a great deal of additional information to test the effectiveness of the programs scientifically. But it will take years to obtain that information and, even if the information is as positive as anticipated, it will still be subject to hardheaded criticisms regarding experimental validity and generalizability. In short, the debate regarding the scientific significance of the programs will go on and on. And it should go on, and it should be informed by even better and more extensive evaluation studies.

But if the programs continue to exist mainly as objects of social and behavioral science scrutiny, they will effect the lives of only those few Black families who happen to be available for the research studies. There is little doubt that these few families will benefit, because the programs empower Black parents with the kinds of information and skills that are helpful in raising proud and healthy Black children. But only a handful will be so empowered and so helped if the programs do not become widely available.

And there is evidence that these types of self-help programs are needed on a wide-scale basis.

The 1985 Children's Defense Fund publication *Black and White Children in America* chronicles one appalling fact after another about how Black children continue to lag behind White children on every indicator of well-being. For example, a Black child is more likely today than just five years ago to come into this world without the benefits of prenatal care and to be born to an adolescent or single mother who is unemployed. His or her brothers and sisters are less likely to be immunized before starting school, less likely to be employed as teenagers, and less likely to go to college. In short, compared to five years ago, life is worse for more Black children and families today, at the very same time when the lives of most White children and families are improving.

As the Children's Defense Fund points out, the economic depression of Black families not only makes them less able to provide the basics for their children, it makes them less able to shape a future for their children and to convince their children that the future is worth planning for.

And here's where these programs for Black parents may be most helpful. Through their potential to empower Black parents of all economic conditions with important information and skills, these programs could serve as vehicles for helping Black parents convince their children that the future is worthwhile. The programs may not change the socioeconomic and political forces that hold Black families back, but they can provide a stronger knowledge base from which these forces can be fought.

There is evidence right now that the Black leadership in our country would be receptive to these programs and to the self-help that they can stimulate and provide.

Over the last few years, national Black organizations have become more concerned about the status of Black families. In 1982, the Black Leadership Forum published a powerful document that emerged out of an overriding concern for the integrity of the Black family. The document is titled *The Black Leadership Family Plan for the Unity, Survival and Progress of Black People* (National Black Leadership Round Table, 1982). It contains detailed instructions for how Black institutions and groups can work to provide for more secure and higher achieving Black families. The plan contains very specific instructions for Black churches and labor organizations; youth groups; colleges; the Black media; businesses; corporate professionals; civil rights groups; law enforcement and senior citizens groups; Blacks in government; in entertainment; in sports; in prisons; in social, fraternal, and Greek letter

164   Kerby T. Alvy

organizations; Black elected and appointed officials; and Black political
and voter registration groups. The instructions from the Leadership
Forum make it clear that there is much that these Black groups can do to
help Black families. But there are no instructions for what the heads of
Black families—Black parents—can do. Possibly, the Black parenting
programs with the Pyramid of Success approach can fill this instructional void.

The 1982 Leadership Forum document is a call for Blacks to help
Blacks. This theme was heard again last year at the Black Family
Summit conference, where leaders of over 100 of America's top Black
organizations came together to discuss what the Black community could
do to strengthen Black families (Jacob, 1984). They vowed to halt what
they termed the crisis facing Black families, a crisis that one leader
referred to as threatening the survival of Blacks as a race. They were clear
that much of the crisis was a result of White racism. But they also
recognized that some problems were self-inflicted. As one leader said,
"We may have allowed our anger at what America has done to obscure
our own need for self-discipline and strengthening community values. . . . We may have neglected the fact that there is a lot we can do about
our own problems ourselves" (Jacob, 1984, p. 17).

This type of consciousness, and a commitment to strengthen Black
families, creates a new climate of receptivity to Black parenting
programs. Because of this, we cannot simply let these programs have
their impact on the few Black families who are involved in the research
studies. Efforts must be made to make the programs more widely
available and to have Black organizations sponsor them.

For our part, CICC is planning to apply for funds that will enable us
to transform the training materials into instructor and parent manuals
and books, and into audio- and videotapes, that will facilitate the use of
the programs nationwide. We are also planning to connect with
national Black organizations to develop sponsorship relations.

These activities, along with the stability that the NIDA research grant
provides for our organization, may be what is needed to begin to bring
the informational and training benefits of these programs to thousands
of Black families. Then it may be easier for Black families to keep the
faith and to instill in their children both the will and the means to
overcome. And then, all of us may find it easier to once again believe in
the American dream of equality and justice for all.

References

Abidin, R. R. (Ed.). (1980). *Parent education and intervention handbook.* Springfield, IL:
    Charles C Thomas.

Aitchison, R. (1976). *Confident parenting workshop leader's guide.* Studio City, CA: Center for the Improvement of Child Caring.

Alvy, K. T. (1975a). Preventing child abuse. *American Psychologist, 30,* 921-928.

Alvy, K. T. (1975b). Indigenous mental health workers for children's services. In R. Simon, S. Silverstein, & B. M. Shriver (Eds.), *Explorations in mental health training* (DHEW Publications No. ADM 74-109). Washington, DC: Government Printing Office.

Alvy, K. T. (1981a). *Effective Black parenting: A review and synthesis of Black perspectives.* Studio City, CA: Center for the Improvement of Child Caring.

Alvy, K. T. (1981b). *The enhancement of parenting: An analysis of parent training programs.* Studio City, CA: Center for the Improvement of Child Caring.

Alvy, K. T. (Ed.). (1981c). *Critiques of parent training manuals: Recommendations for adapting parent training programs for Black poverty-level parents of preschool children.* Studio City, CA: Center for the Improvement of Child Caring.

Alvy, K. T., Fuentes, E. G., Harrison, D. S., & Rosen, L. D. (1980). *The culturally-adapted parent training project: Original grant proposal and first progress report.* Studio City, CA: Center for the Improvement of Child Caring.

Alvy, K. T., Harrison, D. S., Rosen, L. D., & Fuentes, E. G. (1982a). *Black parenting: An empirical investigation with implications for parent trainers and therapists.* Studio City, CA: Center for the Improvement of Child Caring.

Alvy, K. T., Harrison, D. S., Rosen, L. D., & Fuentes, E. G. (1982b). *Black parent training programs: Adapted versions of standard programs for Black parents and pilot test of adapted versions.* Studio City, CA: Center for the Improvement of Child Caring.

Alvy, K. T., & Myers, H. F. (1985). *Drug abuse prevention and Black parent training: Project proposal and description.* Studio City, CA: Center for the Improvement of Child Caring.

Alvy, K. T., & Rosen, L. D. (1984). *Training parenting instructors: A national model for training mental health, social service and educational personnel to deliver group parent training services in their agencies.* Studio City, CA: Center for the Improvement of Child Caring.

Alvy, K. T., Rosen, L. D., Harrison, D. S., & Fuentes, E. G. (1980, September). *Effects of parent training programs with poverty-level minority group parents.* Paper presented at the meetings of the American Psychological Association Convention, Montreal.

Alvy, K. T., & Rubin, H. S. (1981). Parent training and the training of parent teachers. *Journal of Community Psychology, 9,* 53-66.

Arnold, E. L. (Ed.). (1978). *Helping parents help their children.* New York: Brunner/Mazel.

Assembly Bill 251, *The Parent Development Act.* (1985, February 14). Sacramento: California State Legislature.

Atkeson, B. M., & Forehand, R. (1978). Parent behavior training for problem children: An examination of studies using multiple outcome measures. *Journal of Abnormal Child Psychology, 6,* 449-460.

Baumrind, D. (1972). An exploratory study of socialization effects on Black children: Some Black-White comparisons. *Child Development, 43,* 261-267.

Bavolek, S. J., Comstock, C. M., & McLaughlin, J. A. (1983). *The nurturing program: A validated approach to reducing dysfunctional family interactions.* Final report, Grant No. 1RO1MH34862. Rockville, MD: National Institute of Mental Health.

Becker, W. (1971). *Parents are teachers: A child management program.* Champaign, IL: Research Press.

Berkowitz, B. P., & Graziano, A. M. (1972). Training parents as behavior therapists: A review. *Behavior Research and Therapy, 10,* 297-317.

Brim, O. (1965). *Education for child rearing.* New York: Free Press.

Cahill, I. D. (1966). *Child rearing practices in lower socioeconomic ethnic groups.* Doctoral dissertation, Columbia University.

Children's Defense Fund. (1985). *Black and White children in America: Key facts.* Washington, DC: Children's Defense Fund.

Cobb, D. E., & Medway, F. J. (1978). Determinants of effectiveness in parent consultation. *Journal of Community Psychology, 6,* 229-240.

Comer, J. P., & Poussaint, A. F. (1975). *Black child care.* New York: Simon & Schuster.

Coopersmith, S. (1967). *The antecedents of self-esteem.* San Francisco: Freeman.

Croake, J. W., & Glover, K. E. (1977). A history and evaluation of parent education. *Family Coordinator, 26,* 151-158.

Dangel, R. F., & Polster, R. A. (Eds.). (1984). *Parent training: Foundations of research and practice.* New York: Guilford.

Department of Health, Education and Welfare. (1976a). *Child abuse and neglect: An overview of the problem* (Vol. 1) (OHD Publication No. 75-30073). Washington, DC: Government Printing Office.

Department of Health, Education and Welfare. (1976b). *Child abuse and neglect: The roles and responsibilities of professionals* (Vol. 2) (OHD Publication NO. 75-00374). Washington, DC: Government Printing Office.

Department of Health, Education and Welfare. (1976c). *Child abuse and neglect: The community team: An approach to case management and prevention* (Vol. 3) (OHD Publication No. 75-30075). Washington, DC: Government Printing Office.

Dinkmeyer, D., & McKay, G. (1976). *Systematic training for effective parenting: Parent's workbook.* Circle Pines, MN: American Guidance Service.

Durrett, M. E., O'Bryant, S., & Pennebaker, J. W. (1975). Child-rearing reports of White, Black and Mexican-American families. *Developmental Psychology, 11,* 871.

Duvall, E. M. (1971). *Family development.* New York: J. B. Lippincott.

Education Commission of the States. (1976). *Education for parenthood: A primary prevention strategy for child abuse and neglect* (Child Abuse Project: Report No. 93). Denver, CO: Author.

Eimers, R., & Aitchison, R. (1977). *Effective parents—responsible children: A guide to confident parenting.* New York: McGraw-Hill.

Elder, G. H. (1962). Structural variations in the child rearing relationship. *Sociometry, 25,* 241-262.

Eyeberg, S. M., & Johnson, S. M. (1974). Multiple assessment of behavior modification with families: Effects of contingency contracting and order of treated problems. *Journal of Consulting and Clinical Psychology, 42,* 594-606.

Fine, M. J. (Ed.). (1980). *Handbook of parent education.* New York: Academic Press.

Fontana, V. (1973). *Somewhere a child is crying: Maltreatment causes and prevention.* New York: Macmillan.

Fraser, M. W., & Hawkins, J. D. (1982). *Parent training for delinquency prevention: A review* (Report prepared for the National Institute for Juvenile Justice and Delinquency Prevention). Seattle, WA: Center for Law and Justice.

Geismer, L. L., & Gerhart, U. G. (1968). Social class, ethnicity and family functioning: Exploring some issues raised in the Moynihan report. *Journal of Marriage and the Family, 30,* 480-487.

Gil, D. (1973). *Violence against children: Physical abuse in the United States.* Cambridge, MA: Harvard University Press.

Gordon, T. (1970). *Parent effectiveness training.* New York: Wyden.

Gordon, T. (1975). *Parent effectiveness training.* New York: New American Library.

Gordon, T. (1976). *P.E.T. in action: Inside P.E.T. families.* New York: Simon & Schuster.

Gorsuch, R. L., & Butler, M. C. (1976). Initial drug abuse: A review of predisposing social psychological factors. *Psychological Bulletin, 83,* 120-137.

Harmon, D., & Brim, O. C., Jr. (1980). *Learning to be parents: Principles, programs and methods.* Newbury Park, CA: Sage.

Harrison, D. S., & Alvy, K. T. (1982). *The context of Black parenting.* Studio City, CA: Center for the Improvement of Child Caring.

Harrison-Ross, P., & Wyden, B. (1973). *The Black child—A parent's guide.* New York: Peter H. Wyden, Inc.

Haskins, R., & Adams, D. (Eds.). (1983). *Parent education and public policy.* Norwood, NJ: Ablex.

Helfer, R., & Kempe, H. (Eds.). (1974). *The battered child.* Chicago: University of Chicago Press.

Helfer, R., & Kempe, H. (1976). *Child abuse and neglect: The family and community.* Cambridge, MA: Ballinger.

Huba, G. J., & Bentler, P. M. (1982). A developmental theory of drug use: Derivation and assessment of a causal modeling approach. In P. B. Baltes & O. G. Brim, Jr. (Eds.), *Life-span development and behavior* (Vol. 4). New York: Academic Press.

Huba, G. J., Wingard, J. A., & Bentler, P. M. (1980). Longitudinal analysis of the role of peer support, adult models, and peer subcultures in beginning adolescent substance use: An application of stepwise canonical correlation methods. *Multivariate Behavior Research, 15,* 259-280.

Jacob, J. E. (1984, June 22). Black community acts on family issues. *Los Angeles Sentinel,* p. 17.

Johnson, R. C., Brown, C. V., Harris, A., Jr., & Lewis, E. (1980). *Manual of Black parenting education.* St. Louis, MO: Institute of Black Studies.

Kandel, D. (1975). Stages in adolescent involvement in drug use. *Science, 190,* 912-914.

Kaplan, M. S. (1980). Evaluating parent education programs. In M. J. Fine (Ed.), *Handbook of parent education.* New York: Academic Press.

Kellam, S. G., Brown, H. C., Rubin, B. R., & Ensminger, M. E. (1983). Paths leading to teenage psychiatric symptoms and substance use: Developmental epidemiological studies in Woodlawn. In S. B. Guze, F. J. Earls, & J. E. Barrett (Eds.), *Childhood psychopathology and development.* New York: Raven Press.

Kennedy, E. F. (1985, February 7). U.S. must stand for justice in South Africa. *Los Angeles Times,* op. sec.

Lettieri, D. J., Sayers, M., & Pearson, H. W. (Eds.). (1980). *Theories of drug abuse.* Rockville, MD: National Institute of Drug Abuse.

Levine, E. S., & Bartz, K. W. (1979). Comparative child rearing attitudes among Chicano, Anglo and Black parents. *Hispanic Journal of Behavioral Sciences, 1,* 165-178.

Maccoby, E. E., & Martin, J. A. (1983). Socialization in the context of the family: Parent-child interaction. In M. E. Hetherington (Ed.), *Handbook of child psychology* (Vol. 4). New York: John Wiley.

Martin, B. (1975). Child-parent relations. In F. Horowitz (Ed.), *Review of child development research* (Vol. 4). Chicago: University of Chicago Press.

Martin, H. P., & Beesley, P. (1976). Therapy for abusive parents: Its effect on the child. In H. P. Martin (Ed.), *The abused child: A multidisciplinary approach to developmental issues and treatment.* Cambridge, MA: Ballinger.

Mash, E. J., Handy, L. C., & Hamerlynck, L. A. (1976). *Behavior modification approaches to parenting.* New York: Brunner/Mazel.

McLaughlin, C. J. (1976). *The Black parent's handbook.* New York: Harcourt Brace Jovanovich.

Mental health of children: Services, research and manpower. (1973). New York: Harper & Row.

Mitre Corporation [in collaboration with the Mental Health Service Development Branch, National Institute of Mental Health]. (1977). *Challenge for children's mental health services.* McLean, VA: Author.

Moreland, J. R., Schwebel, A. I., Beck, S., & Wells, R. (1982). Parents as therapists: A review of the behavior therapy parent training literature from 1975 to 1981. *Behavior Modification, 6,* 250-276.

Myers, H. F. (1982). Research on the Afro-American family. In B. A. Bass, G. E. Wyatt, & G. J. Powell (Eds.), *The Afro-American family.* New York: Grune and Stratton.

National Black Leadership Round Table. (1982). *The Black leadership family plan for the unity, survival, and progress of Black people.* (Available from National Black Leadership Round Table Box 1965, Washington, DC)

National Institute on Alcohol Abuse and Alcoholism. (1983). *Prevention Plus: Involving schools, parents and the community in alcohol and drug education.* Rockville, MD: Alcohol, Drug Abuse and Mental Health Administration.

Newcomb, M. D., Huba, G. J., & Bentler, P. M. (1983). Mothers' influence on the drug use of their children. *Developmental Psychology, 19,* 714-726.

Patterson, G. (1971). *Families: Applications of social learning to family life.* Champaign, IL: Research Press.

Patterson, G. (1975). *Professional guide for families and living with children.* Champaign, IL: Research Press.

Patterson, G. (1976). *Living with children: New methods for parents and teachers.* Champaign, IL: Research Press.

Patterson, G. R., & Stouthamer-Loeber, M. (1984). The correlation of family management practices and delinquency. *Child Development, 55,* 1299-1307.

Reisinger, J. J., Ora, J. P., & Frangia, G. W. (1976). Parents as change agents for their children: A review. *Journal of Community Psychology, 4,* 103-123.

Rinn, R. C., & Markle, A. (1977). Parent effectiveness training: A review. *Psychological Reports, 41,* 95-109.

Rohner, R. P. (1980). *Handbook for the study of parental acceptance and rejection.* Storrs, CN: Center for the Study of Parental Acceptance and Rejection.

Rose, M., Battjes, R., & Leukefeld, C. (1984). *Family life skills training for drug abuse prevention* (DHHS Publication No. ADM 84-1340). Washington, DC: Government Printing Office.

Rosser, P. L. (1978). The child: Young, gifted and Black. In L. E. Gary (Ed.), *Mental health: A challenge to the Black community.* Philadelphia, PA: Dorrance and Company.

Schuster, D. V., Amdurer, D., Fallon, S., & Hare, J. (1981). *Curriculum outline for parent training program.* New York: Family Dynamics, Inc.

Szalay, L. B. (1978). *The Hispanic American cultural frame of reference: A communication guide for use in mental health education and training.* Washington, DC: Institute of Comparative Social and Cultural Studies.

Szalay, L. B., & Bryson, J. A. (1973). Measurement of psychoculture distance: A comparison of American Blacks and Whites. *Journal of Personality and Social Psychology, 26,* 166-177.

Szalay, L. B., & Maday, B. C. (1973). Verbal associations in the analyses of subjective culture. *Current Anthropology, 14,* 151-173.

Tavormina, J. B. (1980). Evaluation and comparative studies of parent education. In R. R. Abidin (Ed.), *Parent education and intervention handbook.* Springfield, IL: Charles C Thomas.

Timnick, L. (1980, November 13). Success in breaking child abuse reported. *Los Angeles Times.*

Tramontana, M. G., Sherrets, S. D., & Authier, K. J. (1980). Evaluation of parent education programs. *Journal of Clinical Child Psychology, 7*, 40-42.

Wingard, J. A., Huba, G. J., & Bentler, P. M. (1980). A longitudinal analysis of personality structure and adolescent substance use. *Personality and Individual Differences, 1*, 259-272.

Wolfe, D., Kaufman, K., Aragona, J., & Sandler, J. (1981). *The child management program for abusive parents*. Winter Park, Florida: Anna.

7

How to Think, Not What to Think: A Cognitive Approach to Prevention

Myrna B. Shure

There are different ways to change the behavior of children. While the approach one takes corresponds directly to the hoped-for outcome, some approaches are very situation-specific, such as those that teach particular behavioral skills to children who lack them (e.g., Oden & Asher, 1977). Other approaches are more target-specific, such as those that teach specific child-rearing skills to parents (e.g., Alvy, this volume; Gordon, 1970), specific teaching skills to teachers (e.g., Dinkmeyer & Dinkmeyer, 1982), or specific clinical skills to clinicians (e.g., Wolpe, 1969). Our approach is a more generic one, primarily because it focuses on thought, not action. It focuses on *a process* of that thought, not the content of it. It focuses on *how* a person thinks, not what a person thinks. I will describe our approach to behavior, a prevention approach; how it is relevant to family functioning; and my own appraisals about the conditions under which it works and those under which it does not.

Our approach introduces problem solving to children. Specifically, it helps children develop the ability to think through and solve typical everyday problems that arise with peers and figures of authority. Through a series of correlational studies, we have identified a set of interpersonal cognitive problem-solving (ICPS) skills that distinguish good from poor problem solvers as early as age four (see Spivack & Shure, 1982, for a review). But most important, these cognitive skills also relate to specific indices of mental health, indices predictive of later psychological dysfunction. What are these skills, and why are they important to mental health?

One skill that is significantly related to overt behaviors is the ability to think of alternative solutions to real-life problems, as measured by the Preschool Interpersonal Problem Solving (PIPS) test (Shure & Spivack, 1974). In children aged four and five, the problems tested were (a) how one child could get to play with a toy another child has, and (b) how to avert mother's anger after having broken an object of value to her. While the content of the presented problem varied to hold the child's interest, we were interested in the *process* of the child's thinking. Therefore, we were just as interested in solutions such as "hit" or "grab" to obtain a toy as we were in solutions such as "ask," "say please," or offer a bribe or trade. All children could *think* of forceful ways to obtain a toy. But better adjusted youngsters could also think of more nonforceful ways. Moreover, for every behaviorally aggressive youngster who could think of only hit or grab, there was a socially withdrawn youngster who could think of only "say please." Although one solution is more socially acceptable than another, children who perseverated on any one of them were, behaviorally, equally maladaptive.

So our interest turned to *how*, not what the child thinks. Is he or she able to turn to another idea if the first one does not work? Behaviorally, is the child prone to do that, or does he or she give up too soon? We found that across the age span, in both sexes, and regardless of IQ, general language skills, and measured test verbosity (motivation to try), the ability to think of multiple alternative solutions to interpersonal problems relates to positive peer relations, as well as to negative impulsive and inhibited behaviors (see Spivack, Platt, & Shure, 1976), and that these relationships are independent of the content of offered solutions. These findings have been documented in populations of four-year-olds (e.g., Granville et al., 1976; Olson, Johnson, Belleau, Parks, & Barrett, 1983; Rubin & Daniels-Beirness, 1983; Schiller, 1978; Shure, Newman, & Silver, 1973; Turner & Boulter, 1981), kindergartners (Arend, Gove, & Sroufe, 1979; Shure & Spivack, 1980), first- to third-graders (Elias, 1978; Gesten & Weissberg, 1979; Johnson, Yu, & Roopnarine, 1980), second- to fifth-graders (Asarnow & Callan, 1984; Richard & Dodge, 1982), fifth-graders (Shure, 1984), eighth-graders (Marsh, 1981), adolescents (Platt, Spivack, Altman, Altman, & Peizer, 1974), adults (Platt & Spivack, 1974), and the elderly (Spivack, Standen, Bryson, & Garrett, 1978).

A second ICPS skill is that of considering the consequences of one's social acts, in terms of their effect both on other people and on oneself. The process is one of thinking beyond an act to what might happen if it is carried out: "If I grab the toy from Johnny, he might grab it back, or, he might tell the teacher, or he might not be my friend." When young children are asked, "What might happen next?" if one child takes a toy from another, better adjusted youngsters can think of more different consequences than can those more behaviorally aberrant (Shure, Newman, & Silver, 1973). But what we learned about consequential thinking is fascinating. Impulsive children are more aware of what might happen than inhibited ones. This makes sense when I recall how many times I've heard a child who was warned "You can't hit; he'll hit you back" respond with "I know, but I don't care; he won't give me that truck!" Awareness of such consequences does not stop these children because other than making a request, which is often refused, they cannot or do not think of what else to do. Instead of pursuing a new course of action, they may create a new problem with their quick and sure way to get what they want "now." Inhibited children, on the other hand, do not seem able to think of either solutions or consequences. Perhaps these children have experienced failure so often that they just withdraw from other children and from problems they cannot solve.

Given all this, we learned something important about another skill, that of role-taking, the ability to appreciate another point of view even if different from one's own. It turned out that the combination of role-taking and solution skills best identified deficiencies of impulsive children; as we had observed, these children may not allow their awareness of consequences to stop them from performing an impulsive act. If awareness or concern for another's distress is disregarded, there is more reason for these children to behave the way they do. Inhibited youngsters turned out to be better role-takers but not better adjusted than impulsive youngsters. It is possible that their awareness or sensitivity to others' feelings without the wherewithal to deal with them (that is, other options) causes them to freeze and socially withdraw. It seems reasonable to assume that knowing how someone feels, while very important, cannot itself resolve a problem; it may even heighten anxiety or frustration unless one then knows what to do about it. The question now is whether role-taking can enrich problem-solving thinking. Does appreciating the viewpoint of others open up a broader repertoire of solutions from which to choose? Does ability to draw upon this repertoire prevent, or at least diminish, continued frustration and subsequent need for impulsive behaviors or withdrawal?

Zachery, who was seen exercising his skills one day, may support these speculations. When Richard refused to let him have a wagon, Zachery did not create a new problem by reacting impulsively. His ability to think of other options led him to another tactic. "If you let me have the wagon, I'll give it right back." When Richard did not answer, Zachery asked him why he couldn't have it. Richard replied, "Because I need it. I'm pulling the rocks." "I'll pull them with you," shouted Zachery. Richard agreed, and they played with the wagon together. In finding out about the other child's motives, Zachery was able to incorporate them into a solution that was successful. Like other good problem-solvers, he may have thought about hitting or pushing Richard, or just pulling the wagon away, but he also may have been able to anticipate the consequences of such acts. Most important, his ability to think of other options prevented Zachery from experiencing frustration and failure. Interestingly, Snyder and Shanks (1982) found in a sample of middle-class preschoolers that both high PIPS (solution) scores and ability to identify emotions in a story situation related to peer sociometric popularity. As Zachery perhaps has shown us, children competent in these skills appear more likely to use prosocial than deviant responses in actual conflict situations.

Michael Chandler once challenged that perhaps one "good" solution would really suffice (in Shure, 1982). Perhaps. But we believe it is the *process* of turning to another that encourages one not to give up too soon. It may be that very flexibility that allows one to generalize a style of thought from one problem situation to another. While in the short run it may be that one "good" solution that solves a given problem, in the long run the issue for social adjustment is the ability to generate the kind of thinking that results in resiliency instead of frustration.

The relationship of cognition to behavioral resiliency has now been supported by Schiller (1978) and Arend et al. (1979). Studying middle-class children, they found that high PIPS scorers were more likely than low scorers to behave flexibly, persistently, and resourcefully, especially in problem situations, on a measure of ego-resiliency developed by Block and Block (1971). Zachery's resilience (ability to bounce back) and flexibility (ability to think of a new solution) is also consistent with the research of N. Wowkanech (1978), who found that four-year-olds trained to generate their own ICPS skills were more likely to try more different ways to resolve real-life conflicts than a behavioral-modeling group of children, who in the face of conflict were told what to do, and then shown how to do it.

A question raised by Rubin and Krasnor (1983) is whether *cognitive* flexibility aids *behavioral* resiliency and flexibility. Using Rubin's (1982) Social Problem Test, they found that lower-middle- to middle-class kindergartners, more than preschoolers, could respond with a new solution to obtain a toy without first stating irrelevancies or repeating earlier responses. Having more spontaneously conceptualized ideas in one's repertoire may reduce the likelihood of repeating earlier, perhaps less successful acts, and thus help avoid appearing as a "nag."

Looking at different behaviors associated with problem-solving skills is important, but in addition to quantity of solutions associated with those behaviors, we must examine other dimensions of the cognitive skills themselves. Rubin and others have argued that equally if not more important than quantity is the *quality* of solutions, consideration of age and sex of child protagonist and child target characteristics, and the nature of the problem to be solved. Rubin and Daniels-Beirness (1983) found, for example, that rejected peers suggest more agonistic strategies (e.g., hit, grab) while nonrejected peers suggest more positive ones. Still, they did find that sociometric status in first grade was also predicted by the total number of relevant solution categories as tested a year earlier, in kindergarten. Rubin and Krasnor (1983) found that to obtain an object, preschoolers were more likely to suggest the use of prosocial strategies (e.g., ask, share) when the target child was depicted as the same age or older than the protagonist, while kindergartners focused these types of strategies more on older targets only. Further, kindergartners suggested agonistic strategies more often with younger than with older target characters.

Regarding problem content, Feldman (1984) found that the effects of the solution skills of first-, third-, and fifth-graders varied with the nature of the problem depicted. On the other hand, Richard and Dodge (1982) found that the problem-solving ability of second- to fifth-graders remained consistent across problem types. Richard and Dodge also discovered that the quantity of solutions was deficient in aggressive and isolated boys compared to popular boys (girls were not studied), and the initial solution given by all boys was an effective one, but, in subsequent responses, aggressive and isolated boys tended to increase the proportion of aggressive and ineffective solutions, solutions characteristics of their behaviors. As Richard and Dodge (1982) state:

> Deviant boys are not deficient in offering a single effective solution to an interpersonal problem, nor are they deficient in evaluating the relative effectiveness of solutions which are presented to them. When more than one effective solution must be generated, however, deviant boys are relatively less skilled in doing so. It may be that the behavioral problems of these children occur in situations when the initial behavioral solution is not sufficient, and alternate behaviors are necessary. At this point, the cognitive problem solving patterns of popular, aggressive, and isolated boys diverge. (p. 232)

While our research was guided by a process-not-content theory that habitual patterns of behavior are guided (in part) by a general capacity to think, our emphasis on the process does not suggest indifference to *what* people think (that is, the content of solutions that comes to mind). After all, it might be argued, is not the issue whether a child in a given situation comes up with an effective solution rather than whether he or she thinks of three or four or five? In the long run, we believe that the issue of style and content are not really independent. Over time, the likelihood that a person will manifest an effective solution to a problem in a particular situation will depend upon that person's ability to exercise ICPS processes. What is effective? That may be in the eyes of the beholder. Effectiveness may be defined in terms of a style of thought that characterizes the child rather than by discrete products of thought that may be arbitrarily defined by others as effective on any one occasion.

Given our emphasis on process, it is theoretically possible that a good problem-solver could be prone to act in ways that are socially unacceptable. But empirically, this is not the case. Perhaps any child who grows up in a culture or specific subculture learns the consequences of certain behaviors, especially those intimately involved in significant social relationships. For most of us, there is also a desire for positive social contacts. High ICPS children consider these issues and weigh them in decision making. To the extent that they desire human contact, it is likely that the strategies they choose to adopt will reflect prior consideration of culturally relevant social acceptability. We have found over and over that better adjusted children are as able as more poorly adjusted children to think of solutions that may have a negative effect on others (e.g., hit a child to get a toy). The better adjusted children, however, are able to generate more alternative solutions from which to draw, to think of consequences, and, as they get older, to conceptualize a plan. This process of planning, called means-ends thinking, is the ability to conceptualize sequenced steps to reach a stated goal, to consider potential obstacles that could interfere with reaching that goal, and to recognize that goal satisfaction may take time. This planning process begins to become associated with behavior at about age eight or nine (Shure & Spivack, 1972), findings confirmed by Pellegrini (1985) and by Ford (1982) in studies of third- through twelfth-graders, and extended by Gotlib and Asarnow (1979) in young adults. While the more poorly adjusted tend to reach immediately and directly for the goal (e.g., make a friend merely by being introduced), the more socially competent think of sequenced plans to achieve their goals, to recognize and to overcome potential obstacles, and they recognize that achieving their goal may take time.

An overview of the ICPS skills measured to date indicates that the consummate problem-solver first identifies the problem (not always an easy task), tends to look back and consider what led up to the problem, considers alternative solutions or plans (taking the perspectives of others into account), looks forward in anticipation of potential consequences of an act, then changes his or her solution or plan, if need be.

ICPS and Family Functioning

I will now describe some research that demonstrates the importance of ICPS to various dimensions of family functioning, and the implications of these findings for preventive intervention. Having identified specific ICPS skills that are associated with various indices of mental health at several age levels, we turned our attention to a primary source of acquisition—the home. We were interested in learning about why some youngsters enter preschool with relatively well-developed ICPS skills while others do not.

Inner-city Black mothers of four-year-olds were tested for their solution, consequential, and means-ends skills. To assess her general problem-solving "child-rearing style," each mother was also asked to describe what both she and her child typically say and do in a real-life problem (e.g., her child wants something she or he cannot have). We learned that a mother's ICPS skills for solving hypothetical *child*-related problems (e.g., "my child has been saying 'no' to me a lot lately") depends upon her ability to solve hypothetical *adult*-related problems (e.g., "a woman has been arguing with her boyfriend"). It turned out that mothers adept at hypothetical *child*-related problems were, when required to handle real problems, more likely to offer suggestions, explain the consequences, and talk to the children about their own and others' feelings—induction techniques far more sophisticated than suggestions without explanation, demands, or belittling.

In two separate studies (see Shure & Spivack, 1978), mothers' ICPS ability and child-rearing style related to the child's ICPS ability and behaviors. But curiously, this was true only if the child were a girl. Why not among boys? We don't know for sure, but as Hoffman (1971) noted, boys are normally more resistant to influence than girls. This may be especially true when the children are fatherless (the case for nearly 70% of our youngsters), because it appears that children adopt parental characteristics to the extent that the parent is an important and relatively consistent source of nurturance and reward (e.g., Mussen & Rutherford, 1963), and Hoffman (1971) reported that mothers are more affectionate to their fatherless girls than to their fatherless boys.

Whether our findings are a function of the age of the child studied, their socioeconomic level, or their family constellation is not known. Certain more recent studies have shown other dimensions of maternal influences, and other familial influences as well. Arend et al. (1979) found in a longitudinal study of middle-SES families that individual differences in security of attachment at 18 months and effective autonomous functioning at two years of age were related to dimensions of ego-control and ego-resilience (including PIPS competency) at ages four and five. Beyond the initial quality of attachment, home atmosphere also becomes critical to the child's functioning ICPS skills. When skills of children in trouble-distressed families are measured, clear ICPS deficiencies are revealed. For example, Perez et al. (1981) found ICPS deficiencies in mixed SES third-graders whose families experienced one or more family background problems, especially separation or divorce, or lack of educational stimulation at home. Whether lack of educational stimulation precedes or follows separation and divorce in homes where they coincide, and whether such emotional turmoil creates dynamics that restrict the child's opportunity to acquire ICPS skills is not known. But low SES nine- to ten-year-olds whose fathers have been absent from at least the age of four to no later than age seven are significantly more ICPS deficient than those from intact families (Fry & Grover, 1982).

Even within intact families, important differences in ICPS capacities occur. Parents who neglect their children revealed substantial deficits in ICPS skills, especially related to matters of child care and child well-being (Dawson, de Armas, McGrath, & Kelly, 1985). Moreover, both neglecting and abusing parents have distorted beliefs about what can be expected from their children, particularly regarding family responsibility and care of siblings, and these unrealistic expectations are accompanied by serious ICPS deficiencies (Azar, Robinson, Hekimian, & Twentyman, 1984).

Among typical mothers, child-rearing practices can have an impact on the ICPS skills and behavior of the children themselves. Jones, Rickel, and Smith (1980) found that regardless of social class, four-year-olds of restrictive mothers (concerned with the child's adherence to adult-imposed rules and expectations) offered evasion strategies to the PIPS mother-type problem (they said, e.g., "I didn't break [the vase]"; "hide it"). Jones et al. argue that these strategies require no attempt to deal with the thoughts, feelings, and needs of the other. In contrast, children of nurturant mothers who were warm and involved, and recognized the child's desires and emotional needs, offered more solutions of personal appeal and negotiation (e.g., "Mom, don't be mad," or, in the peer-type story, "I'll give the truck right back"). These are reciprocal solutions that recognize others' thoughts, feelings, and wishes. Not unexpectedly, a child's tendency to think of force to obtain a toy was independent of maternal child-rearing practices, just as it has been found to be independent of the number of ideas the child conceptualized. Hill (1983) also reported that, compared to mothers who were high in control, mothers of four- to six-year olds who were high in involvement and creative play had children (and especially daughters) who were more ICPS and behaviorally competent. Among retarded ten-year-olds, ICPS skills were higher among those whose mothers often provided opportunities for decision making and social influence; they were lower among those whose mothers tended to direct, interfere, and restrict the child's attempts to accomplish a goal (Herman & Shantz, 1983).

ICPS and Family Functioning: Implications for Intervention

Our initial interventions for parents (Shure & Spivack, 1978) were designed on the basis of our prior correlational research. Although ICPS skills appeared more strongly associated between mothers and their four-year-old daughters, we still asked whether such skills of girls *and* boys could be enhanced if both mother and child were trained. First I'll describe the program itself, the philosophy behind it, and what we learned. Then I'll discuss some new ICPS training in a family context that adds important dimensions to this field.

The goal of our program is to help the mother transmit a problem-solving thinking style to her child that would guide the child to cope with typical day-to-day problems by teaching the child to generate alternative solutions to problems, and to consider potential consequences of an interpersonal act (e.g., pushing another child out of the way). Based on our having learned from our correlational research that the process is more intimately associated with mental health than is the content, children were taught *how*, but not what to think, so they could choose and evaluate for themselves what and what not to do.

The mothers are given a day-to-day script (see Shure & Spivack, 1978), and the children are exposed to three months of daily 20-minute lessons in game form, beginning with simple word concepts, built in for later association in problem solving. For example, the word "not" is taught so children can later decide what and what *not* to do, and whether an idea is or is not a good one. The word "or" helps children to think about the idea that there is more than one way to solve a problem: "I can do this or I can do that." The word "different" helps the child to later think of *different* things to do. Identification of, and sensitivity to, people's feelings is important in problem solving. Children learn that there is more than one way to find out how people feel and what people like—by watching what they do, hearing what they say, and asking when unsure. To help children understand the effect of their behavior on others and of others' behavior on them, games focus on why a child might feel as he or she does: "He's mad *because* I took his toy."

After mastery of these kinds of skills, generally in about eight weeks, children are presented with pictures and puppets depicting interpersonal problem situations and asked to generate as many ways as possible for the portrayed child to deal with the problem, for example, to get someone to let him help feed the hamsters. All solutions are accepted equally—forceful ones such as "hit" or "grab the food" and nonforceful ones such as "say please," "say I'll be your friend," or offer a toy. In subsequent games, the children evaluate for themselves whether an idea is or is not a good one, and explain why. The idea is not to take away from poor problem-solvers what they already know, but to help them think about what they do and then discover that there's more than one way to accomplish their goal. Therefore, solutions are never reinforced for being good, but rather are supported for being *different*.

In addition to formal training, mothers were taught guided dialogues so that they would learn to use the "style" of the program at other times during the day. In helping children solve their own problems and evaluate their own solutions, mothers learned to help draw out their children's thinking. We did this because we learned from our correlational research that many inner-city, low-SES mothers tell their children what to do without an accompanying explanation, usually in the form of a demand or command. A mother whose child said he was afraid to "hit back" simply remarked, "I told you what to do!" End of conversation. Because the mother was not listening, but just thinking of her own point of view, the child did not have to think further about what to do but only worry about how to do what was expected (or prevent his mother from finding out he hadn't). To us, however, giving the opposite advice, for example, "Don't hit back, tell the teacher instead," is also counterproductive. It is doing the thinking for the child. Although inductive techniques (suggestions accompanied by explanations of consequences of acts and people's feelings) are far more sophisticated than the other techniques described, very few parents actively engage the child in a *process* of thinking about the problem and the actions they might take.

Here is a typical dialogue from our mother interviews before training:

Child: Mommy, Tommy hit me.
Mother: Hit him back.
Child: But I'm afraid.
Mother: You have to learn to defend yourself.
Child: O.K. Mommy.

After both mother and child have received training:

Child: Mommy, Tommy hit me.
Mother: Why did he hit you?
Child: I don't know.
Mother: He might have hit you because . . .
Child: He was mad?
Mother: Why was he mad?
Child: 'Cause I took his truck.
Mother: Is that why he hit you?
Child: Yep!
Mother: Grabbing is one way to get that truck. Can you think of something different to do so he won't hit you?
Child: I could tell him I'd just play a little while.
Mother: That's a different idea.

With this kind of dialoguing, the mother gained information that the first dialogue would not have allowed. With the child gaining the habit of thinking of alternatives, the mother can elicit more ideas from the child, in case Tommy should say "no."

The goal is not to teach children simply to get what they want. The games and dialogues also help them cope with frustration when they cannot have what they want.

Before training:

Child: [Starts to finger paint]
Mother: I don't want a mess now; your grandmother is coming for dinner.
Child: [Whining] But I want to! I won't make a mess.
Mother: Why don't you color in your coloring book?
Child: I don't want to! I want to finger paint.

Instead of constant nagging and what now becomes a power play between mother and child, here is a dialogue after training:

Child: Mommy, I'm going out to ride my bike.
Mother: Not now, we're having dinner soon.
Child: I'll come right back.
Mother: [Knowing differently] Can you think of something different to do inside for a little while.

Remember, we're having dinner soon.
Child: I'll go get my fire truck.
Mother: You thought of a different idea.

Before training, when the mother did the thinking for the child, for example, "Why don't you color in your coloring book?," the child's frustration and nagging was only increased. In the second dialogue, the child felt good about his own idea and didn't need to nag. The mother-child power play became unnecessary.

We found in two separate interventions that both boys and girls could learn solution and consequential skills from their mothers (see Table 7.1); this is important because the correlational links had occurred between mothers and daughters, but not mothers and sons. Importantly, youngsters trained by their mothers at home improved in behaviors as observed by their teachers in school.

In our second intervention for use by parents, we added parent training exercises so that the parents could practice problem solving-skills of their own. For mothers, the goals were (a) to increase awareness that the child's point of view may differ from her own, (b) to help mothers recognize that there is more than one way to solve a problem, (c) to appreciate that thinking about what is happening may, in the long run, be more beneficial than immediate action to stop it, and (d) to provide a model of problem-solving thinking—a thinking parent might inspire a child to think. As mothers help their children think about their own and others' feelings and how to consider the effects of their actions upon others, mothers also think about feelings and how their behavior affects others (including their children). As mothers guide their children to think of alternative solutions to child-relevant problems, mothers also think of solutions to parent-relevant problems, particularly when the problem is one created for the mother by the child (e.g., "Johnny won't do what I ask him to lately"). Just as the children are never told solutions to problems or consequences to acts, neither are the mothers. Again, the value is not on *what* they think, but *that* they think.

We found that mother-trained youngsters increased in alternative solution skills significantly more when their mothers had received systematic ICPS training of their own, in addition to their teaching the formal lessons to the children and learning to dialogue (see Table 7.2). While both mother-trained groups of youngsters improved more than controls, our findings suggest that greater (solution) influence on the child occurs when the mother as well as the child are taught how to think.

This finding is important because it was also found that trained mothers' techniques of handling real everyday problems (her "child-

TABLE 7.1

Means and SDs of Two Child Measures from Pre- to
Posttesting by Experimental Group and by Sex

| | PIPS Solutions | | | | | | Consequences | | | | | |
| | Training | | | Control | | | Training | | | Control | | |
Group	Pre	Post	Ch	Pre	Post	Ch	Pre	Post	Ch	Pre	Post	Ch
Boys:												
$\overline{X}$	5.30	9.70	+4.40	4.80	5.40	+.60	4.50	7.30	+2.80	5.30	5.90	+.60
SD	2.54	2.98		2.35	2.37		1.51	1.95		1.64	1.10	
N	10	10		10	10		10	10		10	10	
Girls:												
$\overline{X}$	2.70	8.00	+5.30	3.10	4.50	+1.40	4.00	7.30	+3.30	4.30	5.40	+1.10
SD	1.95	3.40		2.18	1.65		2.40	2.21		2.63	2.32	
N	10	10		10	10		10	10		10	10	
Total:												
$\overline{X}$	4.00	8.85	+4.85	3.95	4.95	+1.00	4.25	7.30	+3.05	4.80	5.65	+.85
SD	2.58	3.23		2.37	2.04		1.97	2.03		2.19	1.79	
N	20	20		20	20		20	20		20	20	

NOTE: There is no ceiling on PIPS or consequences scores (based on two stories each).

TABLE 7.2

Comparison of ICPS Skills of Children Trained by
Mothers Taught "How to Think" and Children Trained
by Mothers Who Were Not

| Child Group | Alternative-Solution Thinking (PIPS) | | Consequential Thinking | |
	Mothers Taught	Mothers Not Taught	Mothers Taught	Mothers Not Taught
Aberrant Pretest-Adjusted Posttest:				
$\overline{X}$ change	5.58	3.00	3.58	2.83
SD	1.88	3.22	1.73	2.32
N	12	6	12	6
	df = 16		df = 16	
	t = 2.17		t = .78	
	p < .05		ns	
All Training Ss:				
$\overline{X}$ change	4.85	3.30	3.05	3.00
SD	1.98	2.47	1.82	2.86
N	12	6	12	6
	df = 38		df = 38	
	t = 2.19		t = .07	
	p < .05		ns	

NOTE: There were no pretest differences in any group: Solution thinking, Aberrant Preadjusted Post, t = .33, df = 16, ns; All Ss, t = .55, df = 38, ns. Consequential thinking, Aberrant Preadjusted Post, t = .33, df = 16, ns; All training Ss, t = .33, df = 38, ns. (from Shure & Spivack, 1978, p. 181).

rearing style") were more likely to incorporate techniques of problem solving, that is, of guiding the *child* to think (see Table 7.3). Moreover, mothers who learned to do this were more likely to have a child who gained in alternative solution skills (see Table 7.4). It is also important to note that a child's *behavioral* improvement related most strongly to his or her improvement in alternative solutions skills, but mother's child-rearing style and (to a lesser extent) her ability to solve hypothetical mother-child problems also related to the child's behavioral gains (see Table 7.5). This suggests that there is more than one mediator of a child's behavioral adjustment with the child's *own* thinking skills (at least solution skills) playing a significant role as such a mediator.

Mothers, then, can become effective training agents, especially when given ICPS training of their own. It is encouraging that many of them, ICPS-deficient at the start, could transmit these skills to children in only three months time. The children's gains may have been greatly

TABLE 7.3

Means and SDs of Two Mother's Measures from Pre- to Posttesting by Experimental Group and by Sex of Child

| G | Child-Rearing Style[a] | | | | | | Means-Ends Thinking[b] Mother-Child Problem Stories | | | | | |
| | Training | | | Control | | | Training | | | Control | | |
	Pre	Post	Ch	Pre	Post	Ch	Pre	Post	Ch	Pre	Post	Ch
Mothers of Boys:												
X̄	18.30	50.00	+31.70	16.20	16.50	+.30	7.70	14.20	+6.50	6.50	6.70	+.20
SD	8.14	16.47		5.35	6.13		3.47	6.00		2.46	1.25	
N	10	10		10	10		10	10		10	10	
Mothers of Girls:												
X̄	12.10	50.10	+38.00	12.20	15.40	+3.20	5.80	14.30	+8.50	5.60	6.00	+.40
SD	6.30	24.38		7.19	5.19		1.40	5.01		2.99	2.11	
N	10	10		10	10		10	10		10	10	
Total:												
X̄	15.20	50.05	+34.85	14.20	15.95	+1.75	6.75	14.25	+7.50	6.05	6.35	+.30
SD	7.76	20.25		6.50	5.56		2.75	5.38		2.70	1.73	
N	20	20		20	20		20	20		20	20	

a. Scale: 0-25 includes demands, commands, belittling; 26-50 includes suggestions without explanation, mothers attributions of child's feelings and thoughts; 51-75 includes mothers suggestions with explanation, encouraging child to consider peoples' feelings; 76-100 includes mothers' guiding child to consider solutions to problems and consequences to acts.
b. Mean of total scores for three stories.

TABLE 7.4
Change in Mother's Child-Rearing Score and ICPS Skills
with Change in Child's ICPS Skills

| | Child Measures | | | | | |
| | PIPS Solutions | | | Consequences | | |
Mother's Measures	r	df	p	r	df	p
Child-rearing style	.45	18	.05	.06	18	.81
Alternative solutions	.36	18	.11	.27	18	.26
Means-Ends thinking						
(mother-child problem situations)	.53	18	.02	.51	18	.02

NOTE: This table includes only measures that showed a significant training effect.

facilitated by the mothers' increased sensitivity to the child's experiences, recognition of the time and difficulties involved in problem solving, and appreciation of the need for flexibility. In any case, that children trained at home could improve their behavior in school is, we believe, due to our approach. If boys were more resistant to modeling their mothers' ICPS skills before training, it is possible that their resistance decreased when they were guided and freed to think for themselves (Shure & Spivack, 1978, 1979b).

As reported in Shure and Spivack (1978), comments by some of the mothers provided important insights for us.

It doesn't tell me what to do. It helps me think better when I have my own problems.

It's fun. And even I can do it. It makes me feel good that I can help Randolph so much.

Before, I just couldn't make him understand how Rachel [his sister] feels when he hits her. Now he understands. I think he really understands.

My son loves these games. He keeps asking me, "Mommy, can we play our games now?" Sometimes he pesters me. [Laughs]. But I know how to handle that now. I might say, "We'll play a different time!" He accepts that. He likes the sound of the word different. Sometimes we say "deefer-ent."

I liked knowing why we played the games. I knew where we were going [what my child would be learning].

James puts the pictures on his wall. He asks me questions about them. One day I heard him telling Whipple [a puppet] all the things he could do so Allie [another puppet] would play with him. I couldn't believe my ears. My eight-year-old reads the script sometimes [to the four-year-old]. She likes to be the teacher.

TABLE 7.5

Means and SDs Pre-Post and Gain for Training Mothers of Children
Who Did and Did Not Improve in Behavior Adjustment

Child Behavior Change	Child-Rearing Style[a]			Alternative Solutions (adult problems)[a]			Means-Ends Thinking (mother-child problems)[a]		
	Pre	Post	Gain	Pre	Post	Gain	Pre	Post	Gain
Aberrant Pre-Adjusted Post									
X	15.43	55.83	+40.41	11.50	14.67	+3.17	6.83	16.33	+9.50
SD	7.09	21.28	20.08	3.75	3.42	3.93	3.01	4.91	6.19
N	12	12	12	12	12	12	12	12	12
Abberant Pre-Aberrant Post									
X	14.60	36.80	+22.20	12.00	12.80	+.80	7.00	11.60	+4.60
SD	11.26	19.04	16.32	2.65	2.77	3.11	3.00	4.10	3.85
N	5	5	55	5	5	5	5	5	5
df	15	15	15	15	15	15	15	15	15
t	.18	1.73	1.79	.27	1.07	1.19	.10	1.89	1.63
p[b]	ns	.07	.05	ns	ns	ns	ns	.05	ns

NOTE: This table includes only mothers' measures that showed an effect of training.
a. Means of total scores for three stories.
b. Significance level, one-tailed.

After a while, I could make up my own games. That made me feel smart.

I even could dialogue with my mother [the child's grandmother], who used to run the show.

These comments help one understand why the program is accepted by parents. The recipients (both parent and child) are not taught what to do or what is right or wrong; rather, they learn a set of thinking skills that allow them to solve their own problems in their own way. The program does not require a change of child-rearing goals, just a shift in how to accomplish them. The curriculum, a step-by-step building process, is easy to learn and can be implemented while learning it. The goals and their relevance to the concerns of the parent are quickly recognized, the materials are usable for many purposes, and parents soon see their children's enthusiasm and progress. And the fact that parents are encouraged to create games suitable for their own children (within program goals) allows flexibility.

The following incident that occurred in a car nicely illustrates how ICPS intervention can affect a family at any given moment: The child (aged seven), sitting in the back seat, cracked a car window while trying to open it. Her mother, using problem-solving dialoguing, asked the child what she would do about it. The child offered several solutions, such as "I could mow the lawn and earn money and give it back to daddy to buy a new window," or, "I could call the fix-it-man," or, "I could say I'm sorry, I won't do it again." The father was stopped in his tracks, amazed because he had never heard his wife and child talk like this before. Previously, the father would have yelled, the child would have cried, and there would have been silence during the rest of the trip. Although not trained himself, it is hoped that this father recognized the importance of freeing his daughter to think about the problem and a plan of action to solve it (or at least to keep emotions from flying out of control).

Extensions of the
ICPS Intervention for Families

Our research to date has consisted of interventions for use by parents (see Shure & Spivack, 1978), and separate interventions for use by teachers (e.g., Shure & Spivack, 1971, in Spivack & Shure, 1974). Borrowing from the Shure and Spivack scripts, however, Larcen (1980) developed a six-week program for second-graders that combines teacher and parent use. While teachers encourage the children, working in small groups, to learn to identify people's feelings and problems at school, parents encourage their children to identify problems that occur at home. During the time teachers elicit alternative solutions, steps to carry them out, and possible consequences, parents are taught to elicit like responses at home—sometimes for hypothetical children, sometimes for their own. Although youngsters trained simultaneously by teacher and mother gained more in ICPS skills than those trained by teacher alone, it was determined that six weeks of intervention is too short a time for optimal application of parent and teacher dialoguing; no significant (teacher-rated) behavior change was found. In fact, Larcen reported that it took the full six weeks for the participants to even absorb the style and develop the techniques to use it. If dialoguing is the key to helping children associate how they think with what they do and how they behave, it is clear that ICPS interventions need adequate time for the trainer and the trainee to assimilate them. Nevertheless, it seems intuitively likely that simultaneous parent and teacher collaboration could add significantly greater increments to training than that provided by either alone.

Working with a more disturbed population, Yu, Harris, Solovitz, and Franklin (1985) implemented the Rochester Social Problem Solving curriculum (Weissberg, Gesten, Liebenstein, Schmid, & Hutton, 1979) with seven- to twelve-year-old male psychiatric outpatients of largely working-class, single-parent (divorced) families; concurrent parent sessions were held. The parent program included information about the concepts the children were learning, encouragement to implement the principles at home, and group discussions about a variety of parent issues. Two parent groups were compared, one that met twice weekly for 50 minutes (over 20 weeks), and one that met once weekly for 90 minutes (over the same 20 weeks). Compared to control groups, who received the normal clinical services, both experimental groups improved in both ICPS skills and behaviors, including greater social competence and less externalizing symptomatology (e.g., delinquent or aggressive be- haviors). The group whose parents attended once a week for 90 minutes had children whose behavior improved even more (presumably because the mothers attended more regularly). This group exhibited less internalizing (e.g., less depressed or uncommunicative behavior), less externalizing, and less overall clinical symptomatology. These children also tended to be more competent in nonschool activities and social functioning. Thus, even with diagnostically disturbed children, added parent training was more beneficial than non-ICPS treatment that consisted of a variety of therapeutic treatment variables assumed to be ameliorative of manifest psychopathology.

ICPS intervention has now been conducted with parents who themselves are experiencing stress and distress. Nesbitt et al. (1980) learned that six- to fifteen-year-old abused youngsters could improve their ICPS skills and decrease their parent-reported behavior problems when trained in ICPS skills by their therapists, and even more so when trained by the (abusing) parents themselves. Although this was only a pilot study, and the parent behavior ratings might have been subject to some bias, such improved parent perceptions of child behavior, real or apparent, might, at the least, translate into lower incidence of abuse. Further research on the issue is warranted.

There is very informal support for the possibility that the ICPS approach may lower incidence of abuse. As a service to parents who harmed their children or feared that they might, workers on a telephone hot line service informally applied ICPS dialoguing (Gonzales, 1977). Although it was not possible to train a parent to use structured lesson-games or to dialogue in a manner that would teach the child to think, the workers could talk with the parents in a way that would stimulate them to think. After waiting for the parents (typically mothers) to calm down, the workers first helped them to focus on their feelings, and then on how they thought their child might feel about the situation (the latter, rarely considered). By being guided to recall, step-by-step, what happened that might have made them angry, some parents came to see the situation as a problem to be solved, and not just an occasion to vent emotion on their child. Others came to understand that sometimes their children may not have been attempting to annoy the parent deliberately but rather may have been fighting or "misbehaving" because they were in actual conflict with the parent. After being helped to see the problem in a new way, several parents called back to express some relief. If they were not yet able to take positive action, at least they were, at times, able to restrain themselves from imposing physical harm. This is a very important start for many parents who would not or could not think of what else to do.

The perception of child behavior as deliberate annoyance is not uncommon in other families experiencing insufferable child-rearing practices. Silver (1977) reported how the ICPS approach helped one family, who were about to place their three children into a foster home. In addition to formal group ICPS meetings, this family was urged to record interpersonal problems that arose at home, how (and if) they applied dialogues, and the success or failure of the outcomes. Parents gained a greater appreciation of their children's point of view, as well as an awareness that children have problems too. The enhanced problem-solving skills of both the parents and their children prevented outside placement of the children. If as Perez et al. (1981) have found, ICPS abilities of troubled-distressed families are limited, perhaps ICPS training can help them build coping strategies that could reduce or even prevent more severe behavioral dysfunction.

If handling interpersonal problems with emotional outbursts is one source of distress in troubled families, neglect of the child is another. Dawson et al. (1985) gave ICPS training to three neglecting mothers who "had come to the attention of the child welfare authorities for abandoning their children with unsuitable care takers, leaving them in potentially dangerous situations and/or failing to provide medication and other health care" (p. 2). Trained individually, these parents not only learned to solve the problem situations skillfully that were practiced in training, but were able to generalize and apply these new skills to novel child care problem situations that never received training attention. Most important, two of the three mothers were judged competent enough to be given return of full custody. There was no evidence of neglect throughout a four-month follow-up.

Earlier it was explained that infant-maternal attachment can predict a preschooler's ego-control and ego-resilience (including ICPS competency). This suggests that a fruitful intervention would be to help mothers of infants develop what it takes to produce attachment. Perhaps the most powerful intervention of all would combine early attachment and ICPS components. For youngsters under the age of four, parents could be trained to problem solve and to use problem-solving communication skills (see Lambie, 1976). This approach holds promise because, from early on, these parents may have an effect on the subsequent interpersonal problem-solving skills and social adjustment of their children.

Interventions: Conditions for Success

ICPS has been identified as a primary prevention program that works. The question now is why, and under what conditions. Having paid careful attention to the inner-workings of our own and others' ICPS interventions, I believe that conditions for success can be subsumed under three types of perspectives: (a) the scientific perspective; (b) the practical, or logistical perspective; and (c) the personal, or consumer perspective.

The Scientific Perspective

Before designing interventions to improve children's behavior by altering ICPS skills, it was first necessary to establish through correlational research that such cognitive skills and behavior were related in the natural course of life, and then to identify which ICPS skills were related to which behaviors, at what age, and in which socioeconomic levels. Having found such relationships (see Spivack et al., 1976) in several different populations, our next step was to test our theory that ICPS skills are mediators of behaviors by experimental manipulation (intervention). Thus, initially, our intervention strategy was guided by a theory, an ICPS/behavioral mediation theory, well grounded by basic (correlational) research.

The scientific perspective goes beyond basic correlations between dependent (ICPS) and independent (behavioral) variables. It also includes a sense of what components should constitute the intervention. Research in other areas has demonstrated the necessity for teaching age-appropriate prerequisite skills in order to promote final targeted skills that are generalizable (e.g., see Roeper & Sigel's, 1967, work on training conservation). We reasoned that ICPS prerequisite skills were the way to go with our intervention as well. Thus, before teaching the final solution and consequential skills to be learned, our curriculum for preschoolers included the key language concepts and perspective-taking skills described in the first section of this chapter. The need for these prerequisite skills for preschoolers has been confirmed by Egan (1979), who found greater ICPS gains among those receiving the total program script than among those receiving the prerequisite skills alone, solution skills alone, or consequential skills alone (each segment expanded to equal the training time of the total program).

We also discovered that the training must consist of informal application of the concepts when real problems arise during the day, as well as formal didactic lessons. During our first teacher-training pilot study with four-year-olds (Shure, Spivack, & Powell, 1972), I noticed teachers asking children for *their* ideas during the formal lesson-games (consistent with the style of the intervention), then creating confusion by telling them what to do when a *real* problem arose. To deal with this problem, we have had the trainer help the children associate newly developed cognitive skills with their behavior by applying what we came to call "problem-solving dialoguing," or "dialoguing" (see examples earlier in this chapter). Weissberg, Gesten, Carnrike et al. (1981) proposed that greater behavior gains in second- to fourth-graders were due, in part, to more systematic incorporation of informal dialoguing into the daily routine. While other factors may account for the results, we have noted in following ICPS interventions of others that those who do incorporate the dialoguing techniques (e.g., Allen, 1978; Mannarino et al., 1982; Wowkanech, 1978) obtain more significant behavioral impact than those who do not (e.g., Durlak & Sherman, 1979; Sharp, 1981).

Although we believe we have demonstrated scientifically that ICPS skills are at least one significant mediator of behavior, and that youngsters from preschool through grade four can improve their behavior from such training within the time frame of one school year, our research with fifth-graders, at least Black, low SES, inner-city fifth-graders (Shure, 1984) led us to examine practical, logistical considerations in evaluating the impact of this kind of preventive programming.

Practical (Logistical) Perspective

In school interventions, issues such as class size, teachers' other responsibilities, and the number of different teachers a child has can differentially affect the ease of implementation. For example, unlike nursery and kindergarten, children have multiple teachers by fifth-grade, leaving less time to the home-room (training) teacher. Also, it is clearly more difficult to dialogue a real problem in a class of 30 children than in a (nursery) class of 15. While kindergarten teachers may also have 30 children, they typically have more consistent aides to help and more total time with the class. Also, unlike teachers of younger children, home-room teachers are less likely to accompany the class to the playground at recess when so many typical problems arise. Because dialoguing is most effective when applied during or shortly after the conflict, it can lose its potency when the conflict is reported and worked through later.

How did we cope with these logistical differences for the fifth-graders? At the suggestion of one of our creative fifth-grade teachers, children role-played problems that came up, a technique that, learned in the formal lessons, was possible and relatively successful. An alternative is to train all school personnel who come in contact with the children, a procedure more costly, but one that met with success by Elardo and Caldwell (1975, 1979). If curriculum demands and other logistical differences affect the style of training, they also affect its intensity. Teachers of younger children could implement the formal 20- to 30-minute lesson-games daily for 12 weeks (allowing for pre-post testing time and holidays within the constraints of the school year). In the higher grades, three times a week over the same 12 training weeks was fortunate.

In fifth-graders, positive prosocial behavior and peer relations did improve after one exposure to the program, but negative impulsive and inhibited behaviors did not (Shure, 1984). Whether behavior of older (versus younger) children is just more habitual, and therefore more resistant to change, whether lack of daily intervention makes the difference, or whether the ICPS approach is less suitable after age eight or nine is still unknown. But we believe that because these negative impulsive and inhibited behaviors are correlated with ICPS skills among fifth-graders as well as among younger children (e.g., Richard & Dodge, 1982; Shure & Spivack, 1972), perhaps a second exposure to ICPS training in grade six would be beneficial. We are analyzing that data now, but the point I want to make is the following: Before abandoning an intervention because of its less than immediate impact or its apparent inadequacy for a particular population, it is important to examine, among other things, the quality of the training package, and the length and intensity of the intervention. Research is clearly showing that sharply curtailed training does not produce desired results (e.g., Dick, 1981: 10 lessons; Weissberg, Gesten, Rapkin et al., 1981: 17 lessons). It has already been seen, even with younger children, that six weeks, for example, is inadequate for parents or teachers to absorb the dialoguing techniques (Larcen, 1980). If time constraints are going to curtail implementation, or if the full curriculum cannot be readministered a year later, perhaps early training, bolstered by intermittent "booster shots" throughout the elementary years might maximize the impact of ICPS intervention on older children (Wienckowski).[1] This, in combination with the Elardo and Caldwell procedure of training all school personnel to at least "dialogue" when real problems arise, would likely produce an optimal ecological environment, as well as the most methodologically sound approach for continued ICPS and behavioral development.

Another practical consideration that can affect the impact of an intervention is the motivation and commitment of the trainer. Any intervention is only as effective as the agent who conducts it. We discovered that some of our fifth-grade teachers initially viewed interpersonal conflict as annoyances or disturbances to be dealt with quickly and be rid of, rather than as problems to be solved. If teachers of younger children are, from the start, more oriented toward helping children adapt behaviorally than are those of older children (due, perhaps, to fewer pressures of curriculum demands), then a pretraining orientation to new perceptions of child conflict could help.

The Personal, Consumer Perspective

While researchers are investigating the validity of a new intervention, its consumers are simultaneously receiving a service. The administrator (e.g., a school principal), the training-agent (e.g., a teacher), and the direct recipients (e.g., the children), however, may have very different needs, any of which, if not met, could influence the effect of an intervention. While the researcher is concerned about theory testing, program validity, measurement reliability, and so on; administrators may be most concerned about staff development; teachers may be concerned about classroom management, improving their teaching skill, and/or adding variety to their day; and children may focus upon "feeling good," or "being smart." It took inquiring about, then recognition of, these different needs to pave the way for initiating, planning, and staging the research phase of our program (Shure, 1979).

When we turned our research to parents, clearance was obtained from the Policy Advisory Committee (PAC), a parent group that provided input on all aspects of the day care activities, operations, policies, and procedures related to service delivery for parents and children. What interested this group and the parents who were eventually trained was essentially the same as what motivated teachers—that the program was flexible, it did not tell people what to do, but rather, it helped parents and children learn to think so they could solve problems that were important to them in ways that were relevant to them.

As for children, our major concern was to obtain and maintain their enthusiasm, especially those who would be trained for two years (see Shure & Spivack, 1979a). To this end, several rounds of prepiloting and piloting the lesson-games were conducted, with revisions based on children's reactions and responses.

While the above considerations are dealt with *before* implementation, others are attended to *during* it. For example, teachers' freedom to create procedural techniques (e.g., the format of a game) made them feel a part of a team developing ways to teach the concepts. Their ideas and some created by the children, themselves, were later incorporated into the script. Although we now disseminate a "final" product, the program script is never final because it emphasizes that flexibility of content (but not concepts) is not only allowed, but encouraged.

It is hoped that our care in meeting the needs of everyone involved, the flexibility of the program script, overcoming logistical difficulties, and the validity of the program script (piloted several times, each time revising it according to the responses [or nonresponses] of the children) all contribute to "what makes ICPS intervention work." But, in the end, perhaps the bottom line is really what we have come to call "constituent validity" (Kelly),[2] that is, the extent to which the recipients can assess the work as meeting their needs, aspirations, and values. For a truly effective intervention, one must strive toward recipient receptivity, and still remain within the boundaries of valid scientific inquiry.

In our research, we have traveled through three domains of Price and Smith's (1985) map, but have just edged inside of the fourth. We have defined the problem and followed it with descriptive (correlational) research (domain 1), chosen and designed our technology (domain 2), implemented and evaluated it (domain 3), and now, with others, we have begun partial diffusion, sometimes with continuing modification (domain 4). We found that "recycling," especially within and between domains 2 and 3, was particularly fruitful. Every time we ran the program, we learned more about how to improve it. Every time we evaluated it, we were challenged to explore even more. Before completing the trip through domain 4 to widespread adoption, we still have more to learn. Why did our intervention help some high-risk children and not others? How long would it take to help them, if at all? For those it did help, how long did the impact really last?

To date we know the impact lasts at least two years in preschoolers (Shure & Spivack, 1982), and at least one year in second- to fourth-graders (Gesten et al., 1982)—each lasting as long as impact had been measured. To us, still longer lasting impact would be optimal, and to learn about that we need time. Regardless of that outcome, intermittent booster shots would still qualify to say a program "works." In any case, by building competencies designed to reduce and prevent behavior problems in relatively normal, but high-risk children, and by discovering that teachers and inner-city mothers can train those skills, perhaps we have taken what Cowen (1977) winsomely calls concrete, feasible "baby steps" toward primary prevention. If we all think about issues that can strengthen our activities, then demonstrate that we can identify and reduce high risk, we may be taking the first important next steps—the long awaited giant steps. But give us time. We need more time.

Notes

1. Expressed by Louis Wienckowski at Research Planning Workshop. Research on Primary Prevention, Ira Iscoe (chair), co-sponsored by the Center for Prevention Research and the Prevention Research Branch, NIMH, and the University of Texas at Austin February 24-26, 1982.

2. Expressed by James G. Kelly, same workshop as in note 1.

References

Allen, R. J. (1978). *An investigatory study of the effects of a cognitive approach to interpersonal problem solving on the behavior of emotionally upset psychosocially deprived preschool children.* Unpublished doctoral dissertation, Union Graduate School, Washington, DC.

Arend, R., Gove, F. L., & Sroufe, A. L. (1979). Continuity of individual adaptation from infancy to kindergarten: A predictive study of ego-resiliency and curiosity in preschoolers. *Child Development, 50,* 950-959.

Asarnow, J. R., & Callan, J. W. (1984, August). Children with peer adjustment problems: Social cognitive processes. In J. R. Asarnow (chair), *Social skills and preadolescents: Assessment and training.* Symposium presented at the meetings of the American Psychological Association, Toronto.

Azar, S. T., Robinson, D. R., Hekimian, E., & Twentyman, C. T. (1984). Unrealistic expectations and problem-solving ability in maltreating and comparison mothers. *Journal of Consulting and Clinical Psychology, 52,* 687-691.

Block, J. H., & Block, J. (1971). *The California Child Q Set: A procedure for describing personological characteristics of children.* Unpublished manuscript, University of California, Berkeley, Department of Psychology.

Cowen, E. L. (1977). Baby-steps toward primary prevention. *American Journal of Community Psychology, 5,* 1-22.

Dawson, B., de Armas, A., McGrath, M., & Kelly, J. A. (1985). *Cognitive problem-solving training to improve the child-care judgement of child neglectful parents.* Unpublished manuscript, University of Mississippi Medical Center.

Dick, A. (1981). *The effects of training in social problem solving and verbal self-instruction on behavioral adjustment, social problem-solving cognition, and cognitive tempo in socially impulsive kindergarten children.* Unpublished doctoral dissertation, New York University.

Dinkmeyer, D., & Dinkmeyer, D., Jr. (1982). *Developing understanding of self and others* (DUSO). Circle Pines, MN: American Guidance Service.

Durlak, J. A., & Sherman, D. (1979, September). Primary prevention of school maladjustment. In J. A. Durlak (chair), *Behavioral approaches to primary prevention: Programs, outcomes and issues.* Symposium conducted at the meeting of the American Psychological Association, New York.

Egan, F. B. (1979). *A components analysis of interpersonal problem solving skills training.* Unpublished doctoral dissertation, Hofstra University, New York.

Elardo, P. T., & Caldwell, B. M. (1975). *Project AWARE: A school program to facilitate the social development of kindergarten-elementary children.* Unpublished manuscript, University of Arkansas, Little Rock, AR, College of Education.

Elardo, P. T., & Caldwell, B. M. (1979). The effects of an experimental social development program on children in the middle childhood period. *Psychology in the Schools, 16,* 93-100.

Elias, M. J. (1978). *The development of a theory-based measure of how children understand and attempt to resolve problematic social situations.* Unpublished masters thesis, University of Connecticut, Storrs.

Feldman, E. (1984). *Assessment of social-cognitive skills in popular, average, rejected and neglected girls and boys.* Unpublished doctoral dissertation, University of Indiana, Bloomington.

Ford, M. (1982). Social cognition and social competence in adolescence. *Developmental Psychology, 18,* 323-340.

Fry, P. S., & Grover, S. C. (1982). The relationship between father absence and children's social problem solving competencies. *Journal of Applied Developmental Psychology, 3,* 105-120.

Gesten, E. L., Rains, M., Rapkin, B., Weissberg, R. G., Flores, de Apodaca, R., Cowen, E. L., & Bowen, G. (1982). Training children in social problem-solving competencies: A first and second look. *American Journal of Community Psychology, 10,* 95-115.

Gesten, E., & Weissberg, R. P. (1979, September). Social problem-solving training and prevention: Some good news and some bad news. In J. Rolf (chair), *Progress in identifying and promoting social competence.* Symposium conducted at the meeting of the American Psychological Association, New York.

Gonzales, R. (1977). Personal communication.

Gordon, T. (1970). *Parent effectiveness training*. New York: Peter H. Wyden.

Gotlib, I., & Asarnow, R. F. (1979). Interpersonal and impersonal problem solving skills in mildly and clinically depressed university students. *Journal of Consulting and Clinical Psychology, 47*, 86-95.

Granville, A. C., McNeil, J. T., Meece, J., Wacker, S., Morris, M., Shelly, M., & Love, J. M. (1976). *A process evaluation of project developmental continuity interim report IV: Vol. 1. Pilot year impact study—instrument characteristics and attrition trends*. No. 105-75-1112, Washington, DC: Office of Child Development.

Herman, M. S., & Shantz, C. U. (1983). Social problem solving and mother-child interactions of educable mentally retarded children. *Journal of Applied Developmental Psychology, 4*, 217-226.

Hill, H. (1983, April). *An investigation of indices of competent parenting in Afro-American mothers*. Paper presented at the meeting of the Society for Research in Child Development, Detroit.

Hoffman, M. L. (1971). Father-absence and conscience development. *Developmental Psychology, 4*, 400-406.

Johnson, J. E., Yu, S., & Roopnarine, J. (1980, March). *Social cognitive ability, interpersonal behaviors, and peer status within a mixed age group*. Paper presented at the meeting of the Southwestern Society for Research in Human Development, Lawrence, KA.

Jones, D. C., Rickel, A. U., & Smith, R. L. (1980). Maternal childrearing practices and social problem-solving strategies among preschoolers. *Developmental Psychology, 16*, 241-242.

Lambie, D. Z. (1976). *Parents and educators: Experts and equals*. Ypsilanti: High Scope Educational Research Foundation.

Larcen, S. W. (1980). *Enhancement of social problem-solving skills through teacher and parent collaboration*. Unpublished doctoral dissertation, University of Connecticut, Storrs.

Mannarino, A. P., Christy, M., Durlak, J. A., & Magnussen, M. G. (1982). Evaluation of social competence training in the schools. *Journal of School Psychology, 20*, 11-19.

Marsh, D. T. (1981). Interrelationships among perspective-taking, interpersonal problem solving, and interpersonal functioning. *Journal of Genetic Psychology, 138*, 37-48.

Mussen, P., & Rutherford, E. (1963). Parent child relations and parental personality in relation to young children's sex-role preference. *Child Development, 34*, 589-607.

Nesbitt, A. Madren-Braun, J., Bruckner, M., Caldwell, R., Dennis, N., Liddell, T., & McGloin, J. (1980). *Children's Resource Center: "A problem solving approach"* (Final Evaluation. Report to LEAA 77-2A [1]-36-52). Washington, DC, and Adams County Department of Social Services, Commerce City, CO. (Available from Draft Aid Reproductions, 1088 S. Gaylord, Denver, CO 80209).

Oden, S. L., & Asher, S. R. (1977). Coaching children in social skills for friendship making. *Child Development, 48*, 495-506.

Olson, S. L., Johnson, J., Belleau, K., Parks, J., & Barrett, E. (1983, April). *Social competence in preschool children: Interrelations with sociometric status, social problem-solving, and impulsivity*. Paper presented at the meetings of the Society for Research in Child Development, Detroit.

Pellegrini, D. S. (1985). Social cognition and competence in middle childhood. *Child Development, 56*, 253-264.

Perez, V., Gesten, E. L., Cowen, E. L., Weissberg, R. P., Rapkin, B. D., & Boike, M. (1981). Relationships between family background problems and social problem-solving skills of young normal children. *Journal of Prevention, 2*, 80-90.

Platt, J. J., & Spivack, G. (1974). Means of solving real-life problems: I. Psychiatric patients vs. controls, and cross-cultural comparisons of normal females. *Journal of Community Psychology, 2*, 45-48.

Platt, J. J., Spivack, G., Altman, N., Altman, D., & Peizer, S. B. (1974). Adolescent problem-solving thinking. *Journal of Consulting and Clinical Psychology, 42*, 787-793.

Price, R. H. & Smith, S. S. (1985). *A guide to evaluating prevention programs in mental health* (DHHS Publication No. ADM 85-1365). Washington, DC: Government Printing Office.

Richard, B. A., & Dodge, K. A. (1982). Social maladjustment and problem-solving in school-aged children. *Journal of Consulting and Clinical Psychology, 50*, 226-233.

Roeper, A., & Sigel, I. E. (1967). Finding the clue to children's thought processes. In W. Hartup & N. Smothergill (Eds.), *The young child.* Washington, DC: National Association for the Education of Young Children.

Rubin, K. H. (1982). Social and social cognitive developmental characteristics of young isolate, normal, and sociable children. In K. H. Rubin & H. S. Ross (Eds.), *Peer relationships and social skills in childhood.* New York: Springer-Verlag.

Rubin, K. H., & Daniels-Beirness, T. (1983). Concurrent and predictive correlates of sociometric status in kindergarten and grade 1 children. *Merrill-Palmer Quarterly, 29*, 337-351.

Rubin, K. H., & Krasnor, L. R. (1983). Age and gender differences in solution to hypothetical social problems. *Journal of Applied Developmental Psychology, 4*, 263-275.

Schiller, J. D. (1978). *Child care arrangements and ego functioning: The effects of stability and entry age on young children.* Unpublished doctoral dissertation, University of California, Berkeley.

Sharp, K. C. (1981). Impact of interpersonal problem-solving training on preschoolers' social competency. *Journal of Applied Developmental Psychology, 2*, 129-143.

Shure, M. B. (1979). Training children to solve interpersonal problems: A preventive mental health program. In R. E. Munoz, L. R. Snowden, & J. G. Kelly (Eds.), *Social and psychological research in community settings* (pp. 30-68). San Francisco: Jossey-Bass.

Shure, M. B. (1982). Interpersonal problem solving: A cog in the wheel of social cognition. In F. Serafica (Ed.), *Social cognition and social development in context* (pp. 133-166). New York: Guilford.

Shure, M. B. (1984, August). Building social competence in fifth-graders: Is it too late? In K. H. Rubin & J. R. Asarnow (co-chairs). *Social skills in preadolescents: Assessment and training.* Symposium conducted at the meeting of the American Psychological Association, Toronto.

Shure, M. B., Newman, S., & Silver, S. (1973, May). *Problem solving thinking among adjusted, impulsive and inhibited Head Start children.* Paper presented at the meeting of the Eastern Psychological Association, Washington, DC.

Shure, M. B., & Spivack, G. (1971). *Interpersonal cognitive problem solving (ICPS): A mental health program for four-year-old nursery school children* (Training script). Philadelphia: Hahnemann University, Department of Mental Health Sciences.

Shure, M. B., & Spivack, G. (1972). Means-ends thinking, adjustment and social class among elementary school-aged children. *Journal of Consulting and Clinical Psychology, 38*, 348-353.

Shure, M. B., & Spivack, G. (1974). *Interpersonal cognitive problem solving (ICPS): A mental health program for kindergarten and first grade children* (Training script). Philadelphia: Hahnemann University, Department of Mental Health Sciences.

Shure, M. B., & Spivack, G. (1978). *Problem solving techniques in childrearing.* San Francisco: Jossey-Bass.

Shure, M. B., & Spivack, G. (1979a). Interpersonal cognitive problem solving and primary prevention: Programming for preschool and kindergarten children. *Journal of Clinical Child Psychology, 2,* 89-94.

Shure, M. B., & Spivack, G. (1979b). Interpersonal problem solving thinking and adjustment in mother-child dyad. In M. W. Kent & J. E. Rolf (Eds.), *The primary prevention of psychopathology: Vol. 3. Social competence in children* (pp. 201-219). Hanover, NH: University Press of New England.

Shure, M. B., & Spivack, G. (1980). Interpersonal problem solving as a mediator of behavioral adjustment in preschool and kindergarten children. *Journal of Applied Developmental Psychology, 1,* 29-43.

Shure, M. B., & Spivack, G. (1982). Interpersonal problem solving in young children: A cognitive approach to prevention. *American Journal of Community Psychology, 10,* 341-356.

Shure, M. B., Spivack, G., & Powell, L. (1972, April). *A problem solving intervention program for disadvantaged preschool children.* Paper presented at the meeting of the Eastern Psychological Association, Boston.

Silver, S. (1977). Personal communication.

Snyder, J. J., & Shanks, D. (1982). Social-cognitive skills in preschool children: Relationship to teacher and peer ratings and in-vivo behavior. *Behavioral Counseling Quarterly, 2,* 148-155.

Spivack, G., Platt, J. J., & Shure, M. B. (1976). *The problem solving approach to adjustment.* San Francisco: Jossey-Bass.

Spivack, G., & Shure, M. B. (1974). *Social adjustment of young children.* San Francisco: Jossey-Bass.

Spivack, G., & Shure, M. B. (1982). Interpersonal cognitive problem solving and clinical theory. In B. Lahey & A. E. Kazdin (Eds.), *Advances in child clinical psychology* (Vol. 5, pp. 323-372). New York: Plenum.

Spivack, G., Standen, C., Bryson, J., & Garrett, L. (1978, August). *Interpersonal problem-solving thinking among the elderly.* Paper presented at the meetings of the American Psychological Association, Toronto.

Turner, R. R., & Boulter, L. K. (1981, August). *Social competence: The validity of the PIPS.* Paper presented at the meetings of the American Psychological Association, Los Angeles.

Weissberg, R. P., Gesten, E. L., Carnrike, C. L., Toro, P. A., Rapkin, B. D., Davison, E., & Cowen, E. (1981). Social problem-solving skills training: A competence-building intervention with second- to fourth-grade children. *American Journal of Community Psychology, 9,* 411-423.

Weissberg, R. P., Gesten, E. L., Liebenstein, N. L., Schmid, K. D., & Hutton, H. (1979). *The Rochester Social Problem Solving (SPS) Program: A training manual for teachers of 2nd-4th grade children.* Rochester, NY: Center for Community Study.

Weissberg, R. P., Gesten, E. L., Rapkin, B. D., Cowen, E. L., Davidson, E., Flores de Apodaca, R., & McKim, B. J. (1981). The evaluation of a social problem solving training program for suburban and inner-city third grade children. *Journal of Consulting and Clinical Psychology, 49,* 251-261.

Wowkanech, N. (1978, August 26). Personal communication.

Wolpe, J. (1969). *The practice of behavior therapy.* New York: Pergamon.

Yu, P., Harris, G., Solovitz, B., & Franklin, J. (1985). *A prevention intervention program for children at high risk for later psychopathology.* Unpublished report, Texas Research Institute of Mental Sciences, Office of Primary Prevention.

8

In Search of New Selves: Accommodating to Widowhood[1]

Phyllis R. Silverman

How we understand what happens to people when they are widowed should determine the content and the goals of any preventive interventions provided on their behalf. This understanding is reflected in the vocabulary we choose to describe the widow and widower's grief. We talk of "time healing," of "getting over it," and of "working it through." We say "you will recover." The images associated with these phrases imply that grief is an illness from which one recovers with appropriate treatment. The expectation of such treatment is that it will at the least relieve the mourner's pain and at the most remove it entirely. Implicit too is the idea that grief ends and people will pick up their lives and carry on as before. I think of this approach as resulting in a major deception being played on the bereaved. They often feel defective and stigmatized by their inability to achieve this resolution of their grief. The bereaved's own expectations of themselves cannot be disassociated from the way their larger social network deals with bereavement. They feel that something must be wrong with them when they find that their grief is long and pervasive and that they do not recover (Silverman, 1981). In reality, their pain may be tempered by time but time does not heal. In the words of a widow:

> The loneliness and the vacant feelings stay with you. You realize this is the way it's going to be and you'll be happier making the most of it, rather than trying to fight it. You go on—you just do things and you continue— you do things for yourself and for others and life becomes good again.

The widowed don't recover; rather they make an accommodation to their new situation. When newly widowed, grief is the dominant theme in their lives. Their task at this time is not to give in to the impulse to run from the pain often caused not only by the inner sense of loss but by the silence of those around them. They should instead accept the pain as appropriate given the circumstances. After a while, the widowed seem to get a handle on their feelings and learn to understand them:

> I have gotten used to being alone; I've never learned to like it, but I enjoy my freedom. I really like coming and going as I please.

The pain of the loss becomes a dull ache, an occasional visitor whose visits can be anticipated and are not very worrisome. Coping with widowhood, however, seems to be more than managing sorrow. A way of life is lost as well and the widowed cannot reconstitute their lives or themselves as they were before. It may be more accurate to talk of change. They may be wiser—more aware of both life's joys and sorrows—and in many ways they may become quite different from what they were before:

> I've changed in almost every way. I went back to school. I became active in educational organizations. I travel more and I take the lead in organizations.

In this chapter, I want to examine how men and women are changed as a consequence of being widowed and the direction this change takes. I am particularly interested in whether the direction of the change is the same for men and for women. I am also interested in what conditions make change possible. In my mind, there are two main issues that need emphasizing in discussing widowhood. The first issue involves changing the focus from how to manage sorrow to how to manage growth and change (Marris, 1974). The second issue relates to how to facilitate this change. This chapter is a response to these two issues. The first part of the chapter will focus on the nature of change associated with widowhood. The second part of the chapter will present data on how affiliation with a mutual help group does seem to facilitate this change. There has been a proliferation of mutual help groups for the widowed. The Institute of Medicine (Osterweis, Solomon & Green, 1984) devoted most of a chapter in their recent review of the state of knowledge of bereavement to these intervention efforts by the widowed for the widowed. We need to understand what special value widowed people have for each other and what unique power these programs may have for facilitating change.

The data I will use to exemplify the key points in this chapter were gathered from two mutual help groups for the widowed, To Live Again and The Widowed Persons' Service. Both of these organizations are volunteer efforts in which members come together to find ways to solve their common problems. Services derive from the members' own experience with the problem. Members are helpers, officers, and beneficiaries. In essence, the organizations are owned and operated by the membership and meet the definition of a self help/mutual aid program (Katz & Bender, 1976; Silverman, 1980).

The Widowed Persons' Service (WPS) is a loose federation of 142 organizations throughout the United States sponsored by the American Association for Retired Persons (AARP). Each local group has its own elected officers. The national office is staffed by people employed by the AARP to provide technical assistance to local chapters, to develop training programs for volunteers who do outreach as an essential part of their program, and to help develop new groups. The national WPS publishes a newsletter, program materials, and a directory of organizations throughout the United States and Canada.

To Live Again (TLA) is a regional nonsectarian organization affiliated with the Catholic Archdiocese of Philadelphia with about half a dozen branches serving people in Eastern Pennsylvania and Southern New Jersey. They offer seminars to the newly widowed, and provide extensive educational and social activities for their members. Each branch has its own officers and program committee. Members elect representatives to a regional coordinating council that has its own officers, and the regional executive plans the annual meeting and regionwide activities.

A total of 108 members, 18 widowers and 90 widows, from these two organizations answered a questionnaire that was distributed at their annual meetings. The questionnaire consisted of a set of open-ended questions designed to allow the widowed respondents to answer in their own words how they viewed the experience of widowhood, if they had changed as a result of their being widowed, and if so, in what ways they had changed. The respondents were also asked if they felt affiliating with a mutual help program for the widowed made any difference, and if so, in what way.

Identifying the
Need for Change

Historically, widowhood has been viewed as a temporary status that ended when the widowed individual remarried. Rites of passage in many societies helped people accommodate to their losses. Wherever possible, the end of mourning was marked by remarriage. If marriage did not occur, the widowed person was expected to remain in mourning the rest of his or her life. This was especially true for women. In some societies, they were prohibited from remarrying. Their primary role in society either as widow or as wife was through their relationship to their husband, alive or dead. Widowhood was seen as a restricting condition, even in the more open society of twentieth-century America. An 80-year-old American widow described the position she felt widowhood gave her in this society, "When I was married I was someone, now I'm nobody." It is not only the widow who may feel uncomfortable with her singleness, but so do others around her. The larger society seems unable to cope with the profound and disruptive feelings associated with a death and subsequent bereavement.

In the late twentieth century, with the aging of the general population, there is an increase in the number of people who will grow old in the role of widowed person. The medium age at which a woman is widowed in the United States is her late forties or early fifties. Not only do women continue to outlive men, but those men who are widowed tend to remarry. Therefore, this widowed population is primarily female. In an open society where we are examining anew the role of women and men, attention must be turned to widowhood as a societal phenomenon in which the gender of the survivor may be a factor. In no way does it approximate the reality to talk of widowhood as a mental health problem. We can no longer talk of how people accommodate to their widowhood in terms of the absence of depression, or in terms of remarriage. We must talk instead of change. Widowhood can be viewed as a new stage in the life-style—not only as an ending but as a beginning. Psychological and social growth and development do not end with adolescence but continue to the very end of the life cycle. Widowhood, like marriage, is a life cycle transition, an unwelcome opportunity for continuing development. In the words of a 67-year-old widow six years after her husband died:

> I learned that life goes on and I could not wallow in the past. At first, I didn't believe I could ever reminisce about the past. Later I realized I could cherish many memories and began to count my blessings. The worst had happened (he died), and is over. . . . I have a freedom I never had before.

On what dimensions can we characterize social and psychological growth over the life cycle? We can talk of growth in terms of relationship to ourselves and relationship to others. We no longer talk of a static sense of who we are, as if once formed we remain the same over a life time. Rather we can talk of an evolving self (Kegan, 1982). As we mature, we develop new awareness of ourselves and others. We can talk of growing more empathic, of increased mutuality, and of a new flexibility to respond to changing life conditions.

How does one characterize this change that widowed people experience? Probably the best way to begin is to consider what is lost when a spouse dies. Marriage can be seen as a way of framing and focusing the daily life of each partner. In the roles of husband and wife, partners are provided with social and legal prescriptions of how they relate to each other and to the larger society around them. When a partner dies, the surviving partner loses not only the habits of everyday interaction, but the role of husband or wife as well. If the role of husband or wife was central to how the widowed individual defined and experienced him- or herself, mourning may not be only for the lost person but for the lost self as well. Change for the widowed may thus involve developing a new sense of self (Silverman, 1981; Silverman & Cooperband, 1975; Weiss & Parkes, 1983). Because the role that is lost is that of husband or wife, it is essential to ask whether this change is different for men and for women (Silverman, 1981). To answer this question, it is necessary to look at the context in which growth takes place, and the prior experience of the people involved. Do men and women come to the roles of husband and wife with different experiences and different expectations? If so, then the direction of change men and women make as widowed people may be different as well.

A good deal is being written today about women and their development. Much of this literature focuses on the differences between men's and women's investments in relationships (Gilligan, 1982; Miller, 1976, 1984).

Jean Baker Miller suggests that a woman's sense of identity, or sense of self, grows out of her involvement with others. Her sense of self is primarily organized around her ability to make and then to maintain affiliations and relationships. Miller is writing in response to developmental psychologists who, observing in women this quality of being involved with others, felt that it was an indication that women could not achieve the same level of maturity as men. Maturity was synonymous with the ability to be an independent, autonomous individual. Lidz (1968) explained that Erikson (1956) portrayed women as exempt from the struggle that young men experience to learn who they are in relationship to society. Erikson suggested that women's identities were shaped by the men they married. Women's own characteristics were not important because they would be known through their relationship to others via the roles of wife and mother (Lidz, 1968). Women, in this view, were socialized to be passive and dependent in a male-centered world. To be female meant to be dependent, while being masculine meant being independent and separate. Women, however, were often placed in a double bind. They were criticized for being assertive and independent and equally criticized for being dependent. The latter was looked on as a failure to thrive. For example, one sign of pathological grief was dependent attachment to her deceased spouse (Parkes, 1972). If a woman had been socialized not to develop a sense of self apart from her husband, what other response might one get from a widow even several years after the death? The role of wife was the only one she knew unless she was told of other options.

As recently as 1970, a study was conducted to identify the characteristics of a mentally healthy person. Discussing it, Scarf wrote:

> Abstract notions of what is "mentally healthy" (as long as sex isn't mentioned) seem to emphasize those "masculine" traits and characteristics (such as assertiveness and autonomy) that are prized and more valued in our society. The lesser status, less valued "feminine" personality traits—less aggression, less dominance, more freedom of emotional expression, more excitability, etc.—were not seen as consonant with emotional well-being in the adult individual, sex unspecified. As far as mental health is concerned, the feminine role apparently implies pathology. (Scarf, 1980, p. 361)

If society does not legitimate women's experience, then it is difficult for the woman to legitimate it herself. As long as the model for all human experience is taken from that of the man's experience, women could punish themselves, in the words of Henry Higgins, for "not being more like a man." Can we talk about a male and female way of developing? Does men's and women's development differ so that they see their relationships with others in very different ways?

Gilligan (1982), observing the behavior of children at play, found that boys were more concerned with the rules of the game, arguing them out if need be so that play could continue, while girls were more intent on maintaining the relationships among the players than on resolving such differences. Gilligan concluded:

> The elusive mystery of women's development lies in its recognition of the continuing importance of attachment in the human life cycle . . . while developmental litany intones the celebration of separation, autonomy, individuation, and natural rights. (Gilligan, 1982, p. 23)

Miller (1984) suggests that women have long known the importance of attachments to others but society has portrayed this characteristic as a weakness rather than a strength. She writes that if women do not achieve or even seek the total individuation pursued by men, this should not be seen as a deficit but instead as a trait to be understood and valued.

If women know themselves through their relationships to others, then it is easy to understand how their sense of self can be shattered when a relationship is lost. If being a wife is central to one's identity at the time when this role ceases, the woman can find herself, figuratively speaking, without a self. Using the metaphor chosen by Gilligan (1982), who saw women's development "in a different voice," a widow can feel without a voice. She can feel very uncomfortable as she senses her need to become more assertive and self-reliant, these having been seen as unfeminine characteristics.

I am not suggesting that the metaphor of voice does not apply to men as well. I am suggesting rather than there may be several modes of development associated with the bereavement process. For a man who was taught to prize autonomy and who was socialized both to be independent and to be cared for by women, the kind of change associated with the death of his wife may be different than the kind of change experienced by a woman who has lost her husband. The questionnaire completed by members of TLA and WPS was designed to examine whether this formulation matches the experiences reported by widowed people.

The majority of people who answered the questionnaire were between the ages of 50 and 70. The men ranged in age from 41 to 71, the women ranged from 36 to 83. Most had been widowed about a year and a half, some as little as two weeks. Twelve of the women who were over 70 had been widowed at least 10 years. These were all people who had joined long after they were widowed, and were initiators of programs in their own communities. Incomes ranged from minimal social security, which is well under $10,000 a year, to upward of $35,000. While many were college graduates, most people had finished only high school. Respondents did not represent the better educated or the wealthier of the groups' members. The following is a preliminary analysis of the data. A qualitative approach is used to allow the widowed respondents to speak for themselves as much as possible.

The Direction of Change

If differences emerge between widows and widowers in the accommodations they make to their losses, when do these differences become apparent? Were there differences from the very outset in the way men and women experienced the loss?

During the period immediately after the spouse's death, there seem to be few, if any, differences between the reactions of widows and widowers. Both men and women focused on their pain, on their loneliness, and their feeling of aloneness. In the words of a 75-year-old widower:

> At times I feel like a lost ship being tossed about in a storm. After being with someone for 39 years I found it difficult to find myself again. She was my "safe haven," someone I could talk with, confide in, to love and be loved, to plan for the future. I know it will be a long and rough road to find out my bearing and just and true self again. But I must do it for my peace of mind.

A widow talks about her grief:

> I had been a wife and mother for 47 years. I had never lived alone in my life. I feel lost. I can't seem to care; it is so lonely I just feel as if half of me has been taken away, and I am just a half.

Both report a profound disruption in how they see themselves. What does this mean in terms of their day-to-day lives? Some women found coping with household chores, household business, and finances very difficult. Other women were concerned about their ability to support themselves. While men were concerned about cooking and shopping for themselves, they were not concerned with doing work to maintain their homes, or with supporting themselves. Most of the men seemed comforted by getting back into a routine. This was made easier when they returned to work—those women who worked had the same reactions. Everyone found eating alone difficult.

Differences between men and women regarding the need to make decisions clearly emerged within two or three months after the death. None of the widowers questioned his or her ability in this area, while for the widows making decisions was one of the worst things that they had to deal with:

> At first I did not want to choose to do anything alone. I fought against making any choices.

Part of this reluctance may have been due to their unwillingness to accept the finality of the death (Silverman & Silverman, 1979). For the most part, however, the women talked about it in terms of their inexperience in making decisions on their own. In the light of the analysis presented earlier in this chapter, I would suggest that this reluctance might stem from a fear of being "unfeminine" as they realized their need to act on their own behalf. Many of the widows said that they had always let their husbands decide:

> I deferred to my husband's decision. While my husband was living, he did most of the talking other than the problems that were referred to me.

None of the widowers talked of deferring to his wife, although in many instances both widows and widowers talked about decision making being a shared activity in their family. Even among such women, however, there was reported discomfort in acting on their own.

In response to the question, "What strengths did you develop?," the women mentioned their new found ability to decide and to act:

> I had to get used to taking responsibility for making my own decisions.
>
> Making important decisions for myself was a new concept to me. I now voice my own opinions and I am sometimes surprised that I am doing this—right or wrong.
>
> Now *I* think and *I* decide.

The difference in the experiences of widows and widowers is expressed in the following contrasting views of the ability to act on their own behalf. A young widower of three months describes himself as

> quiet, but very strong in coping and handling financial affairs, in making decisions.

A 36-year-old widow of six months said:

> I was happy, excited by life. I was queen of the shopping mall. My husband adored me, my family protected me. They try to do that now, but it doesn't work. I feel like *MUSH*.

The widower seems able to act in spite of his pain and his loss. His prior experience in managing his life serves him well. Women seem to need to learn something that men already know: how to act easily on their own behalf. A widower of six months described himself since he was widowed:

> I haven't changed too much. I am a self-assured individual. I know what I want and make plans to accomplish my goals—a little bit at a time. I've

had to develop a new support system and I've learned to be independent—self-reliant and self-sufficient (in caring for myself and my home).

One widower described his reactions to the death of his wife and the loss of his job of 30 years:

My whole support structure collapsed and I lost all confidence in myself. I was totally depressed and it was by far the most painful and frightening time in my life.

I knew the feelings did not represent past accomplishments and long-term reality expectations for the future. I had to force myself to get out and try new things.

The men's grief seemed a bit less protracted, and they were more focused in what they could do about it. The women seemed to be more accustomed to acting on someone else's behalf:

I had to learn that I am not just someone's daughter, sister, wife or mother. I described myself as Mrs. all the time, and for a long time after my husband died, as____'s wife.

A widow of 49, widowed for five years, recalled that prior to her husband's death,

I did not do many things on my own, but did most things with my family in mind and could not do some things I wanted to, was not encouraged to go out alone.

The woman who has lost her husband loses the critical relationship that has guided not only how she has lived her life, but how she has known herself. Men did not talk of their loss in terms of losing the role of husband. They talked, as did the women, of their loneliness, and of their need to share their lives with others. Their sense of who they were, however, was not dependent upon their relationship to their wives. While the way they lived their lives may have changed, the way that most of the men experienced themselves was not altered. As a result of the loss, men felt cut off from others but not from themselves. They talked of their need to "get out more." They talked of their need for companionship. They talked of possibly remarrying:

Just a guy looking for a wife and not being a dreamer. I am looking for someone in my generation, with similar interests and reasonably good health.

Many focused on developing their social skills. One man talked about "trying not to get so uptight in large social situations" and another was concerned with "being less of an introvert when among people." One man said: "I am trying to be more understanding of people's problems." Another noted that he was "much more tolerant of others." The direction of change among the men seemed to bring them in closer touch with their own feelings, leaving them more able to acknowledge their pain and their tears and to get in touch with the needs of others.

> I am determined to live out my years in a mood of kindness to others. If I find the right person I will marry again.

For the women, the change was in the direction of a growing independence. They began to discover other selves beyond that of wife, and any other single relationship.

> I was very content to stand in my husband's shadow. Now I am learning that I represent only me.

> There was the slow realization that I am really independent and that while I love and am loved by many people no one really cares what I do on any given day. They have confidence in me—I in myself and slowly I am trying to shed fear, guilt and over concern about "what other people think." I am working on many faces of what I hope will be changes in life-style and personal growth.

When a widow knows herself largely through her relationship to others, a good part of her energy is invested in trying to please these others. She gives priority to their needs and feelings over her own. As Gilligan (1982) said, women do not argue over the rules, they give in in order to maintain the relationship. Women also fear rejection, however, because they both know themselves and are known to others through this relationship. A woman's worst fear is realized when she is widowed:

> I feel that as part of a couple, I was included and listened to. Now I'm an afterthought.

> I found a way to speak up. I did a little before, but I was dependent upon my husband. But now if I don't I'm nothing.

These widows talked about becoming more centered in themselves, more in touch with what they want. Widows talked over and over again about the newfound independence and freedom that they were enjoying:

> I have a freedom I never had before.

> I am a happy single person, independent and enjoying it. I wouldn't say
> that I wasn't independent before but I still depended and leaned on my
> husband.

> Although I felt that I was complete and fulfilled, there were times when I
> was not living up to my potential. I suppose it was because I thought it was
> my role to be my husband's help mate (and I would do the same again) but
> in a sense I was probably not being "true to myself."

Change was born of necessity:

> Yes, I experienced a growth that would not have been possible before, if I
> had continued to be a "submissive" partner. In fact I would not have
> "stepped out." This does not mean that I felt liberated in losing a partner,
> but this is what has happened as a result.

> Widowhood has strengthened many traits I already had. It has made me a
> self-sufficient, independent single lady. But I wanted to survive. I cried
> every day the first year. I wanted to laugh again, to socialize again. I'm still
> working to survive. It sure ain't easy and I would not wish the death of a
> loved one on my worst enemy.

Out of necessity, the need to change emerges, and with time and
appropriate help, as described below, the direction of the change takes
shape. There were widows who felt that they had not lived in their
husband's shadow. They had been able to speak up, and they shared in
the decision making. Nonetheless, they found the need to change, and
they also talked about a different sense of self:

> It has always been easy for me to express myself. However, now there is a
> different reason . . . to express the victories that can be gained in the grief
> process, and the new life that can come out of it.

These widows began to achieve an autonomy that they had not known
before. They became more comfortable with themselves. They were
learning the skills needed to live alone, successfully:

> My kids tell me I have grown and expanded as a person. I know I am more
> generous, accepting and sensitive than before. While I enjoy others, I also
> appreciate my solitude and am content in what I am.

> I am a young widow, although not age-wise, independent, alone, but
> happy.

The women's relationships with others were no longer characterized by
their former dependency, but by a new mutuality. A developmental leap

seemed to have taken place. While they still needed people and were involved, there was a different quality to their connectedness.

> I have become more independent in all areas. I enjoy my ability to decide what my goals are. I probably am closer to my children and grandchildren than I would have been had my husband lived. I am also more community conscious and involved in several volunteer groups.

In conclusion, there does seem to be some evidence that widowhood can be understood as a developmental period in the life cycle, and that men and women do change in very different directions. The men seemed to be more in search of others. They became more appreciative of relationships, and the importance of relationships to their well-being. Women, by contrast, were more in search of themselves. They developed a self-confidence, assertiveness, and independence that they had not known before. They enjoyed the freedom from their dependency and the freedom to develop. They were not only free to grow but free of criticism for the direction in which they were going. What other people thought did not have the same meaning to them as before.

A major point of this chapter has been that being involved with others in caring relationships is central to women's sense of identity. I am not suggesting that they give up this need as a result of the changes associated with their widowhood. Women do not come to need people less; they come to need them for different reasons. In fact, a most interesting and unanticipated finding seems to be that in many ways men and women become more alike as they accommodate to their widowhood. Women develop a new appreciation of themselves as individuals and men develop a new understanding of their need for others. They seem to move toward a more appropriate interdependence that allows for a greater mutuality in their relationships. They seem to find a new excitement in their appreciation of the new dimensions of themselves that they discover in their new involvements in volunteer community projects, and in the widowed groups to which they belong.

In the next section, I want to examine how membership in the widowed groups helped individuals achieve these changes in themselves.

Mutual Help and Change

Elsewhere I have written that people are attracted to mutual help associations at times of critical transitions in their lives (Silverman, 1978, 1980, 1982). Transitions are periods of disruption in individuals' lives during which their prior coping techniques may be ineffective.

Typically in any critical transition the individual has to make a major role shift (Rappaport, 1963). It is possible to talk about the end of a transition when the individual reenters society in his or her new role. For widows or widowers, this happens when they can begin to see themselves as single, formerly married persons and shape their lives accordingly. For widowed people, this involves moving from the acute phase of grief to a time when they can accept the loss, achieve some perspective on their pain, and learn the skills needed to develop the new self described in the previous section.

Help, therefore, has to be available over time. Initially, people need to know that their grief is legitimate. They need to feel supported and to come to understand that what they are going through is typical under the circumstances. These are the elements of social support outlined by Cobb (1976) and Caplan (1976). A widow reflects on what she has gained from membership:

> TLA has given me a good feeling of belonging. I have so many new friends, I feel as if I have known them all my life, though I only met them 10 months ago. TLA has lightened my fears and feelings, helped me overcome the fifth wheel syndrome, given me a means to help others by understanding and listening and sharing myself, and to have an active social life.

An additional element respondents readily identified was the value of another widowed person as helper. TLA members are other widowed people. Finding someone "like themselves" who can share the experience seems to have special meaning for the widowed (Silverman, 1966, 1972, 1978, 1986).

> The wide range of ages and interests means there's someone and something for everyone who all have widowhood in common.

> First it made me feel I wasn't the only one in the same situation. Secondly, it made me more outgoing and inclined to offer whatever I could do to help others.

Hamburg and Adams (1967) observed that learning is made easier when the helper is one step ahead of the person in need of help and the learner has other people's experience to use as a guide. In this context, with peers as role models, a special identification can take place based on the confidence that these peers know what they are talking about, at least in the sense that they too are widowed. The relationship in a mutual help experience between peers is nonhierarchical. As noted in the above quote, the focus is on exchange and mutuality, on not being locked into either a recipient or a helper role. The emphasis is on caring and developing continuing relationships (Silverman, 1980, 1982).

The type of relationship available in a mutual help experience may be particularly suitable to the special needs of women (Kaplan & Surrey, 1984). Simply trying to replace the lost relationship with a new one of the same sort could mean merely exchanging a past dependency for a new one. Relationships available in a mutual help exchange can be seen as linking opportunities (Silverman, 1981) or, in Goffman's words (1963), as a bridge between the past and the future. They can be seen as transitional relationships, with similar functions to those of transitional objects as described by Winnicott (1953). The widowed became engaged, involved, and connected to others.

Based on the analysis in the prior sections of this chapter, we might hypothesize that men would not be as responsive as women to linking relationships as a step in accommodating to the death of a wife in that they are more accustomed to coping on their own and finding resources within themselves. In fact, leaders of mutual help groups for the widowed have observed that widowers do not affiliate in proportion to their numbers in the population. More data is needed to determine why this is so. We cannot ignore the fact that most men will remarry. The new wife may provide this linking function with the future. It is not clear whether this forecloses change, enhances change, or makes change unnecessary. Because some widowers do affiliate, it is important to learn what are the distinguishing characteristics of those who do and those who do not join with other widowed people.

In the study reported in this chapter, both the widows and the widowers found similar values in the helping opportunities available to them. For the reasons described above, both needed peers and valued the opportunities for help available in a mutual help group. These men, all members of mutual help groups, may not have been typical of the larger population of widowers. Where a difference existed between widows' and widowers' responses, it was not in the need for others but in the type of help the men and women needed from others. The men needed others to help them learn to be more connected; the women, to learn how to be more self-confident and self-sufficient. The remainder of this chapter focuses on this helping process and how change occurred.

Support and Understanding

People responded to the invitation to come to a meeting or to meet a member of the organization without knowing what to expect. Some went reluctantly, encouraged by a friend or relative who was already involved. They found the following:

> Everyone attending had the same experience and was searching for so many answers to so many questions.
>
> The people really understood what I was going through. I could bare my soul and *no one turned a deaf ear.*
>
> When I said Sunday was so long—it was nice to have someone else agree with me.

Most of the respondents were actively involved with family and friends. Nonetheless, over and over again, they spoke of the importance of meeting others "in the same boat."

> I have tried and really TLA members or other widows are the only ones who understand; my closest friends who still have their husbands, I can feel—they almost think you can do whatever you please and they can't hear me when I try to let them know, so I have stopped trying.

They met people who understood and could hear what they were saying. They also met people who could legitimate their feelings and they no longer felt so alone:

> I realized for the first time that I am not the only person who lost a spouse.
>
> I learned that the things I was feeling and experiencing are "normal."

Not only were there others to listen, to say "I felt the same way," but the others were there for as long as people needed them:

> Since we take time to listen to each other I got it out of my system by telling it over and over again about his last days—the conversations we had—the finding him dead—the doctor coming—and seeing his body go out of the house. . . .
>
> I often wonder how I would have survived. The first year all we did was share our feelings and emotions every step of the way.
>
> They wouldn't let me run away. They let me cry . . . and finally I believed them when they said it would get better.

People spoke of developing a sense of optimism and hope as a result of this sharing. They also found role models:

> I began to see from others who had coped, who looked happy and had made it, that I had something to look forward to.

An experienced widow said:

> Many people come crying and hurting. You can tell they will probably
> make it. They have taken the first step "reaching out for help."

Beyond talking, they found the information they received important.

> The lectures were helpful and the grief workshop was very good. Widowed
> people need perspective on what is happening to them.
>
> TLA came along at the right time to help me get involved in new
> friendships. It kept me connected to others. My friends had disappeared
> and every other group I went to were couples.

People who had been widowed for a time talked about the trips they were
taking with the group and the other social activities that began to fill
their time. They were "repeopling" their lives so to speak (Silverman,
1970). This was especially true for the men. Men also began to develop a
new empathic quality:

> I became much less selfish with my time for others. I became much more
> understanding of the problems of the newly widowed. It got me out with a
> lot of new friends.

A widower of several years said that men really need help admitting their
feelings. He felt the group needed to do more to get men involved early to
help them recognize and acknowledge a need in this area. The women,
however, talked about the new confidence they were developing, as well
as their growing independence, and how the group helped them achieve
this.

> It gave me "permission" to be a different person. It made me feel and
> understand that there is no written creed that says you have to be married
> to be happy.
>
> Not only did WPS occupy my time and my mind, I began to feel that I can
> do things on my own.
>
> They gave me suggestions, not rules. It became clear I was going to have to
> make a new life for myself.

They began to see alternatives for the way they saw themselves and the
way they lived their lives.

> You have to let widowed people know that there are no quick fixes, no easy
> answers, that through the hurts and upsets of a big adjustment one evolves

into something that surprises even yourself, that each of us is so loaded with gifts and untapped talents.

A widow reflected back on how the group helped her change:

The most important thing a widow must learn is to like herself and believe in herself and her own abilities. She has to learn to choose her own priorities in life. TLA taught me that.

They said never use the word "never," just do it. Tell yourself "I can do this" and it worked.

Helping Others

Reissman (1965) first noted the value of helping others as a way of helping oneself. Both widows and widowers reported new ways of being connected to others through their membership in the mutual help groups, not simply because of the help they received but because of their new opportunities for mutuality. Many of the respondents spoke of how this mutuality developed not only in their social lives but in a newfound ability to help others. One widow said:

Working with WPS has given me a purpose in life. It keeps me busy and allows me to give service to widowed persons, especially the newly bereaved. I need to be needed and I am.

For women, this experience provided them with continuity between the past and the future. They continued to have a need to be needed. The need was met in a way they had not previously considered. They had something very special to offer now:

I can understand the newly widowed because I could not forget such a lost soul feeling as I had. I am better because in turn I am helping someone else.

Then I found I had something to offer others who had lost a spouse. This was a rewarding and uplifting experience.

The men, however, talked of helping themselves by helping others as a brand new experience in their lives:

It's the secret—by helping others you help yourself. Other than my children, TLA and the work I do with it is the most important thing in my life. I feel I am really doing something worthwhile and it makes me feel a sense of real accomplishment.

When asked specifically to comment on what they got out of being a member, half of the respondents mentioned that the feeling of being needed gave them a purpose in life. Some who were now leaders in the organization had come up from the ranks after joining the organization to receive help for themselves. Others joined long after they were widowed because

I wish there had been something like this when I was newly widowed. Others can be spared a little of the pain I went through.

In the role of helper, people have a valuable and meaningful way of being connected to others and to themselves: "In helping others I help myself." This is the real meaning of mutual help—the exchange and mutuality that takes place between people as they cope with their common problems. For the widowed, this is especially important.

As a result of their widowhood, these men and women were typically deprived of the most important person in their social network. In the words of one widow:

I lost my friend, my companion. We did everything together. There's no one to listen to me the way he did.

A widower characterizes the developmental aspect of his new status:

We had 39 good years and a lot of people never have that much. One chapter of my life has closed, and a new one is ongoing.

The development comes only after dealing with difficult and painful feelings.

In the words of widows:

I am once again a whole person (half of me had died). At first I did not know what to do with me. My basic self chooses not to be miserable so I am coping and have learned to be happy again. Although I occasionally still have bad times.

You don't forget the past; after all it is still a part of you. But I am having fun planning for the future. I still have a hard time making decisions, but I am getting there.

In the words of a 75-year-old widow who has found a new direction:

I intend to wear out, not rust out.

Networks become enriched as a result of new involvements with others and with the self. Life is found to be meaningful, with joy and excitement in it; it is not without pain, but even that is manageable.

In conclusion, widowhood can be seen as a developmental stage involving profound changes in how the widowed see themselves. For women, the change seems to be toward a greater sense of their own worth, and an ability to act on their own behalf. For widowers, the change seems to be in the direction of greater relatedness to people and an enhanced ability to express their feelings. Both widows and widowers move toward a new sense of interdependence and mutuality with others. The critical lesson here is that widowed people are bringing about this change for themselves and by themselves. They are being empowered by coping with their own experience and in so doing they are empowering others who come after them. These are the elements of an ongoing chain of preventive efforts to promote competency and the capacity to manage change.

Note

1. A version of this chapter was presented at First World Congress of the International Federation of Associations for the Widowed at Royal Holloway College Egham, England, April 19, 1985.

References

Caplan, G. (1976). The family as support system. In G. Caplan & M. Killilea (Eds.), *Support systems and mutual help*. New York: Grune & Stratton.

Cobb, S. (1976). Social support as a moderator of life stress. *Psychosomatic Medicine, 38,* 300-314.

Erikson, E. H. (1956). The problem of ego identity. *Journal of the American Psychoanalytic Association, 4,* 56-121.

Gilligan, C. (1982). *In a different voice*. Cambridge: Harvard University Press.

Goffman, E. (1963). *Stigma*. Englewood Cliffs, NJ: Prentice-Hall.

Hamburg, D. A., & Adams, J. E. (1967). A perspective on coping: Seeking and utilizing information in major transitions. *Archives of General Psychiatry, 17,* 277-284.

Kaplan, A. G., & Surrey, J. L. (1984). The relational self in women: Developmental theory and public policy. In L. E. Walker (Ed.), *Women and mental health policy*. Newbury Park, CA: Sage.

Katz, A. H., & Bender, E. I. (1976). Self-help groups in western society: History and prospects. *Journal of Applied Behavioral Science, 12*, 265-282.

Kegan, R. (1982). *The evolving self.* Cambridge: Harvard University Press.

Lidz, T. (1968). *The person.* New York: Basic Books.

Marris, P. (1974). *Loss and change.* New York: Pantheon Books.

Miller, J. B. (1976). *Toward a new psychology of women.* Boston: Beacon.

Miller, J. B. (1984). *The development of women's sense of self.* Work in Progress Series. Wellesley, MA: Wellesley College, Stone Center.

Osterweis, M., Solomon, F., & Green, M. (Eds.). (1984). *Bereavement: Reactions, consequences, and care.* Washington, DC: National Academy Press.

Parkes, C. M. (1972). *Bereavement: Studies of grief in adult life.* New York: International Universities Press.

Rappaport, R. (1963). Normal crisis, family structure and mental health. *Family Process, 11*, 68-80.

Reissman, F. (1965). The helper therapy principle. *Social Work, 10*, 27-32.

Scarf, M. (1980). *Unfinished business: Pressure points in the lives of women.* New York: Doubleday.

Silverman, P. R. (1966). Services to the widowed during the period of bereavement. In *Social work in practice: Proceedings.* New York: Columbia University Press.

Silverman, P. R. (1970). The widow as caregiver in a program of preventive intervention with other widows. *Mental Hygiene, 54*, 540-547.

Silverman, P. R. (1972). Widowhood and preventive intervention. *Family Coordinator, 21*, 95-102.

Silverman, P. R. (1978). *Mutual help: A guide for mental health workers* (NIMH, DHEW Publication No. ADM 78-646). Washington, DC: Government Printing Office.

Silverman, P. R. (1980). *Mutual help: Organization and development.* Newbury Park, CA: Sage.

Silverman, P. R. (1981). *Helping women cope with grief.* Newbury Park, CA: Sage.

Silverman, P. R. (1982). Transitions and models of intervention. *Annals of the American Academy of Political and Social Science, 464*, 174-187.

Silverman, P. R. (1986). *Widow to widow.* New York: Springer.

Silverman, P. R., & Cooperband, A. (1975). Mutual help and the elderly widow. *Journal of Geriatric Psychiatry, 8*, 9-27.

Silverman, S. M., & Silverman, P. R. (1979). Parent-child communication in widowed families. *American Journal of Psychotherapy, 23*, 428-441.

Weiss, R., & Parkes, C. M. (1983). *Recovery from bereavement.* New York: Basic Books.

Winnicott, D. W. (1953). Transitional objects and transitional phenomena: A study of first not me possessions. *International Journal of Psychoanalysis, 34*, 89-97.

PART IV

Supporting Families Through Nonnormative Transitions

Each of the chapters in this section describes one or more programs that deal with difficult, nonnormative family transitions. We use the term *nonnormative* to describe these transitions not because they are extremely uncommon in a statistical sense, but because they are occurrences that are not normally anticipated in the course of family life. Certain of these occurrences can be quite painful and disruptive to ongoing family functioning. Nevertheless, even in the face of great adversity, periods of change and upheaval can also be periods of maximum growth and development for individuals and families. A number of the programs discussed in this section are based on the assumption that the situation with which the family is faced is not preventable (for example, George and Gwyther describe programs for families that are caring for memory impaired elderly, and Stein et al. review programs for families with a chronically ill child); thus they emphasize the facilitation of effective coping with the situation. Other chapters in this section are concerned with nonnormative family situations that are at least potentially preventable; thus they document efforts not only to promote effective coping but actually to prevent crises from occurring, as in efforts to prevent family violence (Swift) or divorce (Stolberg).

The first chapter in this section is by Arnold Stolberg, Associate Professor of Psychology at Virginia Commonwealth University, and reviews prevention programs for children of divorce and their families. With the rise in the divorce rate in America in recent years, it is tempting to classify divorce as a normative event. Still, divorce is not normally an expected event and when it occurs, as Stolberg points out, it may give rise to long-term psychological problems for both children and parents.

Stolberg reviews the literature on factors related to postdivorce adjustment in both children and adults, and isolates a number of factors that he considers to be the most appropriate targets for prevention strategies. He then proposes a classification scheme for primary prevention programs that is intended to serve as an aid to understanding which types of programs are most likely to be appropriate, depending on the point in the divorce process at which the family is encountered. Stolberg's critical review of prevention programs for divorcing families is organized in accordance with this scheme, and thus offers a useful summary within a developmental framework.

Carolyn Swift, Director of the Stone Center for Developmental Services and Studies at Wellesley College, provides a theoretical and practical overview of efforts intended to prevent family violence. She, like Stolberg, underlines the importance of efforts both to prevent the family crisis itself, as well as to strengthen the coping skills of persons who have been victimized by sexual and physical abuse. Swift notes that mental health professionals in the area of family violence have long inadvertently taken a "blame the victim" approach, by focusing their helping efforts solely on the abused family member. Although she believes that victim-focused efforts are helpful and necessary, she argues that responsible prevention programming must make every effort to eliminate the root causes of the problem.

To this end, Swift presents an in-depth analysis of the factors related to the development and maintenance of family violence. She also describes a broad array of prevention programs designed to address these risk factors, emphasizing the importance of targeting various levels of social systems: lawmakers, schools, community supports, and so on. Citing evidence that gender differences in socialization perpetuate the use of violence as a solution to interpersonal problems, Swift argues convincingly that, ultimately, only major social change will effectively address the problem of violence in the family.

Ruth Stein, Dorothy Jessup, and Henry Ireys of the Prevention Intervention Research Center (PIRC) for Child Health at Albert Einstein College of Medicine focus their efforts on the promotion of healthy adaptation of children with chronic illness and their families. Stein and her colleagues take a noncategorical approach to the study of these children and families. That is, they hold that factors other than the diagnosis itself will determine just how serious the problems facing families will be: for example, Is the illness life threatening?, Does it require daily routines of care?, Are there unpredictable crises?

Grounded in this approach, Stein et al. specify a number of problematic behaviors common to children with a chronic illness, which are maladaptive and should thus be targeted for reduction or elimination. Importantly, they also specify adaptive and competent responses to be promoted and strengthened in these children. More broadly, they offer three general foci for preventive efforts, with examples of prevention approaches appropriate to each: (a) efforts that focus on the service provision system; (b) efforts to increase the availability of social support; and (c) training in cognitive coping skills. Stein and her colleagues then offer a closer look at programs developed at their PIRC that are examples of efforts to incorporate each of these three foci.

Social support is a coping resource that has been viewed as important in preventing negative adjustment outcomes in relation to each of the nonnormative transitions already discussed: divorce, family violence, and chronic childhood illness. In their chapter, Linda George, Professor of Psychiatry and Sociology at Duke University, and Lisa Gwyther, Director of the Duke University Family Support Program, discuss the importance of social support for caregivers of memory-impaired older adults. George and Gwyther, together with their associates at the Family Support Program, have assisted in the organization and maintenance of 52 support groups in North Carolina, whose purpose is to provide information and mutual support to members and to foster community support for and awareness of the needs of families with memory-impaired elderly. The Family Support Program was organized in response to the needs of the many family caregivers in North Carolina who, as George and her colleagues have documented, experience more social isolation and psychological distress than a random community comparison sample. The idea that community-based support groups could be an effective intervention for these caregivers was based on research that showed that caregiver well-being is related to the level of support received from family and friends.

George and Gwyther describe the steps taken to institute a support group in a typical community, and discuss the assistance offered by the Family Support Program. In addition, they present research findings that offer encouraging documentation of the effectiveness of support groups for this population in need.

9

Prevention Programs for Divorcing Families

Arnold L. Stolberg

The rise in the divorce rate in America and the increasing evidence of psychopathological sequelae have prompted the development and evaluation of myriad prevention programs for divorcing families. Criteria on which to evaluate prevention programs will be articulated and will subsequently be applied to existing and proposed divorce adjustment programs.

Essential Elements of Prevention Programs

Three criteria have been hypothesized to be essential in the development of prevention programs of all kinds (Stolberg & Walsh, in press). (a) Program procedures must reflect the processes identified in basic research on both normal development and crisis event-related maladaptation. For example, important developmental experiences have been found to differ for many children of divorce versus those from intact marriage homes (Hetherington, 1979; Wallerstein, 1983). Program components must address these differences, perhaps by temporarily replacing significant individuals or by providing alternative opportunities to master developmental tasks. (b) rigorous evaluation programs must be conducted. A recent National Institute of Mental Health conference on prevention programming for children of divorce concluded that program evaluations must have several elements (Flynn, Hurst, & Breckinridge, in press). Treatment groups must be composed primarily of individuals who are truly at risk for displaying signs of psychopathology. Outcome measures must directly assess adjustment along relevant psychological dimensions, rather than identifying small changes on indirect measures. The strength of intervention procedures must be demonstrated perhaps through the use of both no treatment and not-at-risk controls. Follow-up periods must be of a sufficiently long duration to assess the durability of intervention effects. (c) Tested vehicles must be developed to facilitate program implementation in intended service facilities.

Psychological Adjustment and the Divorcing Family

Influences on Child Adjustment

Psychological problems common to members of divorcing families and the processes that cause them can be drawn from the existing body of research literature. Cognitive, affective, behavioral, and psychophysiological problems have been reported in many children of divorce (Coddington & Troxell, 1980; Hetherington, 1979; Kurdek, 1981). Cognitive reactions include self-blame, feeling different from peers, and heightened sensitivity to interpersonal incompatibility (Kelly & Berg, 1978; Kurdek & Siesky, 1980a, 1980b). Deficits in prosocial behavior and high frequencies of acting out and aggressive behaviors have also been found among children of divorce (Stolberg, Camplair, Currier, & Wells, in press). Their academic performance is often hampered by classroom behaviors that interfere with performance and require special handling (Guidubaldi, Perry, Cleminshaw, & McLaughlin, 1983). They are more often diagnosed as having serious illnesses than peers from intact families (Coddington & Troxell, 1980; Jacobs & Charles, 1980).

Some children of divorce have also been found to possess a combination of psychological strengths including adaptive activity skills and the ability to self-engage in productive endeavors, adaptive social skills and the ability to make friends, and the absence of internalized pathology (Stolberg et al., in press).

The results of several longitudinal investigations allow us to anticipate children's long-range reactions to their parents' divorce. Two-year (Hetherington, Cox, & Cox, 1977), five-year (Hetherington, Cox, & Cox, 1981), ten-year (Guidubaldi et al., 1983; Wallerstein, 1983), and sixteen-year (Langner, in press) follow-up studies of children allow us to conclude that observable problems exist at ten years postdivorce. Sixteen years after parental divorce, however, most young adults whose parents were divorced do not look significantly different from their intact family peers.

The psychological characteristics of children in the two- through ten-year follow-up studies are similar to those already described. Boys appear to display more acting out and impulse disorders and peer interaction problems than girls at two years postdivorce (Hetherington et al., 1977). The actual adjustment of both boys and girls is roughly equivalent at the five-year marker (Hetherington et al., 1981). Boys continue to be rejected by their peers however. Girls, who have not displayed interpersonal problems earlier in the adjustment process, do not show such peer rejection. Ten-year follow-up studies continue to show a residue of impulse control disorders and problems in the academic setting, particularly in boys. Langner's sixteen-year follow-up failed to show any enduring problems unique to the now young adult population. Counter to expectations, young adults who experienced their parents' divorce sixteen years earlier were found to be more reliable and effective employees. Perhaps the meaning of a job to the integrity of the family is more clearly conveyed to the child in one-parent/one-job families. Young adults whose parents were divorced were found to be married at frequencies equal to their intact home peers. Within the single, young adult sample, however, the divorce subgroup was found to have more difficulty in maintaining meaningful relationships.

Children's postdivorce adjustment has been found to be substantially determined by four factors (Emery, 1982; Stolberg & Anker, 1983; Stolberg & Bush, 1985; Stolberg et al., in press). Marital hostility, life changes brought about by the divorce, parenting skills of the custodian, and postdivorce adjustment of the custodian have been demonstrated to account for a majority of the variance in children's divorce-related behavior. Adaptive adjustment outcome appears to result when hostility between parents is relatively low, both before and after the divorce, and when the custodian possesses optimal single-parenting skills (Stolberg et al., in press). Psychological maladjustment appears to result when life change events are frequent in both the child's and the custodian's lives, when interparent hostility is high, and when efforts to facilitate adult adjustment interfere with child adjustment (Stolberg et al., in press).

Several processes may account for the deleterious effect of parental hostility on child adjustment. Parents who display high levels of marital hostility model poor conflict resolution skills to their children. They might also be expected to be less emotionally available to their children as their energies are invested in their experience of overwhelming anger. These parents might not be available to help their children understand the causes of the marital discord and to assist their children in mastering social development tasks facing them. Externalized pathology may be modeled after observed parent behaviors and may, further, be an attempt by the child to express his or her frustration. Internalized psychopathology may result when children attempt to generate their own intrapunitive interpretations for family problems when accurate explanations are not provided by the parents.

The prolonged deleterious effects of interparent hostility are due, in part, to the continued presence of the antagonism. Conflict between parents has been found to continue after the divorce has occurred (Hetherington et al., 1977). Parents' continued animosity may interfere with their ability to cooperate around normal child development issues and the amelioration of existing psychological problems in their children.

Higher frequencies of children's life change events have been found to correlate with lower prosocial skills and greater externalized psychopathology (Stolberg & Anker, 1983; Stolberg et al., in press). Life change events may disrupt the normal progression of social relationships and the acquisition of social skills and may place unusual demands on children. Relationships with parents may be altered and not cognitively understood by the child. Loss of a parent due to divorce and first-time or full-time job may be interpreted as rejection by the child (Kurdek, 1981). Old friendships may be prematurely terminated and new ones may be dependent on the quick acquisition of new social skills and attitudes. For example, a child might move into a social system that is more socially and sexually precocious than the former peer group. The child will have to acquire new social skills quickly if acceptance is to be possible. The loss of elements of the previous environment that were familiar and satisfying and the demand for the rapid acquisition of new skills and attitudes may be particularly frustrating for the child and may result in acting out behaviors.

Postdivorce adult adjustment has been found to predict only a modest predisposition toward effective single parenting in normal populations (Stolberg & Bush, 1985). Significantly, no direct relationship was found between mothers' and children's adjustment after parenting skills were considered. Mothers' coming to grips with their divorces and personally achieving healthy readjustments were not found to be of any value to their children unless this adjustment was reflected in improved parenting practices.

Influences on Adult Adjustment

Adults' divorce adjustment is mediated by three categories of determinants: (a) individual-cognitive factors, (b) individual-behavioral factors, and (c) environmental-familial factors (Stolberg, Kiluk, & Garrison, in press). The individual-cognitive factor comprises perceptions and expectancies of the divorce as a desirable or undesirable event (Chiriboga, Coho, Stein, & Roberts, 1979), adaptability of the individual to change (Stolberg & Anker, 1983; Stolberg et al., in press), and the individual's coping style. Behavioral skills, including job, home maintenance, and family organization skills, make up the individual-behavioral factor. The presence of a stable social support system (Goldstein, 1981; Heller & Schneider, 1978; Spanier & Casto, 1979), economic stability (Colletta, 1978), and the extent of positively and negatively evaluated environmental change (Stolberg & Anker, 1983; Stolberg et al., in press) make up the environmental-familial factor.

Adults who perceived their divorce as positive reported significant reductions in tension, depression, and physical disorders after the divorce (Hunt, 1969). In contrast, those who evaluated the marital dissolution negatively reported increased role strain and diffuse affective distress (Everly, 1978; Spanier & Casto, 1979).

Cognitive flexibility may be reflected in an adult's perception of his or her divorce. Positive evaluations of the divorce may indicate a willingness to meet new environmental and familial demands, leading to adaptive efforts to control and master problems. Successful mastery efforts result in positive feelings of self-worth and more positive emotional states. Conversely, a negative evaluation may reflect cognitive rigidity, an unwillingness to attempt to master new situations, and a consequent "learned helplessness" response pattern. The continued inability to conquer the new environmental demands successfully, which necessarily results from an unwillingness to try, leads to increasing feelings of low self-esteem, depression, and anxiety.

As in the case of children, environmental change requires adults to acquire new life skills, to experience frustration and other negative affective states when required skills are not available, and to have increased needs for social, tangible skills, and emotional and financial supports. Poor health and deteriorated parenting performance were related to accepting first-time employment and acceptance of replacement, negatively evaluated employment in divorced adults (Stolberg & Anker, 1983).

Social supports have been found to reduce the pathogenic impact of stressful life events (Frydman, 1981). Most divorcing adults seek assistance from others (Jacobson, 1979), with the more distressed individuals seeking more help from social supports (Chiriboga et al., 1979). Greater social interaction, including heterosexual dating and cohabitation, has been found to be related to fewer adjustment problems (Raschke, 1978; Spanier & Casto, 1979). Greater role strain and poorer overall divorce adjustment has been found in women who have less interaction with friends and family (Spanier & Casto, 1979).

Social supports have been described as buffers between the individual and the psychological distress caused by the demands of (life change) events (Wilcox, 1981). The buffer provided by the support system may be more specifically defined as emotional support, concrete and tangible assistance (e.g., tangible resources, physical help), and as information and instructional help that facilitates the acquisition of postseparation-environment required life skills.

Economic stability was observed to have a pervasive effect on the adjustment of divorcing families, particularly on women, and was found to mediate the experienced stress (Albrecht, 1980; Colletta, 1978; Kressel, 1980; Spanier & Casto, 1979). Families of divorce who were financially able to take vacations and to purchase new household appliances were found to have fewer incidences of significant illnesses (Stolberg & Anker, 1983). Further, financial stability has been shown to influence the functioning of children in these families.

The effect of financial stability may be similar to that of social supports. That is, it may serve to decrease the number of environmental demands that the parent faces. Services can be purchased to meet the added responsibilities that follow. Financial stability may be directly related to job security and indirectly to the increased sense of self-worth and competence that job stability brings. It may facilitate the adults' access to outlets for relaxation, which are so necessary in this time of increased responsibility and demands. The parent can enjoy dinners, evenings, outings with friends, and so on. Finally, a permanent improvement in perceptual, economic, and life circumstances through skill development can be facilitated through economic resources. The parent can seek educational and career training with which future income can be ensured.

Divorce Adjustment and Prevention Strategies

Several preliminary conclusions about the content of prevention programs for divorcing families can be drawn from the previous literature. Given that interparent hostility, life change events, parenting skills, and adjustment of custodian are the primary determinants of children's divorce adjustment, prevention strategies must attempt to shape these processes along promotional lines. Interparent hostility must be minimized and parent cooperation around child-rearing issues must be maximized. Parenting skills must be enhanced. Parents require assistance in reaching an optimal balance between their own development and that of their children. Custody arrangements must be designed that minimize environmental changes, including alterations in the relationship with the noncustodian.

Skill acquisition, influencing cognitive processes, and shaping environmental circumstances are necessary components of prevention programs for divorcing adults. Job, home maintenance, and parenting skills are needed. A sense of cognitive flexibility and active problem solving must be instilled. Efforts must be made to develop a stable and supportive environment.

Evaluating Prevention Programs for Divorcing Families

A four-stage model for crisis intervention has been proposed (Auerbach, in press), which is useful for organizing and evaluating prevention programs in general and programs for divorcing families specifically. In this model, intervention and prevention programs are grouped according to the time of their introduction relative to the onset of the crisis event. The first three intervention types are prevention-focused and will be considered. The fourth is more oriented toward the treatment of existing problems. Type 1 interventions (Distal, Prestress) are exclusively primary preventive programs and are intended for individuals who may experience a specific crisis event in their distant future. Many individuals who may reap some benefit from program implementation may never have been at risk for experiencing the crisis event. Such programs are generally educational in nature and are frequently directed at significant community agents. For example, Type 1 drug abuse prevention programs are directed at preventing drug importation and have police, Coast Guard, and drug enforcement agents as the recipients of intervention efforts.

Type 2 interventions (Proximal, Prestress) are exclusively primary prevention programs and are intended for individuals who are *very likely* to experience a specific crisis event in the near future. Such programs tend to be both educational and supportive. Program participants continue to include community agents but are also directed at significant family members and the target individual. For example, programs that attempt to facilitate children's pre- and postsurgical adjustment are designed for hospital staff, parents, and the patient.

Type 3 interventions (Proximal, Poststress) include both prevention and treatment programs. Intervention procedures are both supportive and skill building and become increasingly focused on the individual in crisis and the family. Children whose parents recently divorced, for example, might participate in school-based programs. These programs teach skills necessary to cope with divorce-related demands and also provide emotional support and events clarification. Parents may also be

232

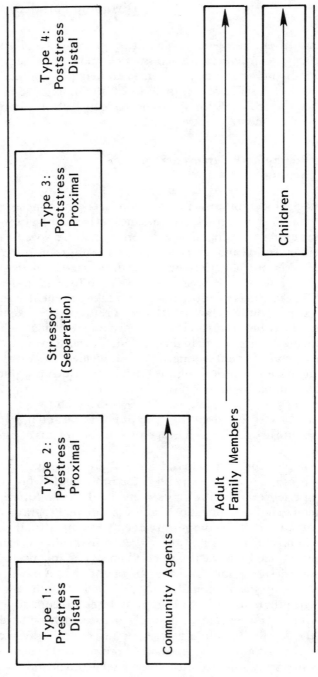

Figure 9.1 Types and Foci of Prevention Programs

included in the prevention strategy, attempting to shape their responses in important parent-child interactions.

Auerbach's four intervention types can be used to categorize preventive interventions for divorcing families. Type 1 interventions are intended for families who have even a slight potential to divorce in the future. Preventive strategies may be directed at increasing the consonance between the behavior of community decision influencers (e.g., professionals, family members, and friends) and the psychological factors shown to facilitate children's divorce adjustment (Camplair & Stolberg, 1985; Stolberg et al., in press). Preventing divorce and enhancing family functioning may also be goals of Type 1 interventions. Type 2 interventions are directed at families for whom divorce is an imminent event. Emotional support and tangible assistance in anticipating, arranging, and becoming behaviorally prepared for the soon-to-be-experienced life changes are integral components of at this stage. Families who have recently separated may benefit from Type 3 prevention programs. Emotional support and relief from external demands, as well as efforts to gain mastery over new life demands, are the primary components of these programs.

Type 1 Interventions

Type 1 interventions programs most clearly fit the criteria for primary prevention programs. Participants come from the general population and include those who may experience the crisis event and those who may not. In all cases, Type 1 programs are intended to enhance the functioning of all participants (Auerbach, in press). Distal prestress interventions for the crisis of parental divorce currently take two forms: those directed at the married couple and those directed at society at large.

Behavioral strategies for preventing marital discord. Several behaviorally oriented strategies have been developed with the goal of preventing divorce (Markman & Floyd, 1980; Nyman, 1982; VanBuren, 1983). Some of the programs are intended for all married partners, before marital conflict is present, and others are designed for couples who have not yet married. The goal of preventing marital dissolution is achieved by enhancing problem-solving and communication skills. Given that program participation occurs before maladaptive interaction patterns have been established, amelioration of existing problems is not necessary. This type of intervention strategy appears to be in its early stages of development and is available in few settings.

The potential impact of divorce prevention programs is on processes that substantially shape divorce adjustment (and the intended marital adjustment). All pathogenic processes associated with divorce are averted. Overt marital hostility is avoided as conflict resolution and problem solving-skills are learned. Participants may learn ways to cooperate around family problems. Thus adaptive conflict resolution styles are modeled for children.

The Premarital Relationship Enhancement Program (PREP, Markman & Floyd, 1980) is a well-articulated and theory-based divorce prevention program. The six group meetings of PREP are behaviorally oriented. Self-monitoring and recording of behavior prior to intervention are followed by presentation of lectures on topics pertaining to conflict resolution, communication, and problem-solving skills. While meetings are held in small groups, program focus is on the interaction of the couple with their individual consultant. Homework and feedback on videotaped interactions supplement other program components. The cognitive restructuring component of the program is broken into seven steps. The communications and skills component is broken into seven additional steps.

Results of evaluations of PREP and other programs are inconclusive (Markman & Floyd, 1980; VanBuren, 1983). The former study failed to show any group differences between intervention participants and no-treatment controls. Methodological weaknesses, including short time span between observations, potential insensitivity of assessment instruments, and the use of subjects who were not and might not marry, may have blurred the potential strength of the intervention. The subjective nature and small sample of the latter study interfere with drawing substantive conclusions. Finally, the full potential of these programs has yet to be realized because vehicles to assist in dissemination and replication of program procedures and benefits are absent.

Little public interest has been expressed for divorce prevention programs, perhaps because it is difficult to motivate people to participate in an intervention when no problem is present. The success of the movement depends upon the developers' abilities to increase its popularity, perhaps through identifying implementation sites where potential participants naturally gather (e.g., churches and synagogues). The relevance of the intervention may be increased by identifying very early markers that a problem may be developing. In addition, populations must be identified who are most receptive to, and who may benefit from, participation.

Shaping community attitudes about divorce. The couple's behavior in divorce settlements is determined by two factors: by interactions with professionals and nonprofessionals in their community (Coogler, 1978; Deredyn, 1977; Kappelman & Black, 1980) and by family interactions prior to the divorce (Lowery, 1985). Attorneys, family members, and friends are the most frequently contacted and most influential decision shapers (Camplair & Stolberg, 1985). Their recommendations, however, rarely reflect the real processes that facilitate children's divorce adjustment (Camplair & Stolberg, 1985). Attorneys, who are the most frequently consulted decision influencers, were not found to weight psychological variables in their deliberations and were retrospectively viewed by their clients as not being helpful in the divorce process. In addition, attorneys' recommendations were frequently adopted as the formal custody and divorce arrangements. Physicians, who are viewed as both helpful and powerful influencers of divorce and custody decisions, are consulted infrequently. Mental health professionals give little weight to psychological variables in their custody recommendations, appear to have little influence on decision-making processes, and are not often approached to assist in divorce planning.

The extent of coparenting prior to the separation, personal goals of the divorcing adults, and the couple's parenting beliefs have been identified as the major intrafamilial determinants of the final custody plan (Lowery, 1985). Active coparenting after the divorce occurs most often when fathers were active participants in child rearing before the divorce and when parents adhere to a belief that shared custodial relationships are important. Continued paternal involvement in child rearing is also common when women seek the divorce and do not ask for their own financial support.

Anger at the former spouse, societal norms, and the adversarial requirements of the legal system are more heavily weighted influences on custody, financial, and residential decisions than are psychological processes demonstrated to facilitate child adjustment (Camplair & Stolberg, 1985). Prior relationships appear to shape future relationships and decisions (Lowery, 1985). As a consequence, many families may be confronted with pathogenic divorce processes. Environmental change and intraparent hostility may be maximized and social supports, financial flexibility, parent availability, and coparenting arrangements may be minimized.

A prevention strategy has been proposed that is aimed at bringing the professional and personal activities of the "primary decision influencers" (e.g., attorneys, physicians, clergy, psychologists, family members, and close friends) in line with the psychological realities of divorce (Benn & Kalter, 1985; Camplair & Stolberg, 1985; Stolberg et al., in press). Educational, skill-building programs are proposed that apprise the primary decision influencer of the psychological processes that mediate child adjustment and that consider the professional and practical constraints on the influencers' behavior.

For example, a preventive role for the pediatrician and family physician is based on the finding that physicians are perceived by custodial parents as very helpful when contacted (Camplair & Stolberg, 1985). They are contacted infrequently, however. Thus enhancing the physicians' role in promoting divorce adjustment must include increasing their awareness of divorce adjustment processes, increasing their sensitivity to signs of impending divorce in their patients, and teaching them how to offer appropriate types of assistance to patients before maladaptive processes are begun (Stolberg, 1985). Such an intervention must also fit a prescriptive format in order to match the tight time constraints facing the physician.

Clergy, too, were found to be helpful when contacted. In addition, their recommendations were generally in keeping with psychological determinants of adjustment. Again, they are used only occasionally. Incorporating religious leaders into the promotive process is more likely when they are *perceived* as being less bound by religious doctrine and thus are more frequently sought by the families in conflict (Camplair, Stolberg, & Worthington, 1985).

Enhancing the role of the primary decision influencer as a strategy to prevent psychopathology in children of divorce is very clearly aimed at the primary determinants of children's postdivorce adjustment. Interactional patterns of the divorcing couple are to be established that increase cooperation and consideration of all family members' needs. Minimizing environmental change, developing coparenting skills, and maximizing the noncustodial parents' contact with the child, to name a few, are the specific goals of this strategy.

This approach is, however, only a hypothetical one and much work is necessary to make it an effective and accepted intervention. The most frequently consulted primary decision influencers have been identified and subjective, retrospective evaluations of their assistance have been conducted (Camplair & Stolberg, 1985). Little is known, however, about the practical and professional constraints that may substantially influence their recommendations. For example, we know that physicians are perceived as helpful, but are infrequently contacted. It may be that many physicians have little time to engage in mental health consultations with their clients and, therefore, do not encourage or seek out such involvement. Many divorcing couples display high levels of anger prior to seeking professional consultations about their future divorce. Is special training required to assist nonmental health professionals in dealing with the hostility that they may encounter while attempting to work with the families in nontraditional ways?

Specific programs for the most powerful decision influencers remain to be developed. Working relationships must be established with professional training programs, professional associations, and licensing boards in order to develop, pilot, evaluate, and implement appropriate interventions.

Type 2 Interventions

Type 2, or Predecision Period, interventions are aimed at families who will experience marital dissolution in the immediate future. In most cases, psychological problems are absent. Thus the programs are preventive in nature.

Needs of adults at this stage in the divorce adjustment process include emotional support, objective information, and assistance in making important divorce arrangements (Stolberg et al., in press). Resolving self-perception conflicts, family castigations, and emotional distress are assisted by a stable support system (Wilcox, 1981). Evaluating the potential for the success of the marriage and separation requires an objective perspective on current circumstances and an informed awareness of future problems. Educational and supportive programs may assist in evaluating current and future circumstances, in building support systems, and in developing future career, economic, and family goals (Stolberg et al., in press).

Children's needs are different. They must be buffered from prolonged and often harmful intraparental hostility (Emery, 1982; Stolberg et al., in press). Continued parenting and supervision are required for normal development. Once the separation has occurred, children will need contact with both parents (Stolberg & Bush, 1985).

Type 2 prevention strategies for children must include maintaining or developing the quality of the parent-child relationships. Only particularly strong parent-child relationships have been observed to mitigate the effects of marital turmoil and discord (Hetherington, Cox, & Cox, 1979). Parents must be assisted in distinguishing anger about parenting and nonparenting issues. Effective coparenting relationships must be developed. Children must be buffered from their parents' overt expressions of hostility.

Existing type 2 prevention programs are of two types: those that assist adults in reaching the decision to divorce (Fine, 1980; Gardner, 1978) and those that assist the separating adults in making concrete postseparation living arrangements (Coogler, 1978).

Predivorce Counseling. Predivorce counseling involves an attempt to help adults involved in disintegrating marriages make a final decision about the future of their marriage. While activities of this type are generally unstructured, *The Divorce Experience* (1977) is one example of a structured program for families considering divorce. Offered by the Domestic Relations staff of the Family Court of Minneapolis, the goals of this program are the development of support systems and facilitation of open, emotional expression in adult participants. The first two of three sessions are devoted to explaining the realities of the legal system and fostering expressions of loss. Adult members are helped to anticipate problems associated with divorce through presentations made by previously divorced adults. Children's adjustment to divorce is the focus of the third session. Participants are organized into small groups based on the age and developmental needs of their children.

No data exist on the effectiveness of the approach. Intervention at this point intuitively appears to be valuable. Programs in other crisis intervention areas, however, suggest treatment directions that are not reflected here. The brevity of the intervention, the relatively heavy weighting on adult decision making, and the minimal emphasis on parent-child interactions lead one to question whether these programs yield the desired outcomes. One wonders if two sessions aimed at decision making will produce results that generalize to the conflicted home. Further, interventions for children in the medical setting (Kupst, in press; Melamed & Bush, in press), sexually abused children (Swift, in press), and children of divorce (Stolberg & Garrison, 1985) are most effective at enhancing children's adjustment when primary emphasis is given to parent-child interactions and relatively little attention is given to adult adjustment and development. In summary, this strategy has potential that requires both further evaluation and greater attention to program development.

Divorce mediation. Divorce Mediation is a process in which divorcing adults voluntarily seek the assistance of an impartial and highly trained third party in order to identify, discuss, and resolve disputes that result from divorce (Coogler, 1978; Emery & Wyer, 1984; Haynes, 1978; Kelly, 1983). This increasingly popular alternative to court-litigated divorces (Fine, 1980) is distinguished from traditional court-mediated interventions in that a single professional is involved, its intent is cooperation rather than competition, and decisions are reached by the divorcing adults themselves rather than being negotiated by attorneys or decided by a judge (Emery & Wyer, 1984).

Mediation may be described as a *philosophy* for planning postdivorce arrangements. It is characterized by cooperation and concern for the future adjustment of all family members. While a wide variety of mediation strategies exist, all seem to share the common thread of being goal-focused, task-oriented, and time-limited (Emery & Wyer, 1984; Kelly, 1983). Goals generally include reaching divorce and custody (when children are in the family) settlements that are mutually beneficial and agreeable to both parties.

Intervention activities are often aimed at developing cooperative and productive coparenting relationships, establishing parent-child relationships to reflect the realities of the divorce, teaching problem-solving skills that will facilitate the cooperative and nonhostile resolution of future conflicts, and promoting the adjustment of all family members (Kelly, 1983). Mediation differs from divorce counseling in that its goal is to prepare for and not prevent the divorce. The mediator takes a very active role, educating the clients, managing conflict, assisting in the development of bargaining proposals, and producing a written divorce agreement. Objective problem solving, rather than emotional expression and improving mental health, is the focus of the intervention (Kelly, 1983).

Many criteria established here for effective divorce interventions are met through the mediation process. Most obviously, the intervention is aimed at promoting the psychological adaptation of all family members. This is accomplished through cooperative efforts to develop living arrangements and parent-child as well as adult-adult interactional patterns that minimize environmental change and marital hostility, and that maximize cooperative problem solving as well as the children's contact with both parents.

Reductions in adults' reliance on activities such as further litigation, which exacerbate hostility and competitiveness, also occur (Emery, 1985). The legal community's divorce activities may be modified. Anticipated reductions in relitigation may be followed by courts demanding cooperative, rather than adversarial, procedures. Psychological determinants of divorce adjustment will thus be given greater consideration (Emery, 1985).

Mediation has been exported to many settings beyond the original development site. The dissemination of mediation procedures requires a significantly more complex plan than many of the interventions described in this chapter, primarily because of the level of sophistication required of the mediator. Extensive training programs are offered nationally, however, to teach these complex procedures (Coogler, 1978).

A positive effect on child adjustment may be anticipated if data on interparental conflict and children's divorce adjustment can be applied to an area (Emery, 1982). Several systematic studies of the impact of mediation on children's divorce adjustment have been conducted. Two studies are currently underway that should shed more light on this question. A court-based mediation program is being evaluated in the Charlottesville, Virginia, area by Emery (1985). In a second study, a nonrandom sample of 150 self-selected mediation participants is being studied (Kelly, 1983).

Emery's project merits an in-depth review. Eighty families petitioning the court for custody or visitation hearings are randomly offered mediation or traditional litigation. Two members of the project staff, one male and one female, are assigned to work with the divorcing couple. Procedures have been articulated in an intervention manual. A series of themes are discussed in sequence. The relative weighting of each is dependent on the needs and abilities of the couple. Assessments are conducted before, after, and one year following either litigation or mediation.

Preliminary results on one-half of the total sample are encouraging (Emery, 1985). At the one-year follow-up, mediation families were found to seek relitigation less often (15%) than litigation families (25%). Further, fathers who participated in mediation reported greater satisfaction with the agreed-upon divorce arrangements. The conservative nature of divorce litigation and decisions in Virginia must be considered in the previous conclusion. Father custody and joint custody are infrequent decisions. The conclusion may be drawn that divorcing fathers in Virginia are more satisfied with the results of mediation because it helps them to achieve some of their goals, perhaps at a cost to what Virginia mothers often are awarded.

Data that investigate the effects of mediation on interadult cooperation and hostility and on child adjustment are still to be analyzed (Emery, 1985). Many important questions will certainly be answered in this well-conceived evaluation project.

Future studies that address the question, "For which divorcing adults is mediation most effective?," are needed. In contrast to the previously described community-oriented divorce intervention strategy, mediation puts a substantial demand on the divorcing couple. Many couples may not possess the prerequisite conflict resolution and problem-solving skills to enter into the process. Their feelings toward each other and their expectations about appropriate behavior during the divorce process may be developed to a point where the cooperation required for successful mediation is unlikely. Such research will allow realistic conclusions to be drawn about the potential power of mediation. It is certainly not, as many advocates and detractors argue, either the answer for all divorcing families or a process that substantially infringes on the rights of some family members (Emery, 1985).

Type 3 Interventions

Children whose parents have recently separated may benefit from Type 3 preventive interventions (Stolberg & Garrison, 1985; Stolberg et al., in press). The emotional state of the now-separated adult dictates their content. Parents are less physically and emotionally available to children, yet their presence is required for children to master developmental tasks successfully (Wallerstein, 1983). Interventions that attempt to enhance the deteriorated parental role and that help the child with the divorce-related stressors are required (Stolberg & Cullen, 1983). Further, the child needs assistance in meeting normal developmental tasks (Stolberg & Cullen, 1983). Teaching single-parenting skills, clarifying the child's role in the divorce, identifying and developing sources of stability and consistency in the child's life, and promoting the development of the child's impulse control skills are important components.

The priority of and perceived viability of prevention programs for families of divorce are demonstrated by the financial support provided recently by the National Institute of Mental Health. Preliminary results of these efforts are encouraging. Improved self-concept (Stolberg & Garrison, 1985), reductions in behavior problems and anxiety (Warren et al., in press), and improved social skills (Stolberg & Garrison, 1985) have been reported for child participants. Improved adult adjustment and greater control over environmental events have been observed in adult participants (Stolberg & Garrison, 1985).

Several strategies have been used to promote the adjustment of children of marital disruption. Interventions have been designed with children as the recipients of the intervention (Brogan & Maiden, 1984; Kalter, 1982; Pedro-Carroll & Cowen, in press; Soehner, 1982; Stolberg & Garrison, 1985), parents/adults as participants (Lemmon & Farrell, 1983; Taylor, Green & Frager, in press; Stolberg & Garrison, 1985; Warren et al., in press), and, in rare cases, parents and their children participating together (Warren et al., in press). Several of these projects are conducted in settings in which the intended participants naturally gather: the schools and divorce courts (Brogan & Maiden, 1984; Pedro-Carroll & Cowen, in press; Stolberg & Garrison, 1985; Warren et al., in press). A representative sample of these programs will be reviewed in this section.

School-based, child-directed programs. The Divorce Adjustment Project: Children's Support Group (CSG) (Stolberg & Garrison, 1985) and the Children of Divorce Intervention Project (CODIP) (Pedro-Carroll & Cowen, in press) are two school-based programs. These two interventions are similar, with the latter project being based on the first and reflecting improvements in program procedures.

The constructive modification of children's responses to the important determinants of child adjustment were of primary consideration when designing these projects. While chronic marital hostility that has already taken place cannot be undone, the child's understanding of such interactions can be modified. Similarly, environmental changes cannot be reversed. The child's perception of these events can, however, be modified and behavioral skills needed to meet the new circumstances can be taught.

Changes in immediate living conditions and family relationships are brought about by divorce. Intervention components were designed to assist children in adaptively responding to such events. Lost support systems must be replaced. Altered living circumstances, and reduced parental availability and financial resources, may result in increased feelings of anger and frustration in children. Communication skills, relaxation skills (Koeppen, 1974), and anger control skills (Novaco, 1975) may help the child to better cope with such feelings. Helping children to understand these confusing events should also serve to reduce their anger, frustration, and self-blame.

Normal developmental processes are interrupted by divorce (Wallerstein, 1983). Thus alternative systems must be developed to help children of divorce establish their identities and build internal control skills. Teaching problem-solving skills may assist in this process (Finch & Kendall, 1979).

The CSG (Stolberg, Cullen, Garrison, & Brophy, 1981) is a twelve-session psychoeducational program designed to help seven- to thirteen-year-old children meet the behavioral and affective demands associated with parental divorce. Each one-hour session is divided into two sections. The first part involves discussion of a specific topic (e.g., Whose fault is it? What do I do on vacations? Do I worry about my dad? I wish my parents would get back together.). The second part focuses on the teaching, modeling, and rehearsing of specific cognitive-behavioral skills, such as problem-solving skills (Finch & Kendall, 1979), anger control skills (Novaco, 1975), communication skills, and relaxation skills (Koeppen, 1974). The groups begin by practicing basic, concrete applications (e.g., problem-solving skills applied to mathematics problems), and end with more complex skills, based on earlier ones, now applied to complex family problems (e.g., communication, anger, and relaxation skills applied to solving the problem of what to say when your father doesn't make his Saturday date).

Procedural revisions introduced in CODIP primarily reflect an increased emphasis on emotional support and diminished attention to rehearsing concrete applications of cognitive-behavioral skills (Pedro-

Carroll & Cowen, in press). These changes are most apparent in the first three sessions. In addition, game playing is the primary vehicle used to teach skills.

The CSG and CODIP programs share an additional characteristic. Detailed manuals specifying all group activities (Pedro-Carroll, 1984; Stolberg et al., 1981) have been developed to facilitate the implementation of the prevention programs in target schools as well as to serve as vehicles to disseminate program procedures to school systems outside of the districts in which they were developed.

School-based interventions, as represented by the CSG and CODIP, meet many of the criteria for effective program design established in this chapter. Most important, evaluation data substantiate claims of immediate and long-term effectiveness of these programs. Participants in the CSG, as compared to no-treatment control children, displayed significant improvements in self-concept at the end of intervention that were maintained at the five-month follow-up. Also, significant increases in adaptive social skills were identified at the follow-up (Stolberg & Garrison, 1985). Significant reductions in problem behaviors (e.g., acting out) and increases in competencies (e.g., effective learning and interpersonal functioning, adaptive assertiveness, appropriate school behavior, coping with failure and social pressures) occurred in children who participated in CODIP, compared to those who did not (Pedro-Carroll & Cowen, 1984; Pedro-Carroll, Cowen, Hightower, & Guare, 1985). Adjustment gains in program children were judged to have taken place by teachers, parents, group leaders, and by the children, themselves. Program participants who were initially assessed to be less well adjusted than their intact home peers prior to intervention were found to be similar following treatment (Pedro-Carroll et al., 1985).

Both programs were firmly founded on the research literature as a source of direction for the program design. Program effectiveness may be attributed to the goodness of fit between the needs of children during parental divorce and the procedures utilized.

Both manuals stand as useful program implementation tools for other service settings. The documents also allow for refinement of the intervention designs, as in the case of the Pedro-Carroll and Cowen refinement of the CSG procedure, with a clear linkage of procedural changes and outcome improvements.

Future evaluation projects must attend to several important questions. First, procedures are needed that ensure the generalization to the home, school, and playground of skills learned and applied in the groups. One such strategy involves parents and teachers as supplemental intervention agents and as group participants. They would be called in at specific times to be instructed in ways to assist the children in applying the skills they have learned and in ways to promote discussion of divorce topics. Workbooks that include exercises for parents that coincide with child tasks might also facilitate skill utilization and topic discussion.

The strength of the prevention programs remains to be demonstrated. Pedro-Carroll and her colleagues have made a significant contribution in identifying the comparability of children of divorce after group participation to the target group of normal, intact family peers (Pedro-Carroll et al., 1985). The durability of these gains remains to be shown. The longest follow-up period studied is five months (Stolberg & Garrison, 1985). A three-year follow-up of the Children's Support Groups is in process (Stolberg, Updegrove, & Camplair, 1985). The long-term psychological effects of program participation on transition through the normal developmental event of puberty is being assessed. Subjects include participants in the original CSG (Stolberg & Garrison, 1985), no-treatment controls for the same project, and a matched group of intact home peers collected during the predata phase of the first evaluation study (Stolberg, Updegrove, & Camplair, 1985).

Community-based programs for single parents. Adults have been targeted as participants in programs intended to promote their own adjustment and that of their children. These interventions have operated under two assumptions: adults who have adjusted to their own divorce are good parents, and children's divorce adjustment is enhanced when parent-child interactions are improved (Stolberg & Garrison, 1985; Taylor et al., in press; Warren et al., in press). The procedures used in parent-directed strategies reflect these assumptions. Enhancing adult adjustment is the goal of some programs (Lemmon & Farrell, 1983; Stolberg & Garrison, 1985; Warren et al., in press) and enhancing single parenting and parent-child communication are the goals of others (Taylor et al., in press; Warren et al., in press). Components of the Parenting After Divorce Project (PAD, Warren et al., in press) and the Divorce Adjustment Project: Single Parents Support Group (SPSG, Stolberg & Garrison, 1985) will be considered as representative of adult-directed strategies.

Two different intervention models have been developed by Warren and her colleagues (in press). The Parent Education component of the PAD project is a structured, five-week, psychoeducational and support group for sets of five-seven single parents. A structured outline is used to direct participants in the discussion of topics relating to the effects of divorce on children, specific parenting skills (i.e., active listening, limit setting, and negotiation), and strategies to promote cooperative co-parenting. The Family Education program includes parents and their children as participants. Single parents and their children met together with two leaders for six sessions. A seventh session is offered for the noncustodial parent, alone. The education and support focus is operationalized by viewing a film on divorce, playing structured games to enhance communication, and discussing family group activities. Thus the PAD project components emphasize single parenting. One involves the discussion of skills; the other reflects the active rehearsal and shaping of optimal parent-child interaction patterns. Subjects were referred from the local courthouse rolls. Recently divorced parents and their children were invited to participate.

The PAD Project meets some of the criteria established for optimal program design. First, its intervention elements attend to a dimension of primary concern in children's postdivorce adjustment, altered parent-child interactions. Second, it is sufficiently structured to allow for dissemination. Last, it has been subjected to rigorous, objective evaluation.

Comparisons of Parent Education group, Family Education group, and self-study control group participants demonstrated that participation in both interventions positively influenced children's overall adjustment, with participation in the Family Education program having the greatest positive effect (Warren et al., in press). A composite, overall adjustment score was derived for each parent-child pair based on parent- and child-reported changes in the child's anxiety, self-concept, social maturity, and school affiliation; feelings about divorce, and behavioral adjustment; and in parenting style, adult anxiety, and depression; and behavioral ratings of family functioning. Thus the conclusion can be drawn that efforts to shape parent-child interactions directly can positively influence children's postdivorce adjustment. Further, the greater the opportunity for monitored application of the skills and interaction patterns, the more positive will be the effect.

The SPSG (Stolberg & Garrison, 1985) provides an important contrast to the procedures and results described by Warren and her associates. The Single Parents' Support Groups (Garrison, Stolberg, Mallonee, Carpenter, & Antrim, 1982) is a twelve-week support and skill-building program for divorced, custodial mothers. Group procedures were intended to focus equally on the development of participants both as individuals and as parents. Participants selected the topics for SPSGs based on a list of 20 options provided by group leaders (e.g., "The Social Me," "The Working Me," "The Sexual Me," "Controlling My Feelings," "Communicating with My Child," "Disciplining My

Child," and "Communicating with My Former Spouse About Child-Rearing Matters"). Procedures associated with each topic were described in a program procedures manual (Garrison et al., 1982).

Mothers in the SPSG were found to display better overall social and emotional divorce adjustment than subjects in child-only interventions and no-treatment controls (Stolberg & Garrison, 1985). They also reported fewer objective life changes and evaluated those changes that occurred as more positive than subjects in the comparison groups. In spite of these improvements, single-parenting skills and the adjustment of their children were not affected.

A more detailed review of topics discussed suggests that most sessions emphasized the development of the adult to the exclusion of parenting issues. Assessment indicated that parenting skills were not altered after intervention. Thus the concurrent consideration of the Warren et al. (in press) and Stolberg and Garrison (1985) data lead to the conclusion that parenting skills and parent-child interactions must be modified if child adjustment is to be enhanced. Facilitating adult adjustment does not automatically affect parenting effectiveness or child adjustment.

These data are consistent with others on divorce and other family crisis events. Path analysis of processes influencing children's post-divorce adjustment clearly indicates that the relationship between adult adjustment and parenting skills is not statistically significant (Stolberg & Bush, 1985). Hospital-based programs for families with a child with leukemia and for children receiving outpatient medical care are most effective when parenting behaviors and parent-child communication patterns are the direct focus of intervention (Kupst, in press; Melamed & Bush, in press).

More research is needed both on parent development and on adult adjustment promotion programs. A strategy for divorced parents must be articulated and evaluated that both assists adults in their own development and promotes effective parenting and child adjustment. We do know that career enhancement facilitates the adult's growth and the economic integrity of the family. In extreme samples, adult adjustment may interfere with effective parenting.

Within parenting skill development groups, exact procedures must be articulated that will promote the desired skill acquisition. Is it best to include children in groups? Is it more effective to allow participants to determine the content of the meetings or should a structured format be followed? Can the noncustodial parent be included? It can be concluded that parent and adult enhancement groups are at an earlier stage of development than those offered for children.

In summary, our review of Type 3 preventive programs suggests two successful directions for intervention; those aimed at the child and operated in the schools and those offered for parents. The latter programs have only been demonstrated to be effective at facilitating child adjustment when attention is directly focused on developing optimal parent-child interactions.

Summary

Three criteria were used to evaluate prevention programs for divorcing families. They were (a) the demonstration of a clear linkage between intervention strategies and more basic research on divorce adjustment, (b) the objective demonstration of program effectiveness, and (c) the availability of a vehicle for program procedure dissemination.

The review of existing prevention programs is very encouraging. A wide array of effective programs exist or are being developed. Some are aimed at preventing the occurrence of psychopathogenic processes and attempt to intervene with significant community resources. Others attempt to promote adaptive responses to the stressful divorce processes. Intervention components are directed at the family members and attempt to teach skills that will help the individuals to master new, divorce-related demands. It is also encouraging that many disciplines, including law (Wexler, 1985) and medicine (Deredyn, 1977), are seeking solutions to divorce problems that are substantially different from those that have traditionally be implemented.

Prevention programs implemented very early in the divorce adjustment process show the greatest promise. Particularly noteworthy are mediation, school-based prevention programs for children, and interventions specifically designed to promote parenting skill competence. The demonstrated success of these three programs may result from attention paid to processes that *directly* influence child adjustment (i.e., parenting skills, environmental change, and marital hostility).

Future program development and evaluation efforts must answer several questions. For example, "Do the benefits yielded from program participation last?" While follow-up data on program outcomes are available, they are generally of no more than five months' duration. Longer follow-up periods are mandatory to demonstrate program effectiveness truly. "Who most and least benefits from available intervention strategies?" Families who can most benefit from existing programs must be identified; new programs for those who do not must be developed. For example, divorcing families with few job and social skills may find that the current array of programs do not meet their needs. Dual professional career, economically stable families may reap maximum benefit from program participation at all levels.

Several untested, primary prevention strategies merit further attention. Relationship enhancement programs for recently married couples may both promote healthy marriages and prevent future divorces. Efforts to integrate psychological considerations into the activities of divorce and custody decision influencers may minimize the intensity of such factors as marital hostility, environmental change, poor parenting skills, and poor coparenting relationships. Practical operationalizations of these strategies merit development and evaluation.

Finally, dissemination programs must be designed and evaluated that will facilitate the implementation of effective interventions in applied settings. While the model programs cited in this chapter have some training programs, none has been tested and few consider such factors as variations in skill levels of service providers and populations served.

References

Albrecht, S. L. (1980). Reactions and adjustments to divorce: Differences in the experiences of males and females. *Family Relations, 1,* 59-68.
Auerbach, S. M. (in press). Stressful life events, psychological crises and crisis intervention: An empirical perspective. In S. M. Auerbach & A. L. Stolberg (Eds.), *Issues in clinical and community psychology: Crisis intervention with children and families.* Washington, DC: Hemisphere.
Benn, R. & Kalter, N. (1985). Personal communication.
Brogan, J., & Maiden, U. (1984). *Who gets me for Christmas: A course on separation, divorce and remarriage.* (Available from Strang Middle School, 2701 Crompond Rd., Yorktown Heights, New York 10598)
Camplair, C., & Stolberg, A. L. (1985). *The role of the primary decision influencer in custody determination.* Manuscript submitted for publication.
Camplair, C., Stolberg, A. L., & Worthington, E. (1985). *The role of family, friends, clergy and other professionals in decisions about child custody after divorce.* Manuscript submitted for publication.
Chiriboga, D. A., Coho, A., Stein, J. A., & Roberts, J. (1979). Divorce, stress and social supports: A study in help-seeking behavior. *Journal of Divorce, 2,* 121-135.
Coddington, R. D., & Troxell, J. R. (1980). The effect of emotional factors on football injury rates: A pilot study. *Journal of Human Stress, 14,* 3-5.
Colletta, N. D. (1978). Divorced mothers at two income levels: Stress, support and childrearing. *Dissertation Abstracts International, 38,* 6114B.
Coogler, O. J. (1978). *Structured mediation in divorce settlement: A handbook for marital mediations.* Lexington, MA: Lexington Books.
Deredyn, A. P. (1977). Children in divorce: Interventions in the phase of separation. *Pediatrics, 60,* 20-27.
The divorce experience. (1977). Unpublished manuscript, Minneapolis, Family Court, Domestic Relations Department.
Emery, R. E. (1982). Interpersonal conflict and the children of discord and divorce. *Psychological Bulletin, 92,* 310-330.

Emery, R. E. (1985, April). Personal communication.

Emery, R. E., & Wyer, M. M. (1984). *Mediated disputes related to divorce*. Unpublished manuscript, University of Virginia, Charlottesville, Virginia.

Everly, K. G. (1978). Leisure networks and role strain: A study of divorced women with custody. *Dissertation Abstracts International, 6,* 3865A.

Finch, A. J., & Kendall, P. S. (1979). Impulsive behaviors: From research to treatment. In A. J. Finch & P. S. Kendall (Eds.), *Clinical treatment and research in child psychopathology.* New York: Spectrum.

Fine, S. (1980). Children in divorce, custody and access situations: The contribution of the mental health professional. *Journal of Child Psychology and Psychiatry, 21,* 353-361.

Flynn, E. J., Hurst, E. F., & Breckinridge, E. (Eds.). (in press). *Impact of divorce on children.* Bethesda: National Institute of Mental Health.

Frydman, J. I. (1981). Social supports, life events and psychiatric symptoms: A study of direct, conditional and interaction effects. *Social Psychiatry, 16,* 69-78.

Gardner, R. A. (1978). *Psychotherapy with children of divorce.* New York: Jason Aronson.

Garrison, K. M., Stolberg, A. L., Mallonee, D., Carpenter, J., & Antrim, Z. (1982). *The Single Parents' Support Group: A procedures manual.* Unpublished manual, Virginia Commonwealth University, Richmond, VA, Department of Psychology, Divorce Adjustment Project.

Goldstein, M. (1981). Major factors acting on the early adolescent. In C. D. Moore (Ed.), *Adolescence and stress.* Bethesda: National Institute of Mental Health.

Guidubaldi, J., Perry, J. D., Cleminshaw, H. K., & McLaughlin, C. S. (1983). The legacy of parental divorce: A nationwide study of family status and selected mediating variables on children's academic and social competencies. *School Psychology Review, 12,* 300-323.

Haynes, J. M. (1978). Divorce mediator: A new role. *Social Work, 23,* 5-9.

Heller, D. B., & Schneider, C. D. (1978). Interpersonal methods for coping with stress: Helping families of dying children. *Omega, 8,* 319-331.

Hetherington, E. M. (1979). Divorce: A child's perspective. *American Psychologist, 34,* 861-858.

Hetherington, E. M., Cox, M., & Cox, R. (1977). The aftermath of divorce. In J. H. Stevens, Jr., & M. Matthews (Eds.), *Mother-child, father-child relations.* Washington, DC: NAEYC.

Hetherington, E. M., Cox, M., & Cox, R. (1979). Family interactions and the social, emotional and cognitive development of children following divorce. In V. Vaughan & T. Brazelton (Eds.), *The family setting priorities.* New York: Science and Medicine.

Hetherington, E. M., Cox, M., & Cox, R. (1981). Effects of divorce on parents and children. In M. Lamb (Ed.), *Nontraditional families.* Hillsdale, NJ: Lawrence Erlbaum.

Hunt, M. (1969). *The world of the formerly married.* New York: Free Press.

Jacobs, T. J., & Charles, E. (1980). Life events and the occurrence of cancer in children. *Psychosomatic Medicine, 1,* 11-24.

Jacobson, D. (1979). The impact of marital separation/divorce on children: III. Parent-child communication and child adjustment, and regression analysis of findings from overall study. *Journal of Divorce, 2,* 175-194.

Kalter, N. (1982, April 17). Personal communication.

Kappelman, M. M., & Black, J. (1980). Children and divorce: The Pediatrician's responsibility. *Pediatric Annals, 9,* 342-351.

Kelly, J. (1983). *Mediation and psychotherapy: Distinguishing the differences.* (Available from Center for Family in Transition, Corte Madera, CA)

Kelly, R., & Berg, S. (1978). Measuring children's relations to divorce. *Journal of Clinical Psychology, 34*, 215-221.

Koeppen, A. S. (1974). Relaxation training for children. *Elementary School Guidance Counseling, 9*, 14-21.

Kressel, K. (1980). Patterns of coping in divorce and some implications for clinical practice. *Family Relations, 2*, 234-240.

Kupst, M. J. (in press). Coping in siblings of children with serious illness. In S. M. Auerbach & A. L. Stolberg (Eds.), *Issues in clinical and community psychology: Crisis intervention with children and families*. Washington, DC: Hemisphere.

Kurdek, L. A. (1981). An integrative perspective on children's divorce adjustment. *American Psychologist, 35*, 856-866.

Kurdek, L. A., & Siesky, A. E. (1980a). Children's perceptions of their parents' divorce. *Journal of Divorce, 3*, 339-378.

Kurdek, L. A., & Siesky, A. E. (1980b). The effects of divorce on children: The relationship between parent and child perspectives. *Journal of Divorce, 4*, 85-99.

Langner, T. S. (in press). Longterm effects of divorce on children. In E. J. Flynn, E. F. Hurst, & E. Breckinridge (Eds.), *Impact of divorce on children*. Bethesda: National Institute of Mental Health.

Lemmon, G., & Farrell, A. D. (1983). *Behavioral rehearsal of partner attention: Social skill remediation of loneliness among the separated and divorced*. Unpublished manuscript, Virginia Commonwealth University, Richmond, VA.

Lowery, C. R. (1985, March). *Traditional and non-traditional custody: Differences in the decision process*. Paper presented at the meeting of the Southeast Psychological Association Conference, Atlanta.

Markman, H. J., & Floyd, F. (1980). Possibilities for the prevention of marital discord: A behavioral perspective. *American Journal of Family Therapy, 8*, 29-48.

Melamed, B. G., & Bush, J. P. (in press). Maternal-child influences during medical procedures. In S. M. Auerbach & A. L. Stolberg (Eds.), *Issues in clinical and community psychology: Crisis intervention with children and families*. Washington, DC: Hemisphere.

Novaco, R. W. (1975). *Anger control: The development and evaluation of an experimental treatment*. Lexington, MA: Lexington Books.

Nyman, J. A. (1982). Divorce: An area for planning of prevention work. *Nordisk Psykologi, 34*, 142-147.

Pedro-Carroll, J.A.L. (1984). *Children of Divorce Intervention Program procedures manual*. (Available from Department of Psychology, University of Rochester, Rochester, NY 14627)

Pedro-Carroll, J.A.L., & Cowen, E. L. (in press). The Divorce Intervention Project: An investigation of the efficacy of a school-based prevention program. *Journal of Consulting and Clinical Psychology*.

Pedro-Carroll, J.A.L., Cowen, E. L., Hightower, A. D., & Guare, J. C. (1985). *Preventive intervention with latency-aged children of divorce*. Manuscript submitted for publication.

Raschke, H. (1978). *The development of a post-separation/post-divorce problems and stress scale*. Paper presented at the National Council of Family Relations Conference, Philadelphia.

Soehner, G. (1982). *The Single Parent Family Project*. (Available from Western Monroe Mental Health Center, Rochester, NY 14626)

Spanier, G., & Casto, R. (1979). Adjustment to separation and divorce: An analysis of fifty case studies. *Journal of Divorce, 2*, 241-253.

Stolberg, A. L. (1985). *The role of the pediatrician in children's divorce adjustment*. Manuscript submitted for publication.

Stolberg, A. L., & Anker, J. M. (1983). Cognitive and behavioral changes in children resulting from parental divorce and consequent environmental changes. *Journal of Divorce, 7*, 23-41.

Stolberg, A. L., & Bush, J. P. (1985). A path analysis of factors predicting children's divorce adjustment. *Journal of Clinical Child Psychology, 14*, 49-54.

Stolberg, A. L., Camplair, C., Currier, K., & Wells, M. (in press). Individual, familial and environmental determinants of children's postdivorce adjustment and maladjustment. *Journal of Divorce.*

Stolberg, A. L., & Cullen, P. M. (1983). Preventive interventions for families of divorce: The Divorce Adjustment Project. In L. Kurdek (Ed.), *New directions in child development: Children and divorce.* San Francisco: Jossey-Bass.

Stolberg, A. L., Cullen, P. M., Garrison, K. M., & Brophy, C. J. (1981). *The Children's Support Group: A procedures manual.* Unpublished manual, Virginia Commonwealth University, Richmond, VA, Department of Psychology, Divorce Adjustment Project.

Stolberg, A. L., & Garrison, K. M. (1985). Evaluating a primary prevention program for children of divorce: The Divorce Adjustment Project. *American Journal of Community Psychology, 13*, 111-124.

Stolberg, A. L., Kiluk, D., & Garrison, K. M. (1986). A temporal model of divorce adjustment with implications for primary prevention. In S. M. Auerbach & A. L. Stolberg (Eds.), *Issues in clinical and community psychology: Crisis intervention with children and families.* Washington, DC: Hemisphere.

Stolberg, A. L., Updegrove, A., & Camplair, C. (1985). *Longterm effects of a prevention program for children of divorce.* Unpublished manuscript, Virginia Commonwealth University, Richmond, VA, Department of Psychology.

Stolberg, A. L., & Walsh, P. (in press). A review of treatment methods for children of divorce. In S. Wolchik & P. Karoly (Eds.), *Advances in child behavior therapy— children and divorce: Perspective and adjustment.* Lexington, MA: Lexington Books.

Swift, C. F. (in press). Community interventions in sexual child abuse. In S. M. Auerbach & A. L. Stolberg (Eds.), *Issues in clinical and community psychology: Crisis intervention with children and families.* Washington, DC: Hemisphere.

Taylor, J. B., Green, A., & Frager, C. (in press). Divorce related pathology: A study in preventive intervention. In E. J. Flynn, E. F. Hurst, & E. Breckinridge (Eds.), *Impact of divorce on children.* Bethesda: National Institute of Mental Health.

VanBuren, D. J. (1983, March). *A behavioral approach for preventing marital discord.* Paper presented at the Southeast Psychological Association Annual Conference, Atlanta.

Wallerstein, J. S. (1983). Children of divorce: The psychological tasks of the child. *American Journal of Orthopsychiatry, 53*, 230-243.

Warren, N. J., Grew, R. S., Ilgen, E. R., Konanc, J. T., VanBourgondien, M. E., & Amara, I. A. (in press). Parenting after divorce: Preventive programs for divorcing families. In E. J. Flynn, E. F. Hurst, & E. Breckinridge (Eds.), *Impact of divorce on children.* Bethesda: National Institute of Mental Health.

Wexler, J. G. (1985). Rethinking the modification of child custody decrees. *Yale Law Journal, 94*, 757-820.

Wilcox, B. L. (1981). Social support, life stress and psychological adjustment: A test of the buffering hypothesis. *American Journal of Community Psychology, 4*, 371-386

10

Stopping the Violence: Prevention Strategies for Families[1]

Carolyn F. Swift

Family violence and prevention, as fields of study in the social sciences, have developed along parallel tracks. Both look at practices that are centuries old. But neither can claim a knowledge base of more than a decade or so. In both fields, initial theories have been simplistic. Today, both benefit from a systems approach. The most powerful prevention programs take place at the macrocosmic level, where interventions are designed to change societal institutions and practices. It is at this level that the issues of inequitable distribution of power and resources are most effectively addressed. Individual human service workers and their agencies, however, have limited resources to devote to systems change. In addition, the realities of their funding bases and community supports rarely permit them to commit resources to institutional change. For these reasons, much of the preventive work of social service agencies and their staffs is with the individuals and families they serve. In support of their work, this chapter focuses attention on efforts to prevent family violence at the micro-cosmic level. The chapter begins by tracing the commonalities shared by the fields of family violence and prevention. A generic model for preventing dysfunctional behavior is then presented. Current beliefs about the causes of family violence are reviewed, and specific programs are discussed as applications of the prevention model.

The idea of prevention is not new. It is embedded in folklore: "A stitch in time saves nine." It is reflected in the wisdom of the sage: "An ounce of prevention is worth a pound of cure." Family violence is not new either. Biblical references, ancient myths, and fairy tales describe violence between husband and wife, parents and children, and siblings. Folk tales are compelling because they embody the collective experience of the human condition. Wicked stepmothers, jealous husbands, and cruel and heartless fathers know no country nor tongue. As characters they crop up

252

in the folk tales of countries around the globe. Their actions speak to the fragility of human relationships, and the need to find ways of ensuring personal health and safety within intimate family bonds.

Theories have only recently begun to emerge to explain the causes of family violence. The serious study of this subject is less than 25 years old, dating from Henry Kempe's identification of the battered child syndrome (Kempe, Silverman, Steele, Droegemueler, & Silver, 1962). As Gelles (1980) points out, there were no articles on family violence in the *Journal of Marriage and the Family* during its first 30 years of publication, nor did the journal review the subject in its decade review of family research and action in the 1960s. One of the consequences of the emergent state of scholarship on family violence is the simplicity of initial attempts to explain it. Early investigators tended to identify a single event or condition as the "cause." They then located this "cause" in the individual—either the abuser or the victim—as a defect in personality or adjustment. Both child abuse and spouse abuse were initially explained as a function of the personalities of the participants (Keller & Erne, 1983; Newberger & Newberger, 1982).

Current etiologies of family violence reflect a systems approach. A variety of integrative models have been suggested. Each assumes that abuse is multidetermined. The imbalance of power between the sexes and sex-role stereotypes are seen as major determinants of abuse, particularly spouse abuse (Breines & Gordon, 1983; Dobash & Dobash, 1979; Straus, 1980b). For both child abuse and spouse abuse, the critical variables include environmental stressors such as life change events, social isolation, poverty and cultural norms; and variables associated with individual family members that may increase the risk of family violence, such as anger proneness and nonnormative status (Gelles, 1973; Justice & Justice, 1976; Keller & Erne, 1983; Young, 1976). More recently, sociopsychological models have looked at repetitive patterns of abuse across generations. In the case of spouse abuse, repetitive cycles of abuse and conciliation within abusing relationships are also thought to perpetuate the abuse (Hilberman, 1980; Walker, 1984).

The field of prevention, as a behavioral science, has undergone a similar process of theoretical development. Preventive health strategies are part of our everyday lives. Most of us know, for example, that exercise, good nutrition, weight control, and stress reduction can prevent the development of some physical and mental illnesses. Prevention, however, has become a bona fide field of study only within the last decade. Scholarly journals and texts devoted to prevention have been in existence for less than five years.

The classic prevention model comes from the field of public health, where the condition to be prevented is physical illness. This classic model casts health outcomes in dichotomous terms: they result from the interactions of (a) persons with (b) their environments. In public health language, disease is caused by the impact of environmental stress on a host population. Given this simple formula, the solution to preventing disease is straightforward. Preventionists intervene to change either the environment, the host population, or both. Environmental interventions are usually aimed at eliminating the noxious stressor or reducing its intensity. Host-focused interventions concentrate on strengthening the defenses of the host population to resist the impact of stress.

Examples illustrate these two classic prevention strategies. Confronted with the problem of preventing malaria, public health officials chose the first option: eliminating the noxious stressor. They destroyed the breeding ground of malaria-carrying mosquitoes by spraying the swamps that served as the insects' habitat. The second strategy, strengthening the host population, is seen in the conquest of polio. Instead of ridding the environment of the noxious stressor—the polio virus—health authorities found it more practical to strengthen the defenses of the host population, primarily children, through inoculation. Both of these examples, each using a different method, achieved the same result. The negative health outcome—disease—was prevented.

Note that the choice between the two prevention strategies in these examples is ethically value-free. Whether to target the stressor or host is a practical issue. The selection is determined by questions, for example, Which strategy is more accessible? Which is less costly? Which is more effective? It is ethically irrelevant, and probably only of interest to cost accountants, whether the stressor is eliminated or the host population strengthened. Either way, the prevention mission is accomplished. Ecologists are not alarmed at the prospect of mosquito-less swamps, and ethicists are not concerned that children are forced into a defensive posture vis-à-vis the polio virus. In the case of physical disease, potential victims are generally at liberty to pursue victim-free status by the most expeditious means available, whether this be by eliminating the stressor or strengthening the host.

The public health prevention model has its major application in preventing the impact of nonhuman stressors on human hosts. It achieves an awkward fit when applied to situations in which both stressor and host are human beings. The discovery that the behavior of other human beings is a source of environmental stress has enormous significance for prevention theory (Cassel, 1974). Once social behavior is seen as a source of psychosocial stress, the dichotomous simplicity of the classic prevention model breaks down.

Family violence is a case in point. If the behavior of one human being or group causes the physical or mental victimization of another human being or group, then prevention strategists are confronted with a dilemma. Their choice of either of the two classic strategies has ethical—and perhaps ecological—implications. Stressor-focused interventions become more complicated, because battering husbands and abusing mothers cannot be targeted for eradication in the same way that mosquitoes or viruses can. Adding humans to the list of environmental stressors complicates prevention analysis because human stressors are, in reality, "double agents." They function both as *sources* of stress for others and as *targets* of stress themselves, from both human and nonhuman sources.

The dilemma is not avoided by choosing the second classic strategy. Strengthening the host population in family violence situations means teaching wives and children at risk for abuse how to negotiate, fight, escape, or mobilize law enforcement or other institutional alternatives. The ethical problem here is that this is a blame-the-victim approach. The responsibility is placed on the potential victim to avoid being criminally attacked by a family member. Table 10.1 traces the consequences of applying the stressor-host dichotomy in the context of battering and sexual assault within the family.

The solution to the preventionists' dilemma goes beyond the classic simplicity of the public health model. Effective prevention programs must incorporate the complexity of the multiple forces that determine behavior.

Prevention Model

George Albee (1981) has developed an equation that incorporates a systems approach to the prevention of mental and emotional illness. The equation has broad applicability for projecting prevention programs across a variety of behavioral and social problems, including family violence. It provides a useful conceptual schema for organizing the major factors associated with health and behavior, and for suggesting ways in which these factors interact to produce health and behavioral outcomes.[2] The formula can be applied to either the stressor or the host, individually; to the family as a system; or to an entire population at risk.

Adapted here for family violence, the equation draws together critical variables and outlines their general relationship to each other:

$$\text{Incidence of Dysfunction} = \frac{\text{Stress} + \text{Risk Factors}}{\text{Social Supports} \times \text{Coping Skills} \times \text{Self-esteem}}$$

TABLE 10.1

Classic Prevention Strategies:

Implications for Battering and Sexual Abuse Within the Family

Applying classic prevention strategies to battering, incest and marital rape leads to radically different interventions, depending on whether the stressor or the host is targeted for prevention efforts. The paradigmatic prevention model involves five steps (adpated from Klein & Goldston, 1977):

1. Identify a behavior or health status judged to be dysfunctional.
2. Document the incidence of the dysfunction in the general population.
3. Identify a population at risk—one in which the incidence of the dysfunction exceeds that for the general population.
4. Intervene with the risk population so as to arrest or stop the development of the dysfunction prior to the occurrence of negative outcomes.
5. Assess the effectiveness of the intervention.

Application to Battering, Incest, and Marital Rape

Stressor	*Host Population*
Step 1	
1. The *acts* of battering, incest, and marital rape are dysfunctional behaviors.	1. The *trauma* of victimization from battering, incest, and marital rape can result in short-term or long-term dysfunction.
Step 2	
2. Incidence of *acts* (est): Battering: 25%-50% of family couples Incest: 2%-12% of children Marital Rape: 10%-14% of couples Perpetrators of these acts are predominately male.	2. Incidence of *trauma* resulting from victimization: unknown. Victims of these acts are predominately female.
Step 3	
3. Males are a population at risk for the development of battering, marital rape, and incestuous behavior.	3. Females are a population at risk for battering, marital rape, and incest.
Step 4	
4. Intervene with males to prevent the development of battering, marital rape, and incestuous behavior.	4. Intervene with females to prevent battering, marital rape, and incest, and/or the trauma resulting from these acts.
Step 5	
5. Assess the effectiveness of the intervention.	

A glance at the equation immediately suggests two prevention strategies: either the value of the numerator must be decreased, or the value of the denominator increased. Note that the top line of the equation contains the factors in the environment and in the person that contribute to the dysfunctional outcome, while the bottom line contains the factors that operate to prevent the unwanted outcome. Because human service workers generally have little control over the life stresses to which their clients are exposed, their efforts are usually focused on "bottom line" activities; that is, increasing the social supports, coping skills, and self-esteem of the people they serve.

A critical issue in designing interventions to prevent family violence is the selection of the disorder—the specific health or behavioral outcome—to be prevented. Is the goal to reduce the incidence of new victims each year, or to reduce the incidence of new abusers? The first goal is directed at preventing victimization, the second, at preventing the development of abusive behavior. As demonstrated in Table 10.1, the choice of outcome determines which populations are identified as at risk, and whether stressor or host-focused strategies are used. Until the very recent past, the victim (host) has the been the major focus for prevention efforts. Societal institutions have traditionally sanctioned, in custom and law, the abuse of wife by husband and child by parent. Increasingly, the professional community has begun to focus on the abusive behavior itself (the stressor) as the appropriate target for prevention efforts. Because the state of the prevention art is imperfect, stressor-focused interventions cannot be guaranteed to eliminate all violence from the home. Therefore, it is appropriate to develop host-focused interventions as well, to protect the safety of potential victims. The assumption here, then, is that both strategies are needed.

Stress is used in the equation to refer to (a) the life change events associated with family violence, such as unemployment, pregnancy, and the onset of parenting, and (b) chronic systemic stressors such as poverty and sexist cultural norms. Risk factors refer to constitutional character-istics of the person or population targeted for prevention efforts. Persons are considered to be at risk if they are members of a group in which the incidence of a specified disorder is above the base rate for that disorder in a population (Vance, 1977). In the case of family violence, sex, age, and nonnormative parental or child status are risk factors. Males are at risk for developing abusive behavior toward other family members. Females and children are at risk for victimization by family violence.

Social supports refer to social networks and resources such as immediate family members, relatives, friends, neighbors, and coworkers. Professionals such as physicians, clergy, counselors, and other human service workers augment natural supportive networks. Coping skills refer both to broad levels of competence as well as to specific skills

258 Carolyn F. Swift

related to the behavior targeted. For example, parenting skills and those involved in negotiating and defusing anger are linked to outcome in situations of family conflict. Self-esteem carries the same meaning here as in the general psychological literature: in general, it refers to the image or assessment of personal resources and capacities.

Programs to Prevent Family Violence

Projecting strategies to prevent family violence, using Albee's formula, involves two basic tasks. The first task is to identify the specific stresses and risks associated with family violence and develop interventions to eliminate or reduce these in targeted families. The second task is to identify the characteristics of supportive networks, the specific coping skills, and the level of self-esteem—or combinations of these factors—associated with healthy family functioning, and develop interventions to increase these in targeted families. In practice, many prevention programs incorporate elements of both tasks.

Reducing Stress

Stress is a major contributor to family violence. Sources of stress include both life change events, such as unemployment and the onset of parenting, and chronic or systemic conditions, such as social isolation, low socioeconomic status, and certain cultural norms. This section reviews the relationship between these sources of stress and family violence, and suggests prevention programs consistent with the prevention model presented.

Unemployment. Marital violence has been found to increase directly with the increase of stressful events experienced by families (Straus, Gelles, & Steinmetz, 1980). A single stressful event does not usually cause breakdown. It is the piling up of stressful events over a short period of time that is damaging. Suddenly losing a job is a major shock. In our country in the last few years, unemployment has affected as many people as the death of a loved one, major illness, and divorce (Buss, Redburn, & Waldron, 1983). The devastating impact of involuntary layoff or termination results from the many changes it brings. Loss of income directly affects the family's capacity to provide for basic human needs such as shelter, food, clothing, and transportation. For many males, unemployment also threatens the ability to fulfill the perceived male role of breadwinner. Anxiety, depression, loss of self-esteem, and alcoholism are commonly found in unemployed males (Buss et al., 1983). Increased levels of both spouse abuse and child abuse have also been found in families in which the male is unemployed (Gil, 1970; Prescott & Letko, 1977; Straus et al., 1980). Inability to provide for his family's needs, together with his reduced social status and the frustrations of constant exposure to the round-the-clock pressures of parenting are believed to contribute to abusive behavior.

The more direct and effective interventions to prevent violence resulting from unemployment are those that eliminate this stressor by returning these men to the work force. While local and federal governmental agencies are assigned this task, a variety of other institutions and human service organizations have entered the field in the last few years. Community job fairs match employers with job seekers, and create an arena in which unemployed peers can exchange information and tips in their search. In some of the communities hardest hit by unemployment, loosely organized barter groups have formed, generally within neighborhoods (Schelkun, 1981). Typically, members of these groups exchange services such as child care, house and car repair, or items such as home-baked or canned goods and used clothing. In one community, a drop-in center located in a union hall served a coordination, education, and referral function (Buss et al., 1983).

These community activities—especially barter groups—serve several preventive functions. They fill the time of the unemployed family member in productive pursuits, they provide for some of the basic needs of the affected families, they maintain the dignity of family members by valuing reciprocal contributions, and they focus the time and energies of family members on events outside the family itself, thus providing a respite from the unaccustomed, constant family presence resulting from sudden unemployment. Widespread integrated social networks in place in communities such as Youngstown, Ohio, provide ready self-help groups in times of crisis: "These networks may assist in fulfilling the financial needs of workers, may provide therapy for problems and may be instrumental in locating and obtaining jobs" (Buss et al., 1983, p. 88).

The Employment Transition Program (ETP) of the University of Michigan's Industrial Development Division is a model prevention program for the unemployed (Hess, 1983). This five-day training program attempts to provide unemployed participants with the skills to control their own careers. The goal is reentry into the labor force. To this end, the classic preventive strategies of stress reduction and skill building are used. By analyzing economic and labor market information, participants come to an understanding of the societal forces underlying their unemployment. This education is designed to reduce their self-blaming behavior and help restore their self-esteem. It also provides them with information needed to consider options for redirecting their careers. The practical skills of job searching, résumé writing, and interviewing are also taught. This program combines the three "bottom line" prevention resources. It provides the added social support of a group of unemployed peers along with expert program staff. It increases the specific coping skills needed to obtain jobs and it aims at restoring self-esteem by reducing self-blaming behavior. A profile of average ETP participants shows them to be middle-aged (49 years), with limited education (11 years), and substantial seniority in previous jobs (19 years). Other unique features of the program include a manual to train trainers, and an experimental design spanning four years, which allows for follow-up of the participants' subsequent attempts to reenter the work force.

Onset of parenting. The onset of parenting marks one of life's major transitions. It signals passage to a generative stage of life. It also brings substantial changes in the economic and social life of the family. Pregnancy is associated with increased levels of spouse abuse (Eisenberg & Micklow, 1977; Gelles, 1975). If the pregnancy is unplanned and unwanted, the baby is at high risk for child abuse.

The most practical prevention strategies to reduce unwanted pregnancies are sex education and birth control. Less than 10% of the children in this country, however, receive any kind of sex education (Dunwoody, 1982b). The continuing opposition of many segments of our society to these prevention strategies means that pregnant women and children will continue to suffer from family violence.

The onset of parenting demands resources and skills that many adults do not have. Alpert, Richardson, and Fodaski (1983) have developed a scale to assess the stresses associated with becoming a parent. Of 21 events, the most stressful was the major illness of a child. The second most stressful event was frequent conflicting demands for time by the spouse and the child. Also ranked as highly stressful were decisions about which one of the parents was responsible for child care tasks, the conflicting demands between the needs of the self and the child, and loss of sleep in the months following childbirth.

Preventive interventions to reduce the stress of pregnancy and of the onset of parenting include prenatal classes, early intervention programs (see below), and parent education. While these programs all involve the strategy of building supportive networks—through classes or home visits—the major prevention strategy employed is an increase in parents' skills in coping with the responsibilities of parenthood.

Comprehensive prevention programs for expectant families include three components. The first two are classic examples of teaching coping skills through anticipatory guidance, a process in which persons about to experience a stressful situation rehearse the anticipated sequence of events and plan coping strategies to meet the crisis (Bloom, 1971). These skills prepare parents for the experiences of birth and child care. First, the prospective parents are recruited for classes covering the stages of pregnancy and the birth experience itself; classes on natural childbirth are among the most popular. Second, child development and parenting skills are taught. Skills such as feeding and bathing the baby are often included in the prenatal curriculum, because capturing the parents' time after the baby is born is difficult.

The third component deals with the practices and procedures of the hospitals' maternity unit. Under optimum conditions, the mother participates actively; this means with little or no anesthesia, and with the option to view the delivery (e.g., through overhead mirrors), hold the baby immediately after birth, and breast-feed if she wishes. It is important to include the father in the birth process as well. This accomplishes two preventive aims: it provides for mutual support between the parents, and it ensures the father's participation in the bonding process. The family should be encouraged to spend time alone with the baby within the first few hours of birth. There should be rooming-in arrangements that include the mother's option to assume major care of the infant as well as extended visiting privileges for the father. Ideally, the hospital or related agency maintains a schedule of follow-up visits for the family in order to answer questions about child care and to put the family in touch with community resources. Gray (1982) describes three current models of perinatal positive parenting programs: The Institute for Family and Child Study at Michigan State University, Vanderbilt University School of Medicine, and the Rural Family Support Project in Indiana.

Parent education takes many forms, ranging from formal curricula in secondary schools and college-level courses in child development, to short courses offered by mental health centers or other community agencies, to brief pamphlets distributed by mail, such as the classic Pierre the Pelican Series. Parenting classes are generally targeted to mothers or couples. In increasing recognition of the importance of the father's role in parenting, some 100 U.S. firms are providing parent education programs at the work site (Klinman & Kohl, 1984). Two models of parent education programs are described here. One is a grass-roots program (USEP), and one (PET) was developed by a professional.

United Services for Effective Parenting (USEP) is an organization of over 170 parenting programs in Ohio (Badger & Burns, 1982). USEP began in 1974 as an advocacy organization for birth-to-three programs and the families they serve. Almost 16,000 children under age three and their families are served annually in the state. A third of the staff members are volunteers, and most of these volunteers are parents. Program activities include short courses on Infant Enrichment Through Mother Training, newsletters, surveys, resource and referral directories, and annual conferences. USEP has developed an effective model for organizing parents and professionals into a delivery system for parent education and early intervention services.

Thomas Gordon (1983) believes that it is not the earliest years, but the ten years following infancy that are most critical for parenting. He believes that parents go through a behavioral shift—from responder to controller—in experiencing their child's transition from infancy to childhood. He argues that the conventional role of parent as disciplinarian assumes a hierarchy of power in the family, and a system of rewards and punishments that leads to inevitable parent-child conflicts. To prevent such conflicts and their potential for abuse, Gordon teaches a simple model of parenting that shares many components with accepted prevention strategies. First, he teaches parents that the child's behavior is motivated to meet physical and psychological needs, not to annoy or challenge parents. By emphasizing communication skills, he helps parents accept responsibility for their own reactions, while teaching children the consequences of their behavior.

A basic part of Gordon's course is his concept that both parent and child can interact to fulfill the needs of each: his "No-Lose," "Win-Win" method. PET eliminates punishment of children. It is designed to raise their self-esteem, and advocates for their involvement in family problem solving. The model is one of participatory democracy. Over half a million parents in the United States and 15 foreign countries have been exposed to PET. Gordon (1977) cites ten research studies documenting changes in parents resulting from their exposure to the course. Changes mentioned include significant increases in (a) parents' confidence and self-esteem in their role; (b) mutual acceptance, understanding and trust between parent and child; and (c) democratic parental attitudes toward the family as a unit. Significant decreases were found in authoritarian attitudes and behavior on the part of parents. Changes cited in the children of PET graduates include higher self-esteem and improved school performance.

Social isolation. Other major sources of stress for families, in addition to life change events, are chronic deficits in social or material resources. It is generally believed that socially isolated families—those with minimal ties to relatives, neighbors and the surrounding community-show higher rates of both spouse abuse and child abuse than less isolated families (Gelles, 1974; Gil, 1970). There is a greater likelihood of child abuse in families without telephones (Gaines, Sandgrund, Green, & Power, 1978; Newberger, Reed, Daniel, Hyde, & Kotelchuck, 1977). Preventive interventions for socially isolated families include early intervention programs and supportive group experiences. In general, close ties with relatives, friends and neighbors supply a continuing stream of support to family members. Supportive behaviors include listening to problems, giving advice and material supplies, providing favors such as childcare, and seeking these same behaviors in return. This reciprocal aspect of the relationship makes social network support different from, and thus superior to, professional therapeutic services (Mitchell & Trickett, 1980). Providing support to others validates an individual's skills as a problem solver and value as a significant other. The positive consequences of reciprocity in personal relationships are reported in many studies (Cohen & Sokolovsky, 1978; Mitchell & Trickett, 1980; Tolsdorf, 1976), and form the basis of Riessman's Helper Therapy (Riessman, 1965).

Early intervention programs offer a variety of supports for isolated families with children (Bond & Joffe, 1982; Heber, Garber, Harrington, Hoffman, & Falender, 1972; Moss, Hess, & Swift, 1982). Programs are usually targeted to pregnant women and mothers of newborn babies who are considered to be at risk for the development of a range of negative outcomes, including child abuse, retardation, developmental delay and school behavior problems. Most programs use parapro- fessional staff as the primary service deliverers. These parent aides make regular—usually weekly—home visits to targeted families, from the time of the mother's pregnancy through the infant's first year. Visits generally continue, with reduced frequency, until the child enters school. Parent aides are trained to listen to the mother's concerns and assist her in problem solving regarding the family's physical and psychological needs. In addition, they demonstrate parenting skills and specific infant stimulation techniques. The aides are trained to link families to the community's resource and referral networks.

The Optimum Growth project (South County Mental Health Center, 1980), a model early intervention program, won the National Mental Health Association's first Lela Rowland Prevention Award. This is one of the few relatively low-cost preventive programs for families that demonstrate empirical evidence of a reduction in family violence. An evaluation during the third year of the program showed that mothers receiving home visits improved significantly when compared to control group mothers in caring for their children's physical needs and interacting with them. "Less than one percent of test group mothers had been reported for child abuse and neglect as compared with 7.7 percent of comparison group mothers" (1980, p. 7).

Early intervention programs provide one-on-one support for isolated mothers through the use of parent aides. Another way to build the mother's social supports is by expanding her social networks. This has been done by linking her to a variety of peer groups. Mutual support groups are a relatively recent, but extremely important, source of social resources for parents. In an age of increasingly transient and mobile families, many parents find themselves uprooted from home communities—faced with raising children in unfamiliar neighborhoods, separated from their customary resources of relatives and friends. The trauma of divorce adds to the alienation of many of today's parents. Parents Without Partners, by creating social networks for divorced and widowed partners, serves as a resource for members' needs for recreation and childcare, as well as social supports. Compassionate Friends provides support for parents who have lost a child through death (Videka-Sherman, 1982). Parents United is directed to families in which incest has occurred (Giarretto, 1981). Parents Anonymous (PA) is a self-help group for abusing people (Comstock, 1982). The preventive value of the latter two groups is twofold. First, they actively help members to stop abusing their children. Second, their educational outreach programs inform the general public about the problem of child abuse, thus possibly influencing high risk families to seek help prior to the occurrence of abuse. These various self-help groups have chapters nationwide.

Local communities have developed a variety of other supportive groups to reduce the isolation of families in their midst. One of the most promising and creative is the Children's Aid Society of Metropolitan Toronto (Breton, Welbourn, & Watters, 1981). While this group pioneered its model with abuse-prone mothers, its methods are appropriate for use with nonabusing, socially isolated and other high risk mothers as well. Agency staff began with the assumption that abusive mothers are unable to nurture their children because they have not received adequate nurturing themselves. Program strategy was also influenced by findings of a general lack of verbal communication coupled with a reliance on physical contact as a means of control in abuse-prone families (Elmer, 1967). In an attempt to remediate the mothers' supposed early failure experiences, a group model was developed that included socially sanctioned touching and nonthreatening conversation. Since hairdressing combines both of these behaviors, a hairdresser was added to project staff and this activity became the focus of the group. The model is reported to be successful in helping the mothers achieve a series of positive outcomes, e.g., gaining social skills, finding employment, accepting parent aides in their homes, sending children to nursery schools and separating from abusive partners.

Social isolation is also a major issue in elder care. In a recent survey of persons caring for an elderly family member, the average age of the elderly was 82 (Steinmetz, 1982). The caretakers did not report being burdened by performing personal or household services for the elder. But major conflict arose around social activities. Elders were often cut off by death or major illness from significant family members or friends of long standing, and were not interested in developing new social contacts. This insistence on fulfilling all their social needs within the family places immense strain on caretakers. Programs that take elders out of the home for part of the day, such as Senior Citizens' Centers, Golden Age Groups, or those that provide respite care in the home appear most promising in their potential to prevent abuse.

Gender issues have often been overlooked in the literature on family violence. The mother has been delegated the role of primary parent, and the father relegated to the background in terms of child care responsibilities. Sexist biases assume that mothers have an exclusive role in bonding at birth (Arney, 1980), and that a mother's care and supervision continue to be primary through childhood and adolescence. Increasingly in recent years, scientists and practitioners have begun to examine the role of the father, and to restructure that role as a more active, influential one (Baruch & Barnett, 1983, 1984; Pleck, 1984).

The workplace is beginning to recognize the importance of supporting fathers' roles. A fourth of this nation's large firms grant fathers one or more days of paid leave at the time of childbirth (Kamerman, Kahn, & Kingston, 1983). Other innovative benefits related to fathering that are occurring with increasing frequency include part-time work schedules and days off for childcare (Putnam, 1984). It is in the context of new recognition of the importance of fathering that we consider the role of social networks for men, and their potential for preventing family violence.

Straus (1980a) found that men who did not belong to any organizations-such as clubs, business or professional groups, unions or lodges— assaulted their wives at a much higher rate than men who were actively involved in many organizations. The same study showed that men who rarely attended religious services also had a higher rate of spouse abuse than men who attended weekly. These results confirm the supportive effects of social networks. However, these networks can also have negative effects. When the norms of the network support the abusing behavior, then close network ties can maintain rather than reduce family violence: "The assumption that the kin network will be opposed to violence is not necessarily correct. For example, a number of women indicated that when they left their husbands because of a violent attack, their mothers responded with urgings for the wife to deal with the situation by being a better housekeeper, by being a better sex partner, or just by avoiding him, etc. In some cases, the advice was 'You have to put up with it for the sake of the kids—that's what I did'" (Straus, 1980a, p. 246.).

Low socioeconomic status. Early investigators believed that family violence was classless. While it is true that such violence occurs across all socioeconomic classes, it is now clear that it occurs most often in the lower socioeconomic class (Gelles, 1980; Straus et al., 1980). This finding makes sense, since poverty is a source of severe, chronic stress. Most of the preventive approaches described—family planning programs, those focusing on unemployment, early intervention, parent education, building social networks—are useful in working with families across the socioeconomic spectrum, including poor families. A pattern that emerges clearly in working with poor battered women or those whose husbands abuse their children is that many stay in the abusing situation out of economic necessity. Women with higher educations and those who have jobs outside the home—particularly paying jobs—tend not to put up with the abuse (Okun, 1983; Semmelman, 1982; Walker, 1984). It follows that interventions supporting the employment of both husband and wife have preventive potential. The unemployed husband, as noted above, is at risk for developing abusing behavior, and the unemployed wife is without resources or options to escape if abuse develops. For these reasons, the strategy of supporting education or training for either or both marital partners may be effective in preventing family violence.

Cultural norms. Certain cultural norms are a source of systemic stress in families. Two norms that have been linked to family violence are the power imbalance between female and male heads of house, and the use of physical force to discipline or control family members. Both sexes are burdened by discriminatory traditions and practices that dictate the "appropriate" role of each in family life and in the world outside the family. In each case, role restrictions and prescriptions set up situations which increase the likelihood of abuse. Sex role socialization sets up a power imbalance within families, with the male in the dominant role and the female in a subordinate role. This imbalance leads to abuse of power as expressed in economic, social and, in the case of family violence, physical ways.

There is one feature that cuts across all forms of family violence: the misuse of power. The bigger, the stronger and those with the most access to valued resources impose their will on the smaller, the weaker and those with less access to resources. As Finkelhor (1983) puts it, "the most common patterns in family abuse are not merely for the more powerful to abuse the less powerful but for the most powerful to abuse the least. . . . Abuse tends to gravitate to the relationship of *greatest power differential*" (p. 18). The highest incidence of physical child abuse is directed against the most powerless—those under six—and is committed by the most powerful parent: the father (Finkelhor, 1983). Television and movies glamorize violent acts, mirroring the norm that assigns the victim role to women and the aggressor role to men (Greenberg, 1982).

Our culture also has a long tradition of physical discipline and punishment of children. Such punishment has been shown to lead to a variety of negative outcomes: low self-esteem (Coopersmith, 1967), aggression and violence toward siblings (Straus et al., 1980) and delinquency and criminality (McCord & McCord, 1958). In the extreme, physical punishment perpetuates the cycle of abuse that erupts in succeeding generations of families. Parent education courses that teach alternatives to physical punishment are effective preventive interventions for individual families (Gordon, 1977).

What sorts of prevention programs exist to help individual families combat the norms that feed family violence? Programs that support more equal roles for both sexes within the family as well as in the world of work, programs that support the role of fathers in nurturing and caring for their children, and parent education courses that reinforce these responsibilities and job sharing for couples, all contribute to equalizing parental responsibilities between mother and father. The more time fathers spend with their children and in the routine execution of childcare and household tasks, the greater their self-esteem and sense of competence as fathers (Baruch & Barnett, 1983). Programs supporting women's options for careers outside the home, those promoting equal pay for equal work, and programs devoted to eliminating sex discrimination in the workplace should ultimately contribute to equalizing the power balance and reducing the likelihood of abuse between marital partners. Widely available, high quality daycare should be within the means of every family, so that both working and nonworking parents can have respite when needed from the intense, continuous task of child care (Levine, 1984).

Reducing Risk Status for Family Violence

Sex and age. The major risk factor associated with family violence is subordinate status in the family structure. Males are at risk for becoming abusers,[3] and women and children are at risk for becoming victims. Interventions at the macrocosmic level are needed to change the cultural norms and practices that maintain these differential risks through sex-role conditioning. Those working with individual families may find it useful to attempt to reduce the risk status of particular family members through skill-building techniques (see below) and promotion of egalitarian roles for the female and male heads of house.

A major barrier to the development of programs to prevent family violence is the invisibility of women's experience. This invisibility is effectively enforced by patriarchal custom and practice. In the context of family violence, there are three significant areas in which women's experiences differ from those of men: ethics, epistemology, and the use of power. There is evidence that males and females resolve moral problems differently, process information differently, and use power differently.

Carol Gilligan (1982) outlines two major approaches to the resolution of ethical dilemmas. It is clear that both males and females have access to both approaches. It is also clear that in Western patriarchal culture, males tend to use one approach predominantly, while females tend to use both. The first approach sees ethical problems as occasions for the creation or enforcement of rules. These rules spell out the rights of those involved. Rules and rights are seen as necessary both to define the outer limits of and to ensure the exercise of autonomy. Autonomy in this view is a highly desired state or goal, the end of a process that begins the *separation* from the mother in childhood. An ethic that emphasizes rights and rules, and is grounded in autonomy as the organizing principle, is the predominant one in Western patriarchal culture.

Another approach to the resolution of ethical problems sees these problems in the context of the relationships in which they are embedded. In this approach, there is an attempt to identify and assign the responsibilities of those involved in a way that maintains caring and connectedness. In our culture, the ethic of responsibility, caring, and connectedness is most likely to be implemented by women. Gilligan traces the origins of the two ethics to the different relationships the two sexes have with the mother from birth. For my purposes, it is only important to note that men, when faced with an ethical dilemma, are more likely to resolve it by asserting their rights, invoking rules, and, more often than not, preserving their autonomy. Women, on the other hand, are likely to consider the impact of various solutions on the relationship involved and to opt for assigning responsibility in such a way as to preserve these connections, in as caring a way as possible. Women tend to value relationships more highly than autonomy, with the opposite being true for men. This difference is extremely important for an understanding of the topic of family violence, because it means that women will be more devoted to preserving the relationship with the partner even through the stress of violence.

Another area of difference between the sexes that has implications for family violence is epistemology. Feminist scholars (Belenky, Clinchy, Goldberger, & Tarule, in press; Clinchy & Zimmerman, 1985) have identified two approaches to knowing. The first approach, based on Perry's (1970, 1981) work, emphasizes a method of thinking that uses objective criteria to analyze new information. The analysis compares the information with what is already known, notes differences, and tests it against established standards. Clinchy and Zimmerman (1985) call this type of knowing "separate" in reference to the autonomous nature of the self in making comparisons and seeing differences. The second approach to knowing involves not separating the self from what is to be known, but entering into the new frame of reference in order to understand it. It is this second type of knowing, called "connected" knowing, that leads to the experience of empathy. Clinchy and Zimmerman give the example of students studying a poem. Those using the method of "separate" knowing "ask themselves: 'What standards are being used to evaluate my analysis of this poem? What techniques can I use to analyze it?' The orientation is toward impersonal rules and procedures" (p. 3). Those using the method of "connected" knowing ask, "What is this poet trying to say to me?" (p. 3). The orientation here is to place oneself in the poem to understand the author's meaning.

It is the thesis of these scholars that connected knowing is more often found in women, although both separate and connected knowing are used by both sexes. The significance of this difference in understanding situations of family violence is that the woman is more likely to feel and to relate to the pain of the other (i.e., the male partner). This capacity for feeling the other's pain may contribute to the woman's lesser readiness to initiate or return violence, a position that places her at a disadvantage in protecting herself against her partner's violence.

The third area of difference related to the experience of women versus men has to do with power. The discussion here is based on the work of Jean Baker Miller (1976, 1982). Issues of power, like those of morality and knowing, are viewed differently by the sexes. Males tend to define power in terms of the capacity to effect their will, with or without the consent of those involved. Domination is a key concept in the male definition and exercise of power. Miller's definition—and one that more accurately represents women's experience of exercising power—is that power is the capacity to effect change, to move something from point A to point B.

In our patriarchal society, women have not been viewed as needing to exercise power. In fact, women do exercise power. They are more likely than men, however, to do this in the service of others. One primary way women "empower" others is by promoting the growth and development of children, in psychological, social, and intellectual spheres. Another way is by promoting their mate's growth and development. Women have traditionally provided psychological and material support to further their husbands' goals, autonomy, and success in the world outside the home.

For women to use their power to effect change—to move something from point A to point B—*in their own self-interest* threatens patriarchal values, and may invoke frightening images in the women themselves.

Miller (1982) identifies three fears women associate with the exercise of power in their own self-interest: fear of being selfish, fear of being destructive, and fear of being abandoned by those they care about. Enhancing one's own power in our culture is often connected with reducing the power of another. Women fear that to act in their own self-interest risks the possibility of putting down others; such action is seen as selfish. To act in one's own self-interest, when one is a member of a subordinate group, is often to act in ways inimical to the interests of the dominant group; such actions may in fact alter or even destroy the arrangements perpetuated by the dominant group:

> Women have lived as subordinates and, as subordinates, have been led by the culture to believe that their own self-determined action is wrong and evil. Many women have incorporated deeply the inner notion that such action must be destructive. . . . In most institutions it is still true that if women do act from their own perceptions and motivations, directly and honestly, they indeed may be disrupting a context which has not been built out of women's experience. Thus, one is confronted with feeling like one must do something very powerful that also feels destructive. (Miller, 1982, p. 4)

The fear of being abandoned is related to the other two fears. If women do act in their own self-interest, and if these actions disrupt existing relationships, then women may suffer attack or abandonment as a consequence. Miller (1982) points out, "All of us exist only as we need others for that existence" (p. 4). Men tend to deny this; women have incorporated this in an extreme form. "Along with it we women have incorporated the troubling notion that, as much as we need others, we also have powers and the motivations to use those powers, but if we use them, we will destroy the relationships we need for our existence" (Miller, 1982, p. 4).

Women, then, are at an immense psychological as well as physical disadvantage in resolving conflicts in marital situations. First, they place the highest priority on preserving the relationship, on staying connected, when disputes arise. Second, their capacity to "know" the other in connected, empathic ways, rather than in the critical, objective ways characterized by "separate" knowing, makes them more likely to feel the pain of the other, even in the midst of their own pain. And third, in abuse situations, women are double-bound in attempting to use their power in their own interest. If they leave to avoid being battered, they risk destroying their primary relationship, and their psychological and economic security. If they act to preserve the primary relationship and their psychological and economic security, they put themselves at risk for physical destruction. Women in battering situations are forced to choose which parts of themselves they will save: their physical safety and well-being, or their psychological and economic safety and well-being. Is it surprising that many women find this a difficult choice to make?

Prevention approaches to family violence must (a) take into account the differences between the sexes in the three areas of moral judgments, empathy, and the use of power, (b) educate family members to their relative risks, and (c) develop skills to cope with gender differences in the priorities assigned to maintaining the relationship.

Nonnormative status. Nonnormative status also appears to increase the risk of abuse. There is evidence that stepchildren suffer higher rates of abuse (Daly & Wilson, 1980; Hunter et al., 1978), particularly sexual abuse (Finkelhor & Hotaling, 1984; Swift, in press). Premarital counseling for parents contemplating second marriages would provide anticipatory guidance and coping skills for problems commonly found in stepfamilies (Anderson, Larson, & Morgan, 1981). Educational interventions in elementary school that teach children escape and avoidance behavior (Cooper, Lutter, & Phelps, 1983) would be particularly helpful for stepchildren in that it would provide them with protective skills without singling them out as a high-risk population. Premature or low-birth-weight children are also at higher risk for abuse (Parke & Collmer, 1975). Children perceived to be "different" by their parents, as well as handicapped, developmentally delayed, or retarded children, appear to be at higher risk than other children as well (Gelles, 1980; Gil, 1970). Early intervention programs, mutual support groups for parents, respite care, and provision of specific training in the skills needed to care for such children are all sound preventive measures.

Status incompatibilities. The cultural norms that identify the husband as the head of house are challenged when the wife has a high educational or occupational status. Status inconsistencies and incompatibilities have been found to be risk factors associated with abuse in couples

(Hornung, McCullough, & Sugimoto, 1981; Walker, 1984). The highest risk, including life-threatening violence, is associated with asymmetric status pairs, such as a wife whose occupational status is high relative to her husband's, or a husband who is an occupational underachiever. One approach to preventing violence in asymmetric status pairs is to educate the husband to understand that his wife's career achievements do not reduce his own. Utilization of resources such as counseling or male support groups might reduce the husband's feelings of personal threat. In extreme cases, separation or divorce might be necessary to avoid violence.

Intergenerational cycle of abuse. Another risk factor is exposure to abuse in childhood. Family violence cycles through generations, repeating patterns of abuse in succeeding cohorts of victims. The repetitive cycle seems to be associated both with childhood victimization and with exposure to the victimization of other family members. Many studies report that parents who abuse their children are more likely to have suffered abuse as children than other parents (Conger, Burgess, & Barrett, 1979; Gelles, 1980; Hunter & Kilstrom, 1979; Hunter et al., 1978; Lystad, 1975; Melnick & Hurley, 1969; Schneider, Hoffmeister, & Helfer, 1976). Men who batter their wives or female partners are over three times as likely to have grown up in a battering home than nonbatterers, and to have suffered abuse as children (Walker, 1984). Preventing the intergenerational cycle of abuse requires the initiation of secondary prevention in the service of primary prevention.

It is not only the child victims of abuse that are at risk for developing later abusive behavior. Simply observing family violence appears to teach the child violent solutions to interpersonal problems. According to a national survey, those who observed their parents hitting each other were more likely to be abusive toward their own children (Gelles, 1980). Battered women tend to abuse their children at a higher rate than nonbattered women (Walker, 1984). When these women leave their battering partners and enter relationships with nonbattering men, abuse of their children tends to drop (Walker, 1984). Modeling, then, is a significant teacher of violent behavior.

In the case of family violence, secondary prevention in one generation becomes primary prevention in the next. The two classic prevention strategies—reducing stress and strengthening coping and resources— are both relevant to breaking the intergenerational cycle of abuse. To reduce the abused child's experience of stress, the abuse must be stopped and the child's safety guaranteed. Once this is done, there must be careful management of how and what the child is told about the parents' behavior, court decisions, and actions of service agency staff (Aber,

1980). Because many abused children are either aggressive or socially withdrawn (Martin, 1976), training in social skills and anger control strengthens them against the development of later abusive behavior (Keller & Erne, 1983). Strengthening supportive networks for abused children and for their families in the next generation is a promising prevention approach. Hunter and Kilstrom (1979) found that parents with access to more supportive resources did not repeat the abuse of the earlier generation. Strengthening parent-infant bonding may also be effective in breaking the cycle. Nonrepeating parents of newborns were found to visit their premature infants more often than abuse-repeating families (Hunter & Kilstrom, 1979).

Increasing Social Supports

The value of supportive relationships for healthy functioning and their role in buffering the destructive effects of stress have been extensively documented (Gottlieb, 1981, 1983; Mitchell & Trickett, 1980). Albee's formula dictates efforts to increase supportive relationships and networks. In family violence, the opposite occurs. Social supports suffer major decrements. A look at the equation shows why. Because the source of pain is a loved one, that person is effectively shifted from a bottom-line supportive role to a top-line stressor role. A similar process occurs with other conventional sources of support. Relatives and friends may side with the male partner out of custom, thus removing themselves from the woman's supportive network. The professional world, from physicians to lawyers to clergy, often follows suit. In a recent survey of Protestant clergy in the United States and Canada (Alsdurf, 1985), investigators found confirmation that pastors hold a patriarchal attitude toward women, which leads them to distrust victims' accounts of family violence and to discount violence as grounds for dissolving the marriage.

> One third of the respondents felt that the abuse would have to be severe in order to justify a Christian wife leaving her husband, while 21 percent felt that no amount of abuse would justify a separation. . . . Twenty-six percent of the pastors agreed that a wife should submit to her husband and trust that God would honor her action by either stopping the abuse or giving her the strength to endure it. (Alsdurf, 1985, p. 10)

These are sobering statistics in view of the fact that some authorities (Pagelow, 1982) cite clergy as the institutional resource contacted most frequently by battered women. At the microcosmic level, self-help groups and early intervention programs are examples of strategies that increase social supports for members of families where violence exists. Educational interventions, such as parenting courses or workshops for the unemployed, also serve this purpose, because they usually involve meetings with groups of peers and professionals in leadership roles. At the macrocosmic level, the legislative process and related enforcement practices have important consequences for healthy family functioning.

Social supports are usually thought of as rooted in the family, the neighborhood—with its churches and schools—and in the work site. The community at large, through its institutions and practices, is a major source of support for its members. Community attitudes about family violence reflect today's changing mores. This shift is apparent in the expansion of social services and options for victims, such as foster homes and safe houses. These options have only become available in most communities within the last decade. In prevention terms, these services are host-focused interventions that treat the problem rather than prevent it. A signal of increasing community support for preventing family violence is seen in recent legislative changes and enforcement of laws related to this problem.

The law is a powerful force in controlling behavior. The last half of this century has witnessed a parade of causes seeking social justice through legislative change. However, passing laws to prohibit discriminatory practices does not guarantee these practices will end. Attitudes, as expressed in norms and customs, may take generations to change. Victims of family violence have suffered a history of benign neglect, at best, and abandonment at worst, by this nation's legal system. One problem has been the lack of adequate legislation to protect victims of family violence. A second problem has to do with enforcement. Even in situations in which the law provides clear protection to victims, police have traditionally declined to arrest offenders. When police have made arrests, the courts have traditionally failed to convict. Over the last decade, discriminatory laws have been changed and new laws passed that create legal remedies for victims. These changes include eviction of the abuser from the home, mandatory arrest of batterers who violate protection orders, and warrantless arrest for misdemeanor offenders involved in domestic abuse (Lerman, 1982). Enforcement practices have also begun to reflect increasing societal support for the rights of persons to be safe from attack by family members. A number of police departments have been sued because of failure of police officers to make appropriate arrests or to enforce laws ensuring the safety of family members (Lerman, 1982). These changes have major significance for prevention. First, legislation codifies societal norms, even if attitudinal change comes slowly; as Walker (1964, cited in Andenaes, 1975) has stated: "The legislation of one generation may become the morality of the next." In discussing rape reform legislation, Loh (1981) echoes this point:

> The role of rape law as catalyst for attitude change may be greater than any immediate impact on the criminal justice system. The criminal law serves not only a general deterrent function. It also has a "moral or sociopedagogic" purpose to reflect and shape moral values and beliefs of society.... The new rape law symbolizes and reinforces newly emerging conceptions about the status of women and the rights of self-determination in sexual conduct.... Conviction of rape, rather than of some surrogate defense, is a dramatic lesson about society's disapprobation of the act, and helps to strengthen the public code. (p. 50)

The second preventive effect of legislation lies in its power to deter the prohibited act. Research has demonstrated that it is the *certainty* of punishment, not its severity, that is effective in deterring crime (Andenaes, 1975; Erickson & Gibbs, 1973; Tittle, 1969). Unfortunately, the certainty factor has historically operated in reverse in the case of family violence. Abusers have traditionally been able to count on avoiding prosecution. One study found that of 10,000 men who assault their wives annually, only 800 are arrested and only two end up going to jail (Dunwoody, 1982a).

Recent studies demonstrate the effectiveness of the certainty principle in preventing crimes of domestic violence. A majority of domestic assault victims who seek prosecution find the action effective in stopping the violence, according to a Justice Department study conducted in four major U.S. cities (Smith, 1981). The study focused on misdemeanor assaults among family members and friends in Charlotte, North Carolina, Los Angeles, Minneapolis, and Brooklyn. Victims expressed the most satisfaction with outcome in court systems in which judges lectured the defendants on the gravity of the crime and warned them of the legal consequences of continued battering. One of the most frustrating outcomes of domestic disputes for law enforcement personnel—and a reason often given for failure to arrest—is the frequency with which victims bring and then drop charges. The results of the Justice Department study refute the conventional wisdom that sees the time spent processing these cases as wasted. Even cases that ended up being dismissed were found to be effective in stopping violence.

In summary, changes in domestic violence legislation and enforcement are slowly beginning to change society's norms about what is and is not acceptable behavior in families. The hard-won victories of individuals in challenging specific discriminatory laws or enforcement practices serve preventive goals, because these victories set the standards by which subsequent behavior is judged.

Increasing Coping Skills

Most prevention programs for families include some sort of skill component. It should be understood that the incidence of family violence in society at large will be little affected by skill-building programs targeted to specific families, because sex role stereotyping and discriminatory laws and customs, if unchanged, will continue to contribute to intrafamilial violence. Skill-building with individual family members, however, may reduce their personal risk for victimization. The workshops, parenting courses, and other interventions described above are designed to increase the capacity of family members to resolve stressful situations such as unemployment and parenting problems. Skill-building interventions are useful in facilitating normal developmental passages from one life stage to another. Such interventions may also reduce risk status in individual situations. Arming individual women and children with escape, avoidance, or physical defense techniques, for example, may reduce the risk status they occupy because of their sex or age (Bart, 1981; Cooper et al., 1983; McIntyre, 1981). This section considers a skill that is critical to the prevention of family violence in individual situations: the control of anger and aggressive behavior.

There is substantial evidence that men who are violent at home are also likely to be violent outside the home (Fagan, Stewart, & Hansen, 1983; Walker, 1984). Walker (1984) found that the rates of arrest and convictions for violent crimes were twice as high for batterers as nonbatterers. Animals, children, and people encountered in public places such as streets, parks, and bars are targets for such men. A study of rearrests of batterers in Brooklyn an average of two and one-half years after conviction found that approximately 10% of the defendants were rearrested for new crimes committed against the original victim, but that over 30% were arrested for new crimes that did not involve the original victim; approximately half of these crimes were violent (Smith, 1981).

Anger has received comparatively little attention from researchers and scholars. While anger and aggression are not the same, the arousal of anger increases the probability of aggression. A prevention approach applicable to individuals at risk for developing physically abusive behavior is training in anger and conflict management, such as Novaco's (1977) stress inoculation model, which emphasizes gaining control over one's behavior through the use of "self-talk".

Novaco (in press) cites a series of studies demonstrating that the approach he advocates is effective. The technique has been applied to child abusive parents (Novaco, in press). Adolescent anger has also been successfully defused and controlled through stress inoculation (Feindler & Fremouw, 1983). A "think aloud" program based on stress inoculation principles has successfully taught aggressive young boys to modify their responses in social situations (Camp, 1977; Camp, Blom, Herbert, & Van Doorninck, 1977).

Increasing Self-Esteem

Self-esteem refers to the way one feels about oneself, how one values oneself in various life roles. There are few experimental studies in the field of family violence that address self-esteem apart from other measures of subject functioning. Many of the studies cited earlier as demonstrating reductions in stress and increases in social support and/or coping skills also demonstrate increases in self-esteem in subject populations (Breton et al., 1981; Gordon, 1977; Hess, 1983; Mitchell & Trickett, 1980; South County Mental Health Center, 1980).

Current literature reflects conflicting findings related to levels of self-esteem in battered women. The traditional view is that these women suffer from low self-esteem (Carlson, 1977; Duncan, 1982; Hilberman, 1978; Mills, 1985) and that their low self-regard is one of the factors that keeps them in the relationship. Wardell and her colleagues suggest that what appears to observers to be passivity, dependence, and a low self-image may in fact be a normal response to situations of severe threat to health and life in which victims have few options for avoidance or escape: "In such situations, to notice that one lacks alternatives signifies rationality, not a poor self-image" (Wardell, Gillespie, & Leffler, 1982, p. 76). The finding of low self-esteem in battered or sexually abused women is usually interpreted as resulting from the abuse situation (Goldstein, 1983; Shields & Hanneke, 1982).

Several recent studies (Feldman, 1983; Walker, 1984) report finding no differences in self-esteem between battered and nonbattered women.

It was predicted that battered women's self-esteem would be quite low and our results, surprisingly, show the opposite. They perceived themselves as stronger, more independent and more sensitive than other women or men. It is possible that battered women develop a positive sense of self from having survived in a violent relationship, which causes them to believe they are equal to or better than others. (Walker, 1984, p. 100)

Walker notes that these findings appear to be incompatible with the victims' reports of depression and other measures she interprets as demonstrating learned helplessness.

Two studies shed light on this apparent contradiction. Thome (1982) found that battered women felt adequate self-esteem when they dealt with the world outside the home, but felt less self-esteem when they dealt with their mates. This finding suggests that investigators of family violence should assess self-esteem separately in these two arenas of functioning. While Feldman (1983) found no differences in self-esteem between battered and nonbattered women, she found significant differences in self-esteem between battered women who stayed in the battering situation and those who left it (the latter had higher scores). As is often the case with research in a relatively young field, conflicting results may be symptomatic of too simple a formulation of the research issues.

Low self-esteem has also been found in males who abuse partners and/or children (Davidson, 1978; Doherty, 1983). A finding with major implications for prevention is that the self-esteem of children in homes where the mother is physically abused is adversely affected (Lombardi, 1982).

It is clear from this overview that the relationship between self-esteem and family violence is a complicated one. The relationship should be investigated for all family members, not just the abuse victim or the abuser. In addition, the investigator should examine self-esteem (a) both within and outside the abusive situation, and (b) for those who stay in and those who leave the situation. Finally, standard definitions of abuse and measures of self-esteem should be used so as to facilitate comparison of the results of multiple studies.

Until such refinements are incorporated into the methodology of family violence research, it is premature to draw definitive conclusions about the relationship between self-esteem and family violence. Interventions with populations at risk in which either coping skills or social supports or both are increased suggest, however, that these variables contribute to elevating self-esteem and, cumulatively, to preventive outcomes.

Summary

This chapter begins by tracing the development of family violence and prevention as fields of study. A model for preventing family violence is then presented. The model links stress and risk factors as major contributors to family violence and identifies social supports, coping skills, and self-esteem as factors that contribute to healthy family functioning. Specific programs are presented as examples of preventive approaches consistent with the model.

Increasingly, major institutions in our society are advocating for developing resources to prevent family violence rather than continuing to treat its victims. This philosophy is put succinctly in the Report of the Attorney General's Task Force on Family Violence (1984):

> The best of all strategies for dealing with family violence is to prevent it from occurring in the first place. A major part of the battle in preventing family violence is to spread knowledge. Potential victims and abusers must know that family violence is not sanctioned, and is not a private matter, but instead comprises criminal offenses that will be vigorously prosecuted. Potential victims, particularly young children, must be told of ways to protect themselves; potential abusers must learn how to deal constructively with the problems common in relationships and the difficult task of raising children. The public at large must be aware of the magnitude and urgency of the problems represented by family violence and the costs to society if prevention is not given high priority, for many of today's abused children will be tomorrow's abusers, runaways and delinquents. (Attorney General, 1984, p. 64)

In summary, the field of family violence cries out for system change as the most powerful and most logical preventive intervention. Without a reduction in the power differential between the sexes, and a rejection of physical violence as a solution to interpersonal problems, preventive approaches to family violence will amount to little more than Band-Aids.

Notes

1. An earlier version of this chapter appears in *Violence in the Home: Interdisciplinary Perspectives*, edited by M. Lystad (New York: Brunner/Mazel, 1986, pp. 219-249). Reprinted with permission.

2. The equation is not intended—nor does it lend itself easily—to being operationalized in any literal mathematical sense. Conceptual issues (e.g., overlapping variables) and logistical issues (e.g., valid and reliable instruments are not available to measure the variables) are barriers to attempts at mathematical translation.

3. While both mothers and fathers abuse their children, mothers are reported slightly more frequently as abusers. This appears to reflect not so much a sex difference as the relative exposure of each parent to the experience of child care—often unrelieved child care. Studies demonstrating an increase in child abuse by unemployed fathers underscore this point.

References

Aber, J. (1980). The involuntary child placement decision: Solomon's dilemma revisited. In G. Gerbner, C. Ross, & E. Zigler (Eds.), *Child abuse: An agenda for action*. New York: Oxford University Press.

Albee, G. W. (1981). Preventing prevention in the community mental health centers. In *The health care system and drug abuse prevention: Toward cooperation and health promotion* (DHHS Pub. No. ADM 81-1105). Washington, DC: Government Printing Office.

Alpert, J., Richardson, M., & Fodaski, L. (1983). Onset of parenting and stressful events. *Journal of Primary Prevention, 3*, 149-159.

Alsdurf, J. (1985). Wife abuse and the church: The response of pastors. *Response to the Victimization of Women and Children, 8*(1), 9-11.

Andenaes, J. (1975). General prevention revisited: Research and policy implications. *Journal of Criminal Law and Criminology, 66*, 338-365.

Anderson, J., Larson, J., & Morgan, A. (1981). PPSF/Parenting Program for Stepparent Families: A new approach for strengthening families. In N. Stinnett et al. (Eds.), *Family strengths 3: Roots of well-being*. Lincoln: University of Nebraska Press.

Arney, W. (1980). Maternal-infant bonding: The politics of falling in love with your child. *Feminist Studies, 6*, 547-70.

Attorney General. (1984). *Report of the Attorney General's task force on family violence*. Washington, DC: U.S. Department of Justice.

Badger, E., & Burns, D. (1982). A model for coalescing birth-to-3 programs. In L. A. Bond & J. M. Joffe (Eds.), *Facilitating infant and early childhood development*. Hanover, NH: University Press of New England.

Bart, P. B. (1981). A study of women who were both raped and avoided rape. *Journal of Social Issues, 37*, 123-137.

Baruch, G., & Barnett, R. (1983). Correlates of father's participation in family work. In *Working Papers 106*. Wellesley, MA: Wellesley College, Center for Research on Women.

Baruch, G., & Barnett, R. (1984). Father's participation in family work: Effects on children's sex role attitudes. In *Working Papers 126*. Wellesley, MA: Wellesley College, Center for Research on Women.

Belenky, M., Clinchy, B., Goldberger, N., & Tarule, J. (in press). *The other side of silence: The development of women's ways of knowing*. New York: Basic Books.

Bloom, B. (1971). A university freshman preventive intervention program: Report of a pilot project. *Journal of Consulting and Clinical Psychology, 37*, 235-242.

Bond, L. A., & Joffe, J. M. (Eds.). (1982). *Facilitating infant and early childhood development*. Hanover, NH: University Press of New England.

Brazelton, T. (1973). *Neonatal Behavioral Assessment Scale, No. 50. Clinics in developmental medicine*. Philadelphia: J. B. Lippincott.

Breines, W., & Gordon, L. (1983). The new scholarship on family violence. *SIGNS, 8*, 490-531.

Breton, M., Welbourn, A., & Watters, J. (1981). A nurturing and problem-solving approach for abuse-prone mothers. *Child Abuse and Neglect, 5*, 475-480.

Buss, T., Redburn, F., & Waldron, J. (1983). *Mass unemployment: Plant closings and community mental health*. Newbury Park, CA: Sage.

Carlson, G. (1977). Battered women and their assailants. *Social Work, 2*, 455-460.

Camp, B. (1977). Verbal mediation in young aggressive boys. *Journal of Abnormal Psychology, 86*, 145-153.

Camp, B., Blom, G., Hebert, F., & van Doorninck, W. (1977). "Think Aloud": A program for developing self-control in young aggressive boys. *Journal of Abnormal Child Psychology, 5*, 157-169.

Cassel, J. (1974). Psychosocial processes and "stress": Theoretical formulation. *International Journal of Health Services, 4*, 471-482.

Clinchy, B., & Zimmerman, C. (1985). Growing up intellectually: Issues for college women. *Work in Progress*, No. 19, Stone Center Working Papers Series. Wellesley, MA: Wellesley College, Stone Center.

Cohen, C., & Sokolovsky, J. (1978). Schizophrenia and social networks: Ex- patients in the inner city. *Schizophrenia Bulletin, 4*, 546-560.

Comstock, C. (1982). Preventive processes in self-help groups: Parents Anonymous. *Prevention in Human Services, 1*, 47-53.

Conger, R., Burgess, R., & Barrett, C. (1979). Child abuse related to life change and perceptions of illness: Some preliminary findings. *Family Coordinator, 28*, 73-78.

Cooper, S., Lutter, Y., & Phelps, C. (1983). *Strategies for free children: A leader's guide to child assault prevention*. Youngstown, OH: Ink Well Press.

Coopersmith, S. (1967). *The antecedents of self-esteem*. San Francisco: Freeman.

Daly, M., & Wilson, M. (1980). Discriminative parental solicitude: A biological perspective. *Journal of Marriage and the Family, 42*, 277-288.

Davidson, T. (1978). *Conjugal crime*. New York: Hawthorne Books.

Dobash, R. F., & Dobash, R. (1979). *Violence against wives*. New York: Free Press.

Doherty, S. (1983). Self-esteem, anxiety and dependency in men who batter women. *Dissertation Abstracts International, 44*, 1384A.

Duncan, D. (1982). Cognitive perceptions of battered women. *Dissertation Abstracts International, 43*, 245B.

Dunwoody, E. (1982a). Canadian National Clearinghouse in Family Violence. *Response, 5*, 8-9.

Dunwoody, E. (1982b). Sexual abuse of children: A serious, widespread problem. *Response, 5*, 1-2, 13-14.

Eisenberg, S., & Micklow, P. (1977). The assaulted wife: "Catch 22" revisited. *Women's Rights Law Reporter, 3*(3-4), 138-161.

Elmer, E. (1967). *Children in jeopardy*. Pittsburgh: University of Pittsburgh Press.

Erickson, M., & Gibbs, J. (1973). The deterrence question: Some alternative methods of analysis. *Social Science Quarterly, 54*, 534-551.

Fagan, F., Stewart, D., & Hansen, K. (1983). Violent men or violent husbands? In D. Finkelhor et al. (Eds.), *The dark side of families*. Newbury Park, CA: Sage.

Feindler, E., & Fremouw, W. (1983). Stress inoculation training for adolescent anger problems. In D. Meichenbaum & M. Jarenko (Eds.), *Stress reduction and prevention*. New York: Plenum.

Feldman, S. (1983). Battered women: Psychological correlates of the victimization process. *Dissertation Abstracts International, 44*, 1221B.

Finkelhor, D. (1983). Common features of family abuse. In D. Finkelhor et al. (Eds.). *The dark side of families*. Newbury Park, CA: Sage.

Finkelhor, D., & Hotaling, G. (1984). Sexual abuse in the National Incidence Study of Child Abuse and Neglect: An appraisal. *Child Abuse and Neglect, 8*, 23-22.

Gaines, R., Sandgrund, A., Green, A., & Power, E. (1978). Etiological factors in child maltreatment: A multivariate study of abusing, neglecting and normal mothers. *Journal of Abnormal Psychology, 87*, 531-540.

Gelles, R. J. (1973). Child abuse as psychopathology: A sociological critique and reformation. *American Journal of Orthopsychiatry, 43*, 611-621.

282   Carolyn F. Swift

Gelles, R. (1974). *The violent home.* Newbury Park, CA: Sage.
Gelles, R. (1975). Violence and pregnancy: A note on the extent of the problem and needed services. *Family Coordinator, 24,* 81-86.
Gelles, R. (1980). Violence in the family: A review of research in the seventies. *Journal of Marriage and the Family, 42,* 873-885.
Giarretto, H. (1981). A comprehensive child sexual abuse treatment program. In P. Mrazek & C. H. Kempe (Eds.), *Sexually abused children and their families.* New York: Pergamon.
Gil, D. (1970). *Violence against children: Physical child abuse in the United States.* Cambridge, MA: Harvard University Press.
Gilligan, C. (1982). *In a different voice.* Cambridge, MA: Harvard University Press.
Goldstein, S. (1983). Spouse abuse. In A. Goldstein (Ed.), *Prevention and control of aggression.* New York: Pergamon.
Gordon, T. (1977). Parent effectiveness training: A preventive program and its delivery system. In G. W. Albee & J. M. Joffe (Eds.), *Primary prevention of psychopathology: Vol. 1. The issues.* Hanover, NH: University Press of New England.
Gordon, T. (1983). Transforming early parenthood to promote family wellness. In D. Mace (Ed.), *Prevention in family services: Approaches to family wellness.* Newbury Park, CA: Sage.
Gottlieb, B. H. (1981). *Social networks and social support.* Newbury Park, CA: Sage.
Gottlieb, B. H. (1983). Opportunities for collaboration with informal support systems. In S. Cooper & W. F. Hodges (Eds.), *The mental health consultations field* (pp. 181-203). New York: Human Services Press.
Gray, E. (1982). Perinatal support programs: A strategy for the primary prevention of child abuse. *Journal of Primary Prevention, 2,* 138-152.
Greenberg, B. (1982). Television and role socialization: An overview. In *Television and behavior: Ten years of scientific progress and implications for the eighties* (Vol. 1, DHHS Pub. No. ADM 82-1195). Washington, DC: Government Printing Office.
Heber, R., Garber, H., Harrington, S., Hoffman, G., & Falender, C. (1972). *Rehabilitation of families at risk for mental retardation.* Madison: University of Wisconsin.
Hess, R. (1983). Early intervention with the unemployed: Employment Transition Program of the University of Michigan. *Journal of Primary Prevention, 4,* 129-131.
Hilberman, E. (1978, January). *Battered women: Issues of public policy.* Unpublished manuscript, University of North Carolina School of Medicine, Chapel Hill.
Hilberman, E. (1980). Overview: "The wife-beater's wife" reconsidered. *American Journal of Psychiatry, 137,* 1336-1347.
Hornung, C., McCullough, B., & Sugimoto, T. (1981). Status relationships in marriage: Risk factors in spouse abuse. *Journal of Marriage and the Family, 43,* 675-692.
Hunter, R., & Kilstrom, N. (1979). Breaking the cycle in abusive families. *American Journal of Psychiatry, 136,* 1320-1322.
Hunter, R., Kilstrom, N., Kraybill, E., & Loda, F. (1978). Antecedents of child abuse and neglect in premature infants: A prospective study in a newborn intensive care unit. *Pediatrics, 61,* 629-635.
Justice, B., & Justice, R. (1976). *The abusing family.* New York: Human Sciences.
Kahn, M. (1984). Battered women: A 5-year study. *ADAMHA News, 10,* 6.
Kamerman, S., Kahn, A., & Kingston, P. (1983). *Maternity policies and working women.* New York: Columbia University Press.
Keller, H. R., & Erne, D. (1983). Child abuse: Toward a comprehensive model. In A. P. Goldstein (Ed.), *Prevention and control of aggression.* New York: Pergamon.
Kempe, C. H., Silverman, F., Steele, B., Droegemueler, W., & Silver, H. (1962). The

battered child syndrome. *Journal of the American Medical Association, 181*, 107-112.

Klein, D., & Goldston, S. (1977). *Primary prevention: An idea whose time has come* (DHEW Publication No. ADM 77-447). Washington, DC: Government Printing Office.

Klinman, D., & Kohl, R. (1984). The Fatherhood Project. In *Fatherhood U.S.A. The first national guide to programs, services and resources for and about fathers.* New York: Garland.

Lerman, L. (1982). Court decisions on wife abuse laws: Recent developments. *Response, 5*, 3-4, 21-22.

Levine, J. (1984). Day care challenges and opportunities in the 1980s. In N. Stinnett et al. (Eds.), *Family strengths: Positive support systems.* Lincoln: Nebraska University Press.

Loh, W. D. (1981). What has reform of rape legislation wrought? *Journal of Social Issues, 37*, 28-52.

Lombardi, J. (1982). Growing up with violence: An analysis of retrospective accounts of female offspring. *Dissertation Abstracts International, 43*, 2118A.

Lystad, M. (1975). Violence at home: A review of the literature. *American Journal of Orthopsychiatry, 45*, 328-345.

Martin, H. (Ed.). (1976). *The abused child: A multidisciplinary approach to developmental issues and treatment.* Cambridge, MA: Ballinger.

McCord, J., & McCord, W. (1958). The effects of parental modes on criminality. *Journal of Social Issues, 14*, 66-75.

McIntyre, J. J. (1981). *Victim response to rape: Alternative outcomes* (Final Report). Rockville, MD: National Institute of Mental Health, National Center for the Prevention and Control of Rape.

Melnick, B., & Hurley, J. (1969). Distinctive personality attributes of child-abusing mothers. *Journal of Consulting and Clinical Psychology, 33*, 746-749.

Miller, J. B. (1976). *Toward a new psychology of women.* Boston: Beacon.

Miller, J. B. (1982). Women and power. *Work in Progress*, No. 1, Stone Center Working Papers Series. Wellesley, MA: Wellesley College, Stone Center.

Mills, T. (1985). The assault on the self: Stages in coping with battered husbands. *Qualitative Sociology, 8*, 103-123.

Mitchell, R., & Trickett, E. (1980). Social network research and psychosocial adaptations: Implications for community mental health practice. In P. Insel (Ed.), *Environmental variables and the prevention of mental illness.* Lexington, MA: D. C. Heath.

Moss, H., Hess, R., & Swift, C. (Eds.). (1982). *Early intervention programs for infants.* New York: Haworth.

Newberger, C. M., & Newberger, E. H. (1982). Prevention of child abuse: Theory, myth, practice. *Journal of Preventive Psychiatry, 4*, 443-451.

Newberger, E., Reed, R., Daniel, J., Hyde, J., & Kotelchuck, M. (1977). Pediatric social illness: Toward an etiologic classification. *Pediatrics, 60*, 178-185.

Novaco, R. (1977). A stress inoculation approach to anger management in the training of law enforcement officers. *American Journal of Community Psychology, 5*, 327-346.

Novaco, R. (in press). Anger and its therapeutic regulation. In M. Chesney, S. Goldston, & R. Rosenman (Eds.), *Anger and hostility in behavioral and cardiovascular disorders.* New York: McGraw-Hill.

Okun, L. (1982). A study of woman abuse: 300 battered women taking shelter, 119 batterers in counseling. *Dissertation Abstracts International, 44*, 1972B.

Pagelow, M. (1982). *Woman battering.* Newbury Park, CA: Sage.

Parke, R., & Collmer, C. (1975). Child abuse: An interdisciplinary analysis. In M.

284   Carolyn F. Swift

Hetherington (Ed.), *Review of child development research* (Vol. 5). Chicago: University of Chicago Press.

Perry, W. (1970). *Forms of intellectual and ethical development in the college years.* New York: Holt, Rinehart & Winston.

Perry, W. (1981). Cognitive and ethical growth: The making of meaning. In A. Chickering (Ed.), *The modern American college.* San Francisco: Jossey-Bass.

Pleck, J. (1984). A new focus for fatherhood activists. In *Research report* (Vol. IV, No. 1, pp. 1-2). Wellesley, MA: Wellesley College, Center for Research on Women.

Prescott, S., & Letko, C. (1977). Battered women: A social psychosocial perspective. In M. Roy (Ed.), *Battered women: A psychosociological study of domestic violence.* New York: Van Nostrand Reinhold.

Putnam, J. (1984). Men's lives: Changes and choices. In *Research report* (Vol. IV, No. 1, pp. 1-2). Wellesley, MA: Wellesley, College Center for Research on Women.

Riessman, F. (1965). The "helper" therapy principle. *Social Work, 10,* 27-32.

Schelkun, R. (1981, January). Personal communication.

Schneider, C., Hoffmeister, J., & Helfer, R. (1976). A predictive screening questionnaire for potential problems in mother-child interaction. In R. Helfer & C. Kempe (Eds.), *Child abuse and neglect: The family and the community.* Cambridge, MA: Ballinger.

Semmelman, P. (1982). Battered and nonbattered women: A comparison. *Dissertation Abstracts International, 43,* 2716B.

Shields, N., & Hanneke, C. (1982). Battered wives' reactions to marital rape. In D. Finkelhor et al. (Eds.), *The dark side of families.* Newbury Park, CA: Sage.

Smith, B. (1981). *Nonstranger violence: The criminal court's response.* Washington, DC: U.S. Department of Justice, National Institute of Justice.

South County Mental Health Center. (1980). *Optimum Growth Project: A primary and secondary prevention research-demonstration project.* Unpublished manuscript. (Available from South County Mental Health Center, Delray Beach, FL 33435)

Steinmetz, S. (1982). Family care of elders: Myths and realities. In N. Stinnett et al. (Eds.), *Family strengths: Positive support systems.* Lincoln: University of Nebraska Press.

Straus, M. (1980a). Social stress and marital violence in a national sample of American families. *Annals New York Academy of Sciences, 347,* 229-250.

Straus, M. (1980b). The marriage license as a hitting license: Evidence from popular culture, law and social science. In M. Straus & G. Hotaling (Eds.), *The social causes of husband-wife violence.* Minneapolis: University of Minnesota.

Straus, M., Gelles, R., & Steinmetz, S. (1980). *Behind closed doors: Violence in the American family.* New York: Anchor.

Swift, C. (in press). Community intervention in sexual child abuse. In S. Auerbach & A. Stolberg (Eds.), *Crisis intervention with children and families.* New York: Hemisphere.

Thome, M. (1982). An analysis of differences between battered and nonbattered women with respect to sex role acceptance, life histories and personal adjustment. *Dissertation Abstracts International, 43,* 3047B.

Tittle, C. (1969). Crime rates and legal sanction. *Social Problems, 16,* 409-423.

Tolsdorf, C. (1976). Social networks support and coping: An exploratory study. *Family Process, 15,* 407-417.

Vance, E. (1977). A typology of risks and the disabilities of low status. In G. W. Albee & J. M. Joffe (Eds.), *Primary prevention of psychopathology: The issues* (Vol. 1). Hanover, NH: University Press of New England.

Videka-Sherman, L. (1982). Effects of participation in a self-help group for bereaved parents: Compassionate friends. *Prevention in Human Services, 1,* 69-77.

Walker, L. E. (1984). *The battered woman syndrome.* New York: Springer.

Wardell, L., Gillespie, D., & Leffler, A. (1982). Science and violence against wives. In D. Finkelhor et al. (Eds.), *The dark side of families*. Newbury Park, CA: Sage.
Young, M. (1976). Multiple correlates of abuse: A systems approach to the etiology of child abuse. *Journal of Pediatric Psychology, 1*, 57-61.

11

Prevention of Emotional Problems in Children with Chronic Illness and Their Families

Ruth E. K. Stein
Dorothy Jones Jessop
Henry T. Ireys

Over the last several decades, children with chronic illnesses have been beneficiaries of impressive advances in medical technology. Many, who in previous decades would have died, now live well into adulthood. Spina bifida, diabetes, cystic fibrosis, hemophilia, severe asthma, sickle cell anemia: these are only some of the many chronic diseases of childhood. Although each condition is relatively rare, collectively they affect more than 10 million of America's children (Haggerty, 1984). When family members and other caretakers are considered, the number of individuals touched by the presence of a childhood chronic illness increases severalfold.

In this chapter, we aim to define the issues relevant to the prevention of emotional problems secondary to a childhood chronic illness and to the promotion of adaptive responses. Drawing on relevant literature and clinical insight, we seek to describe a broad range of preventive and promotive interventions, to outline what strategies work, and to examine why they work.

(1) What is the evidence for psychological, behavioral, and social distress in this population of children and their families?
(2) Which specific problems can be prevented and which adaptive behaviors enhanced?
(3) What general prevention strategies are appropriate?

286

(4) Where in the developmental trajectory of preventable problems, and where in the genesis of adaptive behaviors, might the most fruitful intervention occur?

(5) What works and for whom?

Serious health problems among infants, children, and adolescents raise formidable challenges for the families and communities in which they live and for the professionals who provide their care. Their care can be expensive, time-consuming, and emotionally exhausting. From a family's point of view, a chronic illness always threatens; it is an ever-present companion, "a constant shadow" (Massie, 1985). These children are always "part well and part ill" (Daeschner & Cerreto, 1985). For much of their lives, children with chronic illnesses may seem like healthy children: able to attend school regularly, to play, to be with friends. Yet, their lives may be punctuated with physical pain, with recurrent trips to the hospital, and with seemingly endless boring periods of waiting (Deford, 1983; Massie, 1985). Most healthy children, at some point in their lives, have a medical crisis, but for them the crisis eventually passes. For chronically ill children, crises typically recur quite often. When a crisis passes, these children only become part well; down the road, another crisis may wait. Communities may also be sources of distress. Myths about childhood chronic illnesses are prevalent. "Don't play with Johnny, you might catch leukemia" is a common example. These many myths, often unexpressed, may sever a family from its friends and a child from his peers.

Children with chronic conditions and their families potentially require many different kinds of services: emotional support as well as good medical care, guidance when difficult treatment decisions are at hand, financial counseling, assistance with school matters, and anticipatory guidance to help negotiate developmental transitions. Moreover, they may require someone to help coordinate the many and various services and link the hospital-based services with those in the community. A single person or profession is insufficient to care for these children and their families. Good care demands that many persons from diverse professions collaborate closely, and do so without disenfranchising the family from its role as primary caretaker of the child.

In using the word *family*, we mean to include the many different living arrangements in which children find themselves, including single-parent families, foster care arrangements, stepfamilies, and extended nuclear families. The weight of the evidence suggests that many families with a chronically ill child rise to the occasion; they live through the ordeals with some degree of acceptance and ability to support each other, yet they do so in the face of a health care system that is peculiarly insensitive to their needs (Drotar & Bush, 1985; Hobbs, Perrin, & Ireys, 1985). In view of the stress that accompanies a childhood chronic illness, it is remarkable that many families—however they may be constituted—function fairly well.

Regardless of their specific situations, children with chronic illness grow up in a complex ecology (Bronfenbrenner, 1979). Their development is shaped by experiences with the medical care system, with the illness itself, and with the community's and family's response to the illness. Hence, effective preventive efforts require an understanding of the many ecological variables that accompany a chronic illness and how these variables impinge upon the complex interaction of physiological and psychological phenomena within the individual. Moreover, because chronic illness continues for many years, repeated interventions and long-term follow-up may be needed.

For many decades, there has been financial support for biomedical advances in the treatment of selected diseases, but attention to the broad range of medical and emotional needs has been meager. A concern with prevention and care of secondary social, behavioral, and emotional consequences has emerged visibly only in the last several years. At this point, many obstacles remain to the development of effective measures to prevent negative outcomes and to enhance the natural resilience of children with chronic conditions and of their families.

Effective prevention strategies are likely to be developed from a confluence of clinical observation, theoretical insight, and applied research—a challenging combination to achieve. But the most formidable obstacle in developing preventive efforts may be the nature of the problem itself. Childhood is supposed to be a time of healthy growth, tempered at worst by self-limiting transitory illness. For many individuals, serious childhood illness is a depressing or emotionally overwhelming topic. A child with a tracheostomy, one who must daily inject himself with insulin, or who lives part of her life in a hospital each violate conventional notions of childhood. Above all, the prevention of the social and emotional sequelae of chronic childhood illness rests on overcoming a deeply ingrained reluctance on the part of both lay persons and professionals to contemplate children whose health is ever fragile.

Within the Preventive Intervention Research Center (PIRC) for Child Health at Albert Einstein College of Medicine, we have the exciting opportunity to challenge these many obstacles in an attempt to develop and evaluate prevention strategies for this population of children and families. Our PIRC, funded by the Center for Prevention Research at the

National Institute of Mental Health (NIMH), is committed to investigating programs designed to promote a healthy adaptation to a child's chronic illness and to prevent secondary mental healthproblems in the child and the family. As Figure 11.1 illustrates, our conceptual model takes into account the illness itself; accompanying stressors, risk factors, and mediating variables; and a child's developmental context. Moreover, because of its location within an active clinical delivery setting, the Center permits continuous and close collaboration between practitioners and researchers. Such a collaboration, absent from many academic efforts, has already produced valuable insights.

Until quite recently, many research and intervention efforts in this field have focused on individual disease entities. This focus has led to significant advances in biomedical therapies for defined physiological disorders. Although this work needs to continue, issues related to the consequences of chronic conditions for children and families require us to take a broader view, one that has been termed a noncategorical perspective (Stein & Jessop, 1982).

The noncategorical approach is based on the concept that, regardless of the specific disease, children with diverse medical problems have great similarities in life experiences and in the preventive and rehabilitative aspects of their lives (Mattson, 1972; Pless & Pinkerton, 1975; Stein & Jessop, 1984; Strauss, 1975) and that these result from common aspects of their conditions, rather than from the unique character of a specific disease entity. The consequences of chronic illness for the child and family are such that two children with the same disease may be as different from each other as two children with different diseases. The lives of children and families seem to be affected by such dimensions as whether the condition is obvious or invisible; whether it is life-threatening, stable, or characterized by unpredictable crises; whether it requires much hospitalization; whether it affects sensory or motor systems; whether it requires intrusive daily routines of care; or whether the family's community can provide needed services and support. Work by our research group has suggested that the uncertainty associated with lack of visibility and with unpredictable crises may be especially difficult for families (Jessop & Stein, 1985).

What Is the Evidence?

A considerable body of empirical work documents that severely ill infants, children, and adolescents and their families are at increased risk for mental disorders (Drotar & Bush, 1985). Epidemiological data

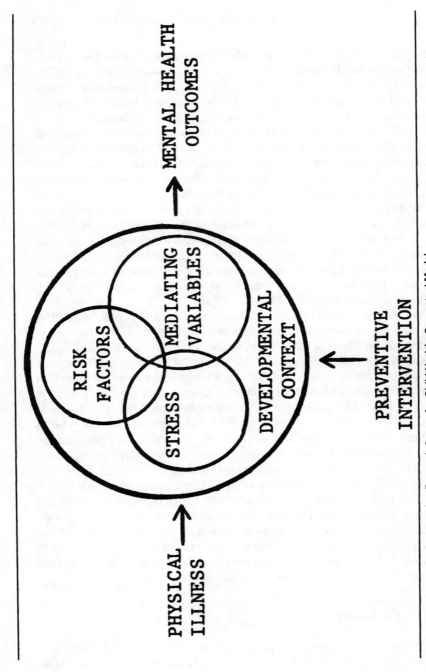

Figure 11.1 Preventive Intervention Research Center for Child Health: Conceptual Model

PHYSICAL
ILLNESS

RISK
FACTORS

MEDIATING
VARIABLES

STRESS

DEVELOPMENTAL
CONTEXT

PREVENTIVE
INTERVENTION

MENTAL HEALTH
OUTCOMES

indicate clearly that children with physical health problems have higher rates of mental health problems. Pless and Roghmann (1971) reviewed three large-scale epidemiological studies and documented an increased incidence of psychological problems among population-based samples of children with chronic health impairments. Data from the Isle of Wight, the national survey of the United Kingdom, and the Rochester Child Health Studies show that children with chronic conditions, in comparison to healthy children, exhibit higher rates of psychiatric disorders, abnormal behavioral symptoms, and school-related adjustment problems. More recently, Walker, Gortmaker, and Weitzman (1981) demonstrated that children with physical health problems have significantly more psychosocial difficulties, including behavior, learning, interpersonal, and school problems. Pless's analysis of the British longitudinal cohorts suggests that the rate of emotional problems is twice the rate in the general population (Pless, 1984). Similarly, in a survey of patients seen in private practice settings, Goldberg, Regier, McAngrney, Pless, and Roghmann (1978) showed that children with chronic physical illness have rates of emotional, behavioral, and school problems twice those of children without ongoing physical illness. A study of school performances of children with a broad range of chronic illnesses demonstrated that these children scored significantly lower on achievement tests in comparison to healthy peers (Fowler, Johnson, & Atkinson, 1985).

These findings, based on a generic or noncategorical approach, are confirmed in disease-specific studies. For example, children with leukemia have been found to be more anxious and isolated than the population of healthy children (Spinetta & Maloney, 1975). According to O'Malley, Koocher, Foster, and Slavin (1979), 59% of children who are long-term survivors of cancer have adjustment problems. Children with renal disease are more likely than healthy children to be isolated, withdrawn, and depressed (Fine et al., 1978); juvenile onset diabetes increases the likelihood of emotional disorder in the child (Johnson, 1980). Many other disease-specific studies might be cited to document this increased risk.

It is worth noting that early case studies of individual children emphasize the serious mental health problems that they faced (e.g., Bruch, 1948; Kubany, Danowski, & Moses, 1956; Toch, 1964; Turk, 1964). More recent studies, however, have shown that seriously ill children and their families have more mental health problems than the general population of children and their families but suggest that severe psychopathology is uncommon. For example, Drotar et al. (1981) studied the psychosocial functioning of children with several different types of chronic illness; they found that the frequency of severe psychopathology was low in all groups, but that the chronically ill children had more psychosocial problems than normal controls.

The reasons for the differences between earlier and later studies may relate to basic improvements in medical outcome and to the presence of comprehensive programs and preventive interventions in the model tertiary care children's hospitals where many of these newer studies have been conducted (Hobbs, Perrin, & Ireys, 1985). In addition, more recent work emphasizes the importance of identifying "characteristics that differentiate patients with adequate versus problematic adjustment and assessment of the effectiveness of emotionally supportive interventions with selected patient groups who appear to be 'at risk' for specific adjustment problems" (Drotar et al., 1981, p. 342). This attention to subgroups with differential risk supports the notion that there are subgroups at increased risk depending on characteristics such as visibility of physical differences (Richardson, 1969), the severity of functional limitations (Pless & Pinkerton, 1975), and uncertainty (Jessop & Stein, 1985).

Work examining the consequences of childhood illness for family life is inconclusive about the degree of impact on the family as a whole and on the mother specifically. Controversy exists particularly in regard to the long- and short-term effects (Haggerty, Roghmann, & Pless, 1975; Klein, 1975; Schulman, 1979). Pratt states that

> in general the limited evidence available indicates that severely disabling and stigmatizing illnesses disrupt roles and relationships in many families, at least during the crisis stage of the illness, although the strenuous coping efforts that are stimulated by illness in the family often result in new patterns of adjustment within the families. (Pratt, 1976, p. 132)

Although a child's illness affects many aspects of family life, the mother generally bears the brunt of the day-to-day care. One analysis of mothers of patients with kidney disease reported that "the emotional impact of the child's disease is greater for parents than children, and greatest for the mother" (Klein, 1975, p. 190). The emotional burden is shared more than the practical burden, which, by reports of all family members, the mother assumes to a greater extent. As the impact on her increases, her husband helps out more with other chores, but not with the burden of the child's care. The mothers studied were found to be more anxious and less happy than mothers from control populations (Klein & Simmons, 1979). A recent study (Breslau, 1983) also found that mothers of children with chronic conditions had more psychiatric symptoms than the mother of well children; these symptoms varied according to the functional status of the child. Another analysis indicated that the child's health status is related to the mother's mental health, but that this relationship is modified by social support and family impact (Jessop, Riessman, Adler, & Stein, 1981).

In addition to emotional stresses, parents of children with chronic illness may feel pressured in various ways by the financial responsibility for care. For example, several reports document that the presence of a chronic illness dissuades fathers from pursuing financially more promising jobs because of a possible loss of insurance coverage or a move away from a familiar medical center (McKeever, 1981; Tiller, Ekert, & Richards, 1977). Mothers may forgo a full-time career in order to care for the child (Hall, 1985). Either spouse may be forced to find a second job to cover expenses.

Siblings of chronically ill children often have strong emotional responses to a severe illness (Cairns, Sussman, & Weil, 1966; Harder & Bowditch, 1982; Lund, 1974; Massie & Massie, 1976; Sourkes, 1981). Various responses have been reported, including guilt that they caused the illness in some magical way, jealousy and anger over the special attention afforded their ill sibling, embarrassment in response to noticeable characteristics, and fear of contracting the illness or of being a carrier (Azarnoff, 1984; McKeever, 1983). Siblings of ill children are more likely to have adjustment problems, behavioral difficulties, and academic troubles (Allan, Townley, & Phelen, 1974; Lavigne & Ryan, 1979; Tew & Laurence, 1975). Recent studies indicate that extra chores fall disproportionately on older siblings who are female (Breslau, Weitzman, & Messenger, 1981; Burton, 1975). To emphasize siblings' negative responses, however, is to provide only a partial account of a complex topic. Many brothers and sisters indicate that experience with a sibling who has a chronic illness has led to greater compassion and a sensitivity to the needs of others (Burton, 1975; Massie & Massie, 1976).

In summary, although controversy exists concerning some specific issues and aspects of risk, the literature strongly supports the notion that children with ongoing serious illness have mental health problems to a greater extent than do children without physical health problems. Moreover, it is possible to postulate variables that increase the risk for these problems: the actual physical symptoms of illness, the therapeutic regimens that the children experience, the unpredictable outcomes and prognosis, periodic medical crises, the potential trauma of hospitalizations and new invasive technologies, the financial status of the family, and the response of the community in which they live. In general, these features can create stress for children and families and may lead to emotional disorders of varying types, including depression, adjustment disorders, acute and chronic anxiety states, mental health problems in other family members, and family discord. Overall, the continued emotional stress of a serious illness interacts in a complex fashion with underlying physiological problems, resulting in potential disturbances to normal physical and emotional development (Drotar, Crawford, & Ganofsky, 1984; Eiser, 1985).

What Specific Problems
Can Be Prevented?
What Adaptive Behaviors Promoted?

The investigation of emotional problems in children with chronic illness and in their families has identified a wide range of emotional distress in response to the illness itself, to the environment of medical institutions, and to demands of daily care. Yet, not all of these responses can or should be prevented. For example, parental anger following the diagnosis of a chronic illness marks an important stage in coming to grips with the child's illness (Drotar, Baskiewicz, Irvin, Kennell, & Klaus, 1975). Denial on the part of parents about the seriousness of an illness, however frustrating this may be for the professionals who try to assist the family, serves an important function for the parents. Would it be wise to prevent the emotional responses of anger and denial, even if it were possible to do so?

Most professionals would agree that the best answer is *no*. What then are appropriate targets for preventive interventions? We can approach this question in several ways. First, we can specify behaviors that are likely to be indicative of a continuing maladaptive response and that are also potentially modifiable. These behaviors include (1) actions reflecting a low self-concept; (2) extreme anxiety; (3) increased absences or decreased performance in school or work; (4) failure to complete age-appropriate developmental tasks; (5) passive or active nonadherence to efficacious medical regimens; (6) severe or repetitive unresolved discord within the family; (7) chronic withdrawal or isolation from family, friend, peers, and community networks; and (8) prolonged depression.

A second approach to answering the question is to emphasize adaptive skills and competent responses to stressful events. Here again it is important to be as specific as possible. What do we mean by the promotion of competency in this population of families and children? What behaviors reflect adaptive coping?

Literature on coping suggests that, in the presence of ongoing stressors, different individuals adopt different types of specific coping strategies. Lazarus and Folkman (1984) and Pearlin and Schooler (1978) indicate that coping generally involves altering the environment that is causing distress and regulating the cognitive and emotional responses to the problem.

Lazarus's "emotion-focused" forms of coping may include avoidance, minimization, distancing, selective attention, positive comparisons, and wresting positive value from negative events, as well as cognitive reappraisal of the event. "Problem-focused" strategies are often directed at redefining the problem, generating alternative solutions, weighing the alternatives, choosing among them, and acting (Lazarus & Folkman, 1984).

Pearlin and Schooler (1978) discusses similar responses, including those that modify the situation (e.g., negotiation in marriage, punitive discipline in parenting, taking an optimistic attitude in work, or seeking advice). If the situation cannot be changed, actors may protect themselves from the stressful impact of the problems by responses that function to control the meaning of the problems. Such responses include cognitively neutralizing a threat by making positive comparisons, selective ignoring, devaluing the relevant area, or substituting rewards in one area for those in another. They suggest that a third type of coping involves management of stress and accommodating to existing stress without being overwhelmed by it. In this area, many techniques are possible (trying not to worry, acceptance, denial, withdrawal, passive acceptance, thinking optimistically, or engaging in diversionary activities, such as watching TV).

Although there are many references to coping strategies in the literature on chronically ill children and their families (e.g., Schulman, 1979), there is no study systematically examining the application of these theoretical mechanisms to chronically ill children and their families. The available literature suggests that, for the chronically ill children themselves, coping is indicated by the continued pursuit of age-appropriate developmental tasks: by the management of stress through play or fantasy, continued involvement in school, the seeking out of peers, and the continuing struggle to achieve appropriate independence from caretakers and parents. Coping, of course, can not be equated with trouble-free compliance or the absence of what parents and providers might label as "problem behaviors." In many respects, a child's active refusal to take medication or to undergo yet another surgical procedure represents an important developmental stage in the child's growth toward independence. Health care professionals frequently view such behavior solely as an impediment to treatment, when in fact it may be an important expression of the child's struggle to cope successfully.

For parents and other family members, competency or successful coping may be demonstrated in a number of ways: by a sustained ability to mediate frightening events for their child and to provide an emotional refuge; by deliberate strategies for seeking and maintaining support; or by an active process of problem solving. Asking questions, confronting the health care team if problems arise, anticipating stressful situations, setting aside time to be alone or for reflection, getting on with life, having fun: these behaviors are indicators of adaptive coping with the issues and problems raised by a chronic illness.

For families, one specific area of coping—requiring a problem-focused approach—involves learning how to negotiate the system of care. This includes the ability to learn how a system works and what to do when a system isn't working. Can a mother initiate questions to her pediatrician? Does she have the phone number of her social worker and does she make calls when necessary? Does she understand how to make the emergency room process work a little faster? Does she know how to reply to the periodic attempts to remove her son from SSI or Medicaid? We have come to appreciate the extraordinary nature of the skills of mothers who are savvy veterans in working the large, complex, stubborn, and often contradictory systems that are embedded in health care institutions.

A second area, understanding the child's illness, refers to the pursuit of knowledge about the illness itself. Do the parents want to read about the illness, or talk with other parents in a similar situation? Can the parents begin to distinguish subtle patterns of behavior in their child and understand and interpret their meaning? For example, some mothers of children with sickle cell anemia report being able to distinguish between different types of crying in their toddler. Some crying expresses the typical fatigue or stubbornness of every toddler; other crying is sensed to be related to pain associated with the illness. The process of adaptive coping becomes apparent when parents report these kinds of distinctions and when they know how to respond.

Available literature and clinical insight suggest that normalization is the central issue for the child and family. To what extent and in what ways are the child treated as "different" from or the "same" as other children? Many problems can be prevented or ameliorated if the family can balance the child's needs to have special arrangements and his or her need to be like other children.

For parents, the process of coping also involves responding to their own emotional needs. Making accurate inferences about how a parent copes emotionally with the demands of a chronic illness requires a deep appreciation for individual differences. No single coping style is best for all parents; no single coping style lacks some drawbacks. The important question is whether the parents' strategies are effective.

What General Prevention and Promotion Strategies Are Effective?

In our work with seriously ill children and their families, we have found three general approaches to be fruitful sources of specific interventions.

Coordination and Continuity of Care

The first general approach rests on the conception of the health care system as a risky environment (Felner, Jason, Moritsugu, & Farber, 1983). Work by this research group (Stein, Jessop, & Reissman, 1983) as well as earlier work by Pless, Satterwhite, and Van Vechten (1978) and Kanthor, Pless, Satterwhite, and Myers (1974) have demonstrated major gaps in the health care of children with chronic conditions. For example, one of the major problems with the health care system for chronically ill children is its disjointed, duplicative, and discontinuous nature; several of our investigations within the Center are based on the hypothesis that improvements in the health care system itself will lead to improvements in the mental health status of children and families (Stein & Jessop, 1984). Coordination of services is essential for any family whose child is dependent on many different medical, social, and educational services.

As Drotar et al. note (1984), continuity is the cornerstone of preventive efforts with children who have a chronic illness or handicap. The development of trust between provider and child, and the provider and family, results in a relationship that will be both buffer and shelter during critical moments. Yet, one of the most persistent observations of the medical care system for children with chronic illness is the lack of coordination and continuity (Pless et al., 1978). As a result, there are many gaps in the provision of services, and some other services are repeatedly duplicated. Problems and disruptions in the doctor-patient relationship are also numerous. Collectively, clinical and research evidence suggest that improvements in the coordination of care and in the continuity of caregiver will themselves reduce stress in families with a chronic illness, and may lead to improved emotional and physiological outcomes.

In the pediatric health care literature, a variety of solutions to coordinated care have been proposed, including the pediatrician who acts as ombudsman (Battle, 1972), the lay family counselor (Pless & Satterwhite, 1975), the health advocate (Klerman, 1981), and comprehensive speciality clinic settings (Kanthor et al., 1974). Some work in social sciences, public administration, and policy analyses suggests that wholesale efforts to coordinate do not in fact accomplish anything for the simple reason that they do not coordinate, but become simply another specialized service. Despite this observation, there is evidence that on a small scale with well-defined groups, such as children with chronic and handicapping conditions, coordination is desirable and effective (Brewer & Kakalik, 1979; Stein & Jessop, 1984; Weiss, 1981).

Social Support

Although there have been various approaches to operationalizing the concept of social support, there is some agreement that the study of social support involves focusing on the helping properties and processes of the social systems in which persons are located (Eckenrode & Gore, 1981). Social support helps maintain social identity, provides emotional reassurance, renders material aid and services, and provides information. Gottlieb (1981) notes that social support may be provided through many vehicles, including dyadic relationships, group settings, or systemwide interventions. It is suggested that social supports have a role in either (a) mediating the impact of the stressor on the person by modifying the negative effects of stress or (b) activating the development of coping strategies that increase the competence of persons involved.

The published literature contains no thorough empirical work on the role of social support specifically focused on children who have ongoing health problems. Closely related studies, however, lead us to hypothesize that social support is a relevant factor for children and their families faced with major ongoing health problems. For example, research indicates that social supports affect physical health (Dimsdale et al., 1979; Killilea, 1982; President's Commission on Mental Health, 1978). Self-help groups have also been found to be useful for parents of these children (e.g., Chesler & Yoak, 1984; Johnson, 1982; Ross, 1978).

Cognitive Competence

One of the general themes in the area of preventive intervention concerns the enhancement of cognitive competence of individuals within specified populations (Felner et al., 1983). This concept refers to a general capacity to acquire and use knowledge in order to help deal with problems. Effective problem-solving skills are among those that characterize "cognitively competent" individuals. Specific abilities may include knowing where to search for information, distinguishing relevant facts, devising alternative approaches, planning ahead, and looking at a problem from different perspectives. One class of intervention strategies has been based on the hypothesis that the enhancement of cognitive competence will prevent certain types of crises or problems from occurring. At this point, a considerable body of clinical and empirical literature indicates that knowledge can help prevent critical disorders that might otherwise have occurred in a child with a chronic illness or in other family members (Ack, 1976; Danilowicz & Gabriel, 1971; Kohlberg & Rothenberg, 1970; Roberts, Wurtele, Boone, Ginther, & Elkins, 1981; Salhoot, 1974; Schowalter, 1971; Siegel & Peterson, 1980; Visintainer & Wolfer, 1975).

The provision of knowledge for children with chronic illness and their families may take one or more of the following tacks:

(1) explanation of the illness and treatment in readily understandable ways, including an explanation of risks and trade-offs between different treatment strategies;
(2) concrete information about upcoming events, including the correction of misconceptions or unrealistic fears in developmentally appropriate ways;
(3) suggestions about the likely feelings that derive from the illness and associated medical procedures and how to identify, label, and manage those feelings through a cognitive problem-solving approach;
(4) provision of resources that will aid in solving the possible problems that might arise, including reading lists, self-help groups, or knowledgeable referral sources; and
(5) specification of the main sources of assistance within the health care system.

Education strategies are likely to have maximum effect in preventing problems if they are presented in an emotionally or intellectually relevant manner and at an appropriate time in the emotional life of the parents or child. For example, Ablin et al. (1971) stress that providing information regarding specific coping strategies for parents of a newly diagnosed leukemic child must be paced after the initial shock has dissipated somewhat, if the information is to have a maximally beneficial effect. These considerations underscore (a) the relationship between cognition and emotion and (b) the importance of a health provider or a knowledgeable lay counselor who can act for the patient and family as a mediator of inherently stressful events by providing appropriate information in an emotionally supportive fashion.

Where in the Developmental Trajectory of Problems Might the Most Fruitful Interventions Occur?

Lorion (1983) has wisely warned that preventive interventions may create more problems than they solve. For example, Gersten, Langner, and Simcha-Fagan (1979) reported that their prevention efforts led to greater risk for dysfunction, rather than less. Preventive interventions for children with a chronic illness and for their families carry a similar risk for generating unexpected problems.

These considerations have led us to ask the question of where in the developmental trajectory of problems would it be best to intervene, in either a preventive or promotive fashion? Generally a chronic illness first makes its presence felt in the form of various symptoms, such as pain, fatigue, or weight loss. The initial symptoms typically lead to considerable anxiety, which is transformed by the actual medical diagnosis into anxiety anchored to specific fears of pain, loss, and death. Professionals in this area universally recognize the stress that the diagnosis of a chronic illness can place on a child and family (e.g., Burton, 1975; Solnit & Stark, 1961). Theories of adaptation to the diagnosis of a chronic illness hypothesize a series of stages, including denial, anger, depression, reorganization, and finally acceptance (Drotar, Malone, & Negray, 1979). Most families assert that stage theories are too linear, that the process is much more cyclical; denial of certain aspects is always present; depression, anger, and anxiety return periodically. Few parents can fully "accept" the illness of their children (Hall, 1985).

Once the initial crisis resolves, however, routines emerge: regular trips to the clinic, special diets, daily self-care procedures. Invariably, these routines are upset by critical incidents, such as a rapid increase in the severity of the symptoms, a sudden hospitalization, or behavioral problems secondary to stress. In most families, relative stability returns, to be upset again by more or less predictable transition points for the child or family. Such transitions might include the birth of another child, starting a new school, moving into a new community, or changing parental employment.

Where in this sequence would a prevention or promotive effort be most effectively initiated: around the times of crisis or in periods of stability? Are different strategies appropriate for different points in this sequence? For example, are social support strategies most effective around the time of diagnosis? Is enhancement of cognitive competence best accomplished during periods of stability? Do children or families differ systematically in their ability to respond to preventive or promotive efforts at different points in time and does this tendency vary from individual to individual? These are questions for which we have no answers yet, but they underscore directions worth pursuing.

We have also come to appreciate the importance of uncertainty in the genesis of emotional problems, an emphasis that has received support from a few empirical studies (Jessop & Stein, 1985) and numerous anecdotal accounts (Deford, 1983; Massie & Massie, 1976). The uncertainty and confusion that follows the diagnosis of an illness or a sudden exacerbation of symptoms may lead to new behaviors. Whether these new behaviors are positive or maladaptive may depend on numerous factors, including the type of assistance found during this time.

What Actually Works?

It would take us beyond the limits of this chapter to detail the many and varied efforts across the country that have potential relevance for prevention of emotional distress for children with chronic illness and for their families. The literature on preparation for surgical or dental procedures, for example, could usefully inform prevention strategies for these children (e.g., Roberts et al., 1981; Visintainer & Wolfer, 1975). The findings from these studies, however, have yet to be applied specifically to children with chronic illnesses.

The preventive interventions that have focused on children with chronic illnesses and that have been successfully implemented and evaluated fall into three general categories. The first focuses on interventions that seek to improve the health care system in order to bring benefits to all or most children with a chronic illness. One such example was the liberalizing of visiting rules (Plank, 1962). Generally, these interventions focus on improving access to care, coordination of care, or strategies for providing comprehensive care, (e.g., Kisker, Strayer, & Wong, 1980: Pierce & Freedman, 1983; Stein, 1983). One program that has been the subject of an extensive randomized evaluation is the Pediatric Home Care program at the Albert Einstein College of Medicine. The program rests on a team consisting of a pediatric nurse practitioner, a pediatrician, and a social worker. This team, targeted for the families of children with severe chronic illnesses, makes home visits as needed and assists in coordinating care between the outpatient clinic, the inpatient service, the emergency room, the school, and community institutions. The members of the home care team may become trusted resources for the family.

302   Stein et al.

Through an extensive evaluation, the Pediatric Home Care program was found to be effective in improving the satisfaction of the family with care, in improving the child's psychological adjustment, and in lessening the psychiatric symptoms of the mother. In comparison to the control group, families receiving care in the PHC program were also more apt to have a consistent provider. Overall, the multidisciplinary PHC team appears to improve the comprehensiveness of care for these children and their families and in so doing to have prevented some of the emotional problems that appeared in the control group (Stein & Jessop, 1984).

A second strategy of preventive intervention efforts builds on the effectiveness of social support in ameliorating the stress of serious medical conditions. The self-help and mutual aid movement that is sweeping the country has spawned many of these efforts (Borman, 1985). Mutual aid groups for parents of chronically ill children (e.g., Chesler & Yoak, 1984) and for the children themselves (e.g., Millspaugh, Kremenitzer, & Lending, 1976) serve many important functions, including socialization, sharing of solutions to common problems, advocacy within the medical care system, and provision of emotional support during times of crisis. Opportunities to facilitate supportive networks range from well-organized "buddy" systems (Family Friends, 1984) to groups that form spontaneously in the waiting rooms of speciality clinics.

A third category of prevention approaches includes those efforts to enhance the competence of individuals to respond to the intellectual and emotional challenges engendered by a child's chronic illness. Programs that focus on the individual (as opposed to the health care system or to the individual's supportive network) tend to rely on (a) education to enhance familiarity with upcoming events or understanding of basic physiological processes of the illness (e.g., Fireman, Friday, Gira, Vierthaler, & Michaels, 1981; Naylor, Coates, & Kan, 1984) or (b) improved methods to cope with the secondary consequences of the illness (e.g., Kolko & Rickard-Figueroa, 1985; Zeltzer & LeBaron, 1982). Problem-solving approaches that have been successfully utilized in other areas (e.g., Shure & Spivack, 1978) have yet to be applied to this population of children and parents.

In our Center we have implemented several interventions that combine the efforts from the various categories noted above. For example, the Center is training individuals to function as family advocates and counselor to parents with chronically ill children. The selected advocates are mothers who themselves have raised a child with a serious long-term illness; they are veterans, able to "work the system" effectively. This program, which builds on previous efforts at a different site (Pless & Satterwhite, 1975), combines several elements, including education, social support, and improved problem-solving skills. We hope to show that family advocates will promote more effective coping in the families with whom they work and in so doing ameliorate the negative effects of a chronic illness on the family's functioning.

A second intervention that incorporates various approaches is peer counseling for adolescents with a chronic illness. In this program, older adolescents who have had a serious illness for many years are trained in basic counseling methods and in interpersonal problem-solving strategies. They then use these skills to assist younger adolescents recently diagnosed with a serious illness. We hope to demonstrate that the peer counseling process will have beneficial preventive effects for both the counselors and the counselees. Here again, this intervention combines elements of social support and education in a fashion tailored to the needs of the individual youngster.

Summary

Efforts toward the prevention of emotional problems of children with chronic illnesses and their families have only just begun. Preventive programs in this area are still new; many reasonable approaches have yet to be put into practice and many ongoing programs have yet to be evaluated. Relevant findings have emerged from diverse professions and research groups, but these findings are poorly integrated and often poorly disseminated outside of the disciplines from which they emerge.

Yet, the need for the knowledge and experience on which to base effective prevention programs remains acute. It is likely that in the next decade the absolute numbers of children with a chronic illness will remain constant (Gortmaker & Sappenfield, 1984), but the technology for treating them will become ever-more sophisticated. The ethnical and legal issues may also become more complex and difficult for this society to resolve. For the first time in the nation's history, for example, there exists a handful of children with complex medical needs whose lives depend on sophisticated medical machines. For these families, intervention efforts should seek to prevent family collapse and to promote the family's ability to cope with persistent stress of relatively high intensity. For families whose chronically ill children are less fragile, intervention efforts should seek to promote as far as possible opportunities for normal child development. Along with new technology for early detection of chronic illness, methods must also be created to lessen unnecessary anxiety and to prevent the emergence of the problems of "stigma."

Over the last several decades, medical research has brought extraordinary opportunities to reduce or prevent some of the most serious physical symptoms of the childhood chronic illnesses; it has also led to the survival of children whose lives depend on treatments unimaginable even a decade ago. It would serve little purpose if the social and emotional problems of these children and their families compromised such remarkable achievement. Prevention programs and research must assure that society's investment in the care of children with chronic illness be preserved by preventing the emotional and family problems that so often characterize their lives.

References

Ablin, A. R., Binger, C. M., Stein, R. C., Kushner, T. H., Roger, S., & Mikkelsen, C. A. (1971). A conference with the family of a leukemic child. *American Journal of Diseases of Children, 122*, 362-366.

Ack, M. (1976). New perspectives in comprehensive health care for children. *Journal of Pediatric Psychology, 1*, 9-11.

Allan, J., Townley, R., & Phelen, P. (1974). Family response to cystic fibrosis. *Australian Pediatrics Journal, 10*, 136-146.

Azarnoff, P. (1984). Parents and siblings of pediatric patients. *Current Problems in Pediatrics, 14*, 6-40.

Battle, C. U. (1972). The role of the pediatrician as ombudsman in the health care of the young handicapped child. *Pediatrics, 50*, 916-922.

Borman, L. D. (1985). Self-help mutual aid groups. In N. Hobbs & J. M. Perrin (Eds.), *Issues in the care of children with chronic illness: A sourcebook on problems, services, and policies*. San Francisco: Jossey-Bass.

Breslau, N. (1983). Care of disabled children and women's time use. *Medical Care, 21*, 620-629.

Breslau, N., Weitzman, M., & Messenger, K. (1981). Psychological functioning of siblings of disabled children. *Pediatrics, 67*, 344-353.

Brewer, G. D., & Kakalik, J. S. (1979). *Handicapped children: Strategies for improving services*. New York: McGraw-Hill.

Bronfenbrenner, U. (1979). *The ecology of human development*. Cambridge, MA: Harvard University Press.

Bruch, H. (1948). Physiological and psychologic interrelationships in diabetes in children. *Psychosomatic Medicine, 11*, 200-210.

Burton, L. (1975). *The family life of sick children*. London: Routledge & Kegan Paul.

Cairns, A., Sussman, A., & Weil, W. (1966). Family interaction, diabetes, and sibling relationships. *International Journal of Social Psychiatry, 12*, 35-43.

Caplan, G. (1984). *Support systems and community mental health*. New York: Behavioral Publications.

Chesler, M., & Yoak, M. (1984). Self-help groups for parents of children with cancer. In H. Roback (Ed.), *Helping patients and their families cope with medical problems: A guide to therapeutic group work in clinical settings*. San Francisco: Jossey-Bass.

Daeschner, C. W., & Cerreto, M. C. (1985). Training physicians to care for chronically ill children. In N. Hobbs & J. M. Perrin (Eds.), *Issues in the care of children with chronic illness: A sourcebook on problems, services, and policies*. San Francisco: Jossey-Bass.

Danilowicz, D. A., & Gabriel, H. P. (1971). Postoperative reactions in children: "Normal" and abnormal responses after cardiac surgery. *American Journal of Psychiatry, 120*, 185-188.

Deford, F. A. (1983). *The life of a child*. New York: Viking.

Dimsdale, J. E., Eckenrode, J., Haggerty, R. J., Kaplan, B. H., Cohen, F., & Dornbusch, S. (1979). The role of social supports in medical care. *Social Psychology, 14*, 175-180.

Drotar, D., Baskiewicz, A., Irvin, N., Kennell, J., & Klaus, M. (1975). The adaptation of parents to the birth of an infant with congenital malformation: A hypothetical model. *Pediatrics, 56*, 710-717.

Drotar, D., & Bush, M. (1985). Mental health issues and services. In N. Hobbs & J. M. Perron (Eds.), *Issues in the care of children with chronic illness: A sourcebook on problems, services, and policies*. San Francisco: Jossey-Bass.

Drotar, D., Crawford, P., & Ganofsky, M. (1984). Prevention with chronically ill children. In M. Roberts & L. Peterson (Eds.), *Prevention of problems in childhood* (pp. 232-265). New York: John Wiley.

Drotar, D., Doershuk, C. F., Stern, R. C., Boat, T. F., Boyer, W., & Matthews, L. (1981). Psychosocial functioning of children with cystic fibrosis. *Pediatrics, 67*, 338.

Drotar, D., Malone, C. M., & Negray, J. (1979). Psychosocial intervention with the families of children who fail to thrive. *Child Abuse and Neglect: The International Journal, 3*, 927-935.

Durlak, J. (1983). Social problem solving as a primary prevention strategy. In R. Felner, L. Jason, J. Moritsugu, & S. Farber (Eds.), *Preventive psychology: Theory, research, and practice* (pp. 87-103). New York: Pergamon.

Eckenrode, J., & Gore, S. (1981). Stressful life events and social support: The significance of context. In B. H. Gottlieb (Ed.), *Social networks and social support*. Newbury Park, CA: Sage.

Eiser, C. (1985). *The psychology of childhood illness*. New York: Springer-Verlag.

Family Friends. (1984, November/December). NCOA Family Friends volunteers enrich lives of handicapped children. *Perspective on Aging*, pp. 5-8.

Felner, R., Jason, L., Moritsugu, J., & Farber, S. (1983). Preventive psychology: Evolution and current status. In R. Felner, L. Jason, J. Moritsugu, & S. Farber (Eds.), *Preventive psychology: Theory, research, and practice* (pp. 3-10). New York: Pergamon.

Fine, R. N., Malezadeh, M. H., Pennisi, A. J., Ettenger, R. B., Wittenbogaart, C. H., Aegrete, V. F., & Korsch, R. M. (1978). Long term results of renal transplantation in children. *Pediatrics, 61*, 641-651.

Fireman, P., Friday, G. A., Gira, C., Vierthaler, W. A., & Michaels, L. (1981). Teaching self-management skills to asthmatic children and their parents in an ambulatory care setting. *Pediatrics, 68*, 341-348.

Fowler, M., Johnson, M., & Atkinson, S. (1985). School achievement and absence in children with chronic health conditions. *Journal of Pediatrics, 106*, 683-687.

Gersten, J., Langner, T., & Simcha-Fagan, O. (1979). Developmental patterns of types of behavioral disturbance and secondary prevention. *International Journal of Mental Health, 7*, 132-149.

Goldberg, I. D., Regier, D. A., McAngrney, T. K., Pless, I. B., & Roghmann, K. J. (1978). The role of the pediatrician in the delivery of mental health services to children. *Pediatrics, 63*, 898-909.

306   Stein et al.

Gortmaker, S., & Sappenfield, W. (1984). Chronic childhood disorders: Prevalence and impact. *Pediatric Clinics of North America, 31*, 3-18.

Gottlieb, B. H. (Ed.). (1981). *Social networks and social support*. Newbury Park, CA: Sage.

Haggerty, R. J. (1984). Forward. *Pediatric Clinics of North America, 31*, 1-2.

Haggerty, R. J., Roghmann, K. J., & Pless, I. B. (1975). *Child health and the community*. New York: John Wiley (Interscience).

Hall, L. (1985, July). *The effects of a disabled child upon the family: A singular testament*. Paper presented to the Crippled Children's Services Institute, Columbus, OH.

Harder, L., & Bowditch, B. (1982). Siblings of children with cystic fibrosis: Perceptions of the impact of the disease. *Children's Health Care, 10*, 116-120.

Heller, K., & Swindle, R. (1983). Social networks, perceived social support, and coping with stress. In R. Felner, L. Jason, J. Moritsugu, & S. Farber (Eds.), *Preventive psychology: Theory, research, and practice* (pp. 87-103). New York: Pergamon.

Hobbs, N., Perrin, J., & Ireys, H. (1985). *Chronically ill children and their families*. San Francisco; Jossey-Bass.

Jessop, D. J., Riessman, C. K., Adler, B., & Stein, R.E.K. (1981, November). *The relation between the mental health of mothers and their children's health status*. Paper presented at the annual meeting of the American Public Health Association, Los Angeles.

Jessop, D. J., & Stein, R.E.K. (1985). Uncertainty and its relation to the psychological and social correlates of chronic illness in children. *Social Science in Medicine, 10*, 993-999.

Johnson, M. (1982). Support groups for patients of chronically ill children. *Pediatric Nursery*, 160-163.

Johnson, S. (1980). Psychosocial factors in juvenile diabetes: A review. *Journal of Behavioral Medicine, 3*, 95-116.

Kanthor, H., Pless, I. B., Satterwhite, B., & Myers, G. (1974). Areas of responsibility in the health care of multiple handicapped children. *Pediatrics, 54*, 779-785.

Killilea, M. (1982). Crisis theory, coping strategies and social support systems. In H. C. Schulberg & M. Killilea (Eds.), *Principles and practices of community mental health*. San Francisco: Jossey-Bass.

Kisker, C. T., Strayer, F., & Wong, L. (1980). Health outcomes of a community-based therapy program for children with cancer. *Pediatrics, 66*, 900-906.

Klein, S. D. (1975). *Chronic kidney disease: Impact on the child and family and strategies for coping*. Unpublished doctoral dissertation, University of Minnesota.

Klein, S., & Simmons, R. (1979). Chronic disease and childhood development: Kidney disease and transplantation. In R. Simmons (Ed.), *Research in community and mental health* (Vol. 1). Greenwich, CT: JAI Press.

Klerman, L. V. (Ed.). (1981). *Research priorities in maternal and child health: Report of a conference*. Waltham, MA: Brandeis.

Kohlberg, I. J., & Rothenberg, M. B. (1970). Comprehensive care following multiple life-threatening injuries. *American Journal of Disease of Children, 119*, 449-451.

Kolko, D. J., & Rickard-Figueroa, J. L. (1985). Effects of video games on the adverse corollaries of chemotherapy in pediatric oncology patients. *Journal of Consulting and Clinical Psychology, 53*, 223-228.

Kubany, A., Danowski, T., & Moses, C. (1956). The personality and intelligence of diabetics. *Diabetes, 5*, 462-467.

Lavigne, J., & Ryan, M. (1979). Psychological adjustment of siblings of children with chronic illness. *Pediatrics, 63*, 616-627.

Lazarus, R., & Folkman, S. (1984). *Stress, appraisal, and coping*. New York: Springer.

Lorion, R. (1983). Evaluating preventive interventions: Guidelines for the serious social change agent. In R. Felner, L. Jason, J. Moritsugu, & S. Farber (Eds.), *Preventive psychology: Theory, research, and practice* (pp. 251-272). New York: Pergamon.

Lund, D. (1974). *Eric*. Philadelphia: J. B. Lippincott.

Massie, R. (1985). A constant shadow: Reflections on the life of a chronically ill child. In N. Hobbs & J. M. Perrin (Eds.), *Issues in the care of children with chronic illness: A sourcebook on problems, services, and policies*. San Francisco: Jossey-Bass.

Massie, R., & Massie, S. (1976). *Journey*. New York: Knopf.

Mattson, A. (1972). Long-term physical illness in childhood: A challenge to psychosocial adaptation. *Pediatrics, 50,* 801-8.

McKeever, P. (1981). Fathering the chronically ill child: A neglected area in family research. *American Journal of Maternal and Child Nursing, 6,* 124-128.

McKeever, P. (1983). Siblings of chronically ill children: A literature review with implications for research and practice. *American Journal of Orthopsychiatry, 53,* 209-218.

Millspaugh, D., Kremenitzer, M., & Lending, M. (1976, September-October). Providing services for adolescents who live with seizures. *Children Today,* pp. 7-9, 34-35.

Naylor, D., Coates, T., & Kan, J. (1984). Reducing distress in pediatric cardiac catheterization. *American Journal of Diseases of Children, 138,* 726-729.

O'Malley, J. E., Koocher, G., Foster, D., & Slavin, L. (1979). Psychiatric sequelae of surviving childhood cancer. *American Journal of Orthopsychiatry, 49,* 608-616.

Pearlin, L., & Schooler, C. (1978). The structure of coping. *Journal of Health and Social Behavior, 19,* 2-21.

Pierce, P., & Freedman, S. (1983). The REACH Project: An innovative health delivery model for medically dependent children. *Children's Health Care, 12,* 86-89.

Plank, E. (1962). *Working with children in hospitals*. Cleveland: Western Reserve Press.

Pless, I. (1984, November). *Childhood chronic illness as a risk factor*. Paper presented at Research Symposium of the Preventive Intervention Research Center for Child Health, Albert Einstein College of Medicine/Montefiore Medical Center, New York.

Pless, I. B., & Pinkerton, P. (1975). *Chronic childhood disorder: Promoting patterns of adjustment*. Chicago: Year Book Medical Publishers.

Pless, I. B., & Roghmann, K. J. (1971). Chronic illness and its consequences: Some observations based on three epidemiological surveys. *Journal of Pediatrics, 79,* 351-359.

Pless, I. B., & Satterwhite, B. (1975). The family counselor. In R. Haggerty, K. Roghmann, & I. Pless (Eds.), *Child health and the community*. New York: John Wiley.

Pless, I. B., Satterwhite, B. B., & Van Vechten, D. (1978). Division duplication and neglect: Patterns of care for children with chronic disorders. *Child Care, Health and Development, 4,* 9-19.

Pratt, L. (1976). *Family structure and effective health behavior*. Boston: Houghton-Mifflin.

President's Commission on Mental Health. (1978). *Report of the task panel on community support systems* (Vol. 2). Washington, DC: Government Printing Office.

Richardson, S. A. (1969). The effect of physical disability on the socialization of a child. In D. A. Goslin (Ed.), *Handbook of socialization, theory and research*. Chicago: Rand McNally.

Roberts, M. C., Wurtele, S. K., Boone, R. R., Ginther, L. J., & Elkins, P. D. (1981). Reduction of medical fears by use of modeling: A preventive application in a general population of children. *Journal of Pediatric Psychology, 6,* 293-300.

Ross, J. (1978). Coping with childhood cancer: Group intervention as an aid to parents in crisis. *Social Work in Health Care, 4,* 381-391.

Salhoot, J. T. (1974). The use of two group methods with severely disabled persons. In R. E. Hardy & J. B. Cull (Eds.), *Group counseling and therapy techniques in special settings*. Springfield, IL: Charles C Thomas.

Schowalter, J. T. (1971). The utilization of child psychiatry on a pediatric adolescent ward. *Journal of the American Academy of Child Psychiatry, 10*, 684-699.

Schulman, J. (1979). *Coping with tragedy: Successfully facing the problems of a seriously ill child*. Chicago: Follett.

Shure, M., & Spivack, G. (1978). *Problem-solving techniques in childrearing*. San Francisco: Jossey-Bass.

Siegel, L. J., & Peterson, L. (1980). Stress reduction in young dental patients through coping skills and sensory information. *Journal of Consulting and Clinical Psychology, 48*, 785-787.

Solnit, A., & Stark, M. (1961). Mourning and the birth of a defective child. *Psychoanalytic Study of the Child, 16*, 523-537.

Sourkes, B. (1981). Siblings of the pediatric cancer patient. In V. Kellerman (Ed.), *Psychological aspects of childhood cancer*. Springfield, IL: Charles C Thomas.

Spinetta, J. J., & Maloney, L. J. (1975). Death anxiety in the outpatient leukemia child. *Pediatrics, 56*, 1034-1037.

Stein, R.E.K. (1983). A home care program for children with chronic illness. *Children's Health Care, 12*, 90-92.

Stein, R.E.K., & Jessop, D. J. (1982). A noncategorical approach to chronic childhood illness. *Public Health Reports, 97*, 354-362.

Stein, R.E.K., & Jessop, D. J. (1984). Relationship between health status and psychological adjustment among children with chronic conditions. *Pediatrics, 73*, 169-174.

Stein, R.E.K., Jessop, D., & Reissman, C. (1983). Health care services for chronically ill children. *American Journal of Diseases of Children, 137*, 225-230.

Strauss, A. L. (1975). *Chronic illness and the quality of life*. St. Louis: C. V. Mosby.

Tew, B., & Laurence, K. (1975). Mothers, brothers, and sisters of patients with spina bifida. *Developmental Medicine and Child Neurology, 15*, 69-76.

Tiller, J., Ekert, H., & Richards, W. (1977). Family reactions in childhood acute lymphoblastic leukemia in remission. *Australian Pediatric Journal, 13*, 176-181.

Toch, R. (1964). Management of the child with a fatal disease. *Pediatrics, 3*, 418-427.

Travis, G. (1976). *Chronic illness in children: Its impact on child and family*. Stanford, CA: Stanford University Press.

Turk, J. (1964). Impact of cystic fibrosis on family functioning. *Pediatrics, 34*, 67-71.

Visintainer, M. A., & Wolfer, J. A. (1975). Psychological preparation for surgical pediatric patients: The effect on children's and parents' stress responses and adjustment. *Pediatrics, 56*, 187-202.

Walker, D. K., Gortmaker, S. L., & Weitzman, M. (1981). *Chronic illness and psychological problems among children in Genesee County*. Boston: Harvard School of Public Health, Community Child Health Studies.

Weiss, J. A. (1981). Substance vs. symbol in administrative reform: The case of human services coordination. *Policy Analysis, 7*, 21-45.

Zeltzer, L., & LeBaron, S. (1982). Reduction of nausea and vomiting associated with chemotherapy in children with cancer: Combined hypnotic and nonhypnotic intervention. *International Journal of Clinical and Experimental Hypnosis, 30*, 327-335.

12

Support Groups for Caregivers of Memory-Impaired Elderly: Easing Caregiver Burden[1]

Linda K. George
Lisa P. Gwyther

This chapter addresses two complex and controversial issues: primary prevention and program evaluation. Great minds disagree about the definition of primary prevention, strategies for implementing primary prevention (e.g., modifying social systems versus promoting individual competence), and appropriate criteria for evaluating the effects of primary prevention interventions (see Albee, 1980; Cowen, 1978; Goldston, 1977). Similarly, attempts to document the effectiveness of intervention programs (whether they are primary prevention interventions or not) typically are accused of improper design, use of inappropriate outcome measures, and, especially, failure to account for the effects of extraneous variables and predisposing characteristics of program participants (see Estes & Freeman, 1976; Gordon & Morse, 1975; Lieberman & Bond, 1979).

All of these issues are relevant to this chapter. We did not set out to establish a primary prevention intervention. Indeed, we remain unsure of whether or not the service program to be described is a primary prevention program. There also are methodological limitations associated with our evaluation effort. For example, the intervention is unruly by usual research standards, consisting of a loosely related system of geographically dispersed community support groups that share a common focus but do not do the same activities or follow a standardized agenda. In short, our efforts are susceptible to the same kinds of disagreements that characterize the fields of primary prevention and program evaluation more generally.

In 1980, the Duke University Family Support Program was established in response to (a) requests from family caregivers of memory-impaired older adults for information services and mutual support and (b) requests from family physicians who were observing the problems that family caregivers had in managing their memory-impaired patients— an issue that these physicians recognized, but had neither the time nor the professional background to tackle. The Family Support Program (FSP) has grown and evolved during the past five years and now is a statewide technical assistance program for the family caregivers of and health providers for memory-impaired older adults. Throughout its five-year history, the FSP has pursued two primary activities: (a) dissemination of information via a statewide newsletter for family caregivers of memory-impaired adults and (b) the development and sustenance of community-based support groups for family caregivers. FSP now has established 52 support groups throughout North Carolina, three of which now are chapters of the national Alzheimer's Disease and Related Disorders Association (ADRDA).

The research reported in this chapter is an evaluation of the effects of support group participation upon selected caregiver outcomes. Prior to describing the evaluation, however, background information is provided about memory impairment in later life, the role of the family in providing services to memory-impaired adults, and the effects of caregiving upon family members. The Family Support Program and the community support groups also are described in greater detail.

The Target Population

Moderate or severe memory impairment in later life is not a normal part of the aging process, but instead reflects the ravages of organic brain disease. There are a number of forms of dementing illness, among which Alzheimer's Disease is the most prevalent. Alzheimer's disease and other forms of senile dementia affect more than two million older Americans. Although dementing diseases are found among middle-aged and even young adults, they are very rare. From age 65 on, however, significant proportions of older people fall victim to the indignities of organic brain disease. Current epidemiologic estimates suggest that approximately 5% of the population aged 65 and older suffer dementing disorders, with the risk of the disease escalating rapidly at advanced ages. Indeed, it is estimated that one-quarter of the population aged 85 and older suffer Alzheimer's disease or a related disorder (Mortimer, Schuman, & French, 1981).

Intellectual decline is the primary symptom of Alzheimer's disease and related disorders. Other symptoms include impaired judgment, emotional lability, incontinence, paranoia, hallucinations, and impaired ability to manage activities of daily living. Symptoms vary in severity both among patients and within the same patient over the course of the illness. Early in the dementing process, typical symptoms include intermittent memory loss, wandering and getting lost, agitation, sleep disturbance, and depressed affect. By the midpoint of the illness, memory loss has become both more frequent and more debilitating, normal personality has been lost, belligerence and even violence is common, and the capacity to perform instrumental tasks of daily living has atrophied. The final stages of the illness often are characterized by bowel and bladder incontinence, difficulty swallowing, loss of coordination and the ability to walk, and seizures.

Although several promising avenues of investigation are underway, the causes of and cure for dementing diseases remain unknown. Alzheimer's disease and related disorders are progressive, incurable, and terminal. On average, victims of these diseases live six to eight years after diagnosis. This average is somewhat misleading, however, in that the duration of survival ranges from 18 months to more than twenty years. Because there is no effective treatment for the dementias, management remains the cornerstone of care for victims of these diseases. Given the extremely debilitating nature of these diseases, management is difficult and, sometimes, even oppressing to the caregiver who has major responsibility for the patient—regardless of whether that caregiver is a family member or a paid service provider.

Although the victims of dementing disorders constitute over half of our nursing home residents, the vast majority of demented older people remain in the community, cared for by family members (see Bergmann, 1975). Widespread fears that the family support system characteristic of earlier times has become defunct have been laid to rest. As Brody recently noted,

> Accumulated evidence documents the strength of intergenerational ties, the continuity of responsible filial behavior, the frequency of contacts between generations, the predominance of families rather than professionals in the provision of health and social services, the strenuous family efforts to avoid institutional placement of the old, and the central role played by families in caring for the noninstitutionalized impaired elderly. (Brody, 1981, p. 471)

Indeed, the U.S. General Accounting Office recently demonstrated that public dollars provide nearly 80% of the costs of institutional care for older persons, whereas families and friends provide 80% of the value of services provided to impaired older persons who remain in the community (Comptroller General of the United States, 1977). Because the majority of impaired older persons remain in the community, family caregivers constitute the largest single component of the long-term care service delivery system in the United States (see Brody, Poulshock, & Mascioschi, 1978).

Although the social and economic benefits of family caregiving have been recognized for a decade, awareness of the true costs of family caregiving is much more recent. Caregiving often is a highly taxing responsibility. The term "caregiver burden" was coined by Zarit and his associates (Zarit, Reeves, & Bach-Peterson, 1980), to refer to the psychological, physical, financial, and social problems that can affect family caregivers as they care for their impaired older relatives. Providing care to victims of dementing diseases probably is especially difficult. Because these diseases are progressive and incurable, caregiving is a lengthy task that becomes increasingly taxing as the illness runs its course. Despite the family's best efforts, the demented patient continues to deteriorate. The lack of effective treatment is difficult for caregivers to cope with and accept. Additionally, available evidence suggests that the cognitive, emotional, and personality impairments characteristic of dementia are more difficult for family members to accept and cope with than are purely physical frailties (Sainsbury & Grad de Alarcon, 1970).

It is against this backdrop that the Family Support Program and our research effort were initiated. When our research began in 1983, there were many clinical and anecdotal reports of the burdens of family caregiving, but startling little research evidence of such. At that time, only two studies of family caregivers had been performed (Fengler & Goodrich, 1979; Zarit et al., 1980). Both of these studies were based on very small samples (i.e., total samples of 40 or fewer caregivers) and both samples had been drawn from the patient populations of medical facilities. We believed it critically important to examine the impact of caregiving in the context of broader, more representative samples. Moreover, the previous studies had included no method of assessing the well-being of caregivers relative to their age peers who were not shouldering caregiving responsibilities. We believed that such a comparison was necessary in order to understand the well-being of caregivers relative to that of random community samples and other subgroups who have been identified as target groups for special services (e.g., mothers with small children, single parents, harried executives).

In light of this paucity of data, we performed an epidemiologic study of the prevalence of caregiver burden, focusing on the four dimensions of well-being suggested by clinical reports and previous research as most at risk for caregiving-related decrements: physical health, mental health/psychological distress, participation in social and recreational activities, and financial resources. Multiple indicators were examined within each well-being dimension. Instruments were chosen to permit comparison of study results with existing norms based on random community samples. In addition, we examined the relationships between well-being and caregiver characteristics, patient characteristics, and the social resources (e.g., social support, use of formal services) available to caregivers. The latter analyses were performed in order to obtain information about individual and situational factors that buffer against and/or exacerbate caregiver burden.

The sampling frame for this research consisted of the mailing list of the Duke University Family Support Program. The mailing list included caregivers of demented older adults throughout the state of North Carolina. Members of the mailing list had been identified from a variety of sources: a media campaign (e.g., radio, newspapers, television); referrals from physicians, nursing homes, and other service agencies; caregivers known to the national ADRDA; and other outreach activities. This sampling frame did not generate a random sampling of family caregivers—and, indeed, the cost of identifying a random sample of caregivers would be prohibitively expensive. The mailing list did, however, yield a large, heterogeneous sample. Representing 89% of the current caregivers on the FSP mailing list—an excellent response rate by usual social science standards—510 caregivers responded to our first survey (see Dillman, 1978). A longitudinal follow-up was performed one year after the initial survey to observe changes in well-being over time. The longitudinal follow-up generated an 82% adjusted response rate (adjusted for nondeliverables, n = 17, and verified caregiver deaths, n = 24).

It is important to note that the only criterion for inclusion in our sample was that the respondent currently be providing some level of care to a memory-impaired older adult. Unlike previous studies, we did not require that the caregiver live with the patient and/or provide full-time caregiving. As a consequence, although a majority (53%) of the caregivers lived with the patients to whom they provided care, the sample also included caregivers who provided services to institutional-ized older relatives (34%) and respondents who were assisting patients who lived with other relatives (13%). It is tempting to consider those caregivers who live with their patients as primary caregivers and other caregivers as secondary caregivers. From our respondents' points of view, however, this conclusion is only partially true. All of the caregivers who lived with their patients described themselves as primary caregivers. Conversely, none of the respondents who provided part-time assistance to patients living with other relatives described him- or herself as a primary caregiver. The pattern was less clear for caregivers of institution-alized patients, however: two-thirds of this subgroup did not describe themselves as primary caregivers; one-third did. As will be noted below, casting this "wide net" in terms of eligibility for sample inclusion generated important information about the relationship between patient living arrangements and caregiver burden.

Sample characteristics will be briefly described. As expected given the results of previous studies (see Cantor, 1983), the majority (71%) of the respondents were women. The age range of the sample was 21-90, with an average age of 57.4 years. Although the age range is very broad, most caregivers were the spouses or adult children of the memory-impaired adults and thus were middle-aged or old. The vast majority of caregivers were White (97%), 2% were Black, and 1% were American Indian or Asian. The vast majority of respondents (88%) were married, with approximately equal and small percentages of widowed, divorced, and never-married caregivers. The modal level of education for the sample was completion of high school. More of the caregivers had attended college, however, than had terminated their schooling prior to high school graduation.

When we compare the caregiver sample with the population of North Carolina, there are some definite demographic differences that appear to reflect two underlying causes. First, the older ages and higher percentage of women in the caregiver sample appear to reflect the process of caregiver selection in this society (see Cantor, 1983; Ikels, 1983). Second, the outreach efforts that generated the FSP mailing list appear to be less effective in reaching members of racial and ethnic minorities and persons of lower-socioeconomic status.

The results of the study indicated that caregiver burden is experienced in two of the four dimensions of well-being examined. In terms of financial resources, the caregiver sample was no worse off than random community samples. This finding undoubtedly reflects, at least in part, the relatively advantaged socioeconomic status of the caregiver sample as a whole. Caregivers also were only slightly and nonsignificantly worse off in terms of physical health than random community samples of their age peers. In terms of social participation and psychological distress, however, significant burden was apparent. Compared to random community samples, caregivers reported spending only one-fourth as much time in social and recreational activities (including visits with friends and relatives, club and church attendance, and time spent relaxing or pursuing hobbies). In addition, the caregivers reported considerable dissatisfaction with their levels and quality of social activities. Burden was most pronounced, however, in the area of mental health or psychological distress. Caregivers reported three times as many psychiatric stress symptoms as their community counterparts—and also reported significantly lower levels of life satisfaction and significantly higher levels of negative affect. Moreover, excluding over-the-counter medications, 28% of the caregivers reported using psychotropic drugs on a regular basis and 23% reported using alcohol regularly to calm down or as a sleep aid. Overall, the caregivers appear to be at considerable risk for social isolation, psychological distress, and substance abuse compared to their age peers who do not have caregiving responsibilities.

Other analyses were performed to identify individual and social factors associated with levels of burden *within* the caregiver sample. A few of these results will be briefly summarized. As expected, burden was greater among caregivers who lived with their patients and presumably provided full-time or nearly full-time care. Surprisingly, however, the caregivers of institutionalized patients were nearly as burdened as the live-in caregivers—and it was the caregivers who provided assistance to other relatives who were relatively free of burden. These findings question one of the most prevalent assumptions in clinical practice: that institutionalization of the patient leads to immediate and substantial relief for the family caregiver.

Compared to adult child caregivers, spouse caregivers exhibited increased burden in the financial, social participation, and physical health dimensions. Moreover, these differences remained significant with the effects of caregiver age statistically controlled, suggesting that the causal factor is the closeness of the relationship between patient and caregiver, rather than age-related vulnerabilities to burden. In the area of psychological distress, however, spouse and adult child caregivers exhibited comparable levels of burden. These findings generally supported the hypothesis that the more central the relationship between patient and caregiver, the greater the burden (see Cantor, 1983).

The factor most closely related to caregiver burden was the perceived adequacy of the social support the caregiver received from other family and friends. Compared to those caregivers who indicated that they were receiving appropriate levels of assistance from their social support networks, those caregivers who perceived their levels of assistance from friends and kin to be inadequate demonstrated decreased well-being in all four well-being dimensions. Causal order is unclear, of course. On the one hand, it may be that perceptions of inadequate social support lead to increased burden. Alternatively, however, it may be that increased burden leads to perceptions of the need for more assistance from friends and relatives.

Contrary to our expectations, men reported less burden than women in all four dimensions, especially in terms of psychological distress. These sex differences, which are unexpected given the assumption that the caregiving role is more compatible with the traditional sex-role orientations of women, remained statistically significant after controlling for resources such as the social support available to the caregiver, and are buttressed by the longitudinal follow-up, which indicated that male caregivers were less likely to institutionalize their patients than female caregivers.

Also surprising, patient characteristics were unrelated to the levels of burden reported by respondents. More specifically, illness duration, length of caregiving, and the severity of the patients' symptoms were all unrelated to levels of well-being in the four dimensions examined. These findings suggest that the personal characteristics and resources of the caregiver are more important factors in determining level of burden than the objective demands placed upon the caregiver by the patient. As has been found in studies of other kinds of stress (see George, 1980; House, 1981), these findings suggest that outcome is less a result of the stressor itself than a reflection of the social context in which the stressor occurs and the personal competencies of the individual to cope with the demands elicited by the stressor.

This description of the target population was presented for two reasons. First, it is important to provide a general overview of the target population in terms of both its heterogeneity and the kinds of problems that caregivers commonly experience. Caregivers of memory-impaired adults are especially likely to experience problems in the areas of social participation and psychological distress. Moreover, the decrements experienced in these dimensions, as well as in the areas of physical health and financial resources, are not randomly distributed among the caregivers. A number of factors—including the relationship between patient and caregiver, the patient's living arrangements, the caregiver's perceived adequacy of social support, and the caregiver's gender—are related to the probability of experiencing decrements in well-being.

Second, the level of psychological distress reported by this sample has implications for conclusions about whether or not family caregivers of memory-impaired older adults are an appropriate target group for primary prevention. That conclusion appears to depend upon whose definition of primary prevention one uses. Cowen (1978), who defined primary prevention at an earlier Vermont Conference, clearly would not view the caregivers of memory-impaired elderly as an appropriate target group for primary prevention. From his purist perspective, any effort to define an at-risk population automatically disqualifies that intervention from consideration as primary prevention. Other authors take a less restrictive view of primary prevention. For example, Goldston, at the first Vermont Conference, defined primary prevention as activities directed toward specifically identified vulnerable high risk groups within the community who have not been labeled psychiatrically ill and for whom measures can be undertaken to avoid the onset of emotional disturbance and/or to enhance their level of positive mental health. Programs for the promotion of mental health are primarily educational rather than clinical in conception and operation, their immediate goal being to increase people's capacities for dealing with crises and for taking steps to improve their own lives. (Goldston, 1977, p. 20)

In contrast to Cowen, Goldston includes interventions targeted to at-risk groups as primary prevention efforts. There are no data suggesting that the stresses of caregiving place one at risk for psychiatric disorder, as defined by conventional diagnostic criteria. Nonetheless, our research results suggest that caregivers are a group at risk for substantial psychological distress. Moreover, as noted below, the intervention that was evaluated is primarily educational, which is compatible with Goldston's definition of primary prevention programs. Thus whether this intervention constitutes primary prevention is a matter of definition. We did not decide to do primary prevention and then search for a strategy to implement. We will proceed with a description of our intervention and leave the decision of whether or not it is primary prevention to others.

The Intervention

The intervention evaluated in this chapter consists of community support groups for the family caregivers of memory-impaired older adults. Though all of the community support groups were established with the technical assistance of the Duke University Family Support Program, each also has its own unique history, tradition, program, and group of participants. We will begin by describing the similarities of purpose and the common procedures used to establish the support groups. Subsequently, we will note some of the factors along which the support groups vary and the implications of those variations for the evaluation effort.

The Duke University Family Support Program has developed a standardized strategy for developing successful community support groups for the caregivers of memory-impaired older adults (with success being defined as long-term survival of the support group, active participation by a substantial proportion of local caregivers, and the ability of the support group to exist in the absence of professional supervision or external funding). A manual describing these methods, and written when more than 20 of the North Carolina community support groups had been established, is available (Gwyther & Brooks, 1983). In North Carolina, this manual has been supplemented by ongoing training sessions for the support group leaders, called support group facilitators, which provide experience-based organizational strategies and information updates to persons responsible for establishing local community support groups or maintaining their momentum.

Scientific literature—both research-based and conceptual/programmatic—suggests that support groups are best equipped to provide two kinds of assistance to participants: information and mutual support (see Lieberman & Borman, 1979; Silverman, 1980). The knowledge function of support groups is based on the facts that (a) persons sharing a common problem frequently report the need for more information about the nature of the problem and/or methods of coping with it and (b) support groups are a potentially useful mechanism for information transfer and exchange. The mutual support function of support groups rests upon the fact that persons experiencing a specific problem— particularly a problem that is nonnormative or somewhat stigmatizing—often feel psychologically (and perhaps socially or physically) isolated. Support groups can be responsive to this need by providing people who share similar problems and/or situations with opportunities to meet together, share experiences and coping strategies, and perhaps experience a sense of mutual understanding and validation. A third potential function of support groups is noted by some authors: an advocacy function (see Lieberman & Borman, 1979; Sagarin, 1969). Some support groups devote part of their efforts to mobilizing community support for their problems and/or educating the community (or relevant segments of it) to their situations and needs.

The community support groups established by the Duke University Family Support Program (FSP) were developed with all three of these functions in mind. The manual for support group development and the training materials provided to support group facilitators recommend seven types of support group activities: providing information about dementing disorders, providing information about available community resources, identifying one's own coping capacities and inner resources, providing opportunities for personal sharing of experiences, encouraging professional education, encouraging the development of community resources, and promoting research. The first two activities address the knowledge function of the support groups, the next two activities address the mutual support function, and the last three activities concern advocacy.

FSP recommends a specified sequence of events in establishing a support group for caregivers of memory-impaired older adults. Given the existence of a small group of caregivers or others concerned about the impact of caregiving on family members, a well-publicized community event is advocated in order to gauge the need and desire for a local support group. Initial efforts consist of a multiagency planning meeting to prepare for the community event. Typically, the planning committee will include one or two family caregivers and representatives from relevant service agencies (e.g., nursing homes, departments of social services, adult day care programs). At this point, a time-limited commitment is made to hold a community event, typically a "Community Information Night on Memory Loss in Later Life." The committee works together long enough to implement the community event (e.g., obtaining guest speakers, making arrangements for a time and place, and publicizing the event).

The community event is used to highlight the importance of the topic of dementing illness. The typical program for the community information event includes a guest speaker who provides information about the nature and prevalence of memory loss in later life and brief descriptions of the functions that a local support group of family caregivers and concerned service providers can serve. Persons who attend the community event are asked to express their interest in the establishment of a local support group and to provide the names of persons who are not present but might be interested in such a group.

Given that a sufficient number of people express interest in developing a local support group, the next step is to concentrate on four important initial tasks: (a) building a knowledge foundation (via audiovisuals, written materials on dementing illness and its management, and learning about the availability of local experts; (b) developing group leadership; (c) planning an agenda of meetings (typically for a year); and (d) cultivating referral sources (i.e., developing outreach mechanisms to identify newly diagnosed patients and families who were missed by previous publicity efforts).

In the North Carolina experience, this process typically has gone quite smoothly. The community information event often generated turnouts of over 100 persons who expressed interest in a local support group, even in small rural communities. Over time, of course, a subset of these people became the backbone of the support group. Progress toward and accomplishment of the four initial goals of the support group are facilitated by the training and technical assistance provided by the Duke Family Support Program.

Once initial decisions are made about support group leadership, leaders are invited to attend the biannual facilitator training sessions hosted by the FSP. At those meetings, group facilitators are provided with new information, research and management updates, opportunities to converse with each other informally, and one-to-one conversations with FSP personnel. FSP recommends that each support group has cofacilitators consisting of one family caregiver and one professional service provider (though the latter frequently performs this leadership role as a community service rather than a part of his or her job duties), with the facilitators being assisted by a steering committee. This leadership strategy is compatible with a more general orientation of the FSP toward the involvement of community agencies as well as family caregivers in support group activities. This strategy benefits the support group in two primary ways. First, involvement of persons from local agencies fulfills part of the advocacy function of the support groups, especially in the areas of professional education and the development of community resources. Second, involvement of community agencies often provides support groups with access to valuable resources such as meeting places, Xerox facilities, and postage at reduced costs or for free.

After the first year or so of operation, the support group must contend with different kinds of issues. Some activities such as program planning and outreach continue. Beyond that, however, two issues are especially likely to crop up after the first bloom of success is fading: (a) developing mechanisms for accommodating newcomers and (b) dealing with attendance problems caused by turnover or by small numbers of participants. The FSP technical assistance program offers support group facilitators assistance with and reassurance about both of these issues. For example, one method of bringing newcomers "up to speed" is to have long-term members present information that previously had to be obtained from outside speakers. Moreover, caregivers' immediate needs and questions change over time; consequently, even previously heard material may have new meaning or special relevance in light of current circumstances. FSP personnel constantly reassure support groups that fluctuating or small attendance is not a major problem and should be expected. Many caregivers have difficulty making alternate arrangements for their patients and must be selective about the meetings they attend. Other caregivers are interested in some, but not other, functions of the support group (e.g., some are more interested in personal sharing than advocacy) and will only attend meetings they believe to be targeted to their interests. From our perspective, the support groups have been unusually capable of attracting cores of dedicated participants from a population that is heavily burdened by competing obligations. Moreover, many caregivers continue active participation in the support groups after their personal circumstances change (i.e., after institutionalization and/or death of the patient).

The development of one-to-one networks is one activity that is specifically recommended by the FSP after the support group itself is firmly off the ground. One-to-one networks consist of dyadic relationships between caregivers with common interests who are matched with the assistance of the support group. These dyadic relationships can serve several functions. First, some caregivers simply cannot participate in support group meetings, but nonetheless would like the opportunity for personal relationships with others who share their problems and concerns. Second, the support group time devoted to mutual support is necessarily limited by the need to serve other functions as well and by the structural characteristics of formal group meetings. Consequently, some caregivers want more mutual support than the support group itself can offer—and can find such support by developing a one-to-one relationship with another caregiver. Third, and most common, some caregivers wish to develop supportive dyadic relationships with caregivers with whom they share more than the common bond of caring for a memory-impaired adults (e.g., two daughters struggling with the decision of whether or not to institutionalize their mothers, two wives whose husbands developed dementing disease at unusually young ages). Most of the North Carolina support groups have developed mechanisms for helping interested caregivers to identify other caregivers with whom they share common interests and who are interested in dyadic relationships.

This description, abstracted from any particular local support group, makes the process of developing and sustaining the support groups sound like a smooth and uniform process. Of course, such has not been the case. Each support group has its unique history and characteristics. Some support groups got off the ground relatively quickly; others were developed more slowly and with difficulty, if not false starts. Support groups vary in the relative emphasis given to knowledge, mutual support, and advocacy, and, within support groups, relative emphasis upon these three types of activities varies over time. Some support groups have been established for as long as five years; others are in their first year of operation. Some support groups have had stable memberships and group facilitators; others have had substantial turnover in both categories. Some support groups have become local chapters of ADRDA; others, which meet all the criteria for becoming local chapters, have resoundingly voted against assuming the responsibilities of national affiliation. Some local support groups take advantage of the technical assistance offered by FSP, but could clearly thrive in its absence; other support groups would not make it a month without FSP personnel helping with program planning or helping to link the support group to appropriate community agencies.

For purposes of the evaluation described below, participation in any local support group is considered exposure to the intervention. Thus we ignored all of the local variations in the nature of the support groups and the potential impact of those variations upon the outcomes of interest. From a research perspective, this is an untidy design indeed. What we are left with is the proverbial "black box." Ignoring any other possible methodological limitations, if support group members demonstrate positive outcomes, we will have no information about the specific aspects of support group participation that brought about these positive outcomes. There are two reasons why we were required to adopt this relatively gross approach to evaluating the impact of support group participation upon family caregivers of memory-impaired adults. First, the Family Support Program was the program being evaluated. FSP needed documentation of its effect and hoped to find some evidence that the program as a whole was having beneficial impact upon support group participants. Given this mandate, we desired evidence that the support groups, as a set, had demonstrable benefits to members—in spite of the fact that program differences were ignored and the causal mechanism underlying the positive outcomes could not be identified. Second, time and resource constraints precluded in-depth examination of the specific activities in which support group members participated. Thus our results are constrained to a very global assessment of the effects of support group membership upon caregiver outcomes.

Evaluation Strategy and Results

Evaluation research typically involves one of two broad design strategies (George & Bearon, 1980; Kent, Kastenbaum, & Sherwood, 1972). One approach—and clearly the preferable one—is to measure intervention participants and a comparable control group before and after the intervention is administered to the former. A second approach involves a cross-sectional comparison of individuals who did and did not receive the intervention or who received different combinations of services. Both of these strategies face methodological difficulties in terms of (a) establishing the comparability of the treatment and control groups and (b) ruling out the impact of extraneous events that affect one group and/or interact with the intervention. These potential methodological problems are exacerbated in natural settings in which participants cannot be randomly assigned to treatment and control conditions and where extraneous variables are not under the control of the research investigator. Both of those conditions apply to this evaluation effort.

Because of the history of this research project, both longitudinal and cross-sectional analysis strategies were used to examine the impact of support group participation upon selected caregiver outcomes. We were originally funded to perform only a cross-sectional study of the caregivers of memory-impaired older adults. In spite of the increased methodological compromises, we examined the impact of participation in caregiver support groups by comparing caregivers who were and were not members of support groups on selected outcomes of interest. Funding constraints not withstanding, a longitudinal study at that point in time would have been difficult. At the time of our initial survey, 22 support groups were operational and study participants either belonged or did not belong to those support groups. (It should be noted, however, that the reason for not participating in a support group was lack of desire for some respondents and lack of availability of a local support group for others.) Thus the timing of the first survey was not geared to the beginning of respondents' participation in support groups and a before-after design would have been precluded even in the absence of funding constraints.

After beginning the initial survey, we were awarded the funds to perform a one-year follow-up survey of the caregiver sample. During the interval between surveys, new support groups were developed in 15 additional North Carolina communities. A sufficient number of re-spondents joined these new support groups that it was possible to examine a subgroup of caregivers before and after they joined community support groups. This presented us with an opportunity to replicate our cross-sectional findings by examining patterns of change in selected outcomes for that subset of caregivers who joined community support groups between the two times of measurement.

We examined four caregiver outcomes in order to assess the impact of the family support groups: (a) knowledge of Alzheimer's disease and related disorders, (b) knowledge about the availability of community-based services especially relevant to memory-impaired older adults and their families, (c) utilization of such services, and (d) feelings of being misunderstood and/or lonely. Clearly these are not the only outcomes that are potentially sensitive to the impact of support group participa-tion. For example, we might have hypothesized that support group participation would affect caregiver well-being, especially social partici-pation and psychological distress.

We chose to examine a more restricted set of outcomes, however. We believed it important to examine only specific outcomes especially likely to be affected directly by the activities of the support groups. One of the primary goals of support groups is to provide opportunities for mutual support—a function that we hypothesized might decrease perceptions of loneliness and being misunderstood, even if it was not sufficient to decrease psychological distress at a broader level. A second goal of support groups is to provide members with information about the problems they face and strategies for managing those problems. Thus we believed that support group members would know more than nonmembers about Alzheimer's disease and relevant community services. The decision to examine utilization of community services was based on somewhat flimsier logic, but we hoped that if support group members knew more about community service programs, they also would utilize those programs more frequently.

Table 12.1 presents the results of the cross-sectional comparisons of the outcome measures for sample members who were and were not support group members. There was a nearly even split in the sample between support group participants (52%) and nonparticipants (48%). It should be noted that we performed empirical checks to determine whether one-to-one network participation also should be taken into account. Those analyses indicated that including one-to-one participation status added no new information to that available through a straightforward comparison of caregivers who did and did not participate in support groups. Significance tests reported in Table 12.1 are based on t-tests for the differences between means and z-tests for the differences between proportions.

As Table 12.1 indicates, most of the outcomes are significantly related to support group participation. Knowledge of Alzheimer's disease and related disorders were measured via a short, 10-item true/false test. As expected, support group members exhibited significantly higher test scores than nonmembers, though the difference was quite modest. Knowledge of community services was ascertained via having caregivers identify the availability of specific types of programs in their communities. As shown in the table, support groups members exhibited significantly greater knowledge of all eight types of community services than nonmembers. Combined, the findings concerning knowledge of Alzheimer's disease and community services suggest that the support groups were adequately performing the knowledge function.

Unfortunately, there is little evidence that the increased knowledge about community services characteristic of support group participants translated into comparable increases in the utilization of those services. Only two of the categories—use of part-time paid helpers and mental health counseling for the caregiver—significantly differed between

TABLE 12.1
Relationships Between Support Group Participation and
Selected Outcomes (cross-sectional findings)

| | Member of Support Group | |
	No	Yes
Knowledge of Alzheimer's disease (means)	7.31	7.92**
Knowledge of community services (percentages)		
visiting nurse services	42	59**
adult day care	31	52**
homemaker services	31	50**
part-time paid help	45	70**
full-time (live-in) paid help	26	48**
hospital-based respite care	19	40**
nursing home-based respite care	15	27*
mental health counseling	46	68**
Utilization of community services (percentages)		
visiting nurse services	20	20
adult day care	11	12
homemaker services	13	15
part-time paid help	39	51*
full-time (live-in) paid help	10	9
hospital-based respite care	9	9
nursing home-based respite care	7	6
mental health counseling	16	29*
Feelings of loneliness (percentages)	55	35**
Feel no one understands (percentages)	46	32**

*$p \leq .05$; **$p < .01$.

support group members and nonmembers. As expected, for those two services, support group members reported higher rates of utilization. Nonetheless, the evidence for effects of support group participation upon service utilization is quite limited and we do not believe that the effects are particularly meaningful.

The final outcomes examined are feelings of loneliness or of being misunderstood as reported by the caregivers. As Table 12.1 indicates, support group members were significantly less likely than nonmembers to report feeling lonely or feeling that no one understands them. These findings suggest that the community support groups also increased feelings of mutual support.

Two cautions need to be kept in mind when considering the data presented in Table 12.1. First, although only about half of the members of our sample were support group members at the initial survey, all respondents were on the FSP mailing list. Consequently, all respondents obtained the quarterly newsletter and other mail information provided by the Duke Family Support Program. Because receipt of these materials is a constant across the sample, these materials are unlikely to result in differences between support group members and nonmembers. Nonetheless, the sample as a whole is probably somewhat more sophisticated about memory impairment and relevant community services than caregivers who do not receive such informational materials.

Second, and even more important, Table 12.1 presents cross-sectional, bivariate relationships between support group participation and selected outcomes. Thus the direction of causal order is unclear and we cannot be sure that better informed and less lonely caregivers were not more likely to participate in support groups than their less well-informed and/or more psychologically isolated peers. Moreover, other personal characteristics may be associated with the decision to join a support group and it may be these personal characteristics that account for the relationships observed in Table 12.1. Although the effects of personal characteristics cannot be definitively eliminated, we statistically examined the relationships between caregivers' personal characteristics (including demographic variables, characteristics of the caregiving context, caregiver resources, and the entire battery of well-being indicators) and support group participation. Much to our surprise—but also to our delight— none of these factors was significantly related to support group participation.

Between the first and second surveys, new support groups were established in 15 North Carolina communities. Thus it was not surprising to find that 49 persons had joined support groups between surveys. Although this subgroup is very small, longitudinal analyses were performed to determine changes in the outcome measures from before to after support group participation; results are presented in Table 12.2. It should be noted that the test of knowledge about Alzheimer's disease and related disorders was not included in the follow-up because of time limitations.

Overall, the results in Table 12.2 support the cross-sectional findings, though fewer of them are statistically significant (primarily because of the decreased sample size). Again, support group participation is associated with increased knowledge about relevant community services and decreased feelings of loneliness or being misunderstood. Also as previously, however, support group participation is not associated with increased utilization of community service programs.

Although we did not consider it an evaluation outcome, we also obtained information about members' satisfaction with their support groups. At the first survey, 96% of support group members rated their support groups as being helpful or very helpful to them; the comparable

TABLE 12.2
Changes in Outcomes Before and After Support Group
Participation (longitudinal findings)

	Time 1	Time 2
Knowledge of community services (percentages)		
visiting nurse services	32	48
adult day care	28	48**
homemaker services	30	46*
part-time paid help	42	60*
full-time (live-in) paid help	18	42**
hospital-based respite care	16	30*
nursing home-based respite care	14	24
mental health counseling	44	62*
Utilization of community services (percentages)		
visiting nurse services	18	20
adult day care	8	12
homemaker services	10	10
part-time paid help	28	46*
full-time (live-in) paid help	4	4
hospital-based respite care	0	0
nursing home-based respite care	2	2
mental health counseling	12	18
Feelings of loneliness (percentages)	44	30*
Feel no on understands (percentages)	42	20**

*p ≤ .05; **p ≤ .01.

percentage at follow-up was 94%. These reports of satisfaction are buttressed by reports of frequency of participation. At Time 1, 90% of the support group members reported regular or frequent attendance at group meetings. By Time 2, this percentage had dropped somewhat to 74%. Ratings of satisfaction and attendance must be interpreted with caution in that persons who are not satisfied with support group activities are likely to drop out of the support groups and their dissatisfactions may be overlooked. Nonetheless, we view the reports of participant satisfaction as corroborating evidence concerning the usefulness of the support groups to members.

Concluding Comments

Having examined the effects of community support groups for caregivers of memory-impaired adults upon selected outcomes, we can return briefly to the link between this project and primary prevention.

We noted earlier that the high levels of psychological distress exhibited by our caregiver sample would lead some observers to reject the community support groups as primary prevention interventions. Other observers might disqualify the support groups from the arena of primary prevention because of our failure to demonstrate that support group participation reduces the incidence of mental health problems.

Our evaluation focused upon outcomes we expected to be directly affected by support group participation: knowledge of dementing disease, knowledge of relevant community services, perceptions of loneliness and being misunderstood, and, to a lesser degree, utilization of community services. In spite of some obvious methodological limitations, the results suggest that support group participation has positive influences upon caregivers' levels of knowledge and perceptions of mutual support. We neither looked for nor found, however, evidence that support group participation is sufficient to decrease the incidence of mental illness or psychological distress. In short, we believe that there is evidence that support groups have useful benefits to members, but we do not claim that they prevent mental illness or psychological distress.

In spite of these reservations, the goals and demonstrable effects of the support groups are closely related to one major strategy advocated in the primary prevention literature: efforts to help individuals achieve competency skills that can see them through rough times (see Albee, 1980; Danish & D'Augelli, 1980). The caregiver support groups are dedicated to the goal of helping members to be more effective caregivers (Gwyther & Brooks, 1983)—more effective in the sense of providing higher quality care to memory-impaired adults and more effective in the sense of protecting the well-being of the caregivers. There is a direct link between the goal of more effective caregiving and caregiver competency.

If support groups provide information about the management of problems such as wandering and incontinence, a competency skill has been transmitted. If support groups teach caregivers how to obtain the most definitive diagnostic tests available for ruling out reversible causes of dementia, the caregivers' competencies have been enhanced. If support groups provide caregivers with opportunities to unbottle their frustrations and resentment to other caregivers such that the inertia of hopelessness is replaced with the comfort of self-validation, competency skills of caregivers have been facilitated. These are the kinds of issues with which support groups grapple and they are highly relevant to caregiver competency. Thus if one accepts the viewpoint that building competence is a legitimate component of primary prevention, we would argue that the community support groups described in this chapter are highly relevant.

Another important feature of bolstering competency is helping people to know when they have reached their own limits. In the context of caregiving for memory-impaired older adults, this issue arises frequently with regard to institutionalization of the demented patient. Research results consistently demonstrate that most family caregivers delay institutionalization for as long as possible—often beyond healthful limits. Indeed, family physicians typically recommend institutionalization of the patient considerably earlier than caregivers are willing to accept it. Support groups typically devote considerable time to educating members about the process of institutionalization and the circumstances under which it is the least undesirable of the options open to the caregiver.

Although we believe that community support groups help to enhance caregiver competency, such programs should not be the only service programs available to family caregivers. Even the best informed and most competent caregiver faces a draining and potentially debilitating situation. Other forms of assistance are needed to help ease caregiver burden. Our surveys, as well as the research of others, suggest that respite care is the service that caregivers desire most but is least available. Respite care refers to temporary relief from the responsibilities of caregiving. Respite care can be delivered as an in-home, a day center, and/or an institutional service and should be available for periods of time ranging from a few hours to a few days. We are currently establishing two respite care demonstration sites that will serve caregivers of demented patients in four North Carolina counties. We believe that the availability and utilization of respite care services will have measurable effects on caregivers' levels of social participation and thus will directly affect one of the two dimensions of well-being most at risk for caregiving-related decrements.

Family caregiving—both for dementing diseases and other chronic conditions—is a situation that affects millions of Americans and will continue to be a family pattern for the foreseeable future. Community support groups appear to be one useful mechanism for enhancing caregiver effectiveness. These and other programs should be encouraged and nurtured. The dedication, commitment, and love of family members struggling to provide the best possible care for relatives whose lives have been destroyed by a cruel trick of nature are inspiring to behold. We should not let their efforts be unnoticed or unassisted.

Note

1. The research reported in this chapter was supported by grants from the AARP Andrus Foundation.

References

Albee, G. W. (1980). A competency model must replace the defect model. In L. A. Bond & J. C. Rosen (Eds.), *Competence and coping during adulthood*. Hanover, NH: University Press of New England.

Bergmann, K. (1975). The epidemiology of senile dementia. *British Journal of Psychiatry, 9,* 100-109.

Brody, E. M. (1981). "Women in the middle" and family help to older people. *Gerontologist, 21,* 471-480.

Brody, S., Poulshock, W., & Mascioschi, F. (1978). The family caring unit: A major consideration in the long-term support system. *Gerontologist, 18,* 556-561.

Cantor, M. H. (1983). Strain among caregivers: A study of experience in the United States. *Gerontologist, 23,* 597-604.

Comptroller General of the United States. (1977). *Report to the Congress on home health—the need for a national policy to better provide for the elderly*. Washington, DC: General Accounting Office.

Cowen, E. L. (1978). Demystifying primary prevention. In D. G. Forgays (Ed.), *Primary prevention of psychopathology: Vol. 2. Environmental influences*. Hanover, NH: University Press of New England.

Danish, S. J., & A. R. D'Augelli (1980). Promoting competence and enhancing development through life development intervention. In L. A. Bond & J. C. Rosen (Eds.), *Competence and coping during adulthood*. Hanover, NH: University Press of New England.

Dillman, D. A. (1978). *Mail and telephone surveys: The total design method*. New York: John Wiley.

Estes, C. L., & Freeman, H. E. (1976). Strategies of design and research for intervention. In R. H. Binstock & E. Shanas (Eds.), *Handbook of aging and the social sciences*. New York: Van Nostrand Reinhold.

Fengler, A. P., & Goodrich, N. (1979). Wives of elderly disabled men. The hidden patients. *Gerontologist, 19,* 175-183.

George, L. K. (1980). *Role transitions in later life: A social stress perspective*. Monterey, CA: Brooks/Cole.

George, L. K., & Bearon, L. B. (1980). *Quality of life in older persons: Meaning and measurement*. New York: Human Sciences Press.

Goldston, S. E. (1977). Defining primary prevention. In G. W. Albee & J. M. Joffe (Eds.), *Primary prevention of psychopathology: Vol. 1. The issues*. Hanover, NH: University Press of New England.

Gordon, G., & Morse, E. V. (1975). Evaluation research. In A. Inkeles (Ed.), *Annual review of sociology* (Vol. 1). Palo Alto, CA: Annual Reviews, Inc.

Gwyther, L., & Brooks, B. (1983). *Mobilizing networks of mutual support: How to develop Alzheimer caregivers' support groups*. Durham, NC: Duke University Center for the Study of Aging and Human development.

House, J. S. (1981). *Work stress and social support*. Reading, MA: Addison-Wesley.

Ikels, C. (1983). The process of caretaker selection. *Research on Aging, 5,* 491-510.

Kent, D., Kastenbaum, R., & Sherwood, S. (Eds.). (1972). *Research, planning and action for the elderly*. New York: Behavioral Publications.

Lieberman, M. A., & Bond, G. R. (1979). Problems in studying outcomes. In M. A. Lieberman & L. D. Borman (Eds.), *Self-help groups for coping with crisis*. San Francisco: Jossey-Bass.

Lieberman, M. A., & Borman, L. D. (1979). Overview: The nature of self-help groups. In M. A. Lieberman & L. D. Borman (Eds.), *Self-help group for coping with crisis*. San Francisco: Jossey-Bass.

Mortimer, J. A., Schuman, L. M., & French, L. R. (1981). Epidemiology of dementing illness. In J. A. Mortimer & L. M. Schuman (Eds.), *The epidemiology of dementia*. New York: Oxford University Press.

Sagarin, E. (1969). *Odd man in: Societies of deviants in America*. New York: Quadrangle.

Sainsbury, P., & Grad de Alarcon, J. (1970). The psychiatrist and the geriatric patient: The effects of community care on the family of the geriatric patient. *Journal of Geriatric Psychiatry, 1*, 23-41.

Silverman, P. R. (1980). *Mutual help groups: Organization and development*. Newbury Park, CA: Sage.

Zarit, S. H., Reeves, K. E., & Bach-Peterson, J. (1980). Relatives of the impaired elderly: Correlates of feelings of burden. *Gerontologist, 20*, 649-655.

PART V

Overviews

13

Integration:
The Preventionist's Craft

Richard H. Price

The chapters in this volume range widely across a great variety of programs and themes. No rigid methodological strategy for summary and integration could possibly do them all justice. The task of summary and integration is much like that faced by a historian or perhaps a literary critic. In that tradition then I will identify themes and patterns that emerged in these chapters and reflect on these themes as they emerge in each contribution. In addition to the manifest themes of the conference, I believe I have detected a number of emergent themes as well. These emergent themes tell us a good deal about the craft of prevention. I will describe each of these emergent themes and try to show how each author has contributed to them and to our understanding of the craft of prevention.

Families and Transitions

First, let us consider some of the themes suggested by the conference itself. These themes are the fertile soil created by Lynne Bond and her colleagues in organizing the conference and they deserve special comment. First, of course, is the theme of the family. Ray Kirk, the Deputy Commissioner of Social and Rehabilitative Services for the State of Vermont, reminded us that all is not well with families and children.[1] As the "official father" of over 3000 children in Vermont for whom he has the responsibility of care and custody, Dr. Kirk was particularly concerned about what he saw as a real increase in the problems of these children. He suggested that we do not have to look too far to identify some of the sources of these children's problems. Holes in the safety net for children and families are growing larger. We may soon have weapons in outer space but, at the same time, more and more families and children are becoming dependent and vulnerable.

On the other hand, Howard Bahr, a sociologist with a historical perspective, warns us not to romanticize the traditional family. In many cases, the circumstances in which children and families lived were far from admirable in the past. We should not try to return to these earlier times. Perhaps the "traditional family" is a mythical entity and perhaps families are doing better than ever. Bahr's perspective is helpful. But creating contrasts with a grim past can lead to complacency about the circumstances of today. Human suffering is a concrete fact today. Preventing that suffering for families and children is one of the critical roles of primary prevention.

Consider the second theme of these chapters, the idea of transitions. Some of the transitions discussed are so obviously painful that the opportunity for prevention is readily apparent. The problems of divorce described by Arnold Stolberg, those of widowhood discussed by Phyllis Silverman, the impact of a child's life-threatening illness on the family described by Ruth Stein and her colleagues, and the burden of care for spouses or children of aging parents described by Linda George and Lisa Gwyther are examples of such transitions. These are transitions where the stresses seem clear and where prevention opportunities abound. In other cases, the consequences may be more subtle. Sylvia Schmidt and Deanna Tate describe the movement of women back into the workplace as creating still another set of transitions and opportunities for prevention.

So the themes of family well-being and transition throughout the life span are well represented in these chapters. At the same time, these scholars have managed, sometimes by intent and sometimes by implication, to paint a second picture. While considering families in their myriad forms and transitions, these chapters provide us with a composite picture of the craft of prevention. In what follows, I want to identify several skills that I believe are critical to the craft of primary prevention.

The Craft of Prevention

Let me now turn to some of the emergent themes in these chapters. I will try to illustrate each of these themes by offering examples from the various chapters.

Reframing the Problem

Many if not all of the prevention programs described in this volume are inspired by *creative insights that reframe the problem* at hand. The process of reframing is something a bit more complicated than the idea implied in Kurt Lewin's dictum that "there is nothing so useful as a good theory." Reframing is not just theorizing. Reframing a problem shifts our attention from one aspect of the problem to another. It reverses figure and ground and makes some aspect of the problem more salient and perhaps more amenable to change. As the reframing takes place, other aspects of the problem may recede into the background.

Reframing a problem can make action seem possible where it didn't seem so before. Consider some examples. Ruth Stein and the research group at Albert Einstein College of Medicine have been concerned with developing prevention programs for children with chronic health problems. They were confronted with dozens of diagnoses, the whole developmental range of problems, and numerous specialists claiming expertise in dealing with these children. These researchers had the intellectual courage to argue that the best way to think about these problems is essentially noncategorically. They did not think about diagnoses as the central fact of the problem or even etiology or prognosis. Instead, they argued that there is at least as much variability within the diagnoses as there is between them. It was then commonalities across diagnostic categories that reframed the problem for them. They argued that there are dimensions of illness that affect psychological and social well-being and go well beyond the question of whether the problem is diabetes or childhood cancer. That is a clear example of creative reframing.

Consider a second example of reframing. Phyllis Silverman described the problems of bereavement and the question of mutual support. She said, "We have to reframe the problem. We have only been focusing on the problem of suffering in bereavement. The suffering is real enough. But the important issue is to change our focus from the management of sorrow to the management of growth and change." The question for those of us concerned with prevention is how to facilitate and to nurture that change. So reframing the problem of widowhood makes it an opportunity, as Silverman suggested, "an unwelcome opportunity," for further growth and development.

Sandra Mitchell provides still another example of creative reframing. She and her research group at the University of Washington are concerned with programs for the newborn. They are centrally concerned with the question of maternal competence. As she described the concept, there was a reframing of the idea of maternal competence, that is, I believe, important for prevention more generally. Her reframing insight was that maternal competence is really dyadic competence between mother and child. Maternal competence is mutual pleasure and mutual interaction. This reframing of the idea of maternal competence does not focus only on attempts to change the mother or the child but on attempts to change the relationship between the two. Considering our very modest capacity to intervene, one of the few chances to make a difference may be to reset those relational trajectories and, perhaps, to create the opportunity for dyadic competence.

In considering the problem of family violence, Carolyn Swift reminded us that there is a growing shift in current thinking about family violence. Swift argues that it does not make sense to think about family violence in conventional prevention terms that focus only on the stress or only on the host. She instead emphasized the issue of subordinate status in the family as a critical aspect of family violence. Power is the issue. When the problem of family violence captured the public's imagination little more than a decade ago, power was not an issue in the debate. It was a forbidden term, people didn't talk much about power, especially because our idealized image of families did not consider power at all. Instead, people concerned with family violence focused on issues of pathology and the observation that somehow family violence was transmitted from one generation to another. To focus on power and status reframes the problem.

Our first theme suggests, then, that those of us concerned with prevention should spend time and energy trying to reframe the problem with which we are concerned. In the act of reframing, we provide ourselves with intellectual leverage and new insights about where the possibilities for change actually lie.

Creating Choices and Alternatives

There is a recurring concern about choices and alternatives in these chapters as well. Providing and enhancing choices and alternatives for families and children was an unexpected but surprisingly common theme. Discovering and creating choices for people lies at the heart of the idea of primary prevention. People with choices have the power to direct their own lives. One of the jobs in primary prevention is to help discover and create those choices. Let me offer some examples.

The work of Shure and Spivack on interpersonal cognitive problem solving is very well known but sometimes not thought of in terms of choices. Central to the idea of interpersonal cognitive problem solving is teaching the skill of generating alternative approaches to solving a problem. In order to enhance the capacity of children to survive in their school and family life, they need access to alternative ways of solving problems. This is a powerful idea and it is at the heart of the interpersonal problem-solving strategy.

Consider another example. Bernard Guerney described his research program on relationship enhancement in terms of choices. He argued that relationship enhancement is not just a group of skills that are taught to people. It is a program designed to provide new skills that give people choices about how to express their deepest feelings and concerns to others.

Sylvia Schmidt described a variety of programs for employers that support families' well-being, including child care programs. Child care provides options for families and primary caretakers in particular. It is only now that the incentives are beginning to develop to provide the possibility of choices for working families. Interestingly, such programs provide choices not only for workers but for employers as well.

Using Research

Many of the chapters in this volume make creative use of research in defining problems. The hard-won insights from systematic and sometimes plodding research can tell us a great many things. It can help us decide whether what we think is a problem really is a problem. Research findings can tell us where to intervene and whether we have accomplished what we had hoped. And, of course, research provides us with a useful antidote to our own assurance that we understand what's going on.

An excellent example of this use of research is Arnold Stolberg's work on prevention programs for divorcing families. His early research began to identify predictors of child maladaption in the context of divorce. He was able to show how marital hostility in divorcing parents created still other effects, including the modeling of hostility for children, the interruption of the critical coparenting process, and the internalization of blame. Who created all that anger, wonders the child. Am I responsible?

Stolberg was also able to show how life changes such as moving to a new neighborhood can contribute to child maladaption. The move produces decreased time with one of the parents, a whole new set of peer relationships to cope with, a caretaking parent who is drawn away from the parenting role by simple geographical dislocation, and the frustration of having fewer resources to go around.

Still another example of insight-producing research is that of George and Gwyther's work on the stresses on caregivers of mentally impaired elderly. Their survey showed that caregivers have only a quarter of the time of their age peers to interact with their social world. The mental health implications of this kind of isolation seem clear, but George and Gwyther's research went farther and focused on the perceived adequacy of social support in this group. For that subgroup of caregivers where social support was not seen as adequate, even more distress was experienced.

George and Gwyther's research provided still other insights. Programs can sometimes be developed that appear well reasoned but can actually add to the demands and the burdens of a vulnerable group. The caregivers in this study already were experiencing enough burdens so that the development of mutual support groups may have in some cases added to the strain. The research results suggest that respite care must be a critical component for this population. So the feedback loop from research to practice continues as an important part of the craft of prevention.

Facing Dilemmas

Facing dilemmas is perhaps inherent in the prevention enterprise. Consider Kerby Alvy's project aimed at developing parenting programs for Black children and their parents. He faced a dilemma in trying to create culturally sensitive parenting programs for Black families. Yet there are divergent views of what is appropriate parenting behavior in different segments of the Black community. Alvy is struggling to solve this dilemma by involving the Black community in the design of the program.

There is another dilemma in the craft of prevention that is beautifully portrayed in the novel *Arrowsmith* by Sinclair Lewis (1982). The important part of the story, for our purposes, involves what I call the "Arrowsmith Dilemma." It is a dilemma that we all face with prevention efforts. Arrowsmith was a tough-minded medical researcher working on a vaccine for the plague; but he had only a laboratory product that had not been field-tested. He had to know if it worked. A plague broke out in the West Indies and he was confronted with a dilemma: Do you give the vaccine to the whole population and hope that it will do some good but never really know, or do you give it to half the population and find out the truth? For Arrowsmith, the truth was most important. He could see beyond the small island in the West Indies to potential plague victims throughout the world.

Creating Incentives

Even after years of committed work to develop prevention programs that address real needs and have evidence of effectiveness, we have no reason to believe that anyone else will be interested in adopting them.

People have to have incentives to do prevention work. As workers in the field of primary prevention, we must be sensitive to the question of incentives—where they are and how to create them. Sometimes incentives are created by a new tax law that gives employers incentives to institute day care. In other cases, it takes on entrepreneurial spirit to do the job.

I consider Charles Roppel and Marion Jacob's work in California as an example of the entrepreneurial spirit that has two aspects. One has to do with seeing an opportunity, the other has to do with creating incentives to get people to act. Roppel reported that 90% of Californians said they thought it was a good idea to seek out someone else who had the same problem they did, but that only 9% of the people actually did so. In that discrepancy, Roppel saw an opportunity. The opportunity turned into his public education campaign called "Friends Can Be Good Medicine."

The other aspect of the entrepreneurial spirit has to do with creating incentives. Roppel's school health contest is a striking example. Having created health-promotion literature, films, and information that could be acted on by children and adolescents, he still had to reach the kids. Roppel created a contest. In California, 1800 schools participated in the contest. One million children had these programs going on in their schools. Roppel created powerful incentives to participate in prevention programs.

Conclusion

Recently, Donald Campbell (1985) observed that researchers concerned with the task of prevention have a very special duty. It is the duty to stay with the problem. We cannot walk away from the problem just because it seems complex or intractable. Basic researchers will frequently leave a problem that does not seem solvable because there are many other tractable problems and only so much time in anyone's life. But preventionists have to stay with the problem. When a problem is poorly defined, it is their own obligation to define it more clearly. If it is poorly understood, our research must make it more understandable.

As practitioners of the craft of prevention, we will have to keep attempting to reframe the problem, to produce intellectual leverage for ourselves. We will always be in the business of creating choices and alternatives for families. And our craft will always face dilemmas and require an entrepreneurial spirit. But above all, we will have to stay with the problem.

342   Richard H. Price

Note

1. Ray Kirk's comments were a part of the introductory remarks to the Vermont Conference on the Primary Prevention of Psychopathology held June 1985 in Burlington, Vermont.

References

Campbell, D. (1985, May 12). Personal communication.
Lewis, S. (1982). *Arrowsmith*. Cutchogue, NY: Buccaneer Books.

14

What Makes Primary Prevention Programs Work?

Lynne A. Bond
Barry M. Wagner

The primary prevention of psychopathology and the promotion of psychological well-being are no longer in their infancy. As the chapters in this and other volumes (e.g., Buckner, Trickett, & Corse, 1985; Joffe, Albee, & Kelly, 1984; Kessler & Goldston, 1986; Rosen & Solomon, 1985) suggest, there is ever-increasing documentation of the effectiveness of prevention and promotion programs. But if these efforts are to thrive, then we need to build on each other's accomplishments. In order to further our efforts, we need to scrutinize our successes carefully to determine those characteristics which distinguish effective from ineffective programs. What can we learn from successful efforts in order to guide our future progress?

In this chapter, we will attempt to extract from successful prevention efforts a number of guidelines and considerations that appear to be important in developing effective programs. These thoughts emerge from our own review of present and past programs, lengthy discussions with our colleagues, and, most important, the contributions from a panel discussion at the 1985 Vermont Conference on Primary Prevention, which included several of the contributors to this volume. Panelists were Lynne Bond, Beverly Long, Richard Price, Myrna Shure, and Carolyn Swift. The guidelines we present in this chapter are far from exhaustive. Moreover, it is not clear that every program could or should encompass them all. Rather, our intention is for these guidelines to be used as a sort of checklist of points to consider when developing and implementing any prevention/promotion effort.

344   Bond, Wagner

General Orientations
Characteristic of Effective
Prevention and Promotion Programs

(1) A multisystem, multilevel perspective. In the past decade, there has been a growing appreciation of the need to consider human functioning from a multisystem, multilevel perspective. That is, in order to understand and foster competent functioning of individuals, it is critical to acknowledge that individuals do not "stand alone," but instead are an integral part of hierarchies of overlapping systems: dyads and family systems that are embedded in subcultures and communities, which are part of even larger, more complex social, political, and legal systems. With the current state-of-the-art of research and programming technology, it is unlikely that one could fully address all of the relevant variables when designing a program. Yet, it is important to consider which of the forces or influences at the many levels of systems interplay most significantly with the functioning of the individuals targeted in any effort. For example, in the case of a child who is experiencing the divorce of his or her parents, it is important to consider not only the family context, but also the attitude of the community to divorce, the orientation of the legal system to divorce, the clergy's perspective, and the changing course of opinion of society at large. Ideally, a prevention program would target as many levels of influence as possible in identifying and targeting agents for change, monitoring program implementation, and evaluating program effects. If practical constraints call for a less than comprehensive effort, then at the very least it is important to be sensitive and open to the potential influences of multiple systems.

(2) An emphasis upon the promotion of competence. Two tactics have been emphasized for preventing the development of psychological and physical disorders (Albee, 1980): (a) modifying the environment in order to reduce or eliminate stressful agents, and (b) enhancing the competence of individuals so that they can deal more effectively with stressful agents. Both are important tactics and may be simultaneously employed in a prevention effort. Because many stressful agents are an unavoidable part of life, and, in fact, are often an integral factor in fostering development (e.g., Danish & D'Augelli, 1980; Lazarus, 1980), however, the promotion of competence is an important goal to keep in mind, even when designing programs in which reduction of environmental stressors is the primary target. The broad-reaching successes of certain prevention efforts that have emphasized promotion of compe-

tence are likely due, in part, to the generalized effects of their outcomes. The individual strengths and skills engendered by these prevention/promotion efforts typically are neither time- nor situation-specific; individuals and groups can apply these competencies to contexts beyond those that inspired the prevention effort. The Relationship Enhancement skills programs described by Guerney (see Guerney, this volume) illustrate this approach.

A process approach to competency building is characteristic of many of the most successful prevention/promotion efforts. Their emphasis is upon providing component skills rather than supplying "answers." In this way, the participants, themselves, develop strategies for adaptively responding to the changing demands of their environments, as well as for creating and restructuring conditions so as to make them conducive to their own well-being and that of the many systems of which they are a part. The work of Shure and Spivack (e.g., Shure, in this volume; Shure & Spivack, 1978, 1982; Spivack, Platt, & Shure, 1976) exemplifies this approach, with its emphasis upon teaching *how* to think rather than *what* to think.

(3) Empowerment of individuals and groups. Often interwoven with the focus on promoting competence is an emphasis upon empowerment, which differs radically from traditional methods of mental health professionals. The expert-helper model is rejected, and replaced by a model in which program participants are empowered to deal with problems of living and provided with opportunities for growth without continued reliance on professional help. In an empowerment model, individuals and groups function within a context in which they have greater options and control—not merely the illusion of alternatives and decision-making opportunities, but actual power to determine the courses of their lives. These programs treat life transitions as not simply crises to be coped with, but as opportunities for change and development. An examination of successful prevention efforts reveals the benefits of incorporating the empowerment model into both the content and the structure of programs. Consider the structure of a mutual support, self-help group: members find that others in situations similar to their own are capable of problem finding, problem solving, and providing help and support. And as individuals engage in group decision making, problem solving, and mutual aid, contributing to the support and development of others, they gain the confidence, power, and skills to make choices in their own lives as well. Empowerment adds greater flexibility and potential for growth beyond the immediately targeted situation.

(4) Sensitivity to the developmental process. Sensitivity to the developmental process includes not only a sensitivity to the chronological age of the participants, but also an awareness of the point in the evolution of the system—whether it be a family system, a dyadic system, a community, or whatever—at which the program is being implemented. If a program sets out to address the needs of individuals during critical transitions, then it is important to take into account the point in the transition at which the individuals are encountered. In this regard, it may be necessary for programs to have the flexibility to address the needs of individuals, families, or larger systems that are at different points in a transition. For example, the needs of families of the chronically ill may differ considerably depending upon how far along family members are in the process of understanding and responding both to the illness and to one another's reactions.

Program Development and Refinement

(5) Guidance by scientific theory. Those prevention programs that have been most successful have been guided by a sound theoretical perspective. Program content as well as structure have been grounded in scientific principles that allow the preventionist to formulate a rationale as to how and why the program should work, and outcomes that should be expected. Working from sound theory has allowed program planners to maintain a focused direction. On the one hand, the theory provides a basis for pinpointing the specific design components that should be most central to guiding the program. On the other hand, it keeps the preventionist grounded in the "big picture" rather than lost in the particulars. This emphasis upon scientific theory is not to suggest that gut feeling and intuition are unimportant in program design. On the contrary, effective practitioners and researchers use their hunches to guide their inquiry, trying to understand why certain strategies feel right while others do not. By linking this inquiry to broader theory, however, they develop a more intensive and extensive framework to guide their work, to structure systematic program modifications, and to generalize their efforts to new contexts. Moreover, they have a framework from which to generalize their results; their program outcomes contribute to a greater network of understanding. Because it is easy to stray from one's guiding scientific principles once enmeshed in the operation of a program, it is important at the outset to identify clearly those principles central to the theoretical perspective of the program and to design a means for monitoring adherence to those principles.

(6) Ensuring replicability of the program. Replication is one of the hallmarks of the scientific method and certainly a characteristic of those programs that "work." In fact, a program must be replicable to permit an adequate test of its merit, that is, to prove that it works. And a program's success may be judged, in part, by its potential for wide-scale use, which, itself, depends upon its replicability. The existence of a sound theoretical base supports the potential for replication because it provides a meaningful context for the details of program implementation; that is, understanding the *spirit* of a program is often critical for replication of the specifics of the program in a meaningful way. At the phase of program design, it is important to incorporate a system for monitoring program implementation, a system that will reveal any distinctions between program design and the actual practice of implementation. For example, interventionists have effectively used daily logs both to oversee program implementation and to document the program for future replication (e.g., see Mitchell, Magyary, Barnard, Sumner, & Booth, this volume).

(7) Field experience by the researcher and program designer. The program designer and/or researcher must spend time directly immersed in the daily workings of the program during both program development (piloting) and program implementation phases. This firsthand experience is important from several perspectives. Translating ideas to practice cannot be done effectively in a vacuum. The program designer must have a true sense of the setting in which the program is being implemented and must have an opportunity to observe, firsthand, the reactions of the targeted population. Direct observation also serves to monitor the program—allowing a determination of whether the program is being implemented as it was intended to be. And watching (or even better, participating in) the daily operation of the program generates the types of insights that lead to creative innovations and modifications for future implementation of the program.

(8) Longitudinal tracking of program operation and effectiveness. As a result of limited resources, the majority of prevention and promotion efforts have been fleeting affairs, lasting a few years at most. While some effective programs have been developed and documented even within these constraints, there is consensus that longitudinal efforts are considerably more likely than short-lived programs to result in effective program development, refinement, implementation, monitoring, evaluation, and dissemination. The mere quantity of time invested in these programs is not their only discriminating factor. The longitudinal plan can also encourage those involved to focus greater energy on *process* issues in development, implementation, evaluation, and dissemination,

building on experience to review and revise current methods, and to identify both intended and unintended program outcomes that occur in the short and long term and that themselves have further effects on the systems in which the target population and the service deliverers are involved. A vision of time tends to generate greater consideration of how one's program fits into other ongoing structures and institutions that, in turn, affects the power, effectiveness, accessibility, and life span of prevention efforts.

Securing Resources for Program Implementation and Maximizing Likelihood of Program Utilization

It is easy to assume naively that if a program is scientifically sound and effective, it will be implemented. As mental health professionals, we typically place too little emphasis on the need to consider operational aspects of our plans. A program may be based on sound scientific principles and guided by an orientation consistent with the broadest goals of prevention, but unless one has the resources necessary to implement the program with integrity, much is in vain. While compromises are often necessary in adopting programs under various conditions, there is a need for great sensitivity to maintaining the integrity of a program. Truncated versions of programs can lead to greater harm than good when their outcomes are generalized to reflect the efficacy (or lack of efficacy) of the larger program model from which they were drawn. Richard Price, in his conference remarks, elaborated upon the notion that the management of prevention activities requires "resource sensitivity," that is, being attuned to locating and attaining resources.

(9) Identifying resources. In embarking upon a prevention effort, one must ask, "What are the most important resources that are needed to get the job done?" A consideration of resources must go beyond finances per se. People, time, legitimacy, and prestige may well be equally important for success. Again, when identifying necessary resources, it is important to think about the success of a prevention program, or more general prevention effort, in the broadest sense—the feasibility of its design, the interworkings of its central and peripheral components, its relationship to ongoing systems and institutions (e.g., social, economic, political, and legal), and so on.

(10) Securing resources. Once necessary resources have been identified, one must ask, "Who are the actors in the environment who have access to

the critical resources?" Both identifying and involving those actors is an essential part of building a successful effort. A desire to stay entirely out of the political arena is understandable but perhaps unrealistic. While mental health professionals are often embarrassed to use political clout, many who have been successful in their efforts stress the absolute necessity of networking and establishing powerful connections and a powerful constituency. It is important to be goal directed, to hook into ongoing structures and organizations that already have resources relevant to one's goals. One should take advantage of the political structure and political organizations, and involve the public and private business sectors. Their resources can play a critical role in contributing legitimacy and prestige to the program and providing access to an entirely new network of resources.

It is useful to identify which of your assets might be valuable to those with clout; which could be offered in exchange for the resources you seek? Recognition, prestige, and legitimacy are commodities that are clearly valued by business and political organizations. Associating a prevention effort with the names of others, even in some minor way, can be a powerful tool for enlisting support and resources. Often, one brief conversation requesting the advice or opinions of others can elicit a sense of ownership sufficient to promote their continued support.

(11) Establishing alternative sources of resources. Once a means of accessing a resource is established, it is important to consider alternative sources for that resource as well. To have only one source is to be dependent and this dependency can place program efforts at great risk. In addition to keeping potential alternative sources of a resource in reserve, having multiple sources that simultaneously contribute to a project is another tack that can help to maintain the commitment of each. For example, two insurance companies involved in a health promotion project will strive to keep pace with one another in an attempt to maintain recognition and goodwill equal to those of their competitor. With this emphasis upon sensitivity to resources, effective program managers view any shift in circumstances surrounding program implementation as opportunity rather than disruption; change suggests the potential for uncovering new means for attaining resources.

Marketing Prevention and Promotion Programs

As noted earlier, a great program is worth little unless it reaches the targeted population. Yet, promoting our work is something for which we have received little guidance. It certainly is easier to market a program once resources are in place, but this may not be the case, particularly when wide-scale dissemination is a goal. Moreover, once the excitement of the program start-up has waned, sustaining the effort can be difficult unless the program has been designed with particular attention to incorporating supportive mechanisms for its maintenance. Marketing a program means arranging contingencies to ensure that it gets used, and use will depend upon those who deliver as well as those who participate in the program.

(12) Assessing the needs of the service deliverers and program recipients. Effective marketing requires taking what Shure has called the "consumer perspective" (see Shure, this volume). One must consider the needs and perspectives of potential program deliverers as well as program recipients, and these considerations must be made with reference to both the content and the structure of the program. Thus in the planning phase it is essential to involve those who have had practical experience both working as a service deliverer and working with the target population. One also benefits from considering the needs and opinions of those more tangentially related to the key players—top-level administrators in service delivery, friends and family of the target recipients, the community. The attitudes of individuals and groups at these levels can powerfully influence the opinions of those who are more directly involved.

(13) Creating translatable, adaptable programming. If a program is to be used, it must be readily defined and adaptable to the requirements of various settings. For example, if a program can be interpreted and implemented only by a sophisticated clinician, then its usefulness is limited. A central aspect of a program's adaptability involves its expense. While a worthwhile program certainly merits allocation of funds, the fact is that limited budgets are available. Thus regardless of how valuable a project may be, its cost will influence its generalizability. The cognitive problem-solving programs of Shure and Spivack (1982) and Weissberg, Gesten, Liebenstein, Schmid, and Hutton (1979) are excellent examples of prevention/promotion efforts that have enjoyed widespread adoption owing to their flexibility, interpretability, and modest expense.

(14) Encouraging a sense of ownership of the program among service deliverers and program recipients. When service deliverers (and pertinent administrators) feel some ownership of a program, they are more likely to use it, and to give it the energy necessary for it to be effective. As mentioned before, a sense of ownership may grow from one brief conversation, whether it involves, for example, consultation during the

program planning phase or discussion about adopting an existing program. Once individuals have played some role in conceptualizing or embracing a program, they are more likely to have a sense of commitment to it and a desire to nurture it. Ideally a program will be flexible enough to allow modifications to fit with the needs and personalities associated with various settings. These modifications provide an avenue for program administrators and deliverers to exercise problem solving and creativity, thereby developing ownership of their venture. Of course, this flexibility must be balanced with sufficient structure inherent in the program to provide firm guidelines for those who want and/or need them, and to maintain the integrity of the program model.

Developing a sense of program ownership among service recipients may be equally important in order to sustain the operation of a project. In considering both the content and the structure of programs, one finds that the great success of process-oriented approaches may stem, in part, from the fact that program recipients often are not simply recipients, but rather are active participants and contributors to the program. The mutual support groups for widows and widowers (see Silverman, this volume) illustrate the active, collaborative role that the target population can play. The incorporation of participant input into program redesign is another means to increase participant ownership as well as the likelihood of program effectiveness in general.

(15) Embedding programs within existing institutions and structures. Several issues raised in this chapter have suggested the benefits of embedding prevention/promotion programs within existing institutions and structures. By incorporating a program into organizations that have close, sustained contact with the targeted population (e.g., places of worship, Girl Scouts and Boy Scouts, schools, businesses), one is more likely to reach that population and maintain the kind of ongoing contact that is essential for effective efforts. There is great potential benefit in involving natural caregivers in the community (e.g., the clergy, or the corner storekeeper) and identifying, educating, and involving the "gatekeepers" of the target population (e.g., funeral directors for the bereaved, lawyers for divorcing families, and physicians for families of the chronically ill).

(16) Making the program engaging for its participants. Despite the quality of a program, it will not be used if it fails to engage its participants. Prevention and promotion programs are sometimes designed to help individuals deal with painful and difficult issues (e.g., death, divorce, illness, unemployment), and/or to persuade individuals to consider or reevaluate certain matters relevant to their lives (e.g., contraception, drug abuse, child stimulation). Thus engaging par-

ticipants and maintaining their involvement is not always a simple accomplishment. Three strategies have proven important: (a) designing a program that allows participants to experience small successes from the start, (b) devising program content that is immediately fun and/or intriguing for participants (e.g., presenting contraceptive information in the context of teen love stories), (c) adopting a program structure that is engaging for participants (e.g., incorporating health education into a game or school competition; see Roppel & Jacobs, in this volume). Both the enjoyment and the accomplishments help to build a motivational base that later strengthens participants' willingness to work through more emotionally or cognitively difficult portions of the program.

Strengthening and Sustaining Prevention and Promotion Efforts

Prevention and promotion programs will be more effective if prevention and promotion efforts, in the broadest sense, are strengthened and sustained. Primary prevention and promotion activities still fail to receive the funding priority they merit. Thus we need to continue to work hard to advocate for our programs. This can be difficult for many of us because, by and large, we have been trained as researchers and/or practitioners and may not feel particularly skilled or comfortable in advocacy work. Yet with the current political and fiscal climates, this work is every bit as important as the energy that goes into the design and implementation of specific programs.

(17) Establishing ties with existing power structures. Again, the need to establish a support network within the existing power structure is apparent. It is naive to imagine that "good science" or "good service" will themselves sustain our efforts. Careful scrutiny of multiple systems can provide insights into ways in which prevention and promotion efforts can be presented as a stand with which those in power want to be associated (e.g., see Roppel & Jacobs, this volume).

(18) Educating policymakers and the public. Both policymakers and the public must be educated about the models and outcomes of prevention efforts. Policymakers must hear of the ways in which their specific constituencies have and/or can prosper from prevention and promotion activities. Education of the public (e.g., see Roppel & Jacobs' use of mass media, in this volume) is also important because prevention and promotion are concepts that are unfamiliar to many, and are seen as entitlements to even fewer. And, of course, as the public increasingly becomes aware of these programs as potential community resources,

elected policymakers will become more responsive to the programs as well—the emphasis on clout reappears!

(19) Training preventionists. Few programs today offer the comprehensive training necessary to develop competent, well-rounded preventionists. In fact, in this chapter, we have suggested that an effective preventionist (or prevention team) needs to wear many hats—those of a sensitive practitioner, a scientist, a politician, a manager, a marketing specialist, and an advocate. Our training programs tend to focus on the first two roles, with little or no attention to the others. And we should emphasize that an effective preventionist needs the skills to serve as a catalyst for change, a stimulus for igniting excitement regarding the implementation of prevention efforts.

How Do We Know
When a Program Has Worked?

As we continue in our efforts to identify the components of prevention programs that work, it will be important to define more clearly what it means to say that a program has "worked." Our focus on narrowly defined quantitative data needs to be broadened to include a greater consideration of qualitative data, as well. By overlooking qualitative data, we often miss the opportunity to explore further which aspects of a program work best for different individuals. Yet at present we have few guidelines for handling qualitative data in any systematic manner. Moreover, we need to look beyond the specific effects we have targeted, to examine ripple effects of our programs. For example, some of the most impressive outcomes of Head Start programs were those involving the parents, families, and communities of the Head Start children; parents returned to school and gained employment, local parks and playgrounds became active community centers, and new community leaders and advocates appeared (e.g., see O'Keefe, 1979). Unexpected Fortuitous Outcomes, or UFO's (a termed coined by Swift in our panel discussion) are often far richer than any effects we had intended. Clearly, these and other issues concerning definition and assessment of program effectiveness will need more attention as we continue to ask, "what makes primary prevention programs work?"

References

Albee, G. W. (1980). The fourth revolution. *Journal of Prevention, 1,* 67-70.
Buckner, J. C., Trickett, E. J., & Corse, S. J. (1985). *Primary prevention in mental health:*

An annotated bibliography (DHHS Publication No. ADM 85-1405). Washington, DC: Government Printing Office.

Danish, S. J., & D'Augelli, A. R. (1980). Promoting competence and enhancing development through life development intervention. In L. A. Bond & J. C. Rosen (Eds.), *Competence and coping during adulthood.* Hanover, NH: University Press of New England.

Joffe, J. M., Albee, G. W., & Kelly, L. D. (Eds.). (1984). *Readings in primary prevention of psychopathology: Basic concepts.* Hanover, NH: University Press of New England.

Kessler, M., & Goldston, S. E. (1986). *A decade of progress in primary prevention.* Hanover, NH: University Press of New England.

Lazarus, R. S. (1980). The stress and coping paradigm. In L. A. Bond & J. C. Rosen (Eds.), *Competence and coping during adulthood.* Hanover, NH: University Press of New England.

O'Keefe, R. A. (1979). What Head Start means to families. In L. G. Katz (Ed.), *Current topics in early childhood education* (Vol. 2). Norwood, NJ: Ablex.

Rosen, J. C., & Solomon, L. J. (Eds.). (1985). *Prevention in health psychology.* Hanover, NH: University Press of New England.

Shure, M. B., & Spivack, G. (1978). *Problem solving techniques in childrearing.* San Francisco: Jossey-Bass.

Shure, M. B., & Spivack, G. (1982). Interpersonal problem solving in young children: A cognitive approach to prevention. *American Journal of Community Psychology, 10,* 341-356.

Spivack, G., Platt, J. J., & Shure, M. B. (1976). *The problem solving approach to adjustment.* San Francisco: Jossey-Bass.

Weissberg, R. P., Gesten, E. L., Liebenstein, N. L., Schmid, K. D., & Hutton, H. (1979). *The Rochester Social Problem Solving (SPS) Program: A training manual for teachers of 2nd-4th grade children.* Rochester, NY: Center for Community Study.

Contributors

Kerby T. Alvy, Ph.D., is the Executive Director of the Center for the Improvement of Child Caring, Inc., Studio City, California, and is a faculty member of the California School of Professional Psychology. He has been active in writing and program development concerning child abuse prevention, parent training, and specifically culturally adapted parent training. He is the Principal Investigator of a NIDA-funded project on Drug Abuse Prevention and Black Parent Training.

Howard M. Bahr, Ph.D., is Professor of Sociology, Brigham Young University. From 1977-1983 he was Director of the Family and Demographic Research Institute at Brigham Young. His extensive research and publications have concerned varied aspects of individual and family development within our changing society. His work has examined Skid Row inhabitants, the disaffiliation of urban females, American ethnicity and religion, divorce and remarriage, and change and continuity over the past 50 years in American family life.

Kathryn E. Barnard, R.N., Ph.D., is Professor of Nursing and Adjunct Professor of Psychology, University of Washington. She is the Principal Investigator of the Seattle Node of the John D. & Catherine T. MacArthur Foundation Research Network on the Transition from Infancy to Early Childhood; she is also principal investigator of the Clinical Nursing Model Project. She is well known for her research involving parent-child interaction, child rearing, and the prevention of developmental dysfunction.

Lynne A. Bond, Ph.D., is Associate Professor of Psychology, and Interim Dean of the Graduate College, University of Vermont. She has chaired several of the Vermont Conferences on the Primary Prevention of

Psychopathology, including that which formed the basis for this volume. She is principal investigator of Listening Partners, a community-based prevention/promotion program designed to support the cognitive and social development of poor rural women and their preschool-aged children. Her research and publications have focused largely on family relationships, infant social and cognitive development, and primary prevention.

Cathryn L. Booth, Ph.D., is Research Associate Professor of Parent and Child Nursing at University of Washington. She is a member of the Seattle Node of the John D. & Catherine T. MacArthur Foundation Research Network on the Transition from Infancy to Early Childhood; she is also coinvestigator of the Clinical Nursing Model Project. Her work has focused on mother-infant interaction, observational methodology, childbirth experiences, and attachment.

Linda K. George, Ph.D., is the Associate Director for Social and Behavioral Programs, Center for the Study of Aging and Human Development, Duke University Medical Center, where she is also Professor of Medical Sociology, Department of Psychiatry, and Professor, Department of Sociology. She has been coprincipal investigator of several projects studying the development of the elderly, as well as of a respite care program for easing the burden of adult caregivers of the elderly. She has published extensively in the fields of aging and mental health aspects of medical sociology.

Bernard G. Guerney, Jr., Ph.D., is Professor of Human Development and Founder and Head of the Individual and Family Consultation Center at the Pennsylvania State University. His research interests include new forms of psychotherapy, marital, and family therapy, with particular interest in those that combine preventive with therapeutic goals. He is also active in mental health problem-prevention programs, the training of professionals and paraprofessionals, training in interpersonal and leadership skills in the workplace, and marital family arbitration.

Lisa P. Gwyther, A.C.S.W., is Coordinator of Continuing Education at Duke University Center for the Study of Aging and Human Development, and Director of the Duke University Family Support Program. Currently she is coordinating 52 support groups for family caregivers of memory-impaired older persons, and is also performing a demonstration evaluation of in-home respite services for family caregivers of persons with Alzheimer's disease. Gwyther has a long history in community service organizations, and program development and training for caregivers of impaired older persons.

Henry T. Ireys, Ph.D., is Codirector for Interventions for the Preventive Intervention Research Center for Child Health at the Albert Einstein College of Medicine, where he is also Assistant Professor of Pediatrics and Psychiatry. A former associate of the Institute for Public Policy Studies at Vanderbilt University, he has been active in analyses of public policies affecting chronically ill children and their families. This work has extended to a concern with secondary problems of young adults with a chronic illness. His recent activities include the development and implementation of a training program in prevention of mental health problems related to child health care.

Marion K. Jacobs, Ph.D., is Codirector of the California Self-Help Center, Coordinator of the Psychology Department Clinic, and Adjunct Professor of Psychology, University of California, Los Angeles. Jacobs is coauthor of the Common Concern Program, a packaged program of audio cassette tapes and printed materials that teach self-help groups how to form and maintain themselves. She is currently engaged in research on group processes in self-help groups.

Dorothy Jones Jessop, Ph.D., is Associate Professor of Pediatrics, and Codirector for Research and Evaluation at the Preventive Intervention Research Center (PIRC) for Child Health, Albert Einstein College of Medicine. She has been involved in an evaluation of the Pediatric Home Care program at Bronx Municipal Hospital Center, and has made major contributions to the development of measurement tools related to the effects of chronic illness on children and families. Currently she is directing, within the PIRC, a program concerned with training lay persons to be family advocates for mothers of children recently diagnosed with an illness.

Diane L. Magyary, M.N., Ph.D., is Assistant Professor of Parent and Child Nursing at the University of Washington and coinvestigator of the Clinical Nursing Model Project. Her research has focused on parent interaction with high risk infants and children and, more recently, parent interaction with chronically ill children.

Sandra K. Mitchell, Ph.D., is Associate Professor of Parent and Child Nursing and Adjunct Associate Professor of Psychology, University of Washington. She is a member of the Seattle Node of the John D. &

Catherine T. MacArthur Foundation Research Network on the Transition from Infancy to Early Childhood; she is also coinvestigator of the Clinical Nursing Model Project. Her work has focused on a variety of aspects of maternal-child health and development including a comparison of different models of prevention programs aimed at fostering the development of high-risk newborns.

Richard H. Price, Ph.D., is Professor and Chairman of the Community Psychology Program at the University of Michigan, where he is also a Faculty Associate of the Institute for Social Research, Survey Research Center. He has long been active in research and training in community psychology and has contributed extensively to the solution of problems involved in evaluating prevention programs. He is Chair of the APA Task Force on Prevention and is Director of the Michigan Prevention Research Center, University of Michigan. His current research includes examinations of occupational stress, and preventive intervention with the unemployed.

Charles E. Roppel is founder and Director of the Mental Health Promotion Branch, Department of Mental Health, for the State of California. In this role, he has been coordinating the establishment of policy guidelines and the development of wellness resources for local county programs, as well as monitoring the implementation of state-funded programs throughout California. He has been extraordinarily successful in developing and implementing mental health mass media preventive education projects.

Sylvia E. Schmidt, Ph.D., is Principal Consultant for Child Care Management Consultants, Inc., Davis, California. Her broad training in family studies and child development led to a concern with employer-supported child care services, and an emphasis upon the benefits of such programs for both families and employers. The specific focus of her professional work has been in planning, developing, and evaluating child care programs in a variety of settings.

Myrna B. Shure, Ph.D., is Professor in the Department of Mental Health Sciences at Hahnemann Medical College, and has been Coprincipal Investigator of the Hahnemann University Prevention Intervention Research Center. She is nationally recognized for the extensive research and writing she has done, in collaboration with George Spivack, on the development and training of interpersonal cognitive problem-solving skills in children. This work has been translated into literally hundreds of prevention programs nationwide.

Phyllis R. Silverman, Ph.D., is Associate Professor at the Massachusetts General Hospital Institute of Health Professions, where she teaches courses on psychosocial development, stress and transitions, social support self-care and mutual help, and living with dying. She is also a Visiting Scholar at the Stone Center for Developmental Services and Studies, Wellesley College. She is well known for her work on widowhood, focusing on mutual support, self-help groups.

Ruth E.K. Stein, M.D., is Professor of Pediatrics, and Director of the Preventive Intervention Research Center (PIRC) for Child Health, Albert Einstein College of Medicine. She has long been interested in issues related to children with a chronic illness, and established one of the first home care programs for these children in the nation, at the Bronx Municipal Hospital Center. As director of the PIRC, she has been involved in a wide variety of preventive intervention programs for infants, children, and adolescents with chronic illness; most recently she has been instrumental in planning a major multi-institutional study of effective programs for preventing emotional problems in these children and their families.

Arnold L. Stolberg, Ph.D., is Associate Professor of Psychology at Virginia Commonwealth University. He has been active in the general fields of community psychology and the primary prevention of psychopathology. Over the past 11 years, his research and writing have focused on children's adjustment to divorce, and the development and assessment of prevention programs for children of divorce and their families.

Georgina A. Sumner, M.S., is Director of Nursing Child Assessment Training at the University of Washington. She is also Coinvestigator of the Clinical Nursing Model Project. She has been actively involved in the continuing education of nurses and other professionals regarding parent-child interaction and its measurement. She has been quite committed to the dissemination of research results to practitioners in the field.

Carolyn F. Swift, Ph.D., is Director of the Stone Center for Developmental Services and Studies, Wellesley College. In 1984, she received the Award for Distinguished Contribution to the Practice of Community Psychology from the Division of Community Psychology, APA. From 1979-1983, she was the Director of Prevention Services, Southwest Community Health Center, Columbus, Ohio. Her work has dealt with a range of issues in community mental health care and primary prevention, and she has twice testified before Congress on child molestation and sexual exploitation of children.

Deanna R. Tate, Ph.D., is Associate Professor in the Department of Family and Consumer Studies, Texas Woman's University. Her research focuses on a variety of family work life issues. She has been working with employee assistance programs, helping them to shift their service delivery focus from individuals to the family unit as a whole. She has also been analyzing the professional capabilities needed by child development professionals who consult with businesses in relation to family work life issues. One of her current projects involves identifying the marketplace for employer supported child care, including cost-benefit analyses and task analyses of the role of the consultant to businesses on these matters.

Barry M. Wagner, Ph.D., is a postdoctoral fellow in the NIMH Training Program in Research and Family Process and Psychopathology. Much of his research has focused upon stress and coping in adolescents and families. He has been involved in evaluating the effects of a program that teaches coping skills to rural adolescents, and is examining gender differences in adolescents' experiences of various types of stress.

Name Index

Subject Index

NOTES

NOTES

NOTES

NOTES

NOTES

NOTES

NOTES

NOTES